GENDER

M000085215

Series editors:
Lynn Abrams, Cordelia Beattie, Pam Sharpe and Penny Summerfield

The expansion of research into the history of women and gender since the 1970s has changed the face of history. Using the insights of feminist theory and of historians of women, gender historians have explored the configuration in the past of gender identities and relations between the sexes. They have also investigated the history of sexuality and family relations, and analysed ideas and ideals of masculinity and femininity. Yet gender history has not abandoned the original, inspirational project of women's history: to recover and reveal the lived experience of women in the past and the present.

The series Gender in History provides a forum for these developments. Its historical coverage extends from the medieval to the modern periods, and its geographical scope encompasses not only Europe and North America but all corners of the globe. The series aims to investigate the social and cultural constructions of gender in historical sources, as well as the gendering of historical discourse itself. It embraces both detailed case studies of specific regions or periods, and broader treatments of major themes. Gender in History titles are designed to meet the needs of both scholars and students working in this dynamic area of historical research.

Modern women on trial

MANCHESTER
1824
Manchester University Press

MODERN WOMEN ON TRIAL

SEXUAL TRANSGRESSION IN THE AGE OF THE FLAPPER

Lucy Bland

Manchester University Press
Manchester and New York

distributed exclusively in the USA by Palgrave Macmillan

The right of Lucy Bland to be identified as the author of this work has been asserted
by her in accordance with the Copyright, Designs and Patents Act 1988.

Published by Manchester University Press
Oxford Road, Manchester M13 9NR, UK
and Room 400, 175 Fifth Avenue, New York, NY 10010, USA
www.manchesteruniversitypress.co.uk

Distributed in the United States exclusively by Palgrave Macmillan
175 Fifth Avenue, New York,
NY 10010, USA

Distributed in Canada exclusively by UBC Press
University of British Columbia, 2029 West Mall,
Vancouver, BC, Canada V6T 1Z2

British Library Cataloguing-in-Publication Data
A catalogue record for this book is available from the British Library

Library of Congress Cataloging-in-Publication Data applied for

ISBN 978 0 7190 8263 4 hardback
ISBN 978 0 7190 8264 1 paperback

First published 2013

The publisher has no responsibility for the persistence or accuracy of URLs for any
external or third-party internet websites referred to in this book, and does not guarantee
that any content on such websites is, or will remain, accurate or appropriate.

Edited and typeset
by Frances Hackeson Freelance Publishing Services, Brinscall, Lancs
Printed in Great Britain
by Bell and Bain Ltd, Glasgow

For my daughter Rosana,
and in memory of my father Tony Bland (1923–89)

Contents

Illustrations

Acknowledgements

This book has taken a number of years to write, competing with demands of motherhood and academic teaching. During this period I have been greatly supported by the interest and encouragement of colleagues/friends at London Metropolitan University (formerly University of North London): Helen Crowley and Irene Gedalof in Women's Studies; Kathy Castle, Kathy Lerman, Paul McGilchrist, Jonathan Moore and Katharina Rowold in History; and Anne Karpt, Megan Stern, Lyn Thomas and Wendy Wheeler. I was also supported intellectually by wonderful colleagues on *Feminist Review*.

Thanks also to the librarians and archivists at the British Newspaper Library, British Library, National Archives, Parliamentary Library, Wellcome Library, Theatre Museum London, British Film Institute Library and The Women's Library for their invariable helpfulness. I am grateful to the Arts and Humanities Research Council for awarding me a Research Leave Grant which enabled me to complete the manuscript. Some of the material for Chapters 1 and 4 has appeared rather differently in two earlier articles: 'Trial by Sexology? Maud Allan, *Salome* and the "Cult of the Clitoris" Case', in Lucy Bland and Laura Doan (eds), *Sexology in Culture: Labelling Bodies and Desires* (Oxford, 1998) and 'The Trial of Madame Fahmy: Orientalism, Violence, Sexual Perversity and the Threat of Miscegenation', in Shani D`Cruze (ed.), *Everyday Violence in Britain, 1850–1950: Gender and Class* (London, 2000). Chapters 3 and 5 have appeared as shorter versions: 'The Trials and Tribulations of Edith Thompson: The Capital Crime of Sexual Incitement in 1920s England', *Journal of British Studies*, 43, 3 (July 2008), and '"Hunnish Scenes" and a "Virgin Birth": a 1920s Divorce Case of Sexual and Bodily Ignorance', in *History Workshop Journal*, 73 (Spring 2012).

Many friends, family members and colleagues have read various versions of my chapters or discussed issues raised in this book; they have given thoughtful commentary, advice and invaluable feedback. Thanks to Sally Alexander, Judith Allen, Susie Balfour, Charlotte Brunsdon, Carolyn Burdett, John Carter Wood, Anna Clark, Ruth Cohen (who helped with the index), Helen Crowley, Joanna de Groot, Irene Gedalof, Judy Greenway, Lesley Hall, Matt Houlbrook, Angus McLaren, Angela McRobbie, Maggie Millman, Frank Mort, Mica Nava, Dave Phillips, Sheila Rowbotham, Richard Smith, Stephen Tifft. Close family friend and writer Micky Burn

(1912–2010) read two chapters in an earlier form; although only ten years old at the time, he vividly recalled the Fahmy trial, such was his extraordinary memory. Thanks to Gail Chester for generously sharing information about Rose Allatini (although in the end, for lack of space, I have not included the 1918 trial of Allatini's book *Despised and Rejected*). I am grateful to Annabel Rathbone and Polly Finch for help with picture research. Thanks to Emma Brennan at Manchester University Press for her good-humoured tolerance at delays in completion. For crucial rock-climbing diversions thanks to my climbing partners/friends Suzanne Ciechomski, David Crawford, Mick Duffield, Mike Fry, Kate Lawrence, David Riley and Catherine Vlasto. For long walks and insightful talks, thanks to Charlotte Brunsdon, Julia Utting and Sophie Watson.

My best and most incisive critics have been my erstwhile collaborator Laura Doan, and my terrific writing group 'The History Girls': Clare Midgley, Alison Oram, Krisztina Robert, Katharina Rowold and Cornelie Usborne. Thank you all so much – I couldn't have done it without you. Finally, endless thanks to Dave Phillips for all his practical and emotional support, and to our daughter Rosana for reminding me that there is life beyond book-writing and research.

Introduction

On 7th January 1923 Virginia Woolf, up from Sussex and staying in Gordon Square, London, reflected on the previous night in her diary: 'the house was too noisy for me to sleep. People seemed to be walking. Then a woman cried, as if in anguish, in the street, and I thought of Mrs Thompson waiting to be executed.'[1] Two days later, Edith Thompson was indeed executed – hanged, along with her lover Freddy Bywaters, for the murder of her husband. After her death, Edith's execution was widely considered a miscarriage of justice, yet at the time the jury, judge, Appeal Court, most of the national newspapers as well as surveys of popular opinion, pronounced her culpable. Evidence of her guilt as to murder is now viewed as non-existent, so why was she deemed a murderer at the time? Six months later, in July 1923, Marguerite Fahmy shot dead her husband, millionaire Egyptian Ali Fahmy, in the corridor of London's Savoy Hotel. It took an Old Bailey jury just one hour's deliberation to find her 'not guilty' of murder or manslaughter, despite clear evidence to the contrary. How was such a verdict possible?

One of the objectives of this book will be to answer this conundrum: why one woman, innocent of murder, was hanged – a woman whose tragic predicament had haunted Woolf, preyed on her mind as she lay unable to sleep – while during the same period another, who was probably guilty, walked free. The conundrum acts as a catalyst, opening up a fascinating terrain of questions concerning the law, the press, the public, young women and issues of morality. These intriguing trials are two of a number of sensational British court trials considered in this book, featuring young female protagonists in the period 1918 to 1924 – 'sensational' because the protagonists were involved in what was widely seen as 'transgressive' sex. Equally fascinating is the obsessive focus on the behaviour of women: the woman in the dock, those women who were part of the courtroom audience, and women generally in the wider society. These trials had extensive press coverage, unsurprising given that in the 1920s – the heyday of the 'dailies' – sensational and scandalous trials were the staple of the popular press. Reports on such trials sold newspapers, 'crime' and 'divorce' (with the accompanying trials) being amongst the subjects cited in contemporary surveys of newspaper readers as the 'most-read' items (along with stories about accidents, human interest, royalty and the weather).[2]

But why examine court trials? I want to explore ideas and possible anxieties regarding the modern woman and her supposed immorality, and I focus on a series of sensational trials as a way in for such an exploration, given that the debates within the law court and on the pages of newspapers reveal (some of the) contemporary attitudes towards women and their sexual mores. The trials are thus taken as a prism through which to identify concerns about modern femininity. Were women thought to have changed/be changing in significant ways? If they were, what threats were perceived to social, economic, moral and domestic order from such a change? I look at these trials not simply in terms of what was said and enacted in court – the facial and bodily expressions, the silences – but also how the trials were represented and commented upon in the wider culture. Thus I analyse not simply the trial transcripts (where they exist), but also police archives, court records, unpublished government memos, public opinion polls, diaries, memoirs, autobiographies and biographies, letters, fictional spin-offs, and most centrally of all, material about the trials in the press: the reportage, commentary, editorials, letters, drawings and photographs. In making the private world of domesticity, sexual relationships, and marriage shockingly public, these accounts generated lively discussion which spilled out beyond the confines of the page into public debate. Reading and talking about sensational trials was a central form of popular cultural entertainment.

The period under consideration is the last year and immediate aftermath of the Great War. This was a period of unemployment, strikes and riots – a time of flux and difficult transition from a war economy and culture to one of peace. Dislocations of work, family and relationships contributed to heightened anxiety and great upheaval for both sexes. On the one hand, men, already mentally and physically scarred by the war, returned to the humiliation of high unemployment; on the other, women, having gained greater independence and skills, were now frustratingly expected to resume pre-war work and conventional gender relations. And their choice of potential husbands was feared to have greatly shrunk with so many dead or shell-shocked.[3] Accounts of the era mention how male veterans, many profoundly transformed by trench warfare, were frequently appalled to find that the women they had left behind were *not* as they had left them: the women had gained in confidence, were sometimes insubordinate, had undertaken so-called men's work during the war, had frequently fared well on their own, and most of those over thirty now had the vote.[4] The younger generation too were demanding greater freedoms and opportunities, the *New Statesman* for example reporting in 1917 that the new women workers 'have a keener appetite for experience and pleasure and a tendency quite new to their class to protest against wrongs'.[5] There was particular resentment by men of the 'pleasure-seeking' attitude that women now seem to have acquired.[6] 'A barrier of indescribable experience' was how Vera Brittain later depicted the gulf between the sexes.[7] One reflection of this gulf lay in the spiralling divorce rate, from just under 1,000 in 1913 to over 5,000 in 1919.[8] (While such figures demonstrate that divorce was still extremely rare, the rate of increase is significant nevertheless.) As for 'bachelor girls', wrote a commentator in the *Daily Mirror*, they were demanding change because they had 'tasted the sweets of liberty'.[9] Relations between men and women did not improve when economic depression set in at the end of 1921, with Britain's staple export industries hard hit.[10] These wider structural problems were linked to Britain's weakened global industrial and political standing, exacerbated by challenges from both socialism (invigorated by the new Soviet Russia) and anti-colonialism, especially in Ireland, Egypt and India.[11] As we shall see, anxiety about Britain's colonial relations, explicitly or implicitly, informed several of the trials considered here.

The modern woman/flapper

The woman of the immediate post-war period, especially the 'bachelor girl', was frequently termed a 'modern woman/girl'. The term 'modern woman' was often used interchangeably with 'flapper' (although strictly the latter referred to girls and women too young to vote, and thus under thirty, while an older woman could still be termed 'modern'). The modern woman-cum-flapper, a figure found across all classes, represented modernity, mobility, new opportunities, a brave new world, a break with the pre-war world of chaperones, Victorian values and restrictive clothing. Above all, she represented female youthfulness and the future. She was associated with short hair, short skirts, dropped waistlines, a flat chest, in fact a look that was decidedly androgynous. Historian Adrian Bingham suggests that this new young androgynous figure symbolised 'a much wider appropriation of masculine traits by women', but as critical historian Laura Doan points out, the boyishness of this new modern girl was seen more as fashion than threat.[12] However, the modern woman-cum-flapper also represented immorality, generational challenge, and the erosion of stability, particularly in relation to gender relations and the family. And she dangerously blurred the boundaries between respectable women and women of a 'certain class' (a coded phrase for prostitutes).[13] Unsurprisingly, while there was much interest in the modern woman-cum-flapper, there was also a deeply felt ambivalence, particularly as far as her sexuality was concerned.[14] In the press, positive commentary sat side by side with more negative sentiments, even in the same publication, where opinion pieces, editorials and fashion pages, for example, might stand in contradiction to each other, suggesting the complexity of 'reading' the modern woman.[15] The press and other commentators categorised women in terms of 'types' – a reductive set of categories which facilitated the telling of a narrative, and helped 'make sense' of certain women's behaviour, but which inevitably straitjacketed any complex or nuanced understanding of the women concerned. In the 1920s the modern woman/flapper was the key 'type'.

Most women over thirty acquired the franchise with the Representation of People Act of February 1918.[16] Why were younger women excluded? It was not as if there was still strong opposition to female suffrage. By 1917 formerly anti-suffrage newspapers such as *The Times* and the *Daily Mail* had been converted, and membership of the Anti-Suffrage League had fallen dramatically. The women munitions workers, having been admonished earlier on in the war for their giddiness, were later in the war thought by many to have 'earned' the vote through their patriotic work.[17] But when it came to drawing up an enfranchisement bill, many politicians were anxious that should women get the vote on the same terms as men, they would greatly outnumber them, and when the bill was negotiated it was agreed that the least objectionable way to keep the numbers of women down was by raising their voting age. Suffragist Millicent Fawcett, who was consulted on the bill, was prepared to go along with this, believing that married women and mothers (the majority of whom were over thirty) in having given their sons and husbands to the war, deserved the vote even more than (the generally younger) industrial workers.[18]

That women over twenty-one but under thirty were not deemed eligible was never properly explained, by the legislators or by the press. While fear of women's numerical superiority was central (the 'surplus woman' problem), there was also the belief held by many politicians and others that young women were insufficiently mature and stable to be party to political decisions – the doubts about the frivolity of the female munitions workers having never fully disappeared, even as they were tempered by recognition of the women's hard work.[19] The flightiness of young women was presented as an inevitable bar to active citizenship. Further, many social commentators were of the opinion that women, particularly young women, had been fundamentally changed by the war: they had become more independent, confident, sensation/pleasure–seeking, selfish, impertinent and uncontrollable. And they were taking on some of the attributes of the opposite sex, as expressed in a popular Sunday paper by a Revd Degen: 'In these days girls knock about the town in the same way as young men. With thoughtless levity, they flutter on the edge of proprieties, the conventions of correct behaviour having been blown sky high.'[20] But although some young women might have been behaving like young men in certain (socially disturbing) respects, they were not thought sufficiently like them to be worthy of the vote, for they were deemed too susceptible, too easily influenced, too prone to hysteria; above all they inherently lacked willpower – a claim prominent in the nineteenth century that carried on into the twentieth.[21]

Early on in the war, certain behaviour of young women had already caused alarm. Working-class girls accused of throwing themselves at soldiers had been held to be suffering 'khaki fever'.[22] There was also believed to have been a huge rise in illegitimacy (an unfounded fear), the offspring labelled 'war babies'. Prostitution had increased, as had the presence of the 'amateur girl/amateur prostitute' (a young woman, across class, giving sexual favours not for money but for presents), the 'amateur' having been seen as a far greater venereal disease threat than her 'professional' equivalent.[23] One response had been the setting up of women's patrols and women police to address issues of immorality. Such women had patrolled parks in search of immoral behaviour, and had been used for the surveillance of women under the Defence of the Realm Act (DORA). In certain areas curfews had been imposed on women 'of a certain class' between 7 p.m. and 8 a.m. However, on grounds of threat to sexual morality and morale the civil liberties of *all* women had been curtailed, with women banned from pubs in London, Cardiff, Sheffield and certain other towns, and their consumption of alcohol prohibited after 6 p.m., even in a restaurant or hotel. There had also been police surveillance of wives and dependents of soldiers and sailors, with the threat of cessation of allowances (given in lieu of pay) if any 'immoral' conduct was discovered – including drinking and consorting with men.[24] As historian Penny Summerfield observes, the State was thereby assuming 'the disciplinary function of the absent husband over his wife'.[25]

There had also been anxiety about women consorting with racially 'other' men. When wounded Indian soldiers, as British imperial subjects, had been sent for treatment to Britain's South coast, rigid rules had been introduced to keep the Indian soldiers apart from local white women.[26]

The concern had not been simply with the Indian soldiers' possible inclinations, but also those of the local white women. Thus the Secretary of State for India (Lord Crewe) had warned the Viceroy of India (Lord Hardinge): 'even if 'Arry [sic] has to some extent enlisted, 'Arriet is all the more at a loose end and ready to take on the Indian warrior'.[27] 'Arriet (the dropped 'h' implying her Cockney provenance) had also been accused of 'taking on' the black sailor. For example, in July 1917 in Canning Town, East London, several black sailors had been attacked in their lodging-houses and on the street by a number of white men and women, the arresting police sergeant in his evidence explaining that 'some of the [local] inhabitants are greatly incensed against the coloured man' because of 'the infatuation of the white girls for the black men'.[28]

Historian Sonya Rose perceptively comments on societal reaction to the behaviour of women in war:

> War's liberating potential threatens the nation that it is imagined to represent. Under such conditions, and in a society with a long history of constructing female sexuality and the pursuit of pleasure as dangerous, women who were perceived to be seeking out sexual adventures might well have been defined as subversive.[29]

The concerns about women during the war can be summarised as anxieties over promiscuity, sensation-seeking and active sexual agency ('khaki fever', the amateur prostitute, women's relationships with men of colour) and irresponsibility (spreading venereal disease and producing illegitimate children). All such behaviour was additionally deemed unpatriotic (although the young women sleeping with soldiers claimed quite the reverse) and, as Rose suggests, dangerously subversive.[30]

At the end of the war, many of the same anxieties about women's morality shifted onto the modern woman/flapper, but also the 'butterfly woman' (a sub-species of the modern woman who frequented nightclubs), the surplus woman, the sterile woman, the promiscuous woman, the female 'dope fiend', and the woman who consorted with men of colour. Representations of these types of women feature in one or more of the trials considered here. Furthermore, each trial, in its reportage and commentary, as well as in the actual content of court proceedings, manifested a critique of some aspect of popular culture and modernity relating to women's leisure and lifestyle: dance, drugs, 'desert romances', sensational fiction, fashion, cinema, nightclubs, etc. The trials in effect became vehicles not simply for the passing of judgement on an individual, or on a particular type of woman, but also entailed the castigation of women more broadly, particularly their pursuit of independence, consumption and sensation.

Historiographical debates

There have been several important studies of young women's representation in inter-war Britain. Billie Melman's *Women and the Popular Imagination in the Twenties,* the classic, invaluable text, was followed a year later by Deirdre Beddoe's *Back to Home and Duty.*[31] Melman, who usefully examines a wide selection of popular novels and magazines read by women, in her first chapter analyses the *Daily Mail* and *Daily Express*'s depictions of the modern woman; these she claims to have been largely negative. Beddoe, as her book title suggests, argues that women were forced back into the home after the Great War, pursuits other than domesticity and motherhood being vigorously discouraged. The arguments of both texts need some revision. In relation to women's inter-war work, while it is true that restrictions were introduced, including the marriage bar in teaching and the civil service, new arenas of work were opening up for women – in white-collar work, in teaching and the civil service (for single women), in finance and in new light industries.[32] Adrian Bingham, in his impressive *Gender, Modernity and the Popular Press in Interwar Britain*, presents a more nuanced picture of press depiction than that given by Melman. He points to how many of the popular newspapers carried articles celebrating sportswomen, and encouraging women to be 'modern' and career-minded.[33] Bingham is certainly correct in pointing to the many positive representations, but I suggest that he underplays the co-existence of negative portrayals, his seeing the inclusion of these as the editors' or owners' desire for controversy rather than indicating ambivalence.

There have also been excellent recent publications on trials. George Robb and Nancy Erber's co-edited *Disorder in the Court* takes as its object the role of the state in regulating sexual morality at the *fin de siècle*, arguing that the various trials analysed in their book provide 'a snapshot of critical moments of social contestation'. This was the era of the 'new woman' – a construct not dissimilar to the later 'modern woman'. Their helpful introduction points out that legal proceedings have too often been overlooked in the study of sexual behaviour and attitudes, but that recent scholarship has began to appreciate the role of 'the judicial contestation of sexual matters'.[34] Such recent scholarship, in addition to Angus McLaren's *The Trials of Masculinity*, now includes two riveting books by Kate Summerscale: one about a murder case, *The Suspicions of Mr Whicher*, the other a divorce case, *Mrs Robinson's Disgrace*.[35] There are also two new books on women accused and acquitted of poisoning: Eleanor Gordon and Gwyneth Nair's study of the nineteenth-century trial of Madeleine Smith, and John Carter Wood's of that of Beatrice Pace in the late 1920s.[36] I follow these important publications in attempting to integrate an examination of the popular press into my analysis of trials, paying attention to the ways in which the press constructed narratives and shaped explanations. Where my project differs is in my placing a series of virtually coterminous trials alongside each other in order to decipher what cultural work these trials and their reportage performed in relation to the construction of, and anxieties about, the modern woman.

The press and other sources

Given that only a tiny minority of people were able to witness the live drama of a sensational court trial, the 'experience' of the trial for the vast majority was via the print media. From the end of the nineteenth century, sensational trials were covered by all the newspapers, frequently reported in great detail, from the so-called 'class' journalism of *The Times*, *Manchester Guardian*, *Morning Post* and *Daily Telegraph* through to the morning and evening popular press, and the Sundays and weeklies.[37] In drawing on a wide range of assorted newspapers I have found much rich material concerning the trials examined here. By the 1920s, the popular 'dailies' had adopted the late Victorian 'new journalism' of sex, crime and scandal, initially the preserve of the Sunday papers.[38] The narrative of the sensational trial, with its ingredients of crime, mystery, detection, sex, and punishment, represented perfect copy for the daily and Sunday papers.[39]

The press was very widely consumed in this period, with the majority of people reading at least one newspaper a day. The daily paper with the highest circulation at this time was the *Daily Mail* (founded in 1896); it had a predominantly middle-class readership, and by 1922 was selling more than 1.75 million copies a day.[40] It was founded by Lord Northcliffe (who also owned *The Times* and the *Evening News*); on his death in 1922 ownership passed to his brother, Lord Rothermere. The brothers (as Amalgamated Press) also controlled the second best-seller the *Daily Mirror* (founded in 1903). Like the *Daily Sketch* (the third in this best-seller list) it was a 'picture' or 'pictorial' newspaper, filling its pages with photographs. By the 1920s, photography was easy, portable and quick, and bold visual images added to the drama of a narrative.[41] Seventy per cent of the readers of both these 'pictorials' were women (and indeed the two papers consciously appealed to women), and both papers had a predominantly lower-middle-class clientele.[42] The fourth and fifth most popular newspapers were the liberal *Daily Chronicle* (bought mainly by the working class) and the conservative *Daily Express* (with a middle-class readership), the latter owned by the other powerful press baron of the time, Lord Beaverbrook.[43] (If we think that press barons are a relatively new phenomenon, we have only to look at the extraordinary political and business careers of Beaverbrook and the Harmsworth brothers (Lords Northcliffe and Rothermere).)[44]

Whereas many of the 'dailies' were relatively new, many of the 'Sundays' were rooted in the early- or mid-Victorian period. The *News of the World* was by far the biggest seller, with sales of 3 million a week in 1924, followed by the *Sunday Pictorial* (the Sunday companion of the *Daily Mirror*) with 2.5 million.[45] The latter was read across class, while the former was cited in surveys as having a mainly working-class readership, although author Paul Ferris claims that its 'three million circulation reached homes at every level. Middle-class households kept it from the children, or slipped their copy under a cushion in the sitting room when visitors came', such was its reputation for scandalous reportage.[46] There were a host of other Sunday papers with large readerships but mostly with names now long forgotten: *Weekly Dispatch, People, Sunday Express, Sunday Graphic, Empire News, Sunday Chronicle, Reynolds's News, Illustrated Sunday Herald, Lloyd's Sunday News*. There was also the hugely popular weekly *John Bull*, which claimed the largest circulation of any weekly British journal – over one million per issue – with a mainly working-class clientele. By the 1920s, with the readership of the popular press (the dailies and the Sundays) increasing rapidly, criminal trials had become mass cultural spectacles delivered directly into the home.[47]

As mentioned, in addition to the press (the main source for the trials), I have also looked at a range of published and unpublished material, which I briefly reference here in relation to their use in each chapter. In my first chapter I examine a libel case, brought by a well-known female dancer against a maverick right-wing MP for the accusation of lesbianism. Although the MP was supposedly on trial, it was the dancer who ended up pilloried and defamed, accused of treachery. I have had access not to official trial transcripts, but to a 'verbatim' report of the libel trial published by the libeller himself. Read alongside press reportage, including that of *The Times*, whose reports on the trial were fairly extensive, and drawing on various diaries and memoirs, I am able to arrive at a sense of the trial's impact, and importantly for my project here, the way in which the trial depicted sexually deviant women as potentially treacherous. I suggest that one aspect of this libel trial involved the drawing up of battle-lines in relation to the construction of a new, post-war womanhood, setting the stage for the trials that were to follow. Further, in studying press omissions of certain 'sexual' terms used in the trial, I am able to register levels of press self-censorship.

Chapter 2 looks at two inquests and three magistrate-court trials that involved women and drugs; young women in relationships with Chinese men were also effectively in the dock. The women discussed in this chapter were all castigated for their sensation-seeking, miscegenation and irresponsibility. I rely largely on the popular press, government memos, various memoirs and popular fiction to arrive at a sense of the anxieties about the dangers *to* the modern woman of her impetuous pursuit of instant gratification, and the dangers *from* the modern woman in her choosing racially 'other' partners. In Chapter 3, on Edith Thompson, one way of accessing court proceedings has been via the account of the trial published as part of the Notable British Trial Series.[48] (The preface's acknowledgement of access to the original transcripts can be read as its offering 'proof' of the account's veracity.) I read this alongside extensive press reportage and commentary, as well as personal memoirs. In Chapter 4, on Marguerite Fahmy, there are no extant trial transcripts, but there are prosecution depositions lodged at the National Archives, much press reportage, and a number of relevant memoirs, all giving a keen sense of the key issues raised by the trial.

Chapter 5 centres on an extraordinary divorce case, that of Christabel Russell, involving cross-dressing, claims of a virgin birth, extreme sexual ignorance, and a particular brand of eccentric modern femininity. As with the libel trial, we again have the opportunity to compare the newspapers' accounts with the supposedly verbatim trial transcripts (the transcript of the second trial being lodged at the Parliamentary Archives) thereby enabling us to see what was considered by the press as publicly unprintable. The case also raises questions about how the 'modern woman' was caricatured at the time, for Christabel Russell was seen, and saw herself, as ultra-modern, yet she disavowed sexuality and embraced maternity.

In the disproportionate space given over to the modern woman-cum-flapper by the press in their reports of these various trials, we gauge other anxieties at large. To pose a 'leading' question: is it possible that the trials' (and newspapers') centring on women's behaviour became a means of expressing a series of concerns about destabilisations in addition to that of gender, namely those of modernity, mass culture, class, race, ethnicity, and the sense of what it meant to be British or English? And is it correct to assume that the female figure, especially that of the 'modern woman', stood as the personification of this sense of instability? During the course of this book, through a detailed examination of a rich array of primary sources, I shall attempt to answer such questions, as well as to explore the role of trials and the press in taxonomising women into a range of modern 'types'.

Notes

1   Anne Olivier Bell (ed.), *The Diary of Virginia Woolf, Volume II, 1920–1924* (London, 1978), pp. 224–5.
2   James Curran and James Seaton, *Power without Responsibility: the Press and Broadcasting in Britain* (5th edition, London, 1998), p. 48.
3   The 1921 Census revelation that there were more than 1.75 million more females than males in the population fuelled fears about the 'surplus women' problem – a concern dating back to the late nineteenth century but now greater than ever. See Katherine Holden, *The Shadow of Marriage: Singleness in England, 1914–60* (Manchester, 2007); Virginia Nicholson, *Singled Out* (London, 2007); *People*, 8th February 1920, p. 7. See Dan Todman, *The Great War* (London, 2005), p. 45 for a contrasting view.
4   See Susan Kingsley Kent, *Making Peace: the Reconstruction of Gender in Interwar Britain* (Princeton, NJ, 1993); Susan Kingsley Kent, *Aftershocks: Politics and Trauma in Britain, 1918–1931* (London and New York, 2009), Chapter 1; Jay Winter and Antoine Prost, *The Great War in History* (Cambridge, 2005).
5   Quoted in George Robb, *British Culture and the First World War* (London, 2002), p. 66.
6   See George E. Pearson, 'The Dream Girl – and the Awakening', *Daily Express*, 16th February 1920, p. 6, about men returning from military service having thought longingly of their 'dream girl', only to find 'pleasure-seeking women'. The article led to a lively correspondence in the paper over the next few days.
7   Vera Brittain, *Testament of Youth* (London, 1933, 1978), p. 143.
8   Royal Commission on Marriage and Divorce, *Report, 1951–1955* (London, 1956, 1968), p. 356.
9   *Daily Mirror*, 6th December 1918, p. 6,
10 Sally Alexander, 'Men's Fears and Women's Work: Responses to Unemployment in London between the Wars', *Gender & History*, 12, 2 (July 2000), p. 406; Sheila Rowbotham, *A Century of Women* (London, 1997), Chapter 3.
11 See Eric Hobsbawn, *Age of Extremes: the Short Twentieth Century, 1914–1991* (London, 1995).
12 Adrian Bingham, *Gender, Modernity, and the Popular Press in Inter-War Britain* (Oxford, 2004), p. 64; Laura Doan, *Fashioning Sapphism: the Origins of Modern English Lesbian Culture* (New York, 2001), p. 105.
13 Billie Melman, *Women and the Popular Imagination in the Twenties: Flappers and Nymphs* (New York, 1988), Chapter 1; Deirdre Beddoe, *Back to Home and Duty: Women between the Wars, 1918–1939* (London, 1989), pp. 22–4. On the Australian modern woman see Liz Coner, *The Spectacular Modern Woman* (Bloomington and Indianapolis, IN, 2004); on the French modern woman see Mary Louise Roberts, *Civilization without Sexes: Reconstructing Gender in Postwar France, 1917–1927* (Chicago and London, 1994); on the Danish modern woman see Birgitte Soland, *Becoming Modern: Young Women and the Reconstruction of Womanhood in the 1920s* (Princeton, NJ, 2000); on the modern woman in Germany see Cornelie Usborne, 'The New Woman and Generation Conflict: Perceptions of Young Women's Sexual Mores in the Weimar Republic', in Mark Roseman (ed.), *Generations in Conflict: Youth Revolt and Generation Formation in Germany, 1770– 1968* (Cambridge, 1995) pp. 137–63; on the modern girl globally see Modern Girl Around the World Research Group, *The Modern Girl Around the World: Consumption, Modernity and Globalization* (London, 2008). On British modernity see Mica Nava and Alan O'Shea

(eds), *Modern Times: Reflections on a Century of English Modernity* (London and New York, 1996); Martin Daunton and Bernhard Rieger (eds), *Meanings of Modernity: Britain from the Late-Victorian Period to World War II* (Oxford and New York, 2001); Lisa Tickner, *Modern Life and Modern Subjects* (New Haven, CT and London, 2000), pp. 190–1.

14 Adrian Bingham suggests that the amount of press attention devoted to the young modern woman after 1918 was exceptional. Bingham, *Gender, Modernity, and the Popular Press*, pp. 45–9. There was also ambivalence about young women who thought too much, especially about feminism: reporting on a twenty-seven year old woman who killed herself, *Empire News* commented: 'She believed in the emancipation of woman. She was not a healthy, normal girl, revelling in sports, pleasure and so forth ... She was over-taxing her brain.' 1st June 1919, p. 7.

15 See Robert Graves and Alan Hodge, *The Long Weekend; a Social History of Great Britain, 1918–1939* (New York, 1940, 1963), p. 113. Establishment figures denouncing the 'modern women' provided perfect copy. Bingham, *Gender, Modernity, and the Popular Press*, p. 52.

16 To be eligible, women over thirty (or their husbands) needed to be paying rent or owning property. This excluded single women living at home with their parents, or working as domestic servants and living in someone else's house.

17 Nicoletta F. Gullace, *'The Blood of our Sons': Men, Women and the Renegotiation of British Citizenship during the Great War* (New York, 2002), pp. 185–7; Gail Braybon, *Women Workers in the First World War* (London, 1981), p. 165.

18 Harold L. Smith, *The British Women's Suffrage Campaign, 1866–1928* (London, 1998, second edition 2007) pp. 83, 132.

19 Once the war had ended, attempts by such women to stay in paid employment were met by press castigation as to their selfish self-interest, their former status as heroines forgotten. Braybon, *Women Workers in the First World War*, pp. 185–6; Deborah Thom, *Nice Girls and Rude Girls: Women Workers in World War One* (London, 1998).

20 *Reynolds's News*, 23rd July 1922, p. 7. Revd Degen presents himself as from 'Coketown'. Presumably this writer wished to be associated with Charles Dickens's *Hard Times*, where 'Coketown' stands in for Preston, a British northern industrial town. I am unfortunately unable to identify Degen. The name, if a penname, may reference degeneration. Thanks to Adrian Bingham for this suggestion.

21 See Lucy Bland, *Banishing the Beast: Feminism and Sexual Morality, 1885–1914* (London, 1995), Chapter 2.

22 Angela Woollocott, '"Khaki Fever" and its Control: Gender, Class, Age and Sexual Morality on the British Home Front in the First World War', *Journal of Contemporary History*, 29 (1994), pp. 325–47. See HO 45/10724/251861, National Archives.

23 Two pieces of regulation under Defence of the Realm Act were introduced to address prostitution and the rise of venereal disease: 13A in 1916 and 40D in 1918. Feminist protest against these acts was effective, because of government fear of renewed militancy.

24 Lucy Bland, 'In the Name of Protection: the Policing of Women in the First World War', in J. Brophy and C. Smart (eds), *Women in Law* (London, 1985); Philippa Levine, '"Walking the Streets in a Way no Decent Woman Should": Women Police in World War One', *Journal of Modern History*, 66 (1994), pp. 34–78; Susan R. Grayzel, *Women and the First World War* (London, 2002), Chapter 5; Susan Grayzel, 'Liberating Women? Examining Gender, Morality and Sexuality in First World War Britain and France', in Gail Braybon (ed.), *Evidence, History and the Great War* (New York and Oxford, 2003); Robb, *British Culture and the First World War*, Chapter 2.

25 Penny Summerfield, 'Women and War in the Twentieth Century', in June Purvis (ed.), *Women's History: Britain, 1850–1945* (London, 1995), p. 309.

26 Philippa Levine, 'Battle Colors: Race, Sex and Colonial Soldiery in World War I', *Journal of Social History* 9, 4 (1998), pp. 104–30; Rosina Visram, *Asians in Britain: 400 Years of History* (London, 2002), pp. 185–92.

27 Letter of 4th December 1914, quoted in Gregory Martin, 'The Influence of Racial Attitudes towards India during the First World War', *Journal of Imperial and Commonwealth History*, 14 (1985), p. 94.

28 *The Times*, 3rd July 1917, p. 5.

29 Sonya O. Rose, 'Sex, Citizenship and the Nation in World War II Britain', *American Historical Review*, 103, 4 (October 1998), pp. 1148–9.

30 E.B. Turner, Chair of the National Council for Combatting Venereal Diseases, declared: 'I believe that a great deal of the going wrong among girls recently is due to what I describe as a wave of patriotic immorality'. Quoted in Grayzel, 'Liberating Women?', p. 128.

31 Melman, *Women and the Popular Imagination in the Twenties*; Beddoe, *Back to Home and Duty*.

32 See Miriam Glucksmann, *Women Assemble: Women Workers and the New Industries in Inter-war Britain* (London, 1990).

33 Bingham, *Gender, Modernity, and the Popular Press*; and see Adrian Bingham, *Family Newspapers? Sex, Private Life and the British Popular Press, 1918–1978* (Oxford, 2009).

34 George Robb and Nancy Erber (eds), *Disorder in the Court: Trials and Sexual Conflict at the Turn of the Century* (London, 1999), p. 3.

35 Angus McLaren, *The Trials of Masculinity: Policing Sexual Boundaries, 1870–1930* (Chicago, 1997); Kate Summerscale, *The Suspicions of Mr Whicher, or the Murder at Road Hill House* (London, 2008); Kate Summerscale, *Mrs Robinson's Disgrace: the Private Diary of a Victorian Lady* (London, 2012).

36 Eleanor Gordon and Gwyneth Nair, *Murder and Morality in Victorian Britain: the Story of Madeleine Smith* (Manchester, 2009); John Carter Wood, *The Most Remarkable Woman in England: Poison, Celebrity and the Trials of Beatrice Pace* (Manchester, 2012).

37 The broadsheet/tabloid dichotomy is not appropriate, since most of the newspapers were broadsheets.

38 Judith Walkowitz, *City of Dreadful Delight: Narratives of Sexual Danger in Late-Victorian London* (London, 1982).

39 See Lynda Nead, 'Visual Cultures of the Courtroom: Reflections of History, Law and the Image', *Visual Culture in Britain*, 3, 2 (2002), p. 135.

40 Tom Jeffery and Keith McClelland, 'A World Fit to Live in: the *Daily Mail* and the Middle Classes, 1918–1939', in James Curran, Anthony Smith and Pauline Wingate (eds), *Impact and Influences: Essays in Media Power in the Twentieth Century* (London, 1987), p. 28.

41 Nead, 'Visual Cultures of the Courtroom', p. 129.

42 Political and Economic Planning, *Report on the British Press* (London, 1938).

43 For class readership of newspapers see H.G. Lyall, *Press Circulations Analysed* (London, 1928). Many thanks to Keith McLelland for access to this fascinating survey undertaken by his great-uncle.

44 Stephen Koss, *The Rise and Fall of the Political Press in Britain, vol.2: Twentieth Century* (London, 1984).

45 A.P. Wadsworth, 'Newspaper Circulations, 1800–1954', *Transactions of the Manchester Statistical Society*, 9 (March 1955), p. 36. Thanks to John Carter Wood for drawing my

attention to this article.

46 Paul Ferris, *Sex and the British* (London, 1993), p. 94.

47 Raymond Williams, *The Long Revolution* (London, 1961), Chapter 3; Jeffery and McClelland, 'A World Fit to Live in'; Bingham, *Gender, Modernity, and the Popular Press*.

48 Filson Young, *Trial of Frederick Bywaters and Edith Thompson* (Edinburgh and London, 1923).

1

The case of the 'Cult of the Clitoris': treachery, patriotism and English womanhood

'A great battle is raging; armies are bleeding and dying; Paris is at stake; and for a week the interest of the British public has been almost entirely centred upon a trial for criminal libel.'[1] The *New Statesman* was referring in disbelief to a six-day trial of May–June 1918, reported extensively in all the British newspapers, and involving a criminal libel brought by the well known 'barefoot' dancer Maud Allan against the right-wing independent MP Noel Pemberton Billing, for his imputation of lesbianism. The successful German offensive of late March on the Western Front had been followed by further German victories in April and May, yet the British public's attention now turned (for diversion presumably) to the Old Bailey. Here hundreds queued for hours in an attempt to secure a seat, although for most, if they gained entry at all, it was standing room only. 'Not since the days of Crippen has any trial so excited the public', declared the popular *Sunday Pictorial*.[2] What was its allure?

The libel suit had been prompted by a paragraph headed 'The Cult of the Clitoris' which in February 1918 had appeared in Billing's paper *The Vigilante*:

> To be a member of Maud Allen's [*sic*] private performance in Oscar Wilde's *Salome* one has to apply to Miss Valetta of 9 Duke St, Adelphi. If Scotland Yard were to seize the list of these members I have no doubt they would secure the names of several thousand of the first 47,000.[3]

Reference to the '47,000' originally appeared three weeks earlier, when *The Vigilante*'s predecessor *The Imperialist* claimed a 'Black Book' was in the possession of the Germans naming 47,000 English men and women vulnerable to German blackmail because of their 'sexual perversions'.[4] Included were: 'The names of Privy Councillors, youths of the chorus, wives of Cabinet ministers, dancing girls, even Cabinet Ministers themselves ... In lesbian ecstasy the most sacred secrets of the state were betrayed.'[5] During the trial the names of former Prime Minister Herbert Henry Asquith, his wife Margot, Lord Haldane and even the presiding judge, Justice Darling, were among those mentioned as listed in the book.[6] The play *Salome*, mentioned in the paragraph, was written by Oscar Wilde in 1891, first in French. Seen as sexually risqué, it had, to date, only been performed in Britain privately.[7]

With this brief summary we can begin to see why the trial must have been so fascinating at the time, for it involved a rich mix: a 'decadent' 1890s play (*Salome*), a notorious figure of those days (Oscar Wilde), a celebrated Edwardian dancer (Maud Allan), and a paranoid rumour about conspiracy, German infiltration and sexual vice in high places (the 'Black Book'). Yet although the trial was famous in its time (referred to by military historian Michael Kettle as 'the libel case of the century'), for many years it surprisingly disappeared almost completely from public view.[8] In her 1948 reminiscences, novelist Marie Belloc Lowndes reflects: 'How completely forgotten is the Pemberton Billing case, and yet in the early summer of 1918 little else was talked of in the world in which I lived.'[9] It was as if it had been an odd blip of eccentricity thrown up by the war. Since the later 1990s, however, the trial has been 'rediscovered' and written about by a number of scholars, the complex intersection of sex and politics being a compelling draw. Thus unlike the other cases considered in this book, the terrain of this trial has been well covered.[10]

In his book-length study *Salome's Last Veil*, Michael Kettle sees Maud Allan as a mere pawn in a wider picture of political conspiracy in which Billing worked with disgruntled British war Generals to overthrow the coalition government, and sabotage its secret peace talks.[11] Cultural critic Philip Hoare's *Wilde's Last Stand* adds to Kettle's study through a far greater focus on the role of Wilde in the trial. Hoare stresses the way in which the Wilde 'cult' was blamed for Britain's moral degeneracy and inability to win the war. Allan is here depicted as Wilde's adjunct. Both books make important contributions to an understanding of the trial, but as literary critic Jodie Medd points out, both exclude the question of female sexuality.[12] One of the most interesting aspects of this case is that its multiple dimensions offer the potential for a range of competing readings, each laying claim to the trial's wider cultural significance. Thus in contrast to Kettle and Hoare, a number of analyses of the trial have focused centrally on the libel of lesbianism. Literary critic Jennifer Travis, for example, claims that the trial was 'the first time in England that lesbianism as a category of sexual identity was the subject of legal discourse'.[13] But while lesbianism did of course feature in the trial, Laura Doan rightly cautions that the libel was primarily a political strategy with political aims rather than a direct attack on, or central portrayal of, female homosexuality.[14] It is perhaps helpful to think of the trial as being simultaneously about what on the one hand was explicitly said in public, both in court and in the press (though these were not always the same), and on the other, what was unsaid but implicit.

In the context of this book's interest in considering some of the key ways in which femininity and female sexual deviancy were debated and contested within and beyond the courtroom, this is clearly a pivotal trial. We must not forget that the libel – and the trial – involved an attack on the reputation of a particular woman, however marginal and beside the point she may ultimately have been in the libellers' scheme of things. During the war, as mentioned in this book's introduction, women in Britain had been subjected to surveillance on an unprecedented scale, but the Billing libel trial was the British war years' most visible attack on the morality of a lone woman. Many aspects of the trial have been considered by previous scholars, such as the debates over sexual perversity, homosexuality, sexology, treachery and patriotism. Yet what has been largely ignored is the role of a second woman, also effectively on trial, namely Margot Asquith. I would suggest that Maud and Margot were together held up as examples of undesirable femininity, exhibiting attributes seen as diametrically opposed to that of a new, refashioned ideal English womanhood, in which patriotic, 'responsible' and moral deployment of the suffrage was now heralded as the crucial aspect of female citizenship of the future. In February 1918, the very month that the 'cult of the clitoris' paragraph was published, most women over thirty gained the vote. Before considering what this new ideal English womanhood entailed, a wider sense of what (else) the trial involved is needed, starting with the obvious questions about the key protagonists: who were Billing and Maud Allan, why had the MP published the offending article and why had he singled out the dancer?

Pemberton Billing as libeller

Noel Pemberton Billing was trained as a barrister, had been an actor, was an aviator and inventor, and since 1916 had represented East Hertfordshire as an independent MP. The following year he had formed the Vigilante Society to promote 'purity in public life' and to root out the 'mysterious influence' (the German fifth column) responsible for Britain's inability to win the war. His organisation fought a series of by-elections with the alliterating slogans: 'Hinder the Huns, Paralyse Profiteers, Purify Politics, Win the War'. Billing and his proto-fascist colleagues, such as Henry Beamish and Arnold White, were explicitly anti-Semitic, claiming that the British war effort was being undermined by the 'hidden hand' of German Jews and sympathisers operating in Britain.[15] What Billing carefully concealed from the court was that his wife was half-German.[16] His assistant editor was a young North American called Captain Harold Spencer, who had been discharged from the British Army for insanity, something else which was not established in the trial, despite Allan's counsel's best attempts.[17] It was Spencer who had written the 'first 47,000' article. Shortly afterwards Billing had received a letter from the romance writer Marie Corelli who had seen a notice in *The Sunday Times* advertising the forthcoming private production of *Salome* starring Allan. Corelli suggested: 'it would be well to secure the list of subscribers to this new "upholding" of the Wilde "cult" among the 47,000'.[18] Spencer then wrote the 'Cult of the Clitoris' paragraph, hoping to raise a libel case and thereby get publicity for their claims of German infiltration and corruption in high places. Billing saw his libelling as a public service:

> I am a libeller ... I have libelled public men for the last two and a half years ... and if you think I am going to keep quiet as a public man while men are being killed at the rate of nine a minute to make a Sodomite holiday, I am not.[19]

When Maud Allan brought the libel suit against him, Billing had no hesitation in presenting a plea of justification. The Libel Act of 1843 decreed that to be found innocent of a criminal libel, the defendant needed to establish both the truth of the libel and its public benefit. This allowed the libeller to assemble diverse witnesses and present incriminating evidence. There were obvious parallels between what was permissible for Billing to do and say, and what had been permissible for the Marquis of Queensberry at the first Oscar Wilde trial in 1895, in which Wilde had brought a libel case against the Marquis (his lover's father) for the accusation of 'posing as a somdomite [*sic*]'.[20] (Another parallel was the presence of Travers Humphreys, who had acted for Wilde in 1895 as a junior counsel.)[21] Billing's plea of justification declared that all the defamatory matter alleged in Allan's indictment was true; firstly, that Allan was 'a lewd, unchaste and immoral woman', who secondly, was about 'to give private performances of an obscene and indecent character', which thirdly, were 'designed as to foster and encourage obscene and unnatural practices among women', and finally, that Allan associated herself with persons 'addicted to obscene and unnatural practices'.[22] Billing was thus in effect stating that Allan was immoral, *Salome* was obscene, *Salome* was designed to encourage obscenity among women, and Allan associated with obscene persons. In a way similar to the libel trial instigated by Wilde, the defence of this criminal libel resulted, in effect, not in Billing being on trial, but Maud and *Salome*.[23]

The libelled Maud Allan

But why had Billing and Spencer selected Maud Allan to libel? Born Maud Durrant in Canada in 1873, the daughter of a shoemaker (although her aggrandising autobiography claims both her parents were wealthy doctors), Maud moved with her family to San Francisco six years later.[24] In 1895, two months after she had gone to Berlin to study classical piano, her brother Theo murdered two young women in a church. He was executed and became one of San Francisco's most notorious criminals. At the time parallels were drawn to Jack the Ripper.[25] To disguise the connection, Maud changed her surname. In 1901 she abandoned the piano and took up dancing, seeing herself as inspired by the ancient Greeks.[26] In 1907 at Marienbad (an Austrian-Hungarian spa visited by royalty) in front of Edward VII, she performed a dance which she had devised called 'the Vision of Salome'.[27] The following year she came to Britain and gave more than 250 hugely popular performances of a series of dances, including the 'Vision of Salome', at the Palace Theatre of Varieties, in London's Soho. Prior to the arrival of Diaghilev's Russian ballet in 1911, dance in Britain, including classical ballet, was consigned to music hall and pantomime, fitted into a programme that included other low-status acts such as jugglers, trained animals and comedians.[28] Allan was not the only Western woman to portray Salome on stage; the biblical character who had figured in many nineteenth-century novels and paintings was now the inspiration for other dancers, such as Louie Fuller, Ruth St Denis, Ida Rubenstein and Mata Hari, all women who were teetering on the edge of respectability.[29] The *New York Times* made tongue-in-cheek references to an outbreak of 'Salomania'.[30]

Maud Allan was patronised by high society, including royalty and the then Prime Minister Asquith and his wife Margot. Maud's fame briefly exceeded that of Isadora Duncan, to whom she was endlessly compared.[31] The two women greatly disliked each other. Isadora Duncan was later to write: 'At least I was not Salome ... I was never a Vampire, but always an Inspirational'.[32] Maud's popularity was reflected in substantial earnings, and her image appeared on a stream of postcards.[33] Flower-pot statuettes of her were sold in Bond Street gift-shops, and her classical sandals and bare legs became high fashion. The Palace Theatre introduced matinees featuring solely Maud, where the vast majority of the audience were female.[34] Lady Diana Manners, a teenager at the time, was enthralled by Maud:

> Maud Allan made a sensation at the Palace Theatre. Greatly daring, she had appeared in a wisp of chiffon and bare legs ... My mother ... sent us to watch and learn, in spite of her number finishing with 'Salome's Dance' – considered scandalous ... [35]

1 Maud Allan as Salome

Maud thus made her own contribution to cosmopolitanism, especially the 'Oriental' look popularised in the fashion world by the French couturier Paul Poiret and the Ballets Russes, the latter having come to Covent Garden in 1911.[36] She also carved out a space for the active physical expression of female sensuality, and along with the Ballets Russes and the arrival of the tango from Latin America, made a central contribution to the cosmopolitan 'dance craze' and night-life of pre-war England.[37] Aided by the opening of numerous dancing schools for all classes, this was a 'dance revolution' that was to carry on into the war and beyond; it was highly significant for many other women considered in this book.[38]

But if Maud was famous, she was also infamous. Two days before her public debut in London, a titillating illustrated pamphlet was circulated focusing solely on the *Vision of Salome* dance: 'The pink pearls slip amorously about the throat and bosom as she moves ... The desire that flames from her eyes and bursts in hot gusts from her scarlet mouth infects the act with the madness of passion'.[39] Even without such a preview, there would have been certain expectations, given that to the Westerner, Salome signified the Orientalist myth *par excellence* of the exotic, erotic, but deadly Eastern female.[40] The many favourable reviews however viewed her as distinct from the 'grossness' of 'authentic' Eastern dancers.[41] The Manchester Watch Committee clearly thought otherwise, for it was quick to ban her from appearing in their home town, and committees in Liverpool and Bournemouth, amongst others, followed suit. The previous year she had been forbidden to dance the 'Vision of Salome' in Munich.[42] There were complaints of her presence at the 1908 Prime Ministerial garden party in London, although as Asquith's private secretary Edwin Montagu wryly noted, it was 'characteristic of our Party that so many members who object to meeting the lady were apparently able to recognise her'.[43] To many in the Liberal Party, the very word 'dancer' had risqué connotations. The following year, in 1909, a pornographic story was published about a wealthy prostitute who dances 'the dance of emancipation' and has four male admirers all of whom she sexually satisfies in various exotic ways. It was no accident that the eponymous heroine is called Maudie.[44] And when Allan travelled to India in 1913 her reputation preceded her: the Viceroy protested that her dancing would be detrimental to 'the prestige of the white woman in India'.[45] Maud's success in England was fairly brief, but within that time period (1908–10) she precariously juggled notoriety with fame and (a degree of) respectability.[46]

The libelled Margot Asquith

Maud's infamy stemmed not only from her 'scorching' eroticised dancing; there were also vague rumours of her lesbianism, largely due to her close friendship with Margot Asquith. Margot was the other woman effectively on trial at the Old Bailey alongside Maud (not counting the third female figure, that of Wilde's Salome). When the 47,000 article mentioned 'lesbian ecstasy' in which 'the most sacred secrets of the state were betrayed', it was clearly Mrs Asquith who was being referred to. For several years gossip had hinted that Margot had sexual relations with women. When Maud was on tour in the USA in 1910, the American newspapers reported that her friendship with Margot was greatly straining the Asquith marriage, although the reports were not reproduced in the British press.[47]

Margot Asquith, née Tennant, was born in 1864, and in her 'reign' in the 1880s and 1890s as effective leader of the Souls, a group of upper-class intellectuals, she had established herself as a key representative of high-minded, permissive, cultural modernity. The group included such influential men as future Prime Minister Arthur Balfour, future Viceroy of India George Curzon, and the great hostesses of the time: Lady Desborough, Lady Elcho, and the Duchess of Rutland (mother of socialite Diana Cooper, née Manners).[48] Margot Tennant married the widowed Asquith in 1894. She was sharp-featured and sharp-tongued, 'a whipcord vitality … tense as a stretched bow; lean and wiry as a whippet' was Virginia Woolf's description, while to Benjamin Jowett, Master of Balliol, she was 'the most educated uneducated woman I ever knew'.[49] She was known above all for her quick wit and unrestrained candour, both of which frequently verged on outright rudeness.[50] She was also known for her generosity.[51] Margot certainly appeared generous in her actions toward Maud, for from 1910 for the next twenty years, Margot paid for Allan to live in West Wing, a grand apartment overlooking Regents Park.

If the *Vigilante* was libellous in relation to Maud, it was also libellous in relation to Margot. In the same issue in which the 'cult of the clitoris' paragraph appeared, a piece headed 'Margot and the Snipers' was placed directly below. Here the 'wife of the ex-Prime Minister' was accused of aspiring to 'the same position in English political life as Madame Caillaux holds in France.'[52] The paragraph suggested she was conspiring with 'Messrs Hogge, Pringle and Roche' – all MPs who supported Asquith as against Lloyd George, the latter having unseated Asquith as Prime Minister in 1916.[53] But why the reference to Caillaux? The French politician Joseph Caillaux had been arrested in January 1918 on the charge of communicating with the enemy – one of a series of treason trials in France at this time.

His wife was already notorious, having shot dead a journalist in March 1914 for publishing incriminating material against her husband. She had been deemed 'not guilty' of the offence, pleading a crime of passion.[54] The short *Vigilante* article was presumably implying that Margot was treacherous, scheming, impulsive and dangerous. Billing had probably hoped that if Maud Allan had not risen to the bait of libel, Margot Asquith might have obliged instead.

It was not the first time that Margot had been libelled for treason. In 1915 the newspaper the *Globe* accused her of treacherously taking presents to German prisoners-of-war. She brought a libel case against the paper and won.[55] Another rumour implicated her in the death of Lord Kitchener: she was accused of secretly signalling to the German submarine that had sunk the ship *Hampshire* in which Kitchener had sailed.[56] The Northcliffe press was at the forefront in accusing the Asquiths of Germanophilia.[57] It was true however that Margot's friends had had to insist that she send away her daughter's German governess, whom she had retained a good year into the war. (Years earlier this governess had apparently saved the life of Margot's daughter Elizabeth.)[58]

Although Margot's husband was widely disliked, she was in some ways seen as the more blameworthy – the insidious power behind the throne, her treachery more overt and calculating: 'Ambitious from her natal hour, And scheming all her life for power', ran William Watson's 1909 vicious poem 'The Woman with the Serpent's Tongue'.[59] It was Margot who represented aristocratic decadence; Asquith was not even born into the upper classes – the first Prime Minister to be without landed property or title. Margot, the daughter of an immensely wealthy Scottish businessman and landowner, had introduced Asquith into smart cosmopolitanism. She had even hosted a Paul Poiret show at Downing Street – the cutting edge of modernist fashion.[60]

Billing's choice of Maud Allan as the person to provoke into a libel suit was perfect for his purposes. The Asquiths' 'good friend', she was non-British, and although not from an enemy country, she had trained in Germany. She was a dancer, famous for performing erotic 'Oriental' dances, and was thus sexually suspect, an appellation reinforced by her friendship with Margot. But it was as Salome, her most famous role, that Allan was judged as essentially 'other', 'foreign' and 'treacherous'. That Salome was Oriental condemned her still further during the war, for the Orient was now seen as part of the enemy. Despite traditional allegiance to England and France, Turkey had entered the war on Germany's side in September 1914. As a result, to be Oriental was to be not only foreign but traitorous.[61] In contemplating the nature of Allan's allegiance, the execution in 1917 for

2 Margot Asquith, dressed in Oriental fancy-dress

espionage of another famous Oriental dancer, Mata Hari, would have been uppermost in many people's minds.[62]

'Reading' the libel

Why was Maud prompted to bring a case of libel; what did she understand the paragraph headed 'The Cult of the Clitoris' to mean? At the preliminary hearing at Bow Street Police Court in April, prior to the Old Bailey trial, Travers Humphreys, one of the two counsel representing Allan, explained why the paragraph's heading was so offensive:

> I find words which I must read, although I see there are some ladies in the court ... The cult of the clitoris ... the words themselves are the filthiest words it would be possible to imagine ... [The heading] can only mean one thing, and that is that the lady whose name is coupled with it ... approves of that which is sometimes described in ... less gross language as lesbianism, and a more horrible libel to publish of any woman ... it is impossible to find.[63]

That Maud understood these 'filthiest words' was the reason for her bringing a libel case in the first place, for she saw them as a challenge to her respectability and honour, but her very comprehension became central to her undoing.[64]

The first day at the Old Bailey was largely devoted to her cross-examination by Billing, who insisted on conducting his own defence without the aid of barristers. The *Daily Express* gave both parties flattering descriptions. Billing 'made a striking figure as he stood erect at the dock-rail, a gaunt, dark-haired, athletic-looking man, bronzed and sharp-featured, wearing an eye-glass and speaking in deep, almost sepulchral tones'.[65] As for Maud Allan, the paper described her as 'a fascinating figure ... tall, slender, delicately featured ... and she speaks with a slight accent – a suggestion of an Irish brogue [surely most unlikely]. She wore a large picture hat and dark cloak revealing a low necked blouse.'[66] Faced with the suggestion of lesbianism, she had conceivably played up her femininity, although the 'immodesty' of her costume was inappropriate for the occasion. She agreed that she had understood the libel at first sight, but when asked whether she was well acquainted with the term 'clitoris', she replied: 'Not particularly.' When she admitted that she had not had to explain the libel to her friends, Billing gleefully informed the court that out of twenty-four people to whom he had shown the libel, only one, a barrister, had known what it meant.[67] Billing's chief medical witness Dr Serrell Cooke said that he had shown it to fifty or sixty friends of his and none of them knew its meaning; (one hopes they were not doctors).[68] Although it is unclear from the reported account whether the solicited persons had not heard of the term 'clitoris', or simply did not understand the meaning of it being a cult, both interpretations seem to have been implied. Also implied was that ignorance indicated lack of perversion, but Maud (and her friends), with their inappropriate sexual knowledge, were sexually deviant.

Billing called on his henchman Captain Spencer to explain his choice of heading, for it was he who had written the paragraph. Spencer reported that he had tried to find a title 'that would only be understood by those by whom it should be understood'.[69] He had telephoned a village doctor and was given the term 'clitoris' and told that it 'was a superficial organ that, when unduly excited or overdeveloped, possessed the most dreadful influence on any woman, that she would do the most extraordinary things'.[70] He added later: 'An exaggerated clitoris might drive a woman to an elephant'.[71] Salome he saw as 'a child suffering from an enlarged and diseased clitoris'.[72] 'Of course, clitoris is a Greek word', elaborated medical witness Dr Cooke, 'it is a medical term … nobody but a medical man or people interested in that kind of thing, would understand the term'.[73] Neither Spencer nor Cooke explicitly linked the clitoris to lesbianism, but another medical witness, Dr J.H. Clarke, when asked whether there was any other term which might have done, replied: 'I cannot think of another … except … "lesbianism" and that word would be equally well known to the initiated and equally unintelligible to the uninitiated'.[74]

This distinction between the initiated and the uninitiated was not as clear cut as Clarke imagined, for it ignored the recent publication, in March, of Marie Stopes' best-seller *Married Love: a New Contribution to the Solution of Sex Difficulties,* which aimed at presenting accessible sex education to married couples. Within a fortnight, the book had sold more than 2,000 copies and by the time of the trial it was into its third edition. The thousands of people who had read the book might well have recognised the term 'clitoris', for it is graphically described and presented as a key factor in women's sexual arousal.[75] Also overlooked was the fact that one of Billing's chief witnesses, Mrs Eileen Villiers Stuart, admitted on the second day of the trial that *she* had immediately understood the libel when she had read it, and had assumed the average person would have too.[76] Yet this knowledge did not apparently deem Mrs Villiers Stuart either a pervert or a medical expert.

Knowing what the word 'clitoris' referred to was one thing; knowing what its use in a heading implied was another. The clitoris was associated with female sexual pleasure separate from both the potential of reproduction, and the 'need' for a man's penis. From the late eighteenth century through into the early twentieth century, one of the most consistent medical characterisations of the anatomy of the lesbian was the claim of an unusually large clitoris, the latter signifying masculinity. In presenting lesbians' bodies as *less* sexually differentiated than the norm – more masculine, the enlarged clitoris as analogous to the penis – it was inferred that lesbians were atavists, namely throwbacks to an earlier evolutionary stage and thereby 'degenerate'. It was held that progressive differentiation of the sexes was one of the hallmarks of evolutionary progress.[77] An enlarged clitoris or the inference of deviant genitalia was also given as the signifier of black women's sexuality and of nymphomania.[78] Lesbians, black women and nymphomaniacs were thereby all grouped together as possessors of a 'primitive' and excessive sexuality.[79] The term 'clitoris' thus carried implications beyond that of a simple anatomical appendage, for it simultaneously suggested autonomous female sexuality, nymphomania, primitiveness and lesbianism.

Unsurprisingly, the word 'clitoris' never appeared in the press, except in the *Vigilante*, available only by private subscription. On day one of the Old Bailey trial the judge, Justice Darling, directed the newspapers to self-censor: 'I hope that in the interests of public decency the press will report as little as possible of this kind of matter.'[80] The print media resorted to euphemism, evasion, even bluff such as when the *Sunday Chronicle* quoted the prosecution counsel: 'the gross heading could only mean one thing ... that which was sometimes described as – (the remainder of the sentence was inaudible)'.[81] They implicitly drew on the claim that oblique language would be unintelligible to the young and sexually ignorant, and 'suggestive' only to those more in the (sexual) know. Thus the popular press could uphold its status as a 'family' read: informative, entertaining yet 'clean', but with a tantalising 'suggestiveness' and sensationalism that had commercial pull.[82]

Maud as German sympathiser, lesbian and sadist

Billing's attempt to discredit Maud via her knowledge of the term 'clitoris' was only one of several ways in which he launched his attack. He implied that she was a German sympathiser by virtue of having undertaken musical training in Berlin. Maud's friendship with Margot Asquith furthered such suspicions because of the rumours of Margot's German sympathies. Maud was tarnished by association. Her friendship with Margot was also mentioned in a manner that suggested lesbianism, or at least intimacy. 'Has she [Margot] ever been to your dressing room at the Palace Theatre?' Billing demanded. Maud denied it. She was asked again; again she denied it. 'You would recognise her?' he facetiously inquired; 'I have eyes', was her frosty reply.[83] Margot was not physically present in the court-room, but she haunted the trial. A few days earlier, at the Front, her sexuality had been discussed by certain English officers, according to Duff Cooper: 'One of my brother-officers ... believed that Mrs Asquith was a "female bugger", that being as near as his limited vocabulary allowed him to get to Sapphist.'[84] The brother-officer then corrected himself and substituted the word 'lesbite'.[85]

Maud was also defamed through reference to her brother. Much to her horror, and the court's amazement (for her brother's crime was not common knowledge in Britain), at the opening of her cross-examination Billing handed her a book entitled *Celebrated Criminal Cases of America*, asking rhetorically whether her brother was executed for 'murdering two young girls and outraging them after death?'[86] With huge insincerity he declared that 'I deeply regret having to put this question', smugly asserting that 'the vices referred to in that book are hereditary'.[87] When Spencer entered the witness box, he likewise referred to Maud as 'a very unfortunate hereditary degenerate', and maintained that as a child, her brother's crime 'was one of the dreadful tales they use to frighten us with in Canada'.[88] Dr Cooke, who had recently worked in the psychiatric wing of Paddington hospital, added scientific authority by describing the crime as 'sadism', and confirming that sadism was indeed hereditary. 'It occurs in families which have an hereditary taint either of insanity or some other neuropathic condition ... The person who has this disease or this condition is probably not aware of it until something or other happens to light up the whole thing in them.'[89] The term 'sadism', Cooke explained, was 'derived from the Marquis of Sade' and had been coined by the Austrian psychiatrist Richard von Krafft-Ebing.[90] (He was in fact wrong on this: Krafft-Ebing admitted that the term was already used in France, but he had coined its companion concept: 'masochism'.)[91]

Probably few in the courtroom (or amongst the readers of the press) would have heard of Krafft-Ebing. Maud denied knowing of him, although she admitted to having read medical books and having heard of sadism. Krafft-Ebing's *Psychopathia Sexualis*, a study of aberrant sex, was written in 1886, translated into English in 1892, and went through a number of editions, but he was explicit on the need to restrict access to its contents. The book was addressed to 'the physician and the jurist', and the preface noted: 'In order that unqualified persons should not become readers, the author saw himself compelled to choose a title understood only by the learned'.[92] In his study he distinguished four main sexual perversions: sadism, masochism, fetishism and what he called 'contrary sexual instinct'. Within the latter he subsumed various different behaviours and identities, but largely

concentrated on homosexuality.[93] He said little specifically about lesbianism and did not link it to sadism. He believed that in many cases perversion
was neither a crime nor a sin, and that punishment was inappropriate.[94]
Unsurprisingly none of this was mentioned in court: the prosecution
appeared ignorant of the book's existence and the defence took from it se-
lectively, so as not to undermine their claims.[95]

One outcome of the exchanges between Billing and his various witnesses in the courtroom was that Maud was declared a sadist by virtue of
her brother's crime. Her alleged sadism was reinforced by Dr Cooke's assertion that any woman acting such a part as Salome would, by definition,
have to be a sadist herself, and if she were to act the part night after night
'it would be a lunatic asylum for [her] within a week'.[96] That the lunacy
resided in the claim itself (in its assertion that an actor who took on the
role of someone perverse or evil would thereby be transformed) went un-
remarked. Justice Darling (referred to by Asquith as 'that little ape') tried
to make a joke about sadism (he was known for his weak jokes in court):
'I suppose you found it interesting as the language of Sodom was a dead
language, to find it being talked'. But the joke fell flat with Billing snapping
back: 'this is not a matter to be flippant upon'.[97]

Salome on trial

The play *Salome* and its eponymous anti-heroine were likewise effectively
on trial. The play involves the young Salome, besotted with the imprisoned
John the Baptist (called Jokanaan in Wilde's version) who rebuffs her advances. She promises to dance the 'dance of the seven veils' before Herod,
her stepfather and uncle, on condition that he gives her anything she demands. Her demand is the head of Jokanaan. She dances before the head,
which is given to her on a platter, and kisses its dead lips. The play ends
with Herod demanding her execution.[98]

Discussion of *Salome* inevitably meant discussion of Wilde. Wilde's
former lover, the quarrelsome Lord Alfred Douglas, was one of Billing's
key witnesses on the immorality of *Salome*. He had become increasingly vehemently opposed to homosexuality, his retrospective rage against
Wilde incandescent, and in one of his typically melodramatic outbursts
he suddenly announced in court that Wilde 'was the greatest force for evil
in Europe in the last 350 years ... the agent of the devil'.[99] According to
the *Daily Express,* when Sir Ellis Hume-Williams, Allan's chief barrister,
mentioned love letters from Wilde to Douglas: 'Lord Alfred blazed with instant fury ... Mr Justice Darling threatened to send him out of court. Then
Lord Alfred, in a voice that had risen to a scream, openly defied the judge:

3 Maud Allan as Salome, with head of John the Baptist, 1907

"I am not here ... to be bullied and browbeaten by you."[100] The audience were agog: 'Even the agitation which followed the revelation of Miss Allan's tragic secret was eclipsed by the sensational conduct of Lord Alfred', announced a shocked *Daily Express*.[101] On the trial's final day he was forcibly ejected from court for shouting that the judge was a liar, when the latter referred to him as *Salome*'s co-author.[102] Douglas was more than happy to condemn the play. He had helped translate it from the French, but that had been half his lifetime ago, when he was 'a wretched silly youth' under the influence of 'a diabolical scoundrel'.[103] When Billing quoted from Robert Ross's preface to *Salome* as to the play's great success in Germany, Douglas agreed that the play appealed to a certain German way of thinking. *Salome* thus followed Allan in being reviled through German associations.

Like Allan, *Salome* was also discredited through being labelled sadistic. But it was apparently more than sadism that was at stake: according to Dr Cooke the play also depicted masochism, fetishism and incest. There was much debate about the effects on people of witnessing or reading the play. In his plea of justification Billing had suggested that *Salome* was designed to encourage obscenity in women, but in the trial this was never focused on (after all, the play is clearly *not* about sexual relations between women). Instead, the issue was how the play might encourage general sexual perversion among women *and men*. Father Bernard Vaughan, a Jesuit priest well-known for his impassioned, sensational sermons on 'the sins of society' and 'the demon drink', felt viewing the play would be calamitous: 'It takes us all our time to keep straight and pure when we are standing in the rear of our animal passions; but when we fan the flames we are ablaze and we are devoured.'[104] Cooke, who claimed to have made a detailed medical synopsis of *Salome* with the help of Krafft-Ebing's work, declared that 'healthy minded people' would not understand it and would simply be disgusted, but if 'they had it in them' (if sexual perversion was lying dormant), they would *become* full-blown perverts. Unfortunately there were inherited sexually perverse tendencies in many people lying unobserved until 'lit up'. (He was keen on repeating this imagery of sexual perversity as akin to hell-fire – a representation closer to Father Bernard's evangelical rhetoric than the scientific discourse of modern medicine.)[105] How many people in England had these latent tendencies? Cooke was asked. 'About a million', he confidently replied.

The attempted defence of Allan, *Salome* and Salome

What defence did Maud manage to mount against the various attacks launched on her, the play *Salome* and its eponymous protagonist? Many of the accusations were difficult to counter. Maud knew the Asquiths; she had trained in Germany; she knew certain sexual terms. Her brother was indeed a murderer and no one attempted to question the 'scientific' assertion that sadism was hereditary. As far as *Salome* was concerned, and as Billing was keen to point out, the prosecution 'has seen fit to call no evidence in support of the play'.[106] In fact Hume-Williams was explicit that 'he had no brief to defend the play', and referred to Wilde as 'a poor perverted genius'.[107] Jack T. Grein, *Salome's* producer, pointed out that some of the greatest actresses and singers had played Salome, and Allan did try to counter the claim that the play was riddled with perversion. She quipped: 'You could say "Mary had a little lamb" in many different ways, and read many different meanings into it if you wished.'[108] But the double entendre of 'having' a little lamb would probably have worked against her, since it again conveyed 'inappropriate' sexual knowledge. She stressed that she was not responsible for what others read into the script, and she also tried to defend the young woman Salome: 'she knows she is innocent but not ignorant', in what was in effect an attempted *self*-defence.[109]

Ironically, the main way in which *Salome* was defended was in Orientalist terms ('ironically' because it was the Oriental aspect of *Salome* that was crucial to its condemnation). To Maud, 'Salome lived in the Eastern world at a time when our rules were not in vogue, and when to see his head in front of her was nothing.'[110] Grein 'looked upon the play as being written in the spirit of Eastern art, and he saw no evidence of criminal vice in it'.[111] Maud and Grein thus both subscribed to the dominant view of the Orient as inherently savage and uncivilised. When asked by Billing if Grein thought 'biting by a girl child of the lips of the severed head of a man an act of sadism?' he replied: 'No ... I do consider that an Eastern characteristic of which I am no judge.'[112] These qualifying remarks would not have diminished the claim of 'sadism' however, for they merely reinforced the idea of Eastern brutality versus Western civility. (See Chapter 4 for much more on this subject.) And when Maud observed that 'it is quite uncustomary for a Westerner to understand the imagery of the Oriental people', *her* implied understanding of the Orient represented additional suspect knowledge, and distanced her still further from any association with patriotic Englishness.[113]

The theatricality of the Black Book

The trial would make a wonderful play, packed as it is with larger-than-life figures and sensational utterings. It was in fact compared to a 'Drury Lane melodrama' at the time, and its theatricality was obvious.[114] In all trials there are parts to play, some more scripted than others. The very layout of the courtroom echoes a theatre's stage and audience, with actors performing in the witness box or on the bench, and the audience listening attentively as the narrative unfolds.[115] In this trial, the acting out of roles was more explicit than in most, and some of the protagonists were keen to perform. Maud admitted that she was attempting to break into acting, hence her taking on the part of Salome in Wilde's play. ('It is my ambition to be an actress as well as a dancer', she told the court.)[116] During the trial, with the aid of her counsel, she played the part of a maligned and defenceless woman falsely accused of a (literally) unspeakable sexual pathology. Billing had previously been an actor for four years, as his many florid orations and ability to play to the gallery testified. During the trial his role was that of patriotic redeemer of true Englishness, intent on exposing corruption and decadence in high places and thereby uncovering the reason for Britain's current failure to win the war.

Spencer took the part of Billing's loyal and valiant sidekick. The description given of him by the *Daily Express* was far less flattering than those given of Billing and Allan, indeed he sounded decidedly seedy: 'A rather small young man of about twenty-eight, with smooth black hair, large deep-set eyes, thick little moustache which he bit incessantly, and an extremely sallow complexion.'[117] Although the libel trial was ostensibly about whether or not Billing was justified in calling Maud Allan and *Salome* immoral and obscene, much space was given over to discussing – or rather, shouting about – the existence of the Black Book, and it was this 'discussion' which was the most theatrical – and bizarre – aspect of the trial. Spencer deployed a language of hysterical righteousness, despite most, if not all, of the assertions about the Black Book very probably being fabrication. He claimed to have been shown this book before the war by the King of Albania, Prince William of Wied, when acting as his Aide de Camp.[118] When asked about names in the book, Spencer replied: 'I will only give the names of those whom I think have been approached and who have succumbed to German agents.'[119] Mrs Asquith and Lord Haldane were the only two he named; he did not remember Mr Asquith's name being in the book. It was a further libel against Margot.

Mrs Eileen Villiers Stuart also claimed to have seen the Black Book; she told the court that it had been shown to her by her friend (in fact her lover) the now dead Hon. Neil Primrose, second son of former Prime Minister Lord Rosebery, at, incongruously, a small hotel in Ripley.[120] Unknown to most in the court, she was in fact an agent provocateur who had been sent by Lloyd George to sexually compromise Billing.[121] Instead she had fallen under Billing's charms and defected, although she was possibly a double agent all along.[122] Initially Darling ruled that mention of the book was inadmissible, unless it could be produced, but he then immediately allowed it to be discussed at great length – one example of his inconsistency and incompetence as a judge. Villiers Stuart appeared as a witness at the trial on days two and five.[123] On her first appearance she caused a sensation by shouting out that Darling's name was in the book, and turning to the judge and 'waving her hand wildly' she exclaimed: 'we have to win this war, and while you sit there we never shall'.[124] Darling demanded that she 'Leave the box', but she simply retorted: 'You dare not hear me' and carried on regardless.[125] On her second appearance she was better behaved (the *Daily Express* found her 'remarkably cool and collected throughout her long ordeal in the box') but dramatically asserted that Neil Primrose and his friend Major Evelyn Rothschild were both dead 'because they knew of the book'.[126] She even claimed that all those named in the book were 'traitors' and would not be listed there if they were not. Up until this point it had been implied that those named in the book were so named because they were open to blackmail, and not that they had necessarily acted treacherously (as yet). The German agents in England listed in the Black Book were meant, she said, 'to create an atmosphere of indecency in England and to spread vice ... so that we should lose the war'.[127]

Whether or not the Black Book actually existed mattered less than how it operated as a site for competing claims. The Black Book was, paradoxically, all the more powerful in the absence of its materiality. Upon the mythical Black Book was projected a set of paranoid fears and fantasies concerning the conduct of the war which were incapable of refutation. Jodie Medd argues that the 'suggestibility' of lesbianism in the trial gave an 'exquisitely elusive means of figuring Britain's political and epistemological crises'; one could equally say the same of the Black Book.[128]

Responses to the verdict

Before the final summing up, Darling announced that all mention of the '47,000' was irrelevant, and the real libel lay with the offending paragraph's title. In effect he was saying that the whole discussion of the Black Book had nothing to do with the case at all. That he permitted so much space to be given to the hypothetical book in the first place demonstrated his sheer incompetence. When Billing came to give his final address to the jury, he took no notice of the judge's directive and insisted urgently: 'For three and a half years a mysterious influence seemed to have dogged our whole footsteps throughout the conduct of the war. German banks were still open in this country ... Germans uninterned ... It was time that that influence was removed.'[129] He expected that some people thought him mad or obsessed. As the *Morning Post* expressed it: 'He was obsessed with one object and that was to bring our Empire out of the war a little cleaner than when we went in. Miss Allan was only an incident.'[130] The newspaper was of course right: Allan was not Billing's real concern. He went so far as suddenly to deny that he had called Allan a lesbian at all, but claimed that she 'ministered' to sexual perverts.[131]

In his final speech, Hume-Williams, one of Allan's two counsel, observed that the '47,000' article had fallen flat; Billing and Spencer 'wanted publicity and they wanted a trial. They knew that if they were to get the publicity to curry favour with the mob with this story ... a name had to be introduced. Let it be a woman's, and if possible a woman without any husband or brother to protect her.'[132] He was castigating Billing for his lack of chivalry. The plea of justification had never been established, Hume-Williams asserted, for Billing had never proved Allan a lesbian (he ignored the MP's denial of such an accusation), and no one had suggested that lesbianism could be found in the play. There was no excuse for questioning Miss Allan about her brother and paining her – it was 'absolutely shameless and unjustifiable', 'most unmanly ... most un-English'.[133] Hume-Williams ended his speech with a plea to the twelve-man jury: 'if you hold that she is the abandoned, lewd woman that he [Billing] says she is ... she will rightly leave this Court condemned by your verdict as a woman who is not fit for decent society ... To you I entrust this lady's reputation.'[134] The jury however clearly cared less about Allan's reputation than the wild claims about the Black Book, and they seemed oblivious or indifferent to Billing's contradictions and lies, for they gave him a verdict of 'not guilty'. He had withdrawn the accusation of lesbianism, but Allan had been labelled a sadist and one who consorted with others of her kind, namely non-patriotic, non-British, sexual perverts. In court, the reaction to the verdict was loud and continuous cheering and excited hat waving ('pandemonium', according to many newspapers) while crowds of thousands awaited Billing outside.

How did the press react to the trial and its verdict? Many newspapers compared the trial's conduct to a 'madhouse', 'Bedlam' or 'Alice in Wonderland', especially the 'Mad Hatter's Tea Party'.[135] The *Westminster Gazette* was concerned that it would be 'gravely damaging to our reputation for sanity and sobriety'.[136] The *Daily Mirror* called the case 'Government by hysteria ... in a time of hysterics', in which you 'scream your way through a court of law, and ... emerge as a Great Hero.'[137] The press castigated Darling for his incompetence, inconsistency, laxity and inappropriate wit, although the right-wing *Morning Post* was less critical, pointing out how a man defending himself is always given greater latitude: 'It is as difficult for a Judge to silence an accused as for a man to silence a woman', was its misogynistic explanation.[138] There was also much objection to Billing's 'monstrous' 'mud-throwing' (the *Daily Mail* called it 'a libel to the nation'), but there was barely a nod to the plight of Maud Allan, who had been flattened by her collision with the law and was now shunned by theatre managers and her once adoring public.[139] The *New Statesman* was the only paper to criticise the 'scientific' evidence presented in court. It observed that the doctors could have got Shakespeare 'branded as a pervert' for *Hamlet*, and as for their views on hereditary traits: 'If people have to go into court with the sins of their relatives upon their shoulders, few indeed will come through'.[140] Yet for all the criticism, most of the papers were in agreement with Billing about *Salome*, and many actually agreed with the verdict, or at least thought the trial gave an important message: that those in high places must behave, for according to *The Times*: 'countless eyes are watching their doings and their associates'.[141]

What did the general public make of the trial? *The Times* noted (rather melodramatically, for *The Times*): 'It is safe to say that no lawsuit of modern times has attracted such universal and painful interest ... Not only in London, but even more in the provincial towns and countryside, the daily reports have been read and discussed with almost as deep anxiety as the news of the war itself'.[142] The trial was widely discussed at the Front as well. Duff Cooper, a young officer, wrote to his future wife Diana Manners: 'No one here speaks or thinks of anything but the Billing case.' But from his account it was not 'deep anxiety' that they were feeling: 'He [Billing] has kept the army amused for several days and provided a topic of conversation to officers who can never find one'.[143] Was this a perverse kind of relief from war fatigue? But not all officers were amused; Siegfried Sassoon wrote in his diary: 'The papers are full of this foul "Billing case". Makes one glad to be away from "normal conditions." And the Germans are on the Marne and claiming 4,500 more prisoners. The world is stark staring mad'.[144] Basil Thomson, Assistant Commissioner of the Metropolitan Police, would have agreed: 'everyone concerned [with the trial] appeared to have been either insane or behaved as if he were.'[145]

The general public may have been fascinated by the trial, but given press censorship and euphemism it is hard to ascertain what was actually known about the sexual contents. No paper reprinted the word 'clitoris' except the *Vigilante*, although Diana Manners informed Duff Cooper that 'Lord Albermarle is said to have walked into the Turf [Club] and said "I've never heard of this Greek chap Clitoris they are all talking of."'[146] That 'they' were 'all talking' about the term indicates that for some at least – the better informed upper classes? Those who had secured a place in the Old

Bailey? – the libel's heading, unnamed in the press, had seeped out into (at least part of) public discourse. And the *Daily Express* referred to 'Mr Hume-Williams' denunciation of the *now notorious* headline',[147] implying that something at least was known. As for the word 'lesbian', the *Vigilante* and *The Times* were the only papers to mention the term, and *The Times* only started using it towards the end of the trial, as if it had had to build up courage. Few of the papers referred to homosexuality. The *Manchester Guardian* used the word 'homosexual', *The Times* and the *News of the World* used 'homosexualists' [*sic*], and *The Times* also wrote of 'sodomy' and 'sodomist'. 'Sadism' was named only in the *Manchester Guardian* and the *Daily Sketch*. Otherwise the newspapers generally wrote darkly of unspecified 'sexual perversions', 'a certain vice', or the favoured term 'moral pervert' (a combination of the older language of morality and the new language of sexology). The sexological information conveyed was thus fragmentary, even garbled. For those not present at the Old Bailey (obviously the vast majority), what sense was made of these hints of sexual deviancy? Diana Manners, who was nursing at Guy's Hospital in London, reflected on precisely this question to her fiancé Duff Cooper: 'The nurses ... ask me all the time about the case and are totally ignorant of any significations. They have a dim vision of Sodom and Gomorrah, which is built for them by the word "vice". But even that is hazy.'[148] As literary critic Deborah Cohler points out, while some of the British elite may have known about 'sapphism' (the likes of Duff Cooper and Diana Manners) for many there was no clear and commonly agreed definition or understanding.[149]

Why Pemberton Billing won: battling the enemies within

If we look at the bare bones of the case, the verdict does not appear a foregone conclusion. For a start, it is unclear how Billing thought he had established the truth and public benefit of the libel. He obviously convinced the jury that the play *Salome* was highly undesirable, but he did not establish that the term 'clitoris' was appropriately linked to Maud Allan. On the contrary, at the end of the trial he had disingenuously denied that he had said she was a lesbian at all. Given too the contradictory nature of the defence's arguments, why was Billing victorious?

The reasons for Billing's success can be divided into those that discredited Allan, and those that fostered approval for the kind of claims made by Billing and his witnesses about 'enemies in our midst'. Allan was discredited as a German-loving, sadistic, sexual pervert.[150] The collective condemnation of *Salome* (including by judge and counsel), combined with the lack of challenge to either the assertion of hereditary sadism, or the extraordinary claim that anyone playing Salome would have to be sadistic herself (surely easy to have countered by reference to a multitude of famous theatrical roles), meant that Allan was effectively left without a defence. The appeal of counsel to male chivalry sounded hollow next to Billing's call to patriotism – it was indeed no defence, merely a weak plea. Allan's lawyers' incompetence was exacerbated by Darling's inability to control or direct his court.[151]

It is too easy (and wrong) to dismiss the trial and its verdict as a mad and paranoid affair, peopled by the extreme and the insane. We need to understand why Billing and his claims had such appeal (novelist Arnold Bennett was certain that Billing 'had a great deal of support from plain people throughout the country').[152] The tales told in the court drew not simply on the age-old narrative of melodrama (and virtually everyone involved in the trial deployed this genre, as we have seen) but also that of 'enemies in our midst', one wartime form of which was the 'hidden' or 'unseen hand' stalling British victory; the Black Book was obviously seen in these terms.[153] The groundwork for the 'hidden hand' idea had been laid by fiction-induced 'spy fever'. This had begun well before the war, with Edwardian spy novels such as Erskine Childers' *The Riddle of the Sands: a Record of Secret Service* (1903), and the writings of prolific William Le Queux, especially his 1906 best-seller *The Invasion of 1910*, which was first serialised in the *Daily Mail*.[154] With the outbreak of war, 'spy fever' became rife. By the beginning of September 1914, the Metropolitan Police had received 8–9,000 reports of suspected espionage, all unsubstantiated. The following month the government decreed that enemy aliens in Britain of military age be interned, but a year later thousands were still at liberty, due to lack of space to intern them, and various exemptions, including lengthy British residency.[155]

With the sinking of the *Lusitania* in May 1915, and its loss of over 1,000 civilian lives, 'spy fever' started to mutate into the more developed conspiracy theory of the 'Hidden', or 'Unseen Hand'.[156] Advocates of this theory envisaged 'concealed' Germans or Germanophiles in high places. Playwright Arthur Pinero wrote to *The Times* demanding loyalty letters from prominent naturalised Germans, and Horatio Bottomley, the right-wing editor of the popular *John Bull,* wrote a highly inflammatory article calling for 'a Vendetta … against every German in Britain, whether "naturalised" or not … you cannot naturalise an unnatural beast – a human abortion – a hellish freak, but you *can* exterminate it'. He recommended that naturalised Germans be 'compelled to wear a distinctive badge, prominently displayed', a suggestion later reiterated by the *Vigilante*.[157] The day of Bottomley's article saw serious anti-German rioting throughout Britain.

For sections of the press the 'enemy in our midst' became an obsession – not just for the journals of the right, such as *John Bull* and *National Review*, but also for the Northcliffe papers: *The Times, Daily Mail, Evening News* and *Weekly Dispatch*.

By spring 1917, MI5 had amassed 250,000 'roneo cards' for all the aliens in Britain, and 27,000 personal files on its chief suspects. (Aliens were classified along a rather infantile if amusing six-point scale: AA: Absolutely Anglised/Allied, A: Anglised/Allied, AB: Anglo-Boche – probably friendly, BA: Boche-Anglo – probably hostile, B: Boche – hostile, BB: Bad Boche – definitely hostile.)[158] Ultimately, at least 32,000 were interned (mostly men of military age), at least 20,000 repatriated (mostly women, children and non-combatant men), and the rest were restricted in their movement.[159] But for some people there were still too many aliens at large. In February 1917 a small group named the Women's Imperial Defence Council held a meeting in a London hotel addressed by William Joynson-Hicks, Conservative MP (later notorious as a repressive Home Secretary, 1924–29) who called for the 20,000 alien enemies 'uninterned in our midst' to be investigated by a Royal Commission so as to identify the 'Unseen Hand'.[160] Interest was so high that the women's group organised another meeting the following month in a bigger venue, and speakers included Billing's chums Arnold White and Corporal Beamish.[161] There was an anti-Semitic side to the campaign: pre-war, the term 'alien' usually meant Jewish; during the war it usually meant German., but for the radical right, Jewish and German were elided, and the term 'Hidden Hand' meant German Jewish conspiracy. The word 'Ashkenaz' meant Germany, the *Vigilante* claimed, and the 'Ashkenazim Germans of Frankfort' were behind the Russian Revolution and in control of the British government: 'Britain is not a democracy … but a Shylockracy'.[162]

In such a climate of 'hidden hands' and 'enemies in our midst', the idea of a German 'Black Book' would not have seemed as absurd or unlikely to the libel trial jury and the general public as it does to us today.[163] No victorious end of the war was in sight; indeed Britain and her allies appeared on the verge of defeat. Explanations and scapegoats were widely sought. Hume-Williams in his summing up was aware of the times: 'We know the wild stories that run from mouth to mouth every day … Your nerves and my nerves, nobody's nerves, are in the condition which they were before. Things are readily believed … which in pre-war times would have been incredible.'[164] As cultural historian Samuel Hynes rightly suggests: 'after four years of war, ordinary English citizens … were … willing to believe in conspiracies and plots; they had been lied to, officially, for so long … that they were ready to believe anything'.[165]

The day that the trial ended, the *Daily Mail* launched a campaign against the Home Office aliens policy, and soon other newspapers were following suit. At two London by-elections in July, the Coalition government candidates narrowly beat those from the Vigilante Society, but only after adopting the radical right demands of denaturalisation and alien internment. Hostility towards Germans reached a peak in the period mid-June through to August. Meetings and rallies throughout the country were organised by either the British Empire Union or the National Party (the latter having been set up the previous year as a right-wing split from the Conservative Party).[166] Legislation was passed to reform naturalisation laws and to close German banks. One million rallied in Hyde Park with the slogan 'Intern them all'.[167]

Homosexuality, treason and resentment of the decadent upper classes

The 'enemies within' were thought to be not solely foreigners; what has been termed the 'home front wars' encompassed a battle against 'sexual perverts' too.[168] The 'Black Book' conspiracy theory drew on the equation of homosexuality and treason which had been in circulation in certain quarters throughout the war. Lord Alfred Douglas had made the link explicit in the last lines of his 1916 poem 'The Rossiad':

> Two foes thou hast, one there, one here,
> One far, one intimately near,
> 2 filthy fogs blot out thy light,
> The German and the Sodomite.[169]

Arnold White explained why the sodomite was 'intimately near': there had been an invasion of Britain by 'German Urnings [homosexuals] for the purpose of undermining ... patriotism', an infection of 'Hunnish erotomania'. He warned: 'if the conception of home life is replaced by the Kulter of Urnings, the spirit of the Anglo-Saxon world wilts and perishes'.[170]

In his evocation of the 'enemy within', Billing expertly mobilised the widespread and deep-seated sentiments of xenophobia, anti-Semitism, homophobia, and popular resentment of officialdom. He also mobilised class hatred of the decadent upper classes. To many, the Asquiths stood for all that was most vilified in these prejudices. At the time of the Billing trial, Asquith's daughter-in-law, Cynthia Asquith, noted in her diary that 'the shop-woman sort of strata were saying "we always knew it of the Asquiths and we're glad they've been exposed"'.[171] As already mentioned, the Asquiths were said to be pro-German; they also had many Jewish friends and colleagues (Asquith had appointed several Jewish men to positions in his cabinet). Asquith had been forced to resign his Premiership in December 1916, but he continued to be held responsible for the war's gross mismanagement. The suffragette Christabel Pankhurst announced in June 1917, for example, that unfortunately 'Asquithism' still dominated Parliament, despite his being 'the most unpopular man in this country'.[172]

Before the war, the Asquiths had been at the heart of what was known as the Edwardian 'smart set'. If elitist, the upper-class grouping was also cosmopolitan in outlook – enthusiasts, for example, of the Russian ballet, experimental French art, and oriental fashion. With the outbreak of war, an argument developed casting the modernism of pre-war England as decadent and self-indulgent. Some believed that such decadence was a cause of the war, but that war, like 'Condy's Fluid', would cleanse society of this foreign pestilence.[173] The Billing trial revealed the cleansing to be incomplete. As the *World* sanctimoniously commented in its reflection on the trial: 'the public ... are shocked by the levity and unabashed *cosmopolitanism* of certain associates of the late government, who even now ... exercise considerable influence'.[174] 'Cosmopolitanism' had become a dirty word, implicitly a deadly mix of Germanophilia and decadence.

The finale of Alfred Douglas's lampooning 1915 poem 'All's Well with England' sums up the various aspersions cast upon the Asquiths:

> Out there in Flanders all the trampled ground
> is red with English blood, our children pass
> Through fire to Moloch. Who will count the loss
> Since here 'at home', sits merry Margot, bound
> with Lesbian fillets, while with front of brass
> 'Old Squiffy' hands the purse to Robert Ross?[175]

'Lesbian fillets' refers to a Grecian hairstyle – strips of ribbon in the hair – but it is also, of course, an inference of lesbianism. As for the other references: Moloch is a Semitic deity to whom parents sacrificed their children; Robert Ross, Oscar Wilde's literary executor, had recently been given a purse of seven hundred sovereigns by friends and admirers for recognition of services to Art and Literature; signatories included the Asquiths. 'Old Squiffy' is Asquith, known for his liking for drink.

Feminism and the radical right

It was not just the political right who attacked Asquith of course; feminists had long loathed Asquith for his opposition to women's suffrage. But opposition to Asquith was not all that feminists had in common with the right.

Historian Nicoletta Gullace convincingly argues that certain prominent feminists, particularly the Women's Social and Political Union (WSPU) leadership (Emmeline and Christabel Pankhurst), developed a right-wing wartime nationalist feminism that successfully reconfigured citizenship and was central to women's (partial) winning of the franchise in February 1918. In decentring manhood, majority and property, these feminists stressed the importance of loyal service, patriotic sentiment and British 'blood' as the legitimate basis for enfranchisement into British citizenship. In the process they were highly active around campaigns to intern all enemy aliens, reform naturalisation laws, confront pacifists and 'shirkers', and advocate the purging from government departments of officials with 'enemy blood' or pro-German connections.[176] It was galling to them that naturalised male aliens could vote, and they jumped on the bandwagon of racial hysteria with fellow right-wingers, such as Horatio Bottomley.[177] Christabel Pankhurst, for example, asserted: 'The Bosch is really made in a different way from the rest of us.' He is 'the enemy of mankind ... sub-human.'[178] She also subscribed to the German Jewish conspiracy idea, informing a public meeting in July 1917 that the 'Unseen Hand' meant 'German Finance': 'the International Financiers ... are Germans and German Jews.'[179] There were other feminists involved in the anti-alien campaign: Mrs Norah Dacre Fox, a close colleague of the Pankhursts and formerly of the WSPU, was a key organiser of anti-aliens meetings and rallies in the summer of 1917 and again in 1918.[180] (Her anti-German stance did not preclude her later joining the British Union of Fascists.)

Like Bottomley, Billing welcomed women's suffrage. A *Vigilante* article headed 'Women, the Centre of Power' predicted that a 'new horizon in the history of Power will be reached when civilisation perceives the significance of utilising the Power of women in the forward march of the world'.[181] Judge Darling too, perhaps surprisingly, favoured women's enfranchisement. Right at the end of the trial he launched into an attack on improper dancing and scanty stage costumes, but was hopeful that women would save the day: 'In a very short time women will be able to use their influence on legislation and then ... I hope they will make it their business to introduce much more purity into public representations than is the case at present, and I hope this verdict may help to bring about some reform in the matter.'[182]

Undesirable womanhood and Englishness

Maud and Margot were both opposed to female suffrage – Maud criticising the suffragettes and holding that 'women should influence rather than dictate', although she favoured equal education and job opportunities.[183] Margot was the more vehemently and vocally opposed. Understandably, feminists tended to loathe Margot. Cynthia Asquith was told by an MP friend that 'the scandal – as to Maud Allan and Margot – had been started and widely diffused by the suffragettes', although whether they actually did spread stories about the two women is difficult to establish.[184] As suggested in the introduction, by early 1918 there were many who held that women's patriotism and war work had demonstrated their fitness for the franchise. 'Women demonstrated their right to the privileges of citizenship by the enthusiasm for service that they have shown since the beginning of the war', enthused the *Daily Express*.[185] Neither Maud nor Margot however had demonstrated any such right. Instead, they had supposedly displayed highly inappropriate female behaviour: sexualised, foreign dancing on Maud's part; scheming, politically manoeuvring on Margot's. Their behaviour towards *each other* was held to be sexually inappropriate, although this was never established. The assumed lack of patriotism, indeed the implicit treachery, of these two well-known women was surely a determining factor in the Billing trial's outcome.

During the trial the definition of Englishness ran as a sub-theme. In his summing up, Hume-Williams had accused Billing of 'un-English' behaviour in the questioning of Allan about her brother: 'most unmanly ... most un-English'.[186] But while lack of chivalry may have been seen as un-English to Hume-Williams, Billing and his radical right colleagues reconfigured Englishness in other terms. 'True' Englishness was open and pure (including sexually): virile or womanly, heterosexual ('perversions of sexual passion have no home in the healthy mind of England' declared the right-wing *Morning Post*) family-orientated (to Arnold White: 'The English conception of their national life is that the home is the unit of the nation') as against the decadence and sexual perversion of the German or Germanophile.[187] In other words, the 'enemy within', who by definition was non/un-English, was not simply an alien other (of hostile nationality, or affiliated to such) but also morally and sexually other. And the boundaries of Englishness were marked by those at the margins – the enemies within, the suspect communities, needing to be watched by the 'countless eyes' referred to in *The Times* editorial. As Sonya Rose points out: 'Wartime is an especially prime historical moment ... for identifying and excluding those who do not exemplify particular national virtues.'[188]

Maud and Margot were seen as part of these condemned, sexually 'other', enemy aliens. Together they represented undesirable femininity – foreign or Germanophile, non-patriotic, non-productive, sexually aberrant, treacherous – as against the ideal Englishwoman who had earned her vote through patriotism, hard work for the war effort, and concern with the pursuit of morality, such as the women patrols mentioned in the introduction to this book, who had been 'cleaning up' parks and other public places. Journalist Austin Harrison writing in the *Sunday Pictorial* after the trial heralded 'The great new England which will be created out of the war, in which purge and movement of regrowth this semi-ridiculous, nauseous extravaganza is at once a symptom and a beginning.'[189] This was a new England without sexual deviancy, in which responsible, moral, family-centred women would have the vote – a vote that women like Maud Allan and Margot Asquith neither desired nor deserved.

The Billing trial acted as a vehicle for the radical right to promulgate its particular brand of nationalism, with specific exclusions pertaining to that which was defined as non-English. When Oscar Wilde was taken to court in 1895, homosexual men throughout England, fearing exposure and conviction, were reported to have fled abroad.[190] The 'cult of the clitoris' case did not of course lead to the conviction of Maud Allan – or Margot Asquith – for 'gross indecency' with women, nor to their flight abroad, but the trial's verdict sent out a message equating sexual conformity with patriotic Englishness, versus sexual perversion, decadence, foreignness and treachery. The degenerate pervert had become racialised – and the racial 'other' was the German barbarian and Oriental sadist rolled into one. As for the newly enfranchised woman, her entitlement to the suffrage appeared to rest not simply on her patriotism and British blood, but also on her disavowal of the treacherous sexual perversity of the likes of Maud Allan and Margot Asquith. Their cosmopolitan modernity, and in Maud's case sexual knowledge and sexualised dancing, were beyond the pale. For the ideal Englishwoman as constructed by the radical right was conventional and moralising, sexually conformist, the mother of the (English) 'race'. And with the vote to her name, she was going to make sure every other woman followed suit – or so the likes of Darling and Billing believed, united on this sole point: their view of a restrictive, ideal femininity. Thus one aspect of the cult of the clitoris trial involved the drawing up of battle-lines in relation to the construction of a new, post-war womanhood – a site of dispute and contestation to be considered further in the chapters that follow.

Despite Maud and Margot's ridicule and humiliation in the Billing trial, and despite their rejection of women's suffrage, they nevertheless had a definite influence on the next generation of women. Maud was an important figure in the 'dance craze' that carried on and expanded in the inter-war years; Margot, in her espousal of cosmopolitan modernity, including modernist dress, was in 1921 referred to as 'the grandmother of the flapper'.[191] Their spirit of assertiveness, their modernity and their seeking of notoriety lived on in the women of the Great War's aftermath.

Notes

1 *New Statesman*, 8th June 1918, p. 183.
2 *Sunday Pictorial*, 9th June 1918, p. 4. Dr Hawley Harvey Crippen had been hanged for the murder of his wife in 1910; remains of what was thought to be her dismembered body were found in their house in North London. See Julie English Early, 'A New Man for a New Century: Dr Crippen and the Principles Of Masculinity', in Robb and Erber (eds), *Disorder in the Court*.
3 *The Vigilante*, 16th February 1918. A small announcement in *The Sunday Times* on 10th February had advertised the play's two forthcoming private performances in April.
4 It is unclear where the idea of '47,000' came from, but reference to the *first* 47,000 was a parody of Ian Hays's *The First Hundred Thousand*, a 1915 patriotic and popular tribute to Kitchener's Army. Philip Hoare, *Wilde's Last Stand: Decadence, Conspiracy and the First World War* (London, 1997), p. 59. Maverick right-winger Arnold White declared that by the time of the trial, the number was nearer 53,000. *The Times*, 1st June 1918, p. 4.
5 *The Imperialist*, 26th January 1918, p. 3.
6 Richard Haldane, a close friend of Asquith's, was at the War Office from August 1914. He had close pre-war ties with Germany (calling it his 'spiritual home'). The *Daily Express* campaigned for his resignation, which Asquith would not accept, but when a coalition government was formed in May 1915, Haldane was dropped.
7 The renowned French actress Sarah Bernhardt was to have given a public London performance in 1892 when it was suddenly banned by the Lord Chamberlain, ostensibly on grounds of blasphemy. Sander L. Gilman, 'Salome, Syphilis, Sarah Bernhardt and the Modern Jewess', in Linda Nochlin and Tamar Garb (eds), *The Jew in the Text* (New York, 1996), pp. 97–120. It was performed privately in Britain in 1905 and 1906, and by the Actresses' Franchise League in 1911. There was a sold-out performance in 1910 of Richard Strauss's opera *Salome*, its German libretto being a condensed version of the play.
8 Martin Kettle, *Salome's Last Veil: The Libel Case of the Century* (London, 1977).
9 Mrs Belloc Lowndes, *A Passing World* (London, 1948), p. 223. Marie Belloc Lowndes, sister of Hilaire Belloc, was a prolific novelist and knew many on the literary scene including Oscar Wilde and Henry James. She was President of the Women's Suffrage League in 1913.
10 There are two books on the trial: Kettle, *Salome's Last Veil* and Hoare, *Wilde's Last Stand*. Other commentaries include Regenia Gagnier, *Idylls of the Marketplace: Oscar Wilde and the Victorian Public* (Aldershot, 1987), Appendix A; Jennifer Travis, 'Clits in Court: Salome, Sodomy and the Lesbian Sadist', in Carla Jay (ed.), *Lesbian Erotics* (New York, 1995); Lucy Bland, 'Trial by Sexology? Maud Allan, *Salome* and the "Cult of the Clitoris" Case', in Lucy Bland and Laura Doan (eds), *Sexology in Culture: Labelling Bodies and Desires* (Oxford, 1998); Angus McLaren, *Twentieth Century Sexuality: a History* (Oxford, 1999), Chapter 1; Doan, *Fashioning Sapphism*, Chapter 2; Gay Wachman, *Lesbian Empire:*

Radical Crosswriting in the Twenties (New Brunswick, NJ, 2001), Chapter 1; Josie Medd, "'The Cult of the Clitoris": Anatomy of a National Scandal', *MODERNISM/Modernity*, 9, 1 (2002), pp. 21–49; Judith R. Walkowitz, 'The "Vision of Salome": Cosmopolitanism and Erotic Dancing in Central London, 1908–1918', *American Historical Research*, 108, 2 (April 2003), pp. 337–76; Deborah Cohler, 'Sapphism and Sedition: Producing Female Homosexuality in Great War Britain', *Journal of the History of Sexuality*, 16, 1 (2007), pp. 68–94; Judith R. Walkowitz, *Nights Out: Life in Cosmopolitan London* (New Haven, CT and London, 2012), Chapter 3. The trial is briefly mentioned in Pat Barker's wonderful novel *The Eye in the Door* (London, 1994).

11 Kettle, *Salome's Last Veil*, Chapter 2.

12 Medd, "'The Cult of the Clitoris"'; p. 24.

13 Travis, 'Clits in Court', p. 147.

14 Doan, *Fashioning Sapphism*, p. 36.

15 Historian G.R. Searle calls him 'the most conspicuous and dangerous of all the war-time jingo demagogues'. G.R. Searle, *Corruption in British Politics, 1895–1930* (Oxford, 1987), p. 256.

16 *Sunday Chronicle*, 9th June 1918, p. 1 mentions that Mr Billing 'is married to a daughter of Mr Theodore Henry Schwetizer of Bristol'.

17 'There was a good deal of sarcastic questioning both by judge and counsel on the subject of Captain Spencer's alleged hallucinations'. *Daily Express*, 31st May 1918, p. 3. Travers Humphreys tried to get some documents brought in to establish whether Spencer was certified insane; the judge refused the request. *The Times*, 3rd June, 1918, p. 4.

18 Quoted during the trial. *Verbatim Report of the Trial of Noel Pemberton Billing, M.P., on a Charge of Common Libel* (London, 1918), p. 167.

19 *Manchester Guardian*, 4th June 1918, p. 8.

20 See Richard Ellman, *Oscar Wilde* (London, 1988).

21 See Merlin Holland, *Irish Peacock & Scarlet Marquess: the Real Trial of Oscar Wilde* (London, 2003), p. 300, fn.40 on how Wilde found Humphreys boring.

22 *The Times*, 30th May 1918, p. 4.

23 See H. Montgomery Hyde (ed.), *The Trials of Oscar Wilde* (London, 1948); Holland, *Irish Peacock & Scarlet Marquess*.

24 Felix Cherniavsky, *The Salome Dancer: The Life and Times of Maud Allan* (Toronto, 1991), p. 21.

25 Cherniavsky, *Salome Dancer*, p. 53.

26 Maud Allan, *My Life and Dancing* (London, 1908), Introduction.

27 She had been influenced by Max Reinhardt's 1904 production of Wilde's *Salome*. Cherniavsky, *Salome Dancer*, p. 142. Earlier that year she had had a terrible trick played upon her. A Hungarian count had dared her to dance in a cage of lions, but she had won the bet by procuring harmless cubs. In revenge he got her to perform the 'Vision of Salome' privately and had her given a real severed head. Cherniavsky, *Salome Dancer*, pp. 146–7.

28 Amy Koritz, *Gendering Bodies/Performing Art: Dance and Literature in Early Twentieth Century British Culture* (Ann Arbor, MI, 1995), p. 15.

29 See Bram Dijkstra, *Idols of Perversity* (Oxford, 1986), Chapter XI; Amy Koritz, 'Salome: Exotic Woman and the Transcendent Dance', in Antony Harrison and Beverley Taylor (eds), *Gender and Discourse in Victorian Literature and Art* (DeKalb, IL, 1992); Elaine Showalter, *Sexual Anarchy: Gender and Culture at the Fin de Siècle* (London, 1991),

Chapter 8; Julie Wheelwright, *The Fatal Lover: Mata Hari and the Myth of Women in Espionage* (London, 1992), Walkowitz, 'The "Vision of Salome"'.

30 *New York Times*, 16th August 1908; 23rd August 1908; 3rd September 1908.

31 Koritz, *Gendering Bodies/Performing Art*, Chapter 2; Lacy McDearmon, 'Maud Allan: the Public Record', in *Dance Chronicle*, 2, 2 (1978), p. 89.

32 Isadora Duncan, *My Life* (London, 1928), pp. 157–8.

33 She was paid £250 a week at the Palace Theatre, and gave private recitals for a minimum of £250. Cherniavsky, *Salome Dancer*, p. 173.

34 Walkowitz, *Nights Out*, p. 80.

35 Diana Cooper, *The Rainbow Comes and Goes* (London, 1958, 1961), p. 77.

36 See Peter Wollen, 'Fashion/Orientalism/The Body', in *New Formations*, 1 (Spring 1987); Kenneth Silver, *Esprit de Corps: The Art of the Parisian Avant-Garde and the First World War* (London, 1989), pp. 167–75; Mica Nava, 'The Cosmopolitanism of Commerce and the Allure of Difference: Selfridges, the Russian Ballet and the tango, 1911–1914', *International Journal of Cultural Studies*, 1, 2 (1998), pp. 163–96.

37 Walkowitz, 'The "Vision of Salome"', pp. 345–6.

38 Allison Jean Abra, 'On with the Dance: Nation, Culture and Popular Dancing in Britain, 1918–1945' (Ph.D. thesis, University of Michigan, 2009).

39 Quoted in *Pall Mall Gazette*, 11th March 1908. No copies of the pamphlet appear to survive. Cherniavsky suggests that the Palace Theatre's manager, Alfred Butt, had all copies destroyed, as he realised their damaging potential. Cherniavsky, *Salome Dancer*, p. 162.

40 See Rana Kabbani, *Europe's Myths of Orient* (London, 1988); Reina Lewis, *Gendering Orientalism* (London, 1996).

41 Koritz, 'Salome: Exotic Woman and the Transcendent Dance', p. 264.

42 Cherniavsky, *Salome Dancer*, pp. 172, 147.

43 Quoted in G.R. Searle, *The Liberal Party. Triumph and Disintegration, 1886–1929* (London, 1992), p. 93.

44 Author of 'Nemesis Hunt', *Maudie* (London, 1909).

45 Quoted in Cherniavsky, *Salome Dancer*, p. 207. The Viceroy's own account is rather different, narrating how Allan modified her clothes and dances accordingly, resulting in him giving her 'full marks … for her behaviour'. Lord Charles Hardinge of Penshurst, *My Indian Years* (London, 1948), p. 88.

46 Amy Koritz, 'Dancing the Orient for England: Maud Allan's "The Vision of Salome"', *Theatre Journal*, 46 (1994), p. 65.

47 Cherniavsky, *Salome Dancer*, pp. 176, 193; Walkowitz, 'The "Vision of Salome"', p. 371. Marie Belloc Lowndes, a friend of Margot's, does not comment on this claim of lesbianism, but notes that 'she [Margot] did not care for women … The only two women she really loved were her sister … and her daughter'. Lowndes, *A Passing World*, p. 112.

48 Angela Lambert, *Unquiet Souls: The India Summer of the British Aristocracy, 1880–1918* (London, 1984). The Souls' offspring went on to rebel in turn, calling themselves the 'corrupt coterie'. Jeanne MacKenzie, *The Children of the Souls: a Tragedy of the First World War* (London, 1986).

49 Anne Olivier Bell (ed.), *The Diary of Virginia Woolf, Vol. 1, 1915–19* (London, 1977), 12th October 1918, p. 201. MacKenzie, *The Children of the Souls*, p. 10. Her prominent, beaky nose (broken in a riding accident) led to her being described as 'looking like a parrot trying to eat a cherry', according to the writer and poet Michael Burn, who knew her

when he was young. Personal communication. 'Margot's wit was as spontaneous and un-
predictable as though she were totally unaware of society's rules for decorum. It flashed
like lightening … many people feared her accurate, sharp tongue.' Lambert, *Unquiet
Souls*, p. 11.

50 'She [Margot] could not conceal what she was feeling, and she was wholly lacking in
the capacity to behave with what may be called the hypocrisy without which life could
scarcely be carried on.' Susan Lowndes (ed.), *Diaries and Letters of Marie Belloc Lowndes,
1911–1947* (London, 1971), p. 263.

51 Frances Horner, *Time Remembered* (London, 1933), p. 169.

52 *Vigilante*, 9th Febuary 1918, p. 1.

53 Thanks to Roland Quinault for identifying these three names as Asquithian MPs.

54 See Edward Berenson, *Trial of Madame Caillaux* (Berkeley, CA and Oxford, 1992).

55 See *Daily Mail*, 18th December 1915, p. 5; 22nd December 1915, p. 2; 22nd March 1916, p. 3.

56 Daphne Bennett, *Margot. A Life of the Countess of Oxford and Asquith* (London, 1984),
p. 288. Another version of this story had her arrange for a bomb to be placed in the ship.
Lowndes, *A Passing World*, p. 74.

57 Lambert, *Unquiet Souls*, p. 210.

58 Lowndes (ed.), *Diaries and Letters of Marie Belloc Lowndes*, pp. 113–14.

59 William Watson, 'The Woman with the Serpent's Tongue', *New York Times*, 30th October
1909, p. 1. See 'A Gentleman with a Duster' [Harold Begbie], *The Glass of Fashion: Some
Social Reflections* (London, 1921, 1922), p. 49.

60 Bennett, *Margot*; Colin Clifford, *The Asquiths* (London, 2002). Judith Walkowitz points
out that Poiret's 'war on corsets' owed much to the Anglo-American health reform tradition, as opposed to being daringly Continental. Walkowitz, 'The "Vision of Salome"', p.
360.

61 Silver, *Esprit de Corps*, p. 177.

62 See Wheelwright, *The Fatal Lover*; Rosie White, '"You'll be the Death of Me": Mata Hari
and the Myth of the *Femme Fatale*', in Helen Hanson and Catherine O'Rawe (eds), *The
Femme Fatale: Images, Histories, Contexts* (London, 2010); Grayzel, *Women and the First
World War*, pp. 43–5.

63 *Vigilante*, 6th April 1918, p. 1.

64 'I am not out for limelight but I will go through the limelight where my honour is concerned'. *Morning Post*, 30th May 1918, p. 7, quoting Maud Allan.

65 *Daily Express*, 30th May 1918, p. 1.

66 *Daily Express*, 30th May 1918, p. 3.

67 *Verbatim Report*, pp. 84–5.

68 *Verbatim Report*, p. 260.

69 *The Times*, 31st May 1918, p. 4.

70 *Verbatim Report*, p. 163.

71 *Verbatim Report*, p. 226.

72 *Verbatim Report*, p. 188.

73 *Verbatim Report*, p. 259. To loud laughter Darling responded: 'You mean, if an indecent
thing is said in Greek, it is not so offensive, except to the Greeks of course.' *Verbatim
Report*, p. 260.

74 *Verbatim Report*, p. 317.

75 Marie Stopes, *Married Love: a New Contribution to the Solution of Sex Difficulties* (London,
1918), p. 50.

76 *Manchester Guardian*, 31st May 1918, p. 8, and many of the other daily newspapers.

77 See Bland, *Banishing the Beast*, p. 71.

78 See Sander Gilman, 'Black Bodies, White Bodies: Towards an Iconography of Female Sexuality in Late Nineteenth-Century Art, Medicine and Literature', in James Donald and Ali Rattansi (eds), *'Race', Culture and Difference* (London, 1992); Thomas Laqueur, 'Amor Veneris', in Michel Feher (ed.), *Fragments for a History of the Human Body*, Part 3 (New York, 1989).

79 See Margaret Gibson, 'Clitoral Corruption: Body Metaphors and American Doctors' Construction of Female Homosexuality, 1870–1900', in Vernon Rosario (ed.), *Science and Homosexualities* (London, 1997). By the late nineteenth century, a number of sexologists were questioning some of these assumptions. See for example Havelock Ellis, *Sexual Inversion* (Watford, 1897), p. 98.

80 *Manchester Guardian*, 30th May 1918, p. 8; *Daily News*, 30th May 1918, p. 5; *Evening News*, 30th May 1918, p. 1.

81 *Sunday Chronicle*, 7th April 1918, p. 4. This report concerned the Bow Street hearing.

82 See Bingham, *Family Newspapers?*

83 *The Times*, 30th May 1918, p. 4.

84 Artemis Cooper (ed.), *A Durable Fire: the Letters of Duff and Diana Cooper, 1913–1950* (London, 1983).

85 John Charmley, *Duff Cooper: the Authorised Biography* (London, 1986), p. 23. During the trial H.H. Asquith's daughter-in-law, Cynthia Asquith, noted in her diary that a friend of hers was being shown furniture in a big store when the showman commented: 'This would make a nice little Lesbian bower for Mrs Asquith – wouldn't it?' It should be noted that the diary was published in 1968 and thus it is possible that she substituted the word 'Lesbian' for the term in her original diary entry. Cynthia Asquith, *Diaries 1915–1918* (London, 1968), 4th June 1918, p. 447.

86 *The Times*, 30th May 1918. The *Daily Express* described the court as 'thunderstruck'. *Daily Express*, 30th May 1918, p. 1, although Lord Alfred Douglas previously knew about her brother, through his own brother, Lord Sholto, who was living in California at the time of the murders. Cherniavsky, *The Salome Dancer*, p. 172.

87 *Verbatim Report*, p. 84; *The Times*, 30th May 1918.

88 *The Times*, 1st June 1918, p. 1.

89 *Verbatim Report*, p. 251.

90 *Daily Sketch*, 1st June 1918, p. 2.

91 McLaren, *Trials of Masculinity*, p. 172

92 Richard von Krafft-Ebing, *Psychopathia Sexualis* (Philadelphia, PN, 1892), p. v. Note that his assumption that only doctors and lawyers would understand the title was undermined by the fact that nearly all upper and upper-middle class British men would have learnt Latin at school.

93 These behaviours were later re-classified by others as hermaphroditism, bisexuality, transvestism, transsexuality etc. Von Krafft-Ebing claimed that homosexuality was either acquired (brought on by certain conditions or behaviour) or was congenital, and a sign of hereditary degeneracy. By 1901 he was arguing that homosexuality was always inborn and not pathological per se. Gert Hekma, 'A Female Soul in a Male Body', in Gilbert Herdt (ed.), *Third Sex, Third Gender* (New York, 1994).

94 See Harry Oosterhuis, 'Richard von Krafft-Ebing's "Step-Children Of Nature": Psychiatry and the Making of Homosexual Identity', in Vernon A. Rosario (ed.), *Science and*

Homosexualities (London, 1997), pp. 67–88; Harry Oosterhuis, *Step-Children Of Nature: Krafft-Ebing, Psychiatry and the Making of Sexual Identity* (Chicago, 2000).

95 See Walkowitz, *City of Dreadful Delight*, p. 207 on W.T. Stead's use of the term 'sadism' in relation to the 1888 Jack the Ripper murders.

96 *Verbatim Report*, p. 259.

97 *The Times*, 1st June 1918, p. 4. Asquith referred to Darling as a 'little ape' in a letter to his daughter Violet in 1911, in Mark Bonham Carter and Mark Pottle (eds), *Lantern Slides: the Diaries and Letters of Violet Bonham Carter, 1904–1914* (London, 1996), p. 255.

98 For an interesting discussion of the play see Gagnier, *Idylls of the Marketplace*; Peter Horne, 'Sodomy to Salome', in Mica Nava and Alan O`Shea (eds), *Modern Times* (London, 1996).

99 *The Times,* 3rd June, 1918, p. 4. The journalist Beverley Nichols, who met Douglas in 1925, described him as 'a very, very nasty little man'. Beverley Nichols, *The Sweet and the Twenties* (London, 1958), p. 230.

100 *Daily Express*, 3rd June 1918, p. 3.

101 *Daily Express*, 3rd June 1918, p. 3.

102 *The Times*, 5th June 1918, p. 4.

103 *Verbatim Report*, p. 297.

104 *The Times*, 3rd June 1918, p. 4. See his obituary in *The Times*, 1st November 1922, p. 13.

105 Dr Arthur Everard, called as a witness after Clarke, also used this imagery: the play would 'light up the latent vices'. *Verbatim Report*, p. 319. See McLaren, *Trials of Masculinity*, Chapter 7 for an excellent discussion of ideas about sadism.

106 *The Times*, 31st May 1918, p. 4. And see *Vigilante*, 15 June 1918, p. 3.

107 *The Times*, 5th June 1918, p. 4. And Hume-Williams told Douglas: 'I should be glad if you did not couple me with Oscar Wilde'. *The Times*, 3rd June 1918, p. 4.

108 *The Times*, 30th May 1918, p. 4.

109 *Verbatim Report*, pp. 103, 105.

110 *Verbatim Report*, p. 103.

111 *Daily News*, 4th June 1918, p. 5.

112 *Verbatim Report*, p. 328.

113 *Verbatim Report*, p. 100.

114 *Daily Mail*, 5th June 1918, p. 2, editorial.

115 Robb and Erber (eds), *Disorder in the Court*, p. 7; Ginger Frost, *Promises Broken: Courtship, Class and Gender in Victorian England* (Charlottesville, VA and London, 1997).

116 *Verbatim Report*, p. 95.

117 *Daily Express*, 31st May 1918, p. 3

118 At the time of learning about the book, Spencer claimed to have reported its existence to Admiral Troubridge, who apparently did nothing. Possibly he had other things on his mind: his wife Una was soon to leave him for her lover Radclyffe Hall. See Sally Cline, *Radclyffe Hall: a Woman Called John* (London, 1997). After the trial, on 1st July, the *Times* printed a report denying that the Prince knew of either Captain Spencer or the Black Book. Kettle, *Salome's Last Veil*, p. 291.

119 *The Times*, 31st May 1918, p. 4.

120 *Verbatim Report*, p. 141.

121 *Verbatim Report*, pp. 479–80.

122 Kettle, *Salome`s Last Veil*, p. 55. Cynthia Asquith had heard a different story: that Villiers Stuart had originally been hired by Allan to discover what Billing knew about her.

Asquith, *Diaries*, p. 448.

123 She was described as 'a good-looking brunette with a pale complexion and a girlish voice.' *Daily Express*, 31st May 1918, p. 3.

124 *Daily Chronicle*, 31st May 1918, p. 3, also same wording in *Manchester Guardian* and *Daily News*.

125 *Verbatim Report*, p. 144.

126 *Daily Express*, 4th June 1918, p. 3; *The Times*, 4th June 1918, p. 4. To Cynthia Asquith: 'The fantastic foulness of the insinuations that Neil Primrose and Evelyn de Rothschild were murdered from the rear makes one sick. How miserably conducted a case, both by that contemptible Darling and Hume-Williams!' Asquith, *Diaries*, p. 448.

127 *Manchester Guardian*, 4th June 1918, p. 8. She named Jack Grein as one of these agents. This accusation was simply left hanging. On previous occasions Allan's counsel Hume-Williams had objected to the mention of persons not present, but Darling had simply carelessly responded: 'So many people have been mentioned a few more or less make no difference.' *Verbatim Report*, p. 172. On this occasion Grein was in court but had no opportunity to defend himself.

128 Medd, '"The Cult of the Clitoris"', p. 44.

129 *Manchester Guardian*, 4th June 1918, p. 8. Similar report in *Daily News*, 4th June 1918, p. 5.

130 *Morning Post*, 4th June 1918, p. 3. As Gay Wachman points out, unlike the Marquis of Queensberry's libel, there was nothing personal about Billing's choice of Allan. Wachman, *Lesbian Empire*, p. 15.

131 Was this similar to Queensbury's denial that he had called Wilde a sodomite, but had said he 'posed' as one, which he claimed was just as bad?

132 *The Times*, 5th June 1918, p. 4.

133 *The Times*, 5th June 1918, p. 4; *Verbatim Report*, p. 420.

134 *Verbatim Report*, p. 420.

135 See *Westminster Gazette*, 5th June 1918, p. 5; *Daily Mail*, 5th June 1918, p. 2; *Sunday Pictorial*, 9th June 1918, p. 4; *Daily News*, 5th June 1918, p. 4; *Daily Herald*, 8th June 1918, p. 2.

136 *Westminster Gazette*, 5th June 1918, p. 1.

137 *Daily Mirror*, 8th June 1918, p. 6.

138 *The Times*, 5th June 1918, p. 7; *Daily Telegraph*, 6th June 1918; *Manchester Guardian*, 5th June 1918, p. 4; *Sunday Chronicle*, 9th June 1918, p. 1; *Morning Post*, 6th June 1918, p. 4.

139 This was despite Justice Darling claiming that she left the court 'without a stain upon her character'. *The Times*, 5th June 1918, p. 7; *Sunday Chronicle*, 9th June 1918, p. 1; *Daily Mail*, 5th June 1918, p. 2; Cherniavsky, *The Salome Dancer*, p. 24.

140 *New Statesman*, 8th June 1918, p. 183.

141 *The Times*, 5th June 1918, p. 7. And see *Daily Mail*, 5th June 1918, p. 2; *Daily Telegraph*, 6th June 1918; *The Times*, 5th June 1918, p. 7; *Morning Post*, 6th June 1918, p. 4; Austin Harrison in *Sunday Pictorial*, 9th June 1918, p. 5. To the *World*: ' If this unsavoury episode has the effect of checking levity in high places … and of producing a revulsion against the "aestheticism" which is apt to degenerate into perversion, it will not have been without its uses.' *The World*, 11th June 1918, p. 516. On agreement with Billing about *Salome*, even the liberal *New Statesman* referred to it as 'that pretentious and pseudo-poetical work'. *New Statesman*, 8th June 1918, p. 183. See *Sunday Chronicle*, 9th June 1918, p. 1; *Sunday Pictorial*, 9th June 1918, p. 5, but also Arnold Bennett's defence: *Lloyd's Sunday News*, 9th June 1918, p. 4.

142 *The Times*, 5th June 1918, p. 7. 'I can recall nothing of recent years which has interested so many different kinds of people, from the austere patriot down to the merest sensation-monger', was the opinion of the *Sunday Chronicle*, 9th June 1918, p. 1.

143 3rd June 1918 and 6th June 1918, in Cooper (ed.), *A Durable Fire*, pp. 67, 71.

144 Siegfried Sassoon, *Diaries, 1915–1918* (London, 1983), p. 259.

145 Diary entry, 4th June 1918, Basil Thomson, *The Scene Changes* (New York, 1937), p. 408.

146 5th June 1918, in Cooper (ed.), *A Durable Fire*, p. 70.

147 *Daily Express*, 30th May 1918, p. 3. My emphasis.

148 Cooper (ed.), *A Durable Fire*, p. 66, 31st May 1918.

149 Cohler, 'Sapphism and Sedition', p. 92.

150 For the role of sexology in the discrediting of Maud Allan, and the way that sexology was itself discredited, see Bland, 'Trial by Sexology?'

151 See Travers Humphreys, *Criminal Days* (London, 1946), p. 146, on Darling's lack of directing of the jury.

152 *Lloyd's Sunday News*, 9th June 1918, p. 4.

153 On melodrama see Walkowitz, *City of Dreadful Delight*, passim for a discussion of the use of melodrama.

154 Erskine Childers, *The Riddle of the Sands: a Record of Secret Service* (London, 1903, 1978). Childers was an Irish Nationalist, executed by the British during the Irish civil war. Queux's book sold a million copies and was translated into 27 languages, Christopher Andrew, *The Defence of the Realm: The Authorized History of MI5* (London, 2009), p. 8. Lord Northcliffe, owner of the *Daily Mail*, in the interests of circulation got Queux to change the original route for the German army's invasion to allow every English town to be included. The paper's circulation rose by 80,000. Andrew, *Defence of the Realm*, p. 9. See David French, 'Spy Fever in Britain, 1900–1915', *Historical Journal*, 21, 2 (1978), pp. 355–70. Queux's other popular fictional works included *Spies of the Kaiser: Plotting the Downfall of England* (1909), *The German Spy* (1914), *German Spies in England* (1915) and *The Spy Hunter* (1916). See *Illustrated Sunday Herald*, February–March 1918 for serialisation of one of his 'hidden hand' stories. And see Mrs Belloc Lowndes, *Good Old Anna* (1915).

155 Andrew, *Defence of the Realm*, Chapter 2.

156 Panikos Panayi, *The Enemy in our Midst* (New York and London, 1991), p. 170.

157 Panikos Panayi, 'Anti-German Riots in Britain during First World War', in Panayi, *Racial Violence in Britain in Nineteenth and Twentieth Centuries* (Leicester, 1996), pp. 73–4.

158 Andrew, *Defence of the Realm*, p. 58.

159 Andrew, *Defence of the Realm*, p. 81.

160 *The Times*, 9th February 1917, p. 3.

161 *The Times*, 5th March 1917, p. 5. A parody of this fear in the form of a play called *The Hidden Hand* by Lawrence Cown ran in the Strand in July 1918. *The Times*, 5th July 1918, p. 9.

162 *Vigilante*, 23rd February and 2nd March 1918; and see Arnold White, *The Hidden Hand* (London, 1917).

163 One real life pre-war German spy, Armgaard Graves, convicted and then recruited as a double agent by Britain's Secret Service Bureau (later to be MI5) in 1912, maintained that at the German intelligence headquarters in Berlin there was a book naming all the German agents in Britain (the basis for the 'Black Book' claim?); the book never materialised. Andrew, *Defence of the Realm*, p. 43.

164 Kettle, *Salome's Last Veil*, p. 247.

165 Samuel Hynes, *A War Imagined: the First World War and English Culture* (London, 1990), p. 232. And see Trudi Tate, *Modernism, History and the First World War* (Manchester and New York, 1998), p. 45. The *Sunday Chronicle* asked a number of 'typical men and women' in the vicinity of Whitehall why they thought Billing had won. One canvassed MP commented: 'I don't suppose anyone believes all the talk about the book. But they do believe in German influences of some kind or another', *Sunday Chronicle*, 9th June 1918, p. 1.

166 Susan McPherson and Angela McPherson, *Mosley's Old Suffragette: a Biography of Norah Dacre Fox* (London, 2010), p. 86.

167 Searle, *Corruption in British Politics*, p. 242. British Nationality and Status of Alien Act, 1918 gave the government power to revoke naturalisation. Despite 'Trading with the Enemy' Acts confiscating most German-owned businesses, German banks stayed open on the procurement of Home Office licences.

168 Hynes, *A War Imagined*, p. 232. Hynes identifies the last of the 'home front wars' as the banning in October 1918 of *Despised and Rejected* by A.T. Fitzroy (Rose Allatini) for its pacifism, although implicitly also for its positive portrayal of homosexuality. Hynes, *A War Imagined*, pp. 232–4.

169 Reprinted in *Vigilante*, 20th April 1918, p. 2. Images of brutal but effeminate Germans appeared in popular fiction, for example in John Buchan's 1916 book *Greenmantle*, which depicts the German officer villain Ulric von Strumm as huge, brutal and effeminate. Hynes, *A War Imagined*, p. 224.

170 'Vanoc' (Arnold White), *Referee*, 2nd June 1918; Arnold White, 'Efficiency and Empire', *Vigilante*, 20th April 1918, p. 3. Roger Casement had been executed for treason in August 1916 for his role in the Irish Easter Uprising, and although few people would probably have known about his homosexuality and the influence of his discovered 'black diary' (detailing his sexual relations with black men) in the rejection of clemency, Darling knew, for he had been on the appeal panel and it may well have added to his prejudice against Wilde and his associates. Jeffrey Dudgeon, *Roger Casement: the Black Diaries* (Belfast, 2002).

171 Asquith, *Diaries*, 2nd June 1918, p. 445.

172 *Britannia*, 29th June 1917, p. 32

173 Hynes, *A War Imagined*, p. 12.

174 *The World*, 11th June 1918, p. 516. My emphasis.

175 Kettle, *Salome's Last Veil*, p. 15.

176 Gullace, 'The Blood of our Sons', Chapter 6.

177 Gullace, 'The Blood of our Sons', p. 132. *John Bull*, 6th March 1915 wished Mrs Pankhurst 'good luck' for her 'splendid work' in recruiting, and Mrs and Christabel Pankhurst sometimes appeared on the same platform as Bottomley. Gullace, 'The Blood of our Sons', p. 125.

178 Gullace, 'The Blood of our Sons', p. 132.

179 *Britannia*, 13th July 1917, p. 47.

180 Panayi, *The Enemy in our Midst*, p. 218; *The Times*, 15th July 1918, p. 3; McPherson and McPherson, *Mosley's Old Suffragette*, p. 84.

181 *Vigilante*, 2nd March 1918, p. 8. Arnold White contrasted the German conception of women: 'lower than that of the Zulus', *Vigilante*, 20th April 1918, p. 3.

182 *The Times*, 5th June 1918, p. 4.

183 See Allan, *My Life and Dancing*, pp. 110–19.

184 Asquith, *Diaries 1915–1918*, 4th June 1918, p. 447.
185 *Daily Express*, 11th January 1918, p. 2.
186 *Verbatim Report*, p. 420.
187 *The Morning Post*, 6th June 1918; *Vigilante*, 20th April 1918, p. 3.
188 Sonja O. Rose, *Which People's War? National Identity and Citizenship in Wartime Britain, 1939–1945* (Oxford, 2003), p. 72.
189 *Sunday Pictorial*, 9th June 1918, p. 5.
190 Ellmann, *Oscar Wilde*.
191 'A Gentleman with a Duster', *Glass of Fashion*, p. 46.

2

Butterfly women, 'Chinamen', dope fiends and metropolitan allure

The susceptible modern woman

I n June 1919 the *Illustrated Sunday Herald* published an article entitled 'Is the Modern Woman a Hussy?' The writer claimed that the country was being subjected to 'a virulent epidemic of Retrospective Morality … that exasperating form of moral criticism which compares the faults of the present with the morals of the past'. He quoted a recent assertion of Judge Darling's as one example: '"between the women of today and their mothers there is the whole width of heaven"'.[1] As seen in Chapter 1, a year earlier Darling had hoped that with the vote, women would 'make it their business to introduce much more purity into public representations'.[2] Presumably to Darling the younger, voteless flapper or modern woman would not be contributing to this 'greater purity' project. If the *Illustrated Sunday Herald* article about the 'modern woman' is indicative of the wide-spread debate over female morality and behaviour that occurred after the war, one theme in this debate related to sensation-seeking, particularly the danger to the modern woman of her impetuous pursuit of instant gratification. She needed protection from *herself*, from her attraction to the entrapping pleasures of modernity, especially those of the Metropolis.

So what were the dangers of the Metropolis thought to beset the modern girl/woman at this time? To Revd Degen writing in a popular Sunday newspaper: 'The supreme obsession of the modern girl is to have a topping time … it is not long before her strongly-developed craving for thrills, variety and excitement drives her into immorality, alcohol, drugs and nightclubs.'[3] Alcohol and drugs were vices associated with nightclubs, along with smoking, unscrupulous men and sexual licentiousness.[4] While these were perceived as primarily dangers of London's West End, there were dangers specific to the East End too. One central danger here was the attraction of young white women to men of colour, and it was the dock area

of Limehouse, home to Chinese sailors and shopkeepers, which was identified by the authorities and the press as the East End's prime geographical
'lure'.

The term 'lure' is used advisedly, for women drawn to the dangers of
nightclubs, drugs, drink, men of colour and Limehouse were all described
in the press as being 'lured'. The dictionary definition of a 'lure' is 'an ap-
paratus used by falconers to recall their hawks', 'something which allures,
entices or tempts'. It also means 'a trap or snare'.[5] This avian analogy of
the lured hawk had a parallel with the idea of young women as 'flappers',
their 'flightiness' and 'fluttering' rendering them insubstantial, unstable
and presumably not worthy of the vote. The press implied that deflection
and 'escape' from these enticing entrapments was socially desirable and
indeed women's pursuit of drugs, gambling and/or men of colour generated extensive media attention. This chapter thus concerns young modern
women/flappers of the Metropolis and the debates and anxieties concerning their susceptibility to and pursuit of sensation, pleasure and desire,
whether these be sought in the bright lights and nightlife of the West End,
or through relationships with Chinese men in East End's Limehouse. The
focus here is on the representation of three different 'types' of modern
woman: the 'butterfly' woman of the West End, the 'lured' young woman
attracted to the 'Chinaman' of the East End, and the female 'dope fiend' who
moved between East and West Ends, trafficking drugs. The extensive press
representation and debate about such women significantly contributed to a
wider discussion about the modern woman across class, her questionable
morality, and her unsuitability, indeed non-eligibility, for full citizenship.

The lure of the West (End): butterfly women and drugs

After the war, the representation of the pleasure-seeking modern girl/
woman who frequented nightclubs and wild parties was most vividly expressed in the image of the 'butterfly woman'. Rather than a symbol of
hope and transformation, it was an image of the butterfly as ephemeral
and flighty (like the 'flapper', of which she was a sub-species). In addition
to the flightiness, a butterfly woman was seen as naive, unstable, irresponsible and easily led. Such a woman was often also referred to as moth-like:
she was drawn to the bright lights of the night-time Metropolis, frequently
singed her wings, and on occasion was fatally burnt. She was seen in effect
as simultaneously butterfly and moth – fragile, short-lived insects of day
and night. And she was susceptible to bad influences and drawn to the
consumption of bad substances (cigarettes, alcohol and drugs).

The *Oxford English Dictionary* (OED) has as its second meaning of 'butterfly': 'a vain, gaudily dressed person (e.g. a courtier who flutters about the court); a light-headed, inconstant person; a giddy trifler'.[6] (The second OED definition of 'flapper' is similar: 'A young girl especially with an implication of flightiness or lack of decorum'.)[7] The term 'butterfly woman' had been used on occasion during the war to refer to frivolous women 'who do not in the least realise that there is a war ... who still spend their time in shop-gazing, planning dainty garments, useless fripperies for personal adornment'.[8] After the war, the term continued to be used about selfish pleasure-seeking ('the cry of pleasure for pleasure's sake') with the 'social butterfly' type of woman deemed 'never ... so prevalent as at present'. According to Dr Murray Leslie (who gave a much-reported lecture at the Institute of Social Hygiene) such a woman was 'the frivolous, scantily-clad, jazzing flapper, irresponsible and undisciplined, to whom a dance, a new hat, or a man with a car were of more importance than the fate of nations', the latter characterisation clearly disqualifying her from the right to the vote.[9] The butterfly woman, flapper, or modern girl (the terms were often used interchangeably) 'lives for dress, "swank", thrills, sensations, dissipation and a rattling good time'.[10] Such women's potential to corrupt men was also an issue: 'they strive by means of dress, or the lack of it, to appeal to man's lower nature', encouraging 'a lowered standard of morality'.[11] Butterfly women may have strived 'to appeal to man's lower nature', but their agency was *impaired* agency, for they were depicted as child-like in their irresponsibility and impetuousness.

Many of the butterfly women were thought to take drugs. Drugs had become a concern in 1916 once it was discovered that Canadian troops based in Folkestone were being sold cocaine by British prostitutes, and that small packets of drugs (cocaine or opium) packed in 'a handy case' could be obtained from various respectable outlets including Harrods; *The Times* advertised such as 'a useful present for friends at the Front'.[12] The authorities feared that soldiers' consumption of drugs would undermine their desire and ability to fight. Thus cocaine and opium, used recreationally by civilians for a number of years, were now recast as a threat to the armed forces.[13] Consequently in July 1916 Regulation 40b under DORA criminalised the possession or sale of opium or cocaine by anyone except licensed chemists, doctors and vets.[14] Once the war ended, cocaine reverted to an association with youthful wild living, seen particularly as a drug favoured by young women, but its criminalisation remained. Some of the drug-taking butterfly women, through their publicised, untimely deaths, entered drug mythology. In the aftermath of the war, the two most prominent in this mythology were Billie Carleton and Freda Kempton. Although their deaths from drugs were separated by over three years – Billie died in November 1918, Freda in March 1922 – they became conceptually linked, as we shall see.

Billie Carleton, the stage name of Florence Stewart, was a twenty-two year old actress who died of a drug overdose on 28th November 1918, having spent the previous night at the Albert Hall's Victory Ball. The Ball, sponsored by the *Daily Sketch*, was celebrating women's wartime achievement, the proceeds going to the Nation's Fund for Nurses.[15] At the ball everyone was clothed in their finery or in fancy dress, Lady Diana Manners, for example, appearing as Britannia, and leading a procession of Society's 'prominent women'.[16] Billie had returned home with friends (she lived in a smart rented flat in Savoy Court, next to the Savoy Hotel), eaten an early breakfast, discussed her promising future (work in Paris for £40 a week – she currently got £20 – and a part in moving pictures in America), and was left to go to bed.[17] She was heard snoring by her maid at 11.30 that morning, but when four hours later Billie had still not surfaced, her maid tried to wake her and found her to be dead.[18]

Billie Carleton had been born illegitimate, the daughter of a chorus singer, and had been raised by her aunt. Although she had left school and home at fifteen to go on the stage, she was fluent in both French and German (presumably self-taught), was well-read, and an excellent pianist.[19] She had had a meteoric rise, and by the autumn of 1918 was the youngest leading lady in the West End.[20] She apparently made her entrance 'by rolling down a long flight of steps to the stage. It was a riotous, successful entry … and very painful'. Detective Annette Kerner suggests that this roll had led to Billie taking drugs.[21] 'How and by what means Billie Carleton came by her death', was, according to the popular Sunday paper the *People*, of enormous national interest.[22] It was suggested that it was cocaine that had killed her (cocaine was discovered in her handbag in a little gold box), and this was the verdict of the inquest, although as writer Marek Kohn points out, it was much more likely to have been veronal, a widely used barbiturate, which Billie had probably taken to bring her down from the cocaine. For the pathologist was wrong in claiming that cocaine could induce sleep and painless death – one indication of the period's general ignorance about drugs and their effects.[23]

The inquest at the Westminster Coroner Court, presided over by coroner Samuel Ingleby Oddie, was lengthy, with five sittings carrying on through December and into late January. The suggestion of suicide was dismissed early on, for witnesses all mentioned Billie's hopes for her future. It was established that she regularly 'doped' – she took opium, cocaine, heroin, morphia, veronal and trional (the last two being barbiturates) – but had inadvertently taken an overdose.[24] Someone other than this 'inno-cent', butterfly-like young woman must be to blame: who had given her the drugs? The spotlight turned on Reggie de Veulle, Billie's dress-designer and fellow-doper, now deemed her corruptor. There were stories of Billie attending dope 'orgies' at de Veulle's home in Dover Street, Mayfair, where a white woman married to a Chinese man, Ada Ping You (of whom more later), 'cooked' opium for the party. Billie was known to take cocaine too. An actress friend, Malvina Longfellow, told the court that she had seen de Veulle give Billie something from a small box, which she sniffed. 'The drug had an instant effect' Malvina recounted, 'for she became very ex-cited, put on a big picture hat, and danced about'.[25] De Veulle was ruthlessly ridiculed in the court and the press, with accusations of effeminacy and hints of improper sexual relationships in his youth with older men (he was now married and in his late thirties). The relevance of these claims to the inquest was never explained, but they were a means to his discrediting, and they gave an impression of him of someone who was decadent, immoral and sexually perverted. De Veulle, accused of having supplied Billie with the (supposedly) fateful cocaine, was found guilty of manslaughter by the inquest jury.

Such a verdict needed confirmation by a higher court, so in early April de Veulle appeared on this charge of manslaughter at the Old Bailey, along with the additional charge of conspiracy to supply cocaine. De Veulle was defended by Huntly Jenkins, who argued that Billie might indeed have committed suicide (we 'did not know what troubles and anxieties she had. People did not take drugs without a reason') and that even had de Veulle supplied Billie with the drug, she, an experienced drug-user, was respon-sible for her own actions: 'Miss Carleton, either by design or by inadver-tence, caused her own death, and they could not make any person liable under the criminal law for the wrongful acts of another'.[26] To the judge, Justice Salter, this argument was insupportable: an older man should pro-tect a young woman, seen by Salter as inevitably immature and in need of guidance (the same argument as to why young women should not have the vote). Like Ingleby Oddie, Salter directed the jury to find de Veulle guilty, but it surprisingly acquitted him of manslaughter, although he got eight months for the conspiracy charge (the heaviest sentence that anyone so far had received for drugs), the judge dramatically proclaiming: 'Traffic in this deadly drug ... leads to ... disease, depravity, crime, insanity, despair, and death.'[27]

From the moment of her death, Billie was constructed as a vulner-able and ephemeral butterfly: 'Miss Billie Carleton ... lies in the cold, dark tomb, her butterfly existence cut tragically short, her brief life ended.'[28]

Three years later, the image was still at large: 'We have but to close our eyes to conjure up visions of bright, beautiful Billie Carleton, flitting through life on butterfly wings'.[29] Billie Carleton became a constant referent in the early 1920s drug narratives. With her frail butterfly appellation to the fore, she was declared emblematic of innocent English girlhood. In his 1922 'revelations', ex-Sergeant Overton, recently retired coroner officer for Westminster, remembered her as 'the very essence of happy English girlhood'.[30] Three years later, 'Dolores', who claimed to have occupied a flat beneath the one figuring in the drug 'orgies', used the same characterisation (or more likely, had such words put into her mouth by a journalist): Billie was 'just the most fragrant specimen of womanhood ... the very essence of English girlhood.'[31] She was written of (and written off) as a lovely butterfly that had been caught in the (butterfly) net of 'vice', and then in death 'pinned' to preserve her delicate beauty, as was the Victorian and Edwardian fashion with butterflies – in her case not literally of course, but 'pinned' onto the canvas of popular memory.

Kohn persuasively argues that Billie's death 'precipitated Britain's first great drug scandal'.[32] There were immediate attempts to explain this (supposed) increased use of drugs. Unsurprisingly the war was blamed: 'Anxiety in connection with the war has driven many people to seek the false solace of drugs ... War has increased the nervous tension to an unheard-of degree.' And with restrictions on alcohol, 'drugs offered an alternative route to oblivion'.[33] Germany was thought to have stimulated the drug traffic, part of its plan 'for the rotting of British manhood', a conspiracy theory on a par with that of the 'hidden hand' discussed in Chapter 1.[34] (The theory did not subside; indeed three years later it was aggrandised: everywhere was being flooded with cocaine as 'a far-flung German plot to accomplish ... the conquest of the world'.)[35] Women were alleged to make up the majority of drug-takers, deemed more susceptible to drugs than men; the *Daily Mail*, for example, authoritatively quoted a 'specialist': 'men do not as a rule take to drugs unless there is a hereditary influence, but women are more temperamentally attracted'.[36] The *Sunday Express* claimed likewise: 'Women, because of their highly strung temperament, fall easy victims to the habit. The first taste is enough. They sink steadily.'[37] The *Daily Mail* asserted that: '"doping" ... is a fashionable habit, an artificial war product, which will disappear with the return of more normal conditions. It is a vice of the neurotic, not a habit of the normal'.[38] It was implied that once women returned to the 'normal' pre-war status quo, their pursuit of drugs (and their neurosis?) would subside.[39] But there was also concern that the butterfly woman/flapper might not wish to 'return'.

Three years on from the Billie Carleton inquest, another butterfly girl drug death captured the news. On the evening of 6th March 1922, Freda Kempton, a 'dance instructress', died in the arms of her landlady in Westbourne Grove, West London. A bottle of cocaine was found nearby. Dance instructresses were employed by nightclubs and dance halls, more as dancing partners than actual instructresses. Paid only a small wage, they made most of their money from tips from clients.[40] Their fortunes were thus precarious, dependent on good looks, dancing ability and stamina, for they had to keep on dancing into the small hours. Freda's exceptional stamina was commented on by a friend: 'She was passionately fond of dancing … she was never tired. I verily believe that she could dance all day and all night without a pause – and still be fit the next morning'.[41] Freda's occupation was not only exhausting, it was stigmatised, 'dance instructress/partner' often seen as a euphemism for prostitute.[42] Freda had worked previously at the Hammersmith Palais de Danse, but more recently had moved to nightclubs: Moody's in Tottenham Court Road, Brett's in Charing Cross Road, and the 43 Club in Gerrard Street, the latter two run by the infamous nightclub owner Kate Meyrick (the 'Night Club Queen') whose clubs were raided and closed on a regular basis for flouting the licensing laws on after-hours drinking, wartime restrictions having continued.[43] Although a dowdy dresser, and 'completely without glamour', Meyrick's 'exploits made luscious Sunday reading for millions'.[44] Her business acumen 'contrasted sharply with her open-handed generosity', and she looked after her 'Merry Maids' (her name for dancing instructresses/hostesses), teaching them class-based social skills, including good 'conversation', grooming and cleanliness.[45] Most of the instructresses were working- or lower-middle-class, but their male clientele included many from the upper strata. The usual pattern for dancing instructresses was to move between two or three nightclubs a night (flitting professionally, so to speak) ending up in a café or restaurant for an early breakfast, then retiring to bed while everyone else was getting up for the day.[46] Freda was twenty-two – the same age on her death as Billie Carleton. She had come from a better-off family than Billie's, having been brought up in Stoke Newington in a house with several servants, for her father had once been a successful jute arbitrator. However, he was downwardly mobile, for according to the *Empire News*, on taking his business to Canada, he lost everything in a forest fire, ran off with 'a half breed girl', and was deported as 'an undesirable'.[47]

The inquest opened on 9th March and was held at Paddington Coroner's court – the same court in which Freda had appeared as a witness six weeks previously on the death by suicide of her friend Mrs Audrey Knowles Harrison. Her friend's death had apparently greatly distressed her.

There were further reasons for her distress. Freda's mother told the court of how her daughter had fallen through a skylight a few months earlier, resulting in bad headaches: she had 'never been really the same since'.[48] Additionally, according to her friend Rose Heinberg, also a dance instructress ('a pale wan little figure' according to the *Daily Express*) three or four weeks prior to her death Freda had separated from a man with whom she had been living for the past ten months: 'She had left him because he had "taken up" with another girl', Rose informed the court.[49] Rose suggested that this 'disappointment in love had driven Freda to take the dope'.[50] (No witness suggested that a significant factor might have been her need for a stimulant to keep her dancing on through the night.) Her friend's suicide, her accident and her broken relationship were in effect presented as joint explanations for why Freda took her life. Between six and seven grains of cocaine were found in the stomach of the deceased, pathologist Dr Bernard Spilsbury asserting that one grain alone was sufficient to cause death.[51]

Although Freda did not possess Billie's celebrity status, her case got the same extensive media coverage, and the two women were described by the press in similar terms. Both women were constructed sympathetically, not censoriously, referred to as youthful, innocent, beautiful and their deaths as 'tragic'. For example, the *Daily Express*'s first mention of Freda's death was headlined 'Tragic Mystery of a Beautiful Girl Dancer'.[52] This 'tragedy' was not deemed of her own making, for she, like Billie, was seen as a passive victim of circumstance, and thereby absolved from blame. That both women had been actively procuring and taking drugs for some time was conveniently overlooked. In the narrative of female passivity and tragic, early death, their own agency was inadmissible.

The 'tragedy' of their short lives was crucially related to their categorisation as butterflies or moths; like Billie, such terms were used in relation to Freda. According to the *News of the World*, Freda was one of the 'leaders of that "butterfly" set which nightly makes a round of the dancing clubs in the West End'.[53] Some papers felt the 'moth' analogy more apt, for example: 'she was one of the hundreds of moths who flutter round the ever brightly burning candle of London night life, taking no thought for the morrow, turning night into day … until her fluttering wings were singed beyond repair'.[54] Other writers, while deploying the image of bright lights and burnt wings used a butterfly analogy nevertheless, the *Empire News* for example referring to 'the last flight of this butterfly before it fell, scorched and dead, from the withering flames of her life of pleasure'.[55] To construct these butterfly girls as innocent victims of forces too great to resist (the lure of unwholesome sensation and excitement) thereby reduced them to pathetic and unthreatening young women in need of sympathy (after all, they had ended up dead). Even the decision to take her own life did not appear to give Freda agency. Freda was also infantilised, James Douglas, editor the *Sunday Express*, implicitly referencing W.T. Stead's (in)famous 1885 exposé of child prostitution 'Maiden Tribute to Modern Babylon' when he evocatively asserted that Freda 'was only a child in years, but she had lost her way in the labyrinth of the merciless minotaur who devours our innocent youth year after year'.[56] The 'minotaur' signified an immoral, ruthless London in which young women could not survive without guidance and protection.

Dance, nightclubs and dope

The demand for 'dance instructresses' had arisen with the new 'mania' for dance, mentioned in Chapter 1.[57] This 'mania', thought to affect all classes, had begun before the war (inspired in part by dancers such as Maud Allan), escalated during the war, and exploded yet further in the inter-war years.[58] 'Everyone in London, young and old, had caught the dance craze', remembered nightclub owner Kate Meyrick.[59] Dancing did not of course only occur in nightclubs; it also took place in public dance halls, hotels, ball-rooms and private sitting-rooms. The *New Survey on London Life and Labour* of 1930 reported that 'people drop into a palais [dance-hall] after the day's work or on Saturday evenings as casually as they go to the cinema'.[60] Dancing, along with the cinema (the 'pictures') and romantic fiction, were young women's key leisure pursuits in this period.[61] Dance had a significant impact on ideal female body image (one of slimness and athleticism) and women's fashion, with shorter and looser dresses made of lighter material – the clothing associated with the flapper. Indeed dance became emblematic of the modern woman/flapper.[62] It was believed to have the potential for good or ill, according to its form and type, and its location. James Donald, President of the British Association of Teachers of Dancing, held that 'when dancing is associated with drinking it ceases to be an art; it is a menace to the community … Modern dancing resembles a pathetic form of imbecility.' He wanted dancing kept out of nightclubs, restaurants and hotels, and confined to the ball-room.[63]

While Billie Carleton's drug-taking was blamed on her unfortunate associations with 'undesirables' such as de Veulle, Freda's drug-taking was additionally blamed on the locale of her profession, namely nightclubs, for Freda was 'a nightclub girl'.[64] Dancing in nightclubs was especially frowned on by moral purists and various commentators in the press, for such clubs were thought to be unhealthy places: dark and airless, often with access to alcohol and drugs and pervaded by criminality. Nightclubs, like dance, had sprung up in London and other cities shortly before the Great War. During the war their activities had been curtailed, but many persisted in selling alcohol illegally. (Licensing hours were reduced in 1915 under Defence of the Realm Liquor Control Act to two short periods: 12–2.30 p.m. and 6–9 p.m.)[65] The clubs were largely located in the West End, especially in Soho, their clientele ranging from soldiers on leave and prostitutes through to figures in high society, indeed they catered for all classes.[66] After the war the wide social mix continued and the clubs expanded; some thought it simply a continuation of the wartime desire to live for the moment, the *Daily Express* for example: 'The craze for anything flashy, cheap, transitory, and daring is … a legacy from the war, when every excitement, no matter how tawdry, how silly, how futile, was greedily seized and cherished. Who knew but that it might be the last? *This spirit has lived on. This is the spirit of the dance den.*'[67] But the increase in clubs was also seen as marking the end of wartime austerity, as well as responding to a new craze for jazz, which had come over from the USA. As one commentator in the *Tatler* noted: 'They say the nightclubs are opening up in rows … And they just can't have enough niggers to play jazz music.'[68] ('Nigger' was widely and uncritically used at the time.) Jazz was highly suspect: 'primitive' and dangerous.[69] To a commentator in one Sunday paper 'the "jazz" den is a rendezvous for dope-traffickers, thugs, crooks and shady women'.[70]

Through the 1920s, nightclubs were associated with drugs. On the front page of the *Sunday Express* it was noted that 'nightclubs of the lowest class are a favourite rendezvous for the traffickers. Young women are lured there, and in the early hours of the morning … they are induced to take their first whiff of the magic "snow"'.[71] To the *Empire News*, Freda's death had 'served one good purpose. For by her passing this innocent victim of London's night life has directed the searchlight of publicity on to the numerous dens of iniquity'. The newspaper admitted there were some nightclubs that were 'licensed, registered, and orderly … But they are outnumbered ten to one by … night dens [where] the sniffing of cocaine is as common as the lighting of a cigarette'.[72] What was now being revealed, according to another popular paper, was 'the mighty undercurrent of sin and shame which flows on while London sleeps'.[73]

After Freda's death there was an increased focus on the dangers of nightclubs, many of which, fearing that they would be raided, became temporarily law-abiding. A *Daily Express* 'Special Representative' on trying to find nightclubs or restaurants selling alcohol or dope was told confidentially by one waiter: 'You see, everybody's got the wind up. The detectives are about.'[74] Those addicted to drugs were described as desperate. 'The most melancholy sight in the dance dens of London is the girl waiting in agony for the drugs which the dope tout is too frightened to hand to her.' The journalist saw a woman he termed 'the Girl with the Tired Eyes. She was typical of the better-class dance den girl [another press 'type'] – the girl who lives for sensation, whose senses have been dulled, whose tired, worn-out nerves must be flogged to life by drugs. She was about twenty-five, pretty … ' But she told him to go away. 'At about two o'clock in the morning things became brighter. More girls arrived … The inevitable Chinaman arrived.' A girl came up to the journalist and asked him to dance: it was the 'Girl with the Tired Eyes' – transformed, radiant and alert.[75] The 'Girl with the Tired Eyes', it was implied, was another Freda Kempton in the making, and her tale a warning to the paper's female readership. The emphasis on 'tired eyes' may have had feminist Rebecca West's approval, for she held that the way to warn young people off drugs was to appeal to their vanity: 'drug-taking is the quickest way to attain the physical condition of one's eldest and most decayed grand-aunt'.[76] The *Evening News* also emphasised the diminishing effects of drugs in its description of the 'girl-addicts' seen in another 'den': 'One was a frail-looking creature of about twenty in a flimsy frock that left three-quarters of her back bare … she gave herself over to almost hysterical attacks of inane, purposeless laughter'.[77] These drugged women, presented as pathetic and absurd, stood in stark contrast to the image of the new sporty, healthy young women of the period, who played vigorous games in the fresh air.[78] The sickly atmosphere of nightclubs took a large part of the blame for Freda's drug-taking, but the question was still posed: who had provided her with the cocaine?

Brilliant Chang

As with Billie Carleton, it was assumed that someone other than the helpless female victim was the perpetrator in the obtaining of drugs. In the case of Freda, the finger was pointed at a particular Chinese man, Brilliant Chang (very likely the 'inevitable Chinaman', referred to by the 'Girl with the Tired Eyes' journalist). Freda's friend Rose Heinberg informed the coroner's court that she believed Freda had refrained from cocaine for about a year, but had recently started using it again. Rose had seen thirteen little white paper packets in Freda's handbag, and had been with Freda on several occasions when she had obtained the drug from a Chinese restaurant. On their last visit to the restaurant, Rose witnessed Brilliant Chang, the restaurant proprietor, give Freda a bottle of powder, and heard his reply to Freda's inquiry as to whether she could die from 'snuffing' cocaine: 'No, the only way you can kill yourself is by putting cocaine in water'.[79] Kate Meyrick, in her reminiscences for a Sunday paper in 1929, noted that she found Chang 'sinister', and forbade him entry to her club. But 'he used to invite girls of the club to supper at his place in Regent Street ... I noticed that when my girls returned ... some of them were decidedly curious in their manner ... and it did not take me long to deduce that they had been taking opium, or cocaine, or some other form of drug.'[80] Freda had been one of Kate Meyrick's 'girls'.

Chang did not appear as a witness at the inquest until April, but he was spotted in the audience by the *Daily Express* at the court's first sitting in March, and photographed: 'a dapper little Chinaman who wore a blue overcoat with fur collar, grey suede shoes and striped socks'.[81] Four days later the paper was mentioning him again, although this time only by inference, in its article 'When the Chinaman takes to the floor'. The scene took place at 1 a.m. on a Sunday morning at a Marble Arch 'expensive' nightclub with 'incoherent Futurist decorations', a good band and a clientele of about two hundred. The latter were characterised in negative and xenophobic terms: 'Round us danced the same old sickening crowd of under-sized

4 Brilliant Chang

aliens, blue about the chin and greasy, the same predominating type of girl, young, thin, underdressed, perpetually seized with hysterical laughter, ogling, foolish.' Suddenly the journalist was surprised by the entry of a Chinese man who was 'not the "Chink" of popular fiction, a cringing yellow man hiding his clasped hands in the wide sleeves of his embroidered gown', but 'in evening clothes … made not far from Savile Row … His long, thin hands … manicured, his manners … too perfect to be described as good'.[82] From other descriptions at the time and subsequently, it is highly likely that this man was Chang. The 'Chinaman' in the fiction and 'fact' of the day was represented as duplicitous, cunning, mysterious, and effeminate – reference to Chang's manicured hands and his small stature being obvious examples of the latter.[83]

When the inquest resumed in April, Chang was called as a witness: '"Is the Chinaman here?" Mr Coroner Oswald peered over his gold-rimmed glasses and amidst stillness that thrilled with expectancy, a black-haired, yellow-faced little man, with the inscrutable eyes of the East … lurched forward'; ('inscrutability' was another regular trope of the 'Chinaman'). The press again commented upon his obvious wealth: 'From his shoulders there hung a heavy coat trimmed with expensive fur, whilst a gold-jewelled watch gleamed from his slender wrist.' Once Chang entered the witness-box: 'A buzz of excitement went round the court … He is an alert, dapper, little man [the latter two adjectives used in the March account were here used again], with long black shining hair brushed back. His eyes gleamed intelligently', noted the *Daily Express*.[84] The *Empire News* had a less flattering description: 'Undersized, yellow, with coal-black straight hair combed back from his wrinkled brow, he was typical of the mysterious East.'[85]

His clothes might have been modern and Western, but the court discussion of how he should be sworn in, other than by using a Bible, revealed to the press and its readers the 'primitiveness' of Chinese custom. 'One method is by wringing the neck of a fowl, another is by breaking a saucer, and another by blowing out a candle.' The *Daily Express* was relieved to report that 'all these picturesque methods were eschewed'.[86] Defining himself as a businessman and proprietor of a Chinese restaurant in West End London's Regent Street, Chang admitted giving money to Freda on several occasions, but never cocaine. He claimed to know nothing about cocaine. With great assurance he asserted: 'I have never done anything wrong in my life.'[87] (To supply or take non-prescribed cocaine or opium remained a crime in 1922, for DORA 40b had been extended under the 1920 Dangerous Drugs Act.)[88] Asked what he did after work, Chang replied that he went to nightclubs. When asked why, he 'shrugged his shoulders and replied: "I

5 *World's Pictorial News*, 'Freda Kempton and "Billy" the Chinaman',
22nd April, 1922 © British Library Board (LON356)

go to enjoy myself".[89] Surely the barrister could not have envisaged Chang
admitting to any other motive?

The court's verdict was that Freda Kempton had 'committed suicide
during temporary insanity, by taking cocaine, which was obtained from
person or persons unknown'. The coroner, whilst finding insufficient evidence to charge Chang with manslaughter, noted his scepticism: if Rose
Heinberg's story *was* untrue, 'she must have a wealth of imagination that one
would hardly expect in a girl like this', he patronisingly remarked.[90] None
of the papers was convinced of Chang's innocence; 'what's there about the
yellow man that fascinates white women, holds them in a spell … makes
them easy victims of remorseless men from the distant East?' wondered the
Evening News.[91] The popular press accused white girls and young women of
'throwing themselves' at Chinese men – for example, the *Empire News* reported that at the end of the coroner's inquest 'fashionably-dressed girls …
rushed to Chang, patted his back, and one … fondled the Chinaman's black
smooth hair and passed her fingers slowly through it'.[92] Other Chinese men

were spotted in the court: 'They had crept into vacant seats, they stood in darkened corners'.[93] If women like Freda were harmless, fluttering moths of the night, Chinese men were their evil counterpoint, vampirically seeking 'darkened corners' into which they 'crept'. And Chang, with his foreignness, 'yellowness', evening clothes, wealth, and mysterious power over women, was like the most famous of vampires, Dracula.[94]

When Chang was eventually sent to prison for fourteen months in 1924 for drug dealing, followed by deportation, particular note was made of his 'inscrutability', the *Daily Express* observing that he 'took the sentence completely unperturbed. He was the unemotional yellow man, his narrow slit eyes blank, his face a mask.'[95] The *Empire News* saw him in a more sinister light: 'the glint in his narrow slits of eyes ... is expressively evil ... he is without question the most dangerous man London has ever housed ... he has the ruin, the degradation and the death of hundreds of young girls upon his conscience'.[96] In this depiction of evil, the cultural referent was the sophisticated but deeply sinister figure of Sax Rohmer's Dr Fu Manchu, the fictitious Chinese master criminal who plots global domination.[97] This menacing cultural representation co-existed within British culture with the more benign image of 'Johnnie Chinaman', whose vices of opium and gambling were seen as simply cultural and only harmful if contagiously spread to whites.

The lure of the East (End): white women, Chinese men, and Limehouse

The 'lure of the East' was an expression used at this time that appeared to convey both geographic and symbolic/metaphorical 'Easts': the lure of the East End of London, in particular Limehouse and its Chinese men, opium, and gambling, and the lure of the (Far) East as personified in the 'Chinaman' and his Oriental drug. Young white women (largely working-class) were 'lured' to a geographical East (London's East End) – travelling there from elsewhere (and for some, taking up residence), drawn by gambling or drugs or the attractions of the 'Chinaman', or a combination of the three. But some women (middle- and working-class) were also 'lured' to/by a *metaphorical* East in their attraction to drugs and/or Chinese men, whether or not the spatial East (End) featured. In the two *causes celebres* involving women who took drugs in the West End discussed in this chapter, their attraction to the 'East' was primarily symbolic, although Billie Carleton apparently went to Limehouse to smoke opium on at least one occasion.[98] And Freda Kempton's relationship with Chang was inferred by some as being more than simply one of drug dealer and client.[99] It is to women's attraction to, and involvement with, Chinese men that this chapter now turns.

Why were there Chinese men resident in East London? During the Great War, the greatly increased demand for seamen had led to a huge rise in sailors coming to Britain from the Indian sub-continent, North and West Africa, the West Indies and China. In the nineteenth century, men of these nationalities had been present in the ports of London, Liverpool and Cardiff, but their numbers had always been small. By 1921, with the increases due to the war, nationally there may have been in the region of 20,000 black men and 2,500 Chinese, although reliable estimates are difficult to obtain.[100] During this period non-white people residing in Britain, be they African, West Indian, South Asian or Arab, were referred to by the interchangeable epithets 'black' and 'coloured', and occasionally 'Negro'. Sometimes Chinese people were also referred to as 'coloured', but more usually as 'yellow'.[101] From 1911 to 1921 the Chinese presence in Britain had more than doubled, while the numbers in London had risen from 247 to 711, although the press was always claiming much larger numbers, the *Daily Mail* for example in 1920 asserting that in Limehouse, where half the Chinese of London lived, there were about 2,000.[102] Given that the presence of black and Chinese was almost entirely due to shipping and soldiery, they were nearly all male. The numbers of men of colour were small, but the anxiety about them, including their relationships with white women, was out of all proportion to their actual numerical presence.

Antagonisms towards the Chinese

When demobbed, white working-class British men returned home, they faced initial unemployment. In Britain's main ports they accused men of colour of having taken their accommodation and their jobs (although in fact there was higher unemployment amongst non-white sailors than white). They also faced the sight of the racial 'other' courting 'their' women. White working-class men, frequently mentally if not physically war-damaged, now came up against challenges to three main definers of British masculinity, namely the ability to work, provide a home, and attract the opposite sex.[103] Their fury on occasion took the form of physical confrontation, the most extensive being in the form of mass street fighting in nine of Britain's main ports in 1919 from late January through to August, the worst rioting occurring in London, Liverpool and Cardiff from April to early July.[104] The 1919 'race riots', as they became known, were instigated by white men, and involved running battles between whites and non-whites, resulting in five deaths, numerous injuries – often serious – and extensive damage to property, especially to houses in which Chinese and black men were lodging.[105] Frequently egged on by demobbed servicemen, the hostile white crowds 'had all the trappings of lynch mobs', to quote historian Paul Rich.[106] For example, in June 1919 a group of white men attacked a house in Poplar, East London where two Chinese men and their white wives were lodging, setting fire to the furniture and assaulting the women.[107] It was rumoured that these inter-racial couples had replaced an evicted white de-mobbed soldier and his wife. After smashing up the house, a mob then wrecked a Chinese laundry, and further street fighting erupted. By the beginning of July the racial violence in Limehouse had escalated to such a degree that virtually the entire East End police force had to be called out.[108]

According to the press, men of colour had tried to displace white men, the *Empire News* suggesting that 'The Chinese have swiftly and cunningly taken advantage of the absence of white men on national service to steal their wives or their daughters, and their honour at the same time.'[109] There was much public condemnation of white women's relationships with men of colour; to the *Western Mail* in June 1919 for example: 'Such consorting is necessarily an *ill*-assorting; it exhibits either a state of depravity or a squal-id infatuation; it is repugnant to all our finer instincts'.[110] The press and the authorities clearly had difficulty explaining why there *were* white women prepared to act in a manner 'repugnant to all our finer instincts'. Declaring such women 'loose', 'of a low type' or 'of a certain class', i.e. prostitutes or akin to such, was one way that the newspapers sought to understand this enigma. But there was still a problem of comprehension: if it was only 'low type' women who were attracted to black and Chinese men, why should there be such concern? The *Sunday Express* explained: 'It is *naturally* offen-sive to us that coloured men should consort with even the *lowest* of white women. Racial antipathy is always present, the sex jealousy inflames it to a violent, unreasoning wave of emotion.'[111] Thus to the press, the relation-ships were demeaning to white males, inciting understandable – indeed instinctive – resentment and anger. To the white sailors and demobbed soldiers, white women were betraying them and their country, while men of colour were stealing their women, their homes and their jobs.

Some papers went so far as to call for the prohibition of Chinese men's contact with white women. For example, a 1920 *Daily Mail* edito-rial headed 'Chinamen and English Girls' declared that the public 'would be glad to see vigorous steps taken by the Government and by the local authorities to deal with these aliens who decoy white girls ... It is even a question whether marriage should be permitted between a white girl and an alien with a totally different standard of living and civilisation.'[112] No ban was forthcoming, but in 1924 the Foreign Office added the category 'Chinese' to those listed in a warning statement given out by marriage registrars to British women. This addition was a response to the case of a British woman who had married a Chinese man in Cardiff, moved with him to Canton, and had been deserted.[113] The warning statement, already operating in relation to 'Hindus, Moslems, African Negroes', advised women that their marriages were unlikely to be recognised in their husband's country of origin, that their husband would be able to have other wives, indeed may already have other wives, and that they would lose British 'protection' and British citizenship once married to an alien.[114] The 1870 Naturalisation Act had ruled, for the first time, that on marriage to foreign men British women would lose their British nationality.[115]

In 1914 antagonism directed at the black and Chinese men also took the form of hostility towards these men's supposedly alien status. Men of colour residing in Britain, whether or not they were formally British subjects, were widely seen as aliens. In the immediate post-war years, the national 'unity' constructed during the war against the 'common enemy' began to disintegrate. Representing black and Chinese men in Britain as 'un-British' contributed to shoring up an imagined national identity.[116] Through racialised nationalism, the equation of Britishness and whiteness was consolidated and social and national cohesion enhanced. (This was to occur again after the Second World War on a larger scale.)[117] The presence of racial 'others' facilitated a sense of who the British were: they were white, *not* black or Chinese or racially 'other', and they (ideally) did not exhibit the various attributes projected onto racial 'others', such as sexual predatoriness, laziness, filthiness or low cunning. In identifying the undesirability of the way that men of colour lived in Britain, the attributes of 'true' Britishness could be drawn in counter-distinction. For example, one journalist writing in a Sunday paper in 1920 lamented: 'I have been back to Chinatown [he was referring to Limehouse] … and I am sick with nausea … in every corner of the world, English dead have built around the name of England qualities of courage, cleanness and high endeavour … Chinatown is an ill monument to the memory of those who died.'[118] In other words, the Chinese, living in the squalor and fecklessness of Limehouse, demonstrated their fundamental non-Englishness against whom the clean, brave English populace could compare itself favourably. Those that lived with or alongside Chinese people in Limehouse were unlikely to have identified with such sentiments, especially women married to Chinese men who had their own collective sense of community and belonging.[119]

Inter-racial relationships appear also to have acted as a visceral challenge to white men's sexuality. Miscegenation fears can be seen in part as a displacement of men's disquiet as to the new demands and behaviour of women. Through a process of disavowal, female sexual desire and agency was simultaneously recognised and denied, with men of colour's 'predatory' sexuality necessitating white male protection and punishment.[120] But it was the contemporary constructions of black and Chinese men's sexuality that indicated most clearly what historian Richard Smith refers to as 'racialised sexual anxiety'.[121] In relation to black men, a man from the Home Office summed up this anxiety in an internal memo: 'The negro is said to be more largely developed than the white man and a woman who has once been with a negro is said to find no satisfaction with anything [*sic*] else'.[122] This representation of black male sexuality is of course familiar, has a long history and is still in circulation today. Less familiar is the early twentieth-century representation of 'Oriental' male sexuality, or rather representations, for there were conflicting depictions of the Chinese, and these differed again from the depiction of the Arab male, to be discussed in Chapter 4.

The 'Chinaman' in Britain was generally seen as effeminate; he was also depicted as less 'bestial' than the black man. Although he was believed to come from an ancient civilisation, it was one defined as inherently immoral and indefinably dangerous. He was a contradictory figure, both emasculated yet simultaneously sexually and racially threatening.[123] This 'yellow peril' image of the 'Chinaman' (embodied in the fictional Fu Manchu) coexisted with the more benign representation of 'Johnnie Chinaman'.[124] Yet as *The Times* was keen to point out, even in relation to the 'thoroughly respectable' 'Chinaman', 'his ways are not our ways'.[125] In addition to gambling and opium-smoking, an example given of how 'his ways are not our ways' was his alleged desire for under-age girls. For instance in 1922 Lily Siddall, who worked in a Chinese laundry, noted that Chinese men desired what they 'regard as a "spring chicken" – a buxom girl of 10 or 11'.[126] And in 1925 and behind the scenes, a Home Office official bemoaned the fact that 'a Chinaman is fastidious, he will not take the battered old prostitute of the seaport, but wants something young, attractive, above all clean and free from venereal disease'.[127] The 1919 film *Broken Blossoms* (released in Britain in 1920) played to this characterisation of the 'Chinaman'.[128] Produced by D.W. Griffith (of *Birth of a Nation* fame), the film was adapted from a short story by journalist and popular author Thomas Burke called 'The Chink and the Child', and portrays the 'pure' love of a Limehouse resident, Cheng Huan (a 'good' 'Chinaman'), for a young, impoverished girl (aged twelve in the short story and fifteen in the film).[129] Literary critic Anne Witchard in her excellent study of Burke's Limehouse writings, suggests that his portrayal of Chinese men as drawn to young girls could be seen as a sexual displacement onto the Chinese of illicit desire.[130]

Explanations for the 'lure of the Chinaman'

Given the feminisation of the 'Chinaman', and his negative cultural depiction as desiring young girls (although *Broken Blossoms* was uncharacteristic in its portrayal of the 'Chinaman', Cheng Huan, as honourable), press and officials alike were endlessly posing the question: 'What is it about the Chinaman that draws white women?' There were a number of explanations offered by the press, most of which denied that the women chose these men for reasons of mutual affection. One explanation was that the women were prompted by materialism and love of finery, and threw themselves at Chinese men because they were generous with their money.[131] For example, in a front-page article in the *Evening News* in 1920 headed 'Chinatown's lure of pretty clothes', the paper claimed: 'the white girl ... seeks out coloured sailors shamelessly ... the Chinese seaman ashore often has £50/£60 to spend ... He is an easy target for women adventurers, and is often more sinned against than sinning.'[132] And a Chinese man told a reporter from the *Daily Graphic* that the Chinese were 'molested time after time' by young white women coming to the East End from elsewhere.[133] Such women were depicted as akin to wartime 'amateur prostitutes', the latter understood as women more interested in presents and sexual pleasure than monetary exchange.[134] In acting as the predator with men as the prey, the amateur prostitute and the woman pursuing Chinese men reversed the rules of sexual pursuit. Both groupings of women were thought affected by an 'attitude problem' spawned by the war, and manifest in their selfishness, pleasure-seeking and defiance. Yet although white women were here presented as initiators of their relationships with Chinese men, they were simultaneously seen as 'lured' ('Chinatown's lure of pretty clothes'), their 'free' agency impaired by their susceptibility.

Another explanation for white women's attraction to Chinese men presented such women as lacking *all* agency: they were seen as victims of their own innate shortcomings, namely their desire for sensation, their lesser willpower, and their greater susceptibility not just to finery but also to drugs, and/or gambling. Such shortcomings enabled them to be overcome by the 'lure of the East/lure of the yellow man'.[135] When in October 1920 a London magistrate, J.A.R. Cairns, fined a Chinese restaurant keeper in Limehouse for 'allowing loose women on his premises', he railed against 'the moral and physical suicide ... of unhappy girls fascinated by the yellow

6 *Daily Graphic*, 7th October 1920 'Chinatown's Happy Wives',
© British Library Board (MLD22)

man'. The *Evening News* front-page headline for the story shrieked out 'White girls "Hypnotised" by Yellow Men'.[136] Chinese men were accused of *luring* women and girls through gambling and drugs, *preying* upon them like vampires. In this scenario, the women were reduced to passive victims in a manner parallel to the white slave narrative.[137] The press recounted that young women under twenty from all over the country were drawn to Limehouse by 'the lure of puck-a-pu', a simple and (initially) affordable form of gambling that was thought 'addictive'. The young women had heard 'stories of easy money to be made'.[138] But as Cairns expressed it a year or so later in his memoirs: 'The lure is more than money ... young girls on the margin of the age of consent come in search of Oriental delight'.[139] He did not elaborate on this 'Oriental delight'. Revd Degen, never hesitant in voicing his opinion on contemporary ethical issues, thought the attraction 'a latent pathological infatuation' – deeply unwise, he opined, for 'the morals and civilisation of the yellow man and the European are fundamentally different'.[140]

There was recognition by some commentators however that women who went on to *marry* Chinese men, as opposed to pursuing them simply for money, did so for perfectly rational reasons, including that these men were kind, good with children, indeed 'good husbands', non-drinkers and non-violent. After Cairns's remarks about social suicide, there were many hostile comments in the press about white women and Chinese men. In contrast, the *Daily Graphic* ran three photographs on its front page entitled 'Chinatown's Happy Wives'. The caption read: 'Chinatown is indignant at the denunciation of the relations between Chinese men and English girls. The English wives declare that their Chinese husbands are models for many English husbands.'[141] One picture shows Mrs Ah Ling sitting 'at tea in her home with her husband and family', although the Chinese husband is turned away from the table and the two women (his wife and her sister?) as if marginal to the scene. Inside the paper a Chinese man living in Limehouse is quoted as saying: 'Some of our men, steady and hard-working people, have married white women and have been very happy and contented with them. Do you ever see a Chinaman in the police courts charged with assaulting his wife? No.' Another white woman married to a Chinese man for fifteen years, Mrs Chow Lan, told the *Daily Graphic* how 'my Chinese husband ... has been an ideal husband to me, and he worships the children. I love him more than when I first married him ... My home life? It is just an ordinary English home ... My husband eats his own food during the week, mostly, but on Sundays we sit down to the good old-fashioned English meal'.[142] The only aspect of 'Chineseness' present in the account is reference to her husband eating 'his own food during the week', and presumably not forcing her to eat it as well. He is represented as a *model* for British men, and nearly completely Anglicised. Thus ironically these Chinese men living in peaceful domesticity were in a sense associated with a *positive* aspect of modernity: the home-loving conservative English modernity of the inter-war years, so brilliantly evoked by cultural historian Alison Light.[143] And in presenting her home life as prosaic and familiar, Mrs Chow Lan implicitly challenged the imaginary construction of Limehouse as alien and threatening.[144]

There were others too who commented positively on the married 'Chinaman'. In his memoir Cairns surprisingly admitted that 'Limehouse has its Chinamen who are industrious and law-abiding citizens. These have driven their stakes deep into the English soil … for they marry English women and beget British children in lawful wedlock. [Children born in Britain did not lose their nationality under the 1870 Naturalisation Act.] They are generous in their behaviour to the women and affectionate towards their children.'[145] Annie Lai, who had married a Chinese man (an opium dealer) in Limehouse in the 1920s, would have agreed. Reflecting back years later on Chinese men's prosaic reliability she noted: 'I always trusted a Chinaman, they were not hard, they weren't sexy or wanting different things. They would always look after the women.'[146] Even the Home Office could be positive, noting in a 1925 memo on the marriage of English women to Chinese men: 'The women are treated with respect and are given far better homes than are provided by English men of the same class'.[147] The following month in a memo to the Foreign Office it changed its tune: 'In spite of the Chinaman's good behaviour these marriages are to be deplored.' No explanation was given as to *why* they were to be deplored; to these parliamentary men the answer was presumably self-evident. The memo continued: 'It is difficult to suggest any remedy. The most we can do is to keep an eye on the Chinese residents and get rid of any who provide sufficient ground for that course [i.e. repatriation] to be taken.'[148] Such 'sufficient grounds' included the provision or possession of opium or cocaine, the latter mobilised against Brilliant Chang in 1924.[149] This deep ambivalence towards inter-racial relationships appears to have been fairly common. For example, a vicar of Limehouse, Revd E.O. James, claimed that 'the Chinaman is as a rule a decent, well-behaved fellow and his treatment of his white wife is generally good', but unaccountably he refused to marry such couples, although he was 'baptising Eurasian children almost every week'.[150]

Progeny resulting from the 'lure of the Chinaman'

While the odd newspaper and a few commentators were prepared to be relatively encouraging about white women's marriages to Chinese men, there were many who were disapproving, particularly of the mixed-race children resulting from those marriages. Indeed it was widely held by British eugenists, anthropologists, biologists and geneticists (groups not necessarily mutually exclusive) that while breeding between races defined as 'close' in evolutionary terms might potentially be a good thing (giving 'hybrid rigour'), breeding between races defined as 'widely divergent' was disastrous, inevitably leading to degeneration. In 1919 eugenist E.J. Lidbetter asserted: 'I think no one who is conversant with East London at the present time can doubt the real danger in which we stand of vitiating the British stock through marriage alliances with Asiatics who make a very undesirable blend with our own people'.[151] At the Eugenics Society's annual general meeting that year the Society's President, Major Leonard Darwin (a son of Charles Darwin), announced that 'what is urgently needed is a thorough scientific study of the mental and physical characteristics of mixed races'.[152] In 1923 Darwin conveyed his concern to the national leaders attending the Imperial Conference (about to be held in London), warning them that 'interbreeding between widely divergent races may result in the production of types inferior to both parent stocks'.[153] Eugenics was not simply espoused to and by the educated middle-classes: the *Sunday Chronicle* (with a working- and lower-middle-class readership) announced that 'any student of eugenics will tell you that the boy in whose blood surges the twin tides of Orientalism and Occidentalism has impulses only the slow process of western civilisation has kept in leash'.[154]

In response to Major Darwin's call for a 'scientific study', the Eugenics Society set up what they called a 'race crossing' project. The Society employed two anthropologists to study Chinese-white mixed-race children in Liverpool, extended to mixed race children with black fathers, and expanded geographically to Cardiff and East London. (In the BBC programme *Mixed Britannia*, broadcast in 2011, Connie Hoe remembered being measured in Limehouse in about 1932 aged nine: 'They measured our heads and the colour of our eyes and noted our complexion.')[155] Possibly much to the surprise of many eugenists, one of the anthropologists, Rachel Fleming, who published her first report in 1927, claimed that some of the Liverpool children with Chinese heritage were exceptionally talented. And social workers' belief that 'the Chinese were good husbands, and especially good fathers', had, she reported, been borne out from her own visits.[156] Many commentators of the time categorised those of mixed race as 'handicapped', but they operated with a hierarchy of handicap predicated on relative distance from the (constructed and idealised) norm of English/Nordic physical appearance. *The Times* made this explicit: 'since the colouring and features [of the Anglo-Chinese children] are far less distinctive than those

of the Anglo-Negroids they are not such a handicap'.[157] That 'the colouring and features are far less distinctive' implies their lesser obtrusiveness
on the ('English') eye, their *difference* was less apparent, and thereby less
threatening. Yet if in inter-war Britain those of Chinese descent had a relative advantage over those of 'Negro' descent, in another context, where
the comparison was not with another racial 'other' but with non-othered
Caucasians, the stereotyped physical features of the Chinese – 'flat nose',
'small, slanty eyes', 'yellow skin' – worked against them. As a man from the
Home Office expressed it in 1925: 'The distressing point to my mind is the
hopeless outlook for the children, who must outwardly bear the physiognomy of the Chinaman in their faces'.[158] Rachel Fleming may have had a
more positive view, but commentary on white women's relationships with
Chinese men generally focused negatively on the problems of and for their
'half-caste' or 'semi-coloured' offspring, suggesting that it was the women,
in choosing to have sex with Chinese men, who were guilty of inflicting on
their children this 'hopeless outlook'.[159]

Women transformed by living with Chinese

If mixed-race children were thought to have a 'hopeless outlook', so too
were their mothers, despite their Chinese husbands' kindness and generosity. Marriage to an 'alien' led to a British woman's loss of British nationality
– as historian Laura Tabili expresses it, she became 'an outsider in the land
of her birth'.[160] The 1914 Aliens Restriction Act forced all aliens to register
with the police; this was reaffirmed in a 1919 Act.[161] It appears to have applied to aliens' wives too, at least in certain geographical regions, for in the
Mixed Britannia programme Doreen and Lynne Ah Foo remembered with
indignation their British-born mother, Emily, having to register with the
Liverpool police in the 1920s.[162] Whether or not a woman had to register, if
she was married to a foreigner, Tabili observes, she 'was not to be trusted:
her loyalty as well as her respectability, bound up as the latter was with
sexual probity, rendered permanently suspect'.[163]

British women's marriages to Chinese men not only deemed them
'aliens' legally and morally, but physically as well, their bodies said to age
prematurely, and their facial features gradually to acquire an Oriental
'look'. Journalist W.A. Mutch on a visit to Limehouse observed: 'two old
women, bent and wrinkled with age, dressed in rags ... They were the favourites of only a few years ago. Women age quickly in Chinatown ... It
is not only their bodies that are befouled. Their brains are benumbed of
all moral sense'.[164] The wife of drug dealer Ching Kow (aka 'Mr King') was
described by a Sunday paper as 'a woman of medium size, with a sad, wan

face', looking 'much older than her years. She is not yet thirty'. Reference to her 'sad, wan face' was repeated further on in the article; it was a representation of the woman as pathetic and pitiable, prematurely aged by her miserable experience of life with 'Mr King'.[165] But it was not just ageing that came about through living with a 'yellow man'. One journalist wrote of 'two Englishwomen who had become so Chinese ... that they had earned the sobriquets "China-faced Nell" and "Chinese Bertha"'.[166] White Scottish Ada Ping You was referred to by de Veulle as 'the Chinese woman';[167] although she was indeed legally Chinese through marriage, de Veulle was more likely to have been referring to her appearance and demeanour. And in an article about a beautiful English woman who married a Japanese man and went to live with him in the Straits Settlement, 'it was noticed by pitying observers that her features, as well as her mind, altered their mould. The abortive nature of the union could be read in the sloping cheeks, the discoloured eyes, and the mannerisms of a race outcast'.[168] In overstepping the racial divide, women who had relations with men from the Far East became quite 'other' – a discourse with echoes of the nineteenth-century idea of the 'fallen' prostitute who was transformed and 'unreclaimable'. While mixed-race offspring were said to exhibit inherited physical 'degeneracy', changes in their mothers' appearance were thought to have been *acquired* rather than inherited – the penalties of 'unnatural', transgressive, inter-racial sex.

East meets West: high priestess, drugs and queens

More than a hundred years after Britain forced China to buy opium, resulting in the opium wars, twelve Chinese men in Liverpool had no doubt as to the allocation of blame: they wrote a letter to the *Liverpool Courier* in September 1916 complaining of their demonisation for smoking opium: 'Who began the opium traffic we ask? Who first forced opium into our country against our wish and will, and made us poor as a nation?'[169] Drugs featured in nearly all of the stories about Chinese men in Limehouse. Thomas Burke's tales (a collection of short stories presented as journalistic, factual vignettes) depict Limehouse as squalid yet lovely, and Chinese men as unscrupulous, addicted to opium and gambling, yet also often kind and lovable – a clear challenge to the 'yellow peril' representation.[170] In Burke's best-selling, 'gritty' realist yet romanticised narratives of Limehouse, inter-racial couples slump together, or lie back languidly, in drug-induced stupor (although years later he admitted that in fact he knew nothing about the geographical area or the Chinese).[171] The linking of inter-racial relations with drugs was common in this period. In many factual and fictional accounts of Britain's drug scene, the belief that drugs dissolved boundaries between the races, breaking down the 'natural' prohibitions and encouraging sexual contact across the colour line, was seen as one strong reason for their condemnation.[172] The 'opium den' represented 'a strange fusion of poverty, filth and pleasure – at once attractive and repellent', to quote historian John Seed.[173] The inter-racial aspect was an important part of what was seen as simultaneously 'attractive and repellent'.

Female officiator at 'disgusting orgies'

Although Brilliant Chang was believed to be a key supplier of opium and cocaine to the West End, he was not thought the only dealer; according to the press, other 'slinky Orientals from Chinatown travelled from East to West, there to ply their ghastly trade'.[174] But a number of white women were also implicated. Who were these female 'dope fiends' who transported drugs, transgressively moving between East and West Ends? One of them, briefly mentioned earlier in this chapter in relation to the Billie Carleton case, was Ada Ping You, charged not with manslaughter, but with provision of opium. In the trials that followed Carleton's death, Ada was the first to be prosecuted. On 13th December 1918, this twenty-eight year old Scottish woman from Limehouse married to a Chinese man was charged with supplying and preparing opium from August to October for Billie's consumption, despite the fact that no one ever suggested that Billie had died of an opium overdose, or indeed had any opium in her flat. Ada was arrested at her home in Limehouse, where she lived with her husband Lau Ping You, and where opium and opium utensils were quickly discovered.

Ada and Lau Ping You were both charged under 1916 DORA 40b, but sent to different regional courts, for Lau Ping was not implicated in the Carleton affair. Ada appeared at Marlborough Police Court before Frederick Mead, a highly moralistic and authoritarian JP.[175] The prosecutor Herbert Muskett set the scene: a small party of men and women would congregate on a Saturday evening at Reggie de Veulle's home in Dover Street, and Billie would arrive later, after her performance at the theatre. They would sit in a circle on cushions, the men in pyjamas, the women in chiffon nightdresses, thereby 'to prepare themselves for the orgy'.[176] They would then communally smoke opium through to Sunday afternoon. In the centre of 'this circle of degenerates', Muskett declared, 'the defendant officiated'.[177] Despite this sensationalist language, Muskett claimed that he desired to present the facts 'in as colourless a manner as possible'.[178] The only example of facts given in a 'colourless' manner was his pedantic account of Ada's preparatory role (in which he also inadvertently demonstrated her skill):

She had an opium tin and the lamp, the opium needle, and all the accessories. She prepared the opium. She used the needle for the purpose of extracting small portions when it was prepared by the heating up of the small pellets ... She placed them on a needle into the bowl of the pipe ... one pipe being used for the whole party for inhaling the fumes of this drug.[179]

Ada pleaded not guilty to supplying opium, but admitted to its preparation; "'they say I have been up West cooking'" was the way that she described the latter.[180] Ada's defence counsel, Barrington Matthews, pointed out that she was young and had 'been married for the past three and a half years to a Chinaman and one could well appreciate what her surroundings had been since her marriage' (implying that they had been awful enough to constitute mitigation). He explained that she had been invited to supper at Dover Street because the people there knew she could prepare opium, but she had not done so for reward. The people 'whom Mr Muskett had described as degenerates' Barrington Matthews labelled 'something worse', thereby shifting the blame away from Ada. He was constructing her as an innocent young woman living under difficult conditions (marriage to a Chinese man in Limehouse) who was shamelessly manipulated by unscrupulous sub-humans (he referred to 'this man de Veulle, whoever or *whatever* he was'). He noted that Ada 'very much regretted what she had done', and he 'hoped the magistrate would take the view that a small fine would meet the case'.[181]

Magistrate Mead did not take such a view, and agreed with Muskett as to the seriousness of the crime, declaring that 'she took a leading part in the most disgraceful proceedings ... She really acted as high priestess in these unholy rites'. Keen to make an example of her, Mead gave her the maximum possible sentence at this time: five months imprisonment with hard labour.[182] Designating Ada a 'high priestess' 'officiating' at 'disgusting orgies' created an image of her as at the very heart of scenes of unspeakable sexual debauchery and religious sacrilege. Matthews' attempt to present her as a passive *victim* of circumstances was countered by a representation of her as a key *villain*. Her transgressions were seen as multiple: not only were the boundaries that she crossed moral, but also racial, in marrying a 'Chinaman'. Further, she had inappropriately moved across geographical boundaries – East (End) to West (End) – bringing the polluting drug of Limehouse with her (although in fact she denied supplying the opium), and she may have been seen as violating gender norms too in her central role as opium facilitator (although 'cooking' opium does of course have a 'feminine' ring). At her appeal, her defence counsel, Huntly Jenkins (who also acted for de Veulle, as we have seen), pointed out that while Ada's husband smoked opium, she did not, and that she had 'endeavoured to dissuade Miss Carleton from taking up the habit', managing to get her to relinquish recently purchased opium-smoking paraphernalia. It was also observed that Ada was 'in a very poor state of health, and had suffered both mentally and physically through the case.' But the Chairman of the London Sessions was neither moved by her abstention, her acts of compassion, nor her ill-health, swiftly dismissing the appeal with the claim that: 'the offence was a very serious one and must be put down'.[183]

The outcome of Ada's husband's trial was very different. Lsu Ping You, who had been in Britain twelve years, was tried the same day as Ada but at a different court and by a different magistrate. He appeared at Thames Police Court before magistrate Henry Rooth, and was also charged with opium possession. Unlike his wife though, he had not been providing white people with the drug – the opium was for his consumption alone. That Rooth saw opium-smoking as the 'national vice' of the Chinese clearly diminished the weight of the crime in his eyes. Further, he must have been impressed that Lsu Ping, who had started smoking opium aged eleven, had reduced his opium 'habit' from 200 or 300 pellets a day down to eight. He was fined only £10.[184] Ada however was sent to Holloway prison.

In December 1918 and January 1919, during the (overlapping) weeks of Ada's trial and Billie Carleton's inquest, the press was full of lurid tales of drug taking, 'vice trusts' controlling the narcotics traffic, visits to 'opium dens' (in West and East Ends), including an artist's impression of such, and for lighter relief, a quirky proposal for addiction cure through the application of 'Pelmanism' (a memory-training and auto-suggestion technique in vogue at the time, which was believed to increase will-power).[185] The stage was set for the public reception of another racy Sax Rohmer volume about the Chinese, conspiracy and drugs, delivered in the 1919 novel *Dope: the Story of Chinatown and the Drug Traffic*, whose parallel to the Billie Carleton case must have been obvious to all.[186] It features Rita Dresden, a beautiful but frail ex-actress, who is addicted to drugs, a dissolute aristocrat, Sir Lucien Pyne, who first introduced her to drugs, and a striking but evil 'Cuban-Jewess' called Lola, who in relation to the novel's Mayfair opium parties is explicitly referred to as 'the officiating priestess'.[187] Lola lives in Limehouse with her one-eyed Chinese master criminal husband, Sin Sin Wa; when Lola kills his beloved (also one-eyed) raven, he strangles her with his pigtail – transforming a key Chinese racial marker, as historian Sascha Auerbach observes, into a tool of violence.[188] Thus in this narrative it is not Rita/Billie who comes to a disastrous end (Rita is subsequently cured of her cocaine addiction), but Lola/Ada. Lola and her husband were of course many removes away from Ada and Lsu Ping You, both

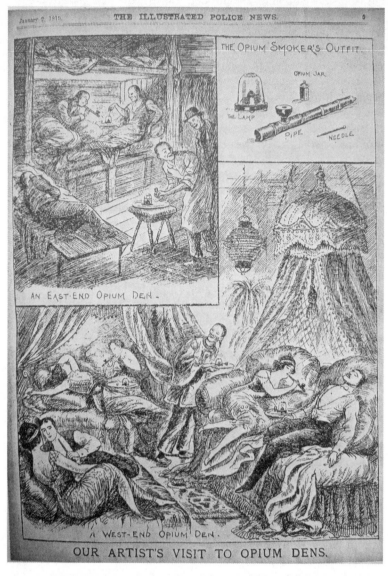

7 *Illustrated Police News*, 2nd January 1919, p.5 'Opium Dens',
© British Library Board (LON261)

in Lola's greater racial 'otherness', and in Sin Sin Wa's central involvement in a global criminal drug syndicate. But both women were sullied and corrupted by their close association with the Chinese, and both, in travelling to Mayfair from the East End, were presented as key to the cult of West End drug taking, indeed corrupters of white West Enders, or that is at least how Rohmer presented Lola, and the prosecution and the judge presented Ada.[189] Sax Rohmer and (at least some of) his readers may have seen the strangulation of Lola as a fitting finish for a woman who transgressed on so many counts.

East End queens

At the end of 1922, May Roberts, described as 'a good-looking well-dressed woman of thirty-one, who stepped smartly into the dock', was charged at Bow Street Police Court for being in possession of a quantity of black opium sufficient 'to satisfy scores of drug-takers'.[190] She had been under police observation for some time. On a Friday evening in December, Detective Charles Owen had seen her leave her house in Limehouse and get into a large private car which was waiting for her nearby. He followed the car to Wellington Street, off the Strand, where she was joined by Albert Ellis, a thirty-five year old commercial traveller who was holding a large brown paper parcel. They were then driven to the nearby Waldorf Hotel, where Ellis alighted. May Roberts's car moved on towards Ludgate Circus, pursued by Owen and two police officers in a taxicab. When her car ground to a halt in heavy traffic, Owen and the officers jumped out of the taxicab, mounted the car's footboard, and opened the car door. May confessed that the paper parcel, on the seat beside her, contained opium. Ellis, arrested later in the evening, at first denied all knowledge of the parcel, but subsequently admitted that he had 'been a mug'.[191] May was given a six-month jail sentence and a £30 fine; Ellis got the same jail sentence but his fine was £40, for in this case he had supplied the opium.

Given the current press obsession with the 'modern woman', it is not surprising that there was far greater media interest in May's background than in Ellis's. The *Empire News* however, presented what it clearly thought were two 'telling' pieces of information about Ellis: he had been a quarter-master in the Chinese Labour Corps during the war, and was a British subject of Jewish origin.[192] He was thus long familiar with the Chinese and was himself almost an 'alien'. May Roberts on the other hand was seen as an intriguing enigma. It was reported that a few years before, she had abandoned her (white British) husband and 'comfortable home' in a middle-class area of Liverpool to live with a Chinese man in the city's Chinese quarter, later moving to London's Limehouse. She still moved between Liverpool and London however, and was known to the Liverpool police for being associated with opium smugglers.[193] The press reported that at her court appearance, May Roberts was 'described as "independent"'.[194] The meaning of 'independent' is unclear (although perhaps only to today's reader). Was the press repeating May's own self-definition or was it that of her counsel? Did it relate to her (lack of) official occupation? Was it a reference to her ambiguous marital status? (She had apparently co-habited with a Chinese man, who was killed in a gang fight, and then with another, also killed, but had married neither. Whether she had divorced her husband was unclear.)

Newspapers' representations of May Roberts varied significantly. The *Empire News* saw May not as a controlling figure, but as simply an agent employed by 'the principals – who are always in the background', and who used 'well and even fashionably dressed people' to avoid suspicion.[195] The paper did not seem able to countenance a mere woman as a drug chief. The *Illustrated Sunday Herald* took a similar line: despite calling her the 'Queen of Limehouse', it labelled her a 'dope decoy'. The term is of course related to the idea of a 'lure', for it means 'anything employed to allure, especially into a trap; an enticement, bait'.[196] May, the article argued (written by 'a special commissioner', thereby conveying authoritative private investigation), had been lured by the 'blandishments' of a 'suave Chinese', but she in turn was used as a lure ('one of the most expert agents and decoys in the kingdom'): 'how many other white women May Roberts has lured to the same doom it is impossible to guess'. The idea of May herself being a 'lure' – as a woman who 'lured' others (into drugs in this case) – spoke of a long history of women being blamed for their 'allure' – 'honey traps' fatally drawing others (usually men) to their downfall. The nature of the 'doom' in the article was not spelt out, but there was mention of how May's 'husband' (inverted commas in the original) had enabled her to 'traverse England as a woman of wealth and culture – when she was not wallowing in the orgies of her bondage'. The latter comment implied drug addiction, although no other paper referred to her taking drugs (as was likewise the case with Ada Ping You). The article also noted how 'it was significant that when she was arrested … it was an Englishman who was her companion in the enterprise … her Chinese "husband" … apparently immune'.[197] This mysterious 'Chinaman' was the power behind the scenes, and May a mere stooge, the paper implied.

In stark contrast, *Reynolds's News* printed an article by 'One who Knew Her' which claimed that May was not a mere 'decoy' but a *leader*, the 'White Queen of Chinatown', who had 'amazing power' over the Chinese.[198]

Her 'word was law in all matters pertaining to the traffic in opium and morphine ... the directing spirit of an almost perfect organisation for "running" supplies of opium into this country, and then distributing it, not only in this country but abroad'. She was described as 'absolutely fearless and could take care of herself in the roughest company', using a pistol when the need arose. Both her 'Celestrial "husbands"'['Celestrial' was a nineteenth-century term for Chinese] had been killed in gang warfare, but she had subsequently managed to unite the rival gangs. Her authority was such that she was asked to be the final arbiter in disputes 'over gambling, opium smoking, rivalry for the affections of white girls'.[199]

Given that May appears to have been more middle-class than most of the women in Limehouse, the question as to why this white woman should choose to live with the Chinese was all the more puzzling. 'One who Knew Her' in *Reynolds's News* asked May to reflect on her preference for Chinese men (although the language of May's 'answer' suggests that it was very probably ghosted):

> There is a subtle charm, a romance and a poetry about [the Chinaman's] love- making that makes the efforts of the average Westerner seem ridiculous ... I prefer Chinamen ... This preference may have its origin in some wild primitive instinct that may or may not be a reversion to a barbarous past, as I have been told by a missionary, but the fact is that the preference is deeply ingrained in my soul and ... I am not going to alter in this respect for anyone.[200]

Whether or not these were indeed her own words, the passage conveyed her defiance against the dictate of others, including that of a missionary ('I am not going to alter in this respect for anyone'). And in claiming her 'preference' as 'ingrained', she was claiming it as unchangeable. While she appears to have adopted the widespread idea of the 'Chinaman' as mysterious and hypnotic, rather than seeing these attributes as sinister she saw them as romantic, and her attraction as instinctive – a fitting retort to the former British colonial administrator who had written to *The Times* in June 1919 that 'it is an instinctive certainty that sexual relations between white women and coloured men revolt our very nature'.[201]

May Roberts was an example of a woman who moved between two worlds geographically and class-wise, masquerading as a society lady (although she was more middle-class, it seems, that many of the women similarly masquerading) when she entered top West-End nightclubs with opium to sell – her intent on the night in question. While some newspapers presented her as under the power of a mysterious and absent Chinese man, *Reynolds's News* gave space to a different portrayal. Here May Roberts was presented as powerful in her own right, holding sway as 'Queen' over Limehouse, and possibly Liverpool's Chinese quarter too. However, the initial draw for May had been the 'subtle charm' of the 'Chinaman', and in that sense, May is presented by the paper as having been 'lured' – an undermining of the agency given in her depiction as 'Queen'.

A year after May's trial, a good friend of May's, Julia Kitt, aged twenty-eight, was charged at Thames Police Court for possession of cocaine. She had been arrested in Limehouse on leaving a public house, expensively dressed, and about to step into a waiting motor-car ('a costly limousine' according to the popular paper *John Bull*); she was found to have 3.6 grains of the drug in her handbag.[202] She was married to Choy Ah Kitt, with whom she had two children. When May Roberts left prison in the summer, she had moved in with Julia, Julia's husband having gone to Hamburg to organise the smuggling of drugs to London. He was believed to be there still. For months detectives had been shadowing Julia and it was claimed that 'for two years [the *Empire News* reported three] she had been engaged in "running" dope to the West End, going by motor-car from Chinatown to expensive West End nightclubs and resorts near Tottenham Court Road'.[203] In this she was similar to May, but it was cocaine rather than opium that she had been selling, Julia appropriately known as the 'Snow Queen' to May's 'White Queen'.[204] Magistrate Cairns gave her a six-month jail sentence (the length of imprisonment given to May).[205]

While the *Reynolds's News* article on May Roberts depicted her as a powerful and central actor in the world of drug trafficking, its report on Julia was explicitly in terms of 'the lure of the East'.[206] She, like May, had come to London from Liverpool: 'Limehouse attracted her and before long she was dragged down into the underworld of Chinatown'.[207] *John Bull's* article 'Broken Blossoms' conveyed the same sentiment: Julia was 'now broken on the iron wheel of Fate', a depiction that hinted at the idea of the butterfly broken on a wheel.[208] But if these two papers conveyed a picture of a pathetic woman under the spell of her domineering Chinese husband, the *Empire News*, which had deemed May Roberts' power insubstantial, treated Julia Kitt very differently. It declared that she was 'the most successful drug runner in the Metropolis', and described her extraordinary and clever metamorphosis with grudging respect: 'One minute Julia was Mrs Kitt, the downtrodden wife of a Chinese, seeking relaxation or temporary forgetfulness in the bars of Chinatown; the next she was a beautiful, fashionably-dressed woman-about-town, sweeping gaily into club or dance hall'. She prospered, and 'invested in a fine-looking car of her own in which to "run" the dope'. In addition, there was 'her ability to wear expensive clothes well and her clever aping of society speech and manner'. It ended the article by suggesting that despite having been caught, 'Julia Kitt, "queen" of the drug-runners, is probably laughing up her sleeve at having escaped with six months after plying for three years a trade calculated to ruin hundreds of patrons and probably bringing death to not a few'.[209] She was thereby invested with an agency on a par with Brilliant Chang, and her cleverness acknowledged, even as she was condemned for the murderous nature of her trade.

It is unclear why the newspapers' accounts of May Roberts and Julia Kitt differed so markedly, given that the women's situations and authority appear to have been equivalent. It is also unclear why *Reynolds's News* and *Empire News* shifted their (opposed) positions in the intervening year between the trials of the two women. It is of course possible that the differences in reporting reflected the particular and contrasting views of the different reporters, but it also surely demonstrates that for each newspaper there was no clear and agreed position on how to 'understand' the actions of these women other than through the concept of the 'lure'. That the *Empire News*, a right-wing newspaper inclined to overt racism, should endow Julia Kitt with some respect was perhaps indicative of the wide range of responses to the modern woman – responses that were unstable, shifting, indecisive and confused. There was no monolithic position on the modern women's capabilities, no definite idea as to her limitations or potential.

Chapter 1 ended with a reference to how the construction of a new, post-war modern womanhood as a site of dispute and contestation would be considered further in the chapters that follow. This chapter has focused particularly on the anxiety felt as to the modern young woman's apparent impetuous pursuit of pleasure – whether it be drugs and dance in nightclubs, or Chinese men, easy virtue and gambling in Limehouse. Concern with the modern woman as consumer and/or seller of drugs and/or pursuer of the 'Chinaman' was played out in various sites, especially in the press, in popular culture (novels and film) and in the law courts. The three different 'types' of modern woman that are examined here – the 'butterfly' woman of the West End, the 'lured' young woman attracted to the 'Chinaman' of the East End, and the female 'dope fiend' who moved between East and West Ends, trafficking drugs – were all to some degree cast as victims. The butterfly women were depicted as child-like in their irresponsibility and impetuousness, unable to resist the pull of illicit pleasures; they were implicitly if not explicitly thought ineligible for active citizenship. As passive victims of circumstance, they were absolved from blame for their drug taking. The white women who pursued Chinese men were deemed pests, but simultaneously victims of the 'lure of the East'. The white women who married Chinese men lost their British citizenship on marriage, and were presented as pitiful – transformed and diminished legally, morally and physically, the mothers of 'handicapped' children, even while their husbands were praised for good behaviour. There was less consensus about the female 'dope fiends'. Although they too were thought under the spell of the 'yellow man', this view co-existed with one in which the women concerned had acted with some agency. Ada Ping You was condemned in court by prosecution and judge for her transgressions, and given the maximum sentence permitted under the 1916 Act. Yet the transgressions of May Roberts and Julia Kitt extended beyond those of Ada, for in addition to selling drugs, 'polluting' the West, and partnering Chinese men, the two women masqueraded as West End Society women, disguising themselves through dress, smart cars, and 'aping' of 'society speech and manner'. Despite or perhaps because of this, some of the press reports gave them grudging respect, recognising the women's power, entrepreneurial skills, fearlessness and cleverness in a manner missing from most other accounts of the modern young woman of the day.[210]

The women considered in this chapter were of course the exception: most modern women did not die from drugs, or form inter-racial relationships, or act as 'dope fiends'. But the consequences of these women's actions were taken as indicative of the potential dangers facing *all* young women. These 'deviant' women were presented as a warning to others of the dire straits facing those who dared to act on impulse and succumb to the 'lure' of nightclubs, dope, or 'Chinamen'. The narratives surrounding these women acted as morality tales: should young women get caught up with drugs they would lose their looks and their health, and probably their lives too; should they marry Chinese men, their looks and health would also be compromised, and their lives would become pitiful. And if they became 'dope fiends' and went into the business of selling drugs, they would inevitably end up as imprisoned criminals. The dominant message was that young women could not help themselves, and left to their own devices, would be sucked into an immoral abyss. They needed regulation and protection, for they were too susceptible, and too intent on seeking sensation. In Chapters 3 and 4 the crimes that the female defendants are accused of are much more serious, namely the murder of their husbands. Arguably the sensation-seeking, modernity, sexuality and adultery of the first of these women assured her culpability. The narrative of the second of these women, charged with the murder of her Egyptian husband, is presented, like the drug narratives, as a morality tale: the danger besetting white women who rashly choose to overlook the fundamental incompatibility of 'East' and 'West'.

Notes

1 Robert Blatchford, 'Is the Modern Woman a Hussy?', *Illustrated Sunday Herald*, 15th June 1919, p. 5. And see Lady Burbidge, 'Women and the War', *The Sunday Times*, 1st June 1919, p. 9.

2 *The Times*, 5th June 1918, p. 4.

3 *Illustrated Sunday Herald*, 30th April 1922, p. 6.

4 On modern women and smoking see Penny Tinkler, *Smoke Signals: Women, Smoking and Visual Culture* (Oxford and New York, 2006), Chapter 4; Penny Tinkler and Cheryl Krasnick Walsh, 'Feminine Modernity in Interwar Britain and North America', *Journal of Women's History*, 20, 3 (2008), pp. 113–43.

5 *Oxford English Dictionary*, Vol. IX (Oxford, 1989), p. 114.

6 *Oxford English Dictionary*, Vol. II (Oxford, 1989), p. 713.

7 *Oxford English Dictionary*, Vol. V (Oxford, 1989), p. 1008.

8 Edith Barton and Marguerite Cody, *Eve in Khaki: the Story of the Women's Army at Home and Abroad* (London, 1918), p. 48. Thanks to Krisztina Robert for this reference.

9 *People*, 8th February 1920, p. 7.

10 *People*, 4th March 1923, p. 6.

11 *The Times*, 5th December 1920, p. 9.

12 Virginia Berridge, 'Drugs and Social Policy: the Establishment of Drug Control in Britain, 1900–30', *British Journal of Addiction*, 79, 1980, p. 20. An example of the ease with which one could obtain cocaine before the 1916 law is given in David Garnett's autobiography, where he recounts buying cocaine from a chemist for his lover Betty May, an artist's model. He refers to her as 'a tough little dope-fiend', who when asleep, 'seemed like a butterfly spreading its wings in the sun'. *The Golden Echo: 2: The Flower of the Forest* (London, 1955), pp. 44–5.

13 See *The Times*, 12th Febuary 1916. Consuming cocaine in the 1880s had been largely acceptable, for example when consumed by Sigmund Freud or the fictitious Sherlock Holmes. But by 1896 the story 'The Missing Three-quarters' has Dr Watson referring to Holmes's syringe as 'an instrument of evil'. Virginia Berridge and Griffith Edwards, *Opium and the People* (London, 1981), pp. 218, 223.

14 Terry M. Parssinen, *Secret Passions, Secret Remedies: Narcotic Drugs in British Society, 1820–1930* (Manchester, 1983), p. 139; Berridge, 'Drugs and Social Policy', p. 21. The Metropolitan Commissioner deployed women patrols to investigate the sale of cocaine by women to soldiers in London parks. Joan Lock, *The British Policewoman: Her Story* (London, 1979), p. 39. On prostitutes selling drugs in London in the 1920s see Lillian Wyles, *A Woman at Scotland Yard* (London, 1952), pp. 77–8.

15 *Daily Sketch*, 28th November 1918.

16 *The Times*, 28th November 1918; Juliet Nicolson, *The Great Silence, 1918–1920: Living in the Shadow of the Great War* (London, 2009), p. 133.

17 *Lloyd's Sunday News*, 23rd February 1919, p. 4. Detective Annetter Kerner claims she earned £100 a week, but that seems rather unlikely. Annette Kerner, *Further Adventures of a Woman Detective* (London, 1955), p. 12.

18 *Daily Chronicle*, 4th December 1918, p. 3.

19 Marek Kohn, *Dope Girls: the Birth of the British Drug Underground* (London, 1992), p. 67. This compelling book has been invaluable for my knowledge and thinking about young women and drugs.

20 Kohn, *Dope Girls*, p. 76.

21 Kerner, *Further Adventures of a Woman Detective*, p. 12. On Kerner see Louise A. Jackson, 'The Unusual Case of "Mrs Sherlock". Memoir, Identity and the "Real" Woman Private Detective in Twentieth-Century Britain', *Gender & History*, 15, 1 (April 2003), pp. 108–34.

22 *People*, 19th January 1919.

23 Kohn, *Dope Girls*, pp. 99–100. Not everyone at the time agreed that it was inevitably death from cocaine. Dr G.A. Hamerton, divisional police surgeon, for example, said that the state of the dead woman's body could also indicate death from veronal. And De Veulle's defence lawyer, Huntly Jenkins, also suggested that Billie might have died from veronal poisoning. *The Times*, 1st March 1919, p. 2.

24 *Lloyd's Sunday News*, 2nd March 1919, p. 6.

25 *Star*, 18th February 1919, p. 12.

26 *The Times*, 5th April 1919, p. 6.

27 *The Times*, 5th April 1919, p. 6; 8th April 1919, p. 7.

28 *News of the World*, 15th December 1918.

29 *World's Pictorial News*, 7th January 1922.

30 *World's Pictorial News*, 18th March 1922, p. 12.

31 *World's Pictorial News*, 27th March 1925, p. 10.

32 Kohn, *Dope Girls*, p. 67.

33 *Daily Express*, 7th December 1918, p. 1.

34 *Daily Express*, 7th December 1918, p. 1.

35 *World's Pictorial News*, 29th July 1922, p. 8.

36 *Daily Mail*, 16th December 1918, p. 3.

37 *Sunday Express*, 12th March 1922, p. 1.

38 *Daily Mail*, 16th December 1918, p. 3.

39 In Sax Rohmer, *Yellow Claw* (1915) a doctor explains: 'Women who acquire a drug habit become more rapidly and more entirely enslaved by it than does a man … all other claims, social and domestic, are disregarded', quoted in Sascha Auerbach, *Race, Law and the 'Chinese Puzzle' in Imperial Britain* (New York, 2009), p. 110. And see Susan Zeigler, '"How far am I Responsible?" Women and Morphinomania in Late-Nineteenth Century Britain', *Victorian Studies*, 48, 1 (2005), pp. 59–81.

40 See Mrs Meyrick, *Secrets of the 43: Reminiscences* (London, 1933), pp. 210–13 on how she paid dance 'hostesses' £3 a week, but that they could make small fortunes from tips, although needed to stay healthy and drink little.

41 *Empire News*, 12th March 1922, p. 2.

42 Abra, 'On with the Dance', pp. 206–7. And see Kate Meyrick on dance instructresses, *Sunday Sentinel*, 13th February 1929, p. 13.

43 *Daily Express*, 8th March 1922, p. 7, and *Illustrated Police News*, 20th April 1922, p. 2. Kate Meyrick (1875–1933) had opened Brett's in 1919, but had soon sold it and founded the 43 Club in November 1921. Its clientele included aristocracy, members of Bohemia, such as Augustus John and Jacob Epstein, and criminals. Meyrick, *Secrets of the 43*, pp. 31, 41. And see D.J. Taylor, *Bright Young People: the Rise and Fall of a Generation: 1918–1940* (London, 2007), pp. 43–4; Walkowitz, *Nights Out*, Chapter 7. The Palais had opened in October 1919, followed by many others around the country. See Samantha Moles, '"Going down the Pally": a Comparative Study of a Working Class "Girls' Night Out" at the Hammersmith Palais from the 1940s to 1980s', unpublished MA dissertation, London

Metropolitan University (2007), deposited in The Women's Library.

44 Jack Glicco, *Madness After Midnight* (London, 1952), p. 23

45 Glicco, *Madness After Midnight*, p. 21; Meyrick, *Secrets of the 43*, p. 210.

46 'like a butterfly of the night she would flit from club to club', *World's Pictorial News*, 11th March 1922, p. 2; She 'flitted like a butterfly from flower to flower.' *Reynolds's Newspaper*, 30th April 1922, p. 10. And see Charlotte Simpson, 'Dope Girls, the Yellow Peril and Mormonism: Young Women and Moral Panics in the Early 1920s English Press', unpublished MA dissertation, London Metropolitan University (2008), p. 49, deposited in The Women's Library.

47 *Empire News*, 23rd May 1926, p. 11.

48 *Empire News*, 12th March 1922, p. 2.

49 *Daily Express*, 18th April 1922, p. 6; *Evening News*, 17th April 1922, p. 1.

50 *World's Pictorial News*, 22nd April 1922, p. 1.

51 On Spilsbury see Jane Robins, *The Magnificent Spilsbury and the Case of the Brides in the Bath* (London, 2010).

52 *Daily Express*, 8th March 1922, p. 7.

53 *News of the World*, 12th March 1922, p. 5.

54 Reynolds's Special Correspondent, *Reynolds's Newspaper*, 12th March 1922, p. 7. However, the following month this paper referred to her as a 'nightclub butterfly'. *Reynolds's Newspaper*, 23rd April 1922, p. 9. And see James Douglas, 'The Night Club Girl', *Sunday Express*, 12th March 1922, p. 8: 'she called herself a dance instructress, but it is evident that she was a foolish little moth whose wings were scorched by the flame of vicious luxury'.

55 *Empire News*, 23rd April 1922, p. 7. See Lady Norah Bentinck in the *Pall Mall Gazette*: Freda was 'a London butterfly who ... fluttered a little too near the flame of the city's night life, burnt her wings, and died with a cry of despair', *Pall Mall Gazette*, 25th March 1922, p. 3. And see Kate Meyrick: 'London's nightlife has many butterflies, and often, too often, they are scorched by the flame'. *Sunday Sentinel*, 17th March 1929, p. 12.

56 *Sunday Express*, 12th March 1922, p. 8. On the 'Maiden Tribute' see Walkowitz, *City of Dreadful Delight*. Most of the papers likewise emphasised her youth, claiming her to be twenty-one when in fact she was to be twenty-three that year.

57 *Daily Mail*, 8th January 1919, p. 7, and see *Daily Mail*, 15th January 1919, p. 4, and *Daily Express*, 30th October 1919, p. 7.

58 See Graves and Hodge, *The Long Weekend*; James J. Nott, *Music for the People: Popular Music and Dance in Interwar Britain* (Oxford, 2002); Jill Julius Matthews, 'Dancing Modernity', in Barbara Caine and Rosemary Pringle (eds), *Transitions: New Australian Feminisms* (Allen & Unwin, 1995), pp. 74–87. It is estimated that 11,000 dance halls and nightclubs opened in Britain in the period 1919–26. Abra, 'On with the Dance', p. 134.

59 Meyrick, *Secrets of the 43*, p. 23.

60 Quoted in Christopher Breward, *Fashioning London: Clothing and the Modern Metropolis* (Oxford, 2004), p. 111.

61 See Claire Langhamer, *Women's Leisure in England, 1920–1960* (Manchester, 2000), p. 58, Ross McKibbin, *Classes and Cultures: England, 1918–1951* (Oxford, 1998), p. 395; Jill Julius Matthews, *Dance Hall and Picture Palace: Sydney's Romance with Modernity* (Sydney, 2005).

62 See Hsu-Ming Teo, 'Women's Travel, Dance and British Metropolitan Anxieties, 1890–1939', *Gender & History*, 12, 2 (July 2000), pp. 366–400; and Abra, 'On with the Dance' for an excellent discussion of dance in all its forms.

63 *Reynolds's News*, 24th June 1923, p. 2.

64 *Sunday Express*, 12th March 1922, p. 8.

65 Stella Moss '"Wartime Hysterics"? Alcohol, Women and the Politics of Wartime Social Purity in England', in Jessica Meyer (ed.), *British Popular Culture and the First World War* (Boston, MA, 2008), p. 149.

66 Sally Alexander, 'A New Civilization? London Surveyed 1928–1940s', *History Workshop Journal*, 64 (2007). Judith Walkowitz points out that for 1890–1945 Soho was seen by journalists and social commentators as a prime spot for crime and vice. Walkowitz, *Nights Out*, Chapter 7.

67 *Daily Express*, 16th March 1922, p. 7. Emphasis in original.

68 'Eve' in the *Tatler*, 15th January 1919.

69 See James Nott, *Music for the People*; Martin Pugh, *'We danced all Night': a Social History of Britain Between the Wars* (London, 2008), Chapter 11; Cathy Ross, *Twenties London: a City in the Jazz Age* (London, 2003), pp. 27–32; Ethel Mannin, *Young in the Twenties: a Chapter in Autobiography* (London, 1971), pp. 31–4; Walkowitz, *Nights Out*, Chapter 7. See Petrine Archer-Straw, *Negrophilia: Avant-Garde Paris and Black Culture in the 1920s* (London, 2000) for jazz and nightclubs in Paris.

70 *Illustrated Sunday Herald*, 4 November 1923, p. 5.

71 *Sunday Express*, 12th March 1922, p. 1. And see *Reynolds's Newspaper*, 30th April 1922, p. 10. The term 'snow' was an American import.

72 *Empire News*, 12th March 1922, p. 1.

73 *Reynolds's Newspaper*, 30th April 1922, p. 10. A few weeks earlier, the paper had suggested that many London's nightclubs were run by convicted criminals: *Reynolds's Newspaper*, 29th January 1922, p. 2. In January of the following year a 'war on nightclubs' was declared by the Metropolitan police that would entail stricter supervision and increased numbers of raids: *Reynolds's News*, 28th January 1923, p. 12.

74 A taxicab driver responded similarly: 'This Freda Kempton business had properly put the lid on things!' *Daily Express*, 13th March 1922, p. 1. The *Evening News*'s 'Special Representative' likewise had difficulty finding a nightclub selling drink and drugs.

75 *Daily Express*, 15th March 1922, p. 7. See Trevor Allen, *Underworld: the Biography of Charles Brooks Criminal* (London, 1932), p. 225: 'There were no more tragic people in the whole of London in those days than the women dope-fiends.'

76 *Illustrated Sunday Herald*, 19th March 1922, p. 5.

77 *Evening News*, 14th March 1922, p. 1.

78 See Bingham, *Gender, Modernity, and the Popular Press*, pp. 69–78; Mike Huggins, '"And Now for Something for the Ladies": Representations of Women's Sport in Cinema Newsreels, 1918–1939', *Women's History Review*, 16, 5 (2007), pp. 681–700.

79 *Daily Express*, 18th April 1922, p. 6.

80 *Sunday Sentinel*, 24th February 1929, p. 13.

81 *Daily Express*, 10th March 1922, p. 8.

82 *Daily Express*, 14th March 1922, pp. 1, 4.

83 See for example Otto Weininger, *Sex & Character* (London, 1910), p. 302 on the Chinese: 'One might feel tempted to believe in the complete effeminacy of the whole race.'

84 *Daily Express*, 23rd April 1922, pp. 4, 8. And see *World's Pictorial News*, 29th April 1922, p. 3: 'He has been well-educated, and to the questions that were rained upon him in rapid succession he replied with that imperturbable calm which one associates with the mystic East.'

85 *Empire News*, 30th April 1922.

86 *Daily Express*, 25th April 1922, p. 4. See image 'London's Chinatown: Taking the Oath', *Daily Graphic*, 2nd August, 1913, reproduced in Auerbach, *Race, Law and the 'Chinese Puzzle'*, p. 163.

87 *Daily Express*, 25th April 1922, p. 4.

88 Virginia Berridge, 'The Origins of the English Drug "Scene", 1890–1930', *Medical History*, 32 (1988.)

89 *World's Pictorial News*, 29th April 1922, p. 3. And see Glicco, *Madness after Midnight*, p. 55.

90 *Daily Express*, 25th April 1922, p. 4.

91 *Evening News*, 30th April 1922.

92 *Empire News*, 30th April 1922.

93 *World's Pictorial News*, 22nd April 1922, p. 1. 'Never in my long and varied experience have I seen so many Easterns in a court of justice', observed the *Empire* reporter. *Empire News*, 23rd April 1922, p. 7.

94 Bram Stoker, *Dracula* (London, 1897); Judith Halberstam, 'Technologies of monstrosity: Bram Stoker's *Dracula*', in Sally Ledger and Scott McCracken (eds), *Cultural Politics at Fin de Siecle* (Cambridge, 1995)

95 *Daily Express*, 11th April 1924, p. 1.

96 *Empire News*, 13th April 1924, p. 1.

97 Sax Rohmer was the pseudonym of English writer Arthur Henry Ward. Rohmer wrote a series of thrillers in the early twentieth century about the evil Dr Fu Manchu, starting with *The Mystery of Dr Fu Manchu* in 1913. As an example of witty inter-textuality, Fu Manchu is pursued by Sherlock Holmes's nephew, Dennis Nayland Smith. See Sax Rohmer, *The Mystery of Dr Fu Manchu* (London, 1913, 1985); see Anne Veronica Witchard, *Thomas Burke's Dark Chinoiserie: Limehouse Nights and the Queer Spell of Chinatown* (Farnham, 2009), p. 105; Clive Bloom, *Cult Fiction* (London, 1996), Chapter 9.

98 Virginia Berridge, *Opium and the People* (London, 1981, 1999), p. 281; Kohn, *Dope Girls*, p. 79.

99 *Empire News*, 23rd April 1922, p. 7, and see *Daily Express*, 11th March 1924, p. 1.

100 Peter Fryer, *Staying Power: the History of Black People in Britain* (London, 1984), p. 296; John Seed, 'Limehouse Blues: Looking for Chinatown in the London Docks, 1900–1940', *History Workshop Journal*, 62 (2006), p. 63; Hg Kwee Choo, *The Chinese in London* (Oxford, 1968), pp. 7–12.

101 As Laura Tabili points out: 'This diverse population shared neither physiognomy nor culture; they were united by a political and historical relationship of colonial subordination.' Laura Tabili, *'We Ask for British Justice': Workers and Racial Difference in Late Imperial Britain* (Ithaca, NY, 1994), p. 9.

102 Seed, 'Limehouse Blues', p. 63; *Daily Mail*, 5th October 1920, p. 7.

103 On men's experiences of the Great War, see J.M. Winter, *The Experience of World War I* (Oxford, 1988); Joanna Bourke, *Dismembering the Male: Men's Bodies, Britain and the Great War* (London, 1996); Santanu Das, '"Kiss Me, Hardy": Intimacy, Gender, and Gesture in World War I Trench Literature', *Modernism/Modernity* 9, 1 (2002), pp. 51–74; Margaret Millman, 'In the Shadow of War: Continuities and Discontinuities in the Construction of the Masculine Identities of British Soldiers, 1914–1924', unpublished Ph.D. thesis (Greenwich University, London, 2003); Richard Smith, *Jamaican Volunteers in the First World War: Race, Masculinity and Development of National Consciousness*

(Manchester, 2004); Santanu Das (ed.), *Touch and Intimacy in First World War Literature* (Cambridge, 2008).

104 The ports where riots occurred were London, Liverpool, Cardiff, Newport, Barry, Salford, Hull, South Shields and Glasgow. There had been earlier confrontations too, such as the destruction of all but one of the twenty-two Chinese laundries in Cardiff in July 1911, when it was held that Chinese seaman were undercutting their British equivalents. Auerbach, *Race, Law and the 'Chinese Puzzle'*, p. 55–56. John Seed's figure are a little different: he states that 'all thirty-three laundries in the town were destroyed'. Seed 'Limehouse Blues,' p. 73.

105 See Roy May and Robin Cohen, 'The Interaction between Race and Colonialism: A Case Study of the Liverpool Race Riots of 1919', *Race and Class XVI*, 2 (1974), pp. 111–26; Neil Evans, 'The South Wales Race Riots of 1919', *Llafur*, 3 (1980), pp. 5–29; Fryer, *Staying Power*, pp. 298–311; Jacqueline Jenkinson, 'The 1919 Riots', in Panikos Panayi (ed.), *Racial Violence in Britain in the Nineteenth and Twentieth Centuries* (Leicester, 1996), pp. 92–111; Michael Rowe, 'Sex, "Race" and Riot in Liverpool, 1919', *Immigrants and Minorities*, 19, 2 (2000), pp. 53–70; Jacqueline Jenkinson, *Black 1919: Riots, Racism and Resistance in Imperial Britain* (Liverpool, 2009).

106 Paul Rich, *Race and Empire in British Politics* (Cambridge, 1986; 2nd edition 1990), p. 121.

107 *The Times*, 17th June 1919, p. 9.

108 Auerbach, *Race, Law and the 'Chinese Puzzle'*, p. 157.

109 *Empire News*, 1st June 1919, p. 8.

110 *Western Mail*, 13th June 1919.

111 *Sunday Express*, 15th June 1919. Emphasis in the original.

112 *Daily Mail*, 1st October 1920, p. 6.

113 PRO: HO 45/25404. And see *Daily Mail*, 7th October 1920, p. 6.

114 PRO: HO 45/25404. In 1913 the India Office had instructed British marriage registry offices to 'explain to British women contemplating marriage with Hindus, Mohamedans and other subjects or citizens of countries where polygamy is legal, the risk attendance on such marriages.' Quoted in Shompa Lahiri, *Indians in Britain: Anglo-Indian Encounters, Race and Identity, 1880–1930* (London 2000), p. 122. See *People*, 10th October 1920, p. 8: '"Johnnie" invariably makes a model husband – providing his white spouse does not accompany him to his native land! For the Chinaman is a polygamist'.

115 The 1870 law was consolidated with the 1914 British Nationality and Status of Aliens Act, and was only finally changed in 1948 with the British Nationality Act. Pat Thane, 'The British Imperial State and the Construction of National Identities', in Billie Melman (ed.), *Borderlines: Genders and Identities in War and Peace, 1870–1930* (London, 1998), pp. 35–8; Laura Tabili 'Outsiders in the Land of their Birth: Exomamy, Citizenship, and Identity in War and Peace', *Journal of British Studies*, 44, 4 (October 2005). There was no parallel requirement for British men marrying foreign-born women to change their nationality; on the contrary, at the discretion of the Home Office these foreign-born women could acquire British nationality.

116 On the idea of a national identity or community being 'imagined' see Benedict Anderson, *Imagined Communities: Reflections on the Origins and Spread of Nationalism* (London, 1983).

117 See Rose, *Which People's War?*; Chris Waters, '"Dark Strangers" in Our Midst: Discourses of Race and Nation in Britain, 1947–1963', *Journal of British Studies*, 36 (April 1997), pp. 207–38.

118 *Illustrated Sunday Herald*, 10th October 1920, p. 5.

119 See Laura Tabili, *Global Migrants, Local Culture: Natives and Newcomers in Provincial England, 1841–1939* (New York, 2011) which charts the inclusion and integration of migrants into the working-class community of South Shields over a period of a hundred years.

120 Lucy Bland, 'White Women and Men of Colour: Miscegenation Fears in Britain after the Great War', in *Gender & History*, 17, 1 (2005), p. 38.

121 Smith, *Jamaican Volunteers in the First World War*, p. 116.

122 15th October 1925, PRO: HO 45/25404.

123 Witchard, *Thomas Burke's Dark* Chinoiserie, p. 18.

124 See Gina Marchetti, *Romance and the 'Yellow Peril': Race, Sex and Discursive Strategies in Hollywood Fiction* (Berkeley, CA, 1993).

125 *The Times*, 14th September 1916, p. 5.

126 *Empire News*, 10th December 1922, p. 5. And see *Empire News*, 24th December 1922, p. 7. In 1907 a Liverpool Council Inquiry noted: 'The evidence shows that the Chinese appear to much prefer having intercourse with young girls, more especially those of undue precocity.' Witchard, *Thomas Burke's Dark* Chinoiserie, p. 115.

127 15th October 1925, PRO: HO 45/25404. Memo from Home Office to the Foreign Office; the author's signature is illegible.

128 See Julia Lesage, '*Broken Blossoms*: Artful Racism, Artful Rape', *Jump Cut: A Review of Contemporary Media*, 26 (1981), pp. 51–5; Jon Burrows, '"A Vague Chinese Quarter Elsewhere": Limehouse in the Cinema, 1914–1936', *Journal of British Cinema and Television*, 6, 2 (August 2009), pp. 281–301.

129 The story is in Thomas Burke, *Limehouse Nights* (London, 1916, 1926). The book was instantly banned by circulating libraries on grounds of immorality. Concern about the propriety of fictitious depictions of adult-child sexual relations influenced actress Lillian Gish when she took the star role in the film, and she insisted on raising the girl's age to fifteen. But her portrayal was still one akin to the sexualised girl-child of the Victorian stage. Witchard, *Thomas Burke's Dark* Chinoiserie, pp. 1, 235. Griffith never visited Limehouse before making the film, but did so three years later, and was reported as finding 'Limehouse so much more interesting than our own "Chinatowns" because in America the white and coloured people do not mix as in London.' *Evening News*, 26th April 1922, p. 1. His comments seem fundamentally at odds with the racist depictions of African Americans in his 1915 film *Birth of a Nation*. See Everett Carter, 'Cultural History written with Lightening: the Significance of the Birth of a Nation', *American Quarterly*, 12, 3 (Autumn 1960).

130 Witchard, *Thomas Burke's Dark* Chinoiserie, pp. 129–32.

131 Lily Siddall commented on this generosity: 'They [Chinese men] are thoughtful of their wives, they will spend far more money on their clothing and in providing them with finery than most other husbands do.' *Empire News*, 24th December 1922, p. 7.

132 *Evening News*, 7th October 1920, p. 1.

133 *Daily Graphic*, 7th October 1920, p. 3.

134 In the nineteenth century the prostitute had also been noted as loving 'finery'. See Lynda Nead, 'The Magdalen in Modern Times: the Mythology of the Fallen Woman in Pre-Raphaelite Painting', in Rosemary Betterton (ed.), *Looking On: Images of Femininity in the Visual Arts and Media* (London, 1987). On the amateur prostitute, see Lucy Bland and Frank Mort, 'Look out for the "Goodtime" Girl: Dangerous Sexualities as Threat to

National Health', in *Formations of Nation and People* (London, 1984), pp. 139–40; Bland, 'In the Name of Protection'; Levine, '"Walking the Streets in a Way no Decent Woman Should"', pp. 34–78; Woollocott, '"Khaki Fever" and its Control', pp. 325–47.

135 For example, *Illustrated Sunday Herald*, 10th October 1920, p. 5; *Daily Express*, 1st October 1920, p. 1.

136 *Evening News*, 5th October 1920, p. 1.

137 For 'white slave' narratives, see Mariana Valverde, *The Age of Light, Soap and Water* ((Toronto, 1991), Chapter 4; Walkowitz, *City of Dreadful Delight*, Chapter 3; Bland, *Banishing the Beast*, pp. 297–302.

138 *Evening News,* 5th October 1920, p. 1.

139 J.A.R. Cairns, *The Loom of the Law: the Experiences and Reflections of the Metropolitan Magistrate* (London, 1922), p. 219.

140 *Illustrated Sunday Herald*, 30th April 1922, p. 6. And see *Reynolds's Newspaper*, 8th January 1922, p. 2.

141 *Daily Graphic*, 7th October 1920, p. 1.

142 *Daily Graphic*, 7th October 1920, p. 3.

143 Alison Light, *Forever England: Femininity, Literature and Conservatism between the Wars* (London, 1991).

144 See Seed, 'Limehouse Blues' for a very useful discussion of the ideological construction of Limehouse.

145 Cairns, *The Loom of the Law*, p. 222. Lily Siddall likewise commented: 'Where Chinese have married white women they have usually made very good husbands'. *Empire News* 24th December 1922, p. 7. And see Wyles, *A Woman at Scotland Yard*, p. 92.

146 Annie Lai in Steve Humphries and Pamela Gordon, *Forbidden Fruit: Our Secret Past, 1900–1960* (London, 1994), p. 29.

147 Home Office to Secretary of State for Commissioner, 26th September 1925, HO 45/25404.

148 Memo from Home Office to the Foreign Office (author's signature is illegible), 14th October 1925, HO 45/25404.

149 *Daily Express*, 11th April 1924, p. 1.

150 *Evening News*, 6th October 1920, p. 5.

151 E.J. Lidbetter, *Eugenics Review*, XI, 3 (1919), p. 132.

152 *Eugenics Review*, XI, 3 (1919), p. 126.

153 Quoted in *Eugenics Review* (January 1924), p. 647.

154 *Sunday Chronicle*, 23rd March 1919, p. 3, quoted in Bingham, *Family Newspapers?*, p. 103.

155 *Mixed Britannia (1910–39)* directed and produced by Fatima Solaria, BBC2, October 2011.

156 R.M. Fleming, 'Anthropological Studies of Children', *Eugenics Review* (January 1927), p. 298.

157 *The Times*, 16th June 1930, p. 7.

158 Home Office to Secretary of State for Commissioner, 26th September 1925, HO 45/25404.

159 Lucy Bland, 'British Eugenics and "Race Crossing": a Study of an Interwar Investigation', in Special Issue on 'Eugenics Old and New', *New Formations,* 60 (2007). See *Daily Mail*, 5th October 1920, p. 6.

160 Tabili, 'Outsiders in the Land of their Birth', p. 802. Widowed wives of aliens could apply for their reinstatement as British subjects, but the process was cumbersome and lengthy,

although eased somewhat with the 1914 Act. Tabili, 'Outsiders in the Land of their Birth', pp. 806–7.

161 The Aliens Restriction (Amendment) Act, 1919. M. Page Baldwin, 'Subject to Empire: Married Women and the British Nationality and Status of Aliens Act', *Journal of British Studies*, 40 (October 2001), p. 534.

162 *Mixed Britannia (1910–39)*. Campaigning against British women's loss of British nationality on marriage became a concern of feminists in the inter-war years. See Baldwin, 'Subject to Empire'.

163 Tabili, 'Outsiders in the Land of their Birth', pp. 807–8.

164 *Illustrated Sunday Herald*, 10th October 1920, p. 5.

165 *World's Pictorial News*, 25th March 1922.

166 *Star*, 9th January 1919.

167 *People*, 19th January 1919.

168 '*Reynolds's Newspaper*, 8th January 1922, p. 2. In Charles Dickens' unfinished novel *The Mystery of Edwin Drood* it is the partaking of the Chinese 'vice' of opium-smoking that brings about the transformation: a woman who runs an opium den in Chinatown is described as having 'opium-smoked herself into a strange likeness of the Chinaman. His form of cheek, eye and temple, and his colour, are repeated in her'. Quoted in Auerbach, *Race, Law and the 'Chinese Puzzle'*, p. 84.

169 National Archives: HO45/24683. See Julia Lovell, *The Opium War: Drugs, Dreams and the Making of China* (London, 2011); Andrew Blake, 'Foreign Devils and Moral Panics: Britain, Asia and the Opium Trade', in Bill Schwarz (ed.), *The Expansion of England* (London, 1996), p. 253.

170 For example, Tai Ling, who is describes as 'a loveable character' but 'non-moral'. Thomas Burke, *Nights in Town* (London, 1915, 1925), p. 63. He appears again in 'The Father of Yoto' in *Limehouse Nights* where he is described as 'by our standards, a complete rogue; yet the most joyous I have known' (p. 28). The idea of the 'yellow peril' was challenged by the *People*: 'the so-called "yellow peril" exists more in the mind of the imaginative writer than in actual fact.' *People*, 10th October 1920, p. 8.

171 Thomas Burke, *Son of London* (1946), referenced in Seed, 'Limehouse Blues', pp. 77–8 .

172 Kohn, *Dope Girls*, p. 2.

173 Seed, 'Limehouse Blues', p. 69.

174 *World's Pictorial News*, 22th March 1925, p. 10.

175 Kohn, *Dope Girls*, p. 87.

176 *Daily Chronicle*, 21st December 1918, p. 3.

177 *Daily Chronicle*, 21st December, 1918, p. 3.

178 *Daily Chronicle*, 21st December 1918, p. 3.

179 *The Times*, 21st December 1918, p. 3. Burke presented the Chinese ritual of opium preparation as civilised, compared to the quick fix of the Westerner taking cocaine. Witchard, *Thomas Burke's Dark Chinoiserie*, p. 124.

180 *Daily Chronicle*, 14th December 1918, p. 5; 21st December 1918, p. 3.

181 *The Times*, 21st December 1918, p. 5. My emphasis.

182 *The Times*, 21st December 1918, p. 5.

183 *The Times*, 11th January 1919, p. 3, and see, *Lloyd's Sunday News*, 12th January 1919, p. 7. I am indebted to the perceptive analysis of this case given by Auerbach, *Race, Law and 'The Chinese Puzzle'*, pp. 129–35.

184 *The Times*, 21st December 1918, p. 5.

185 For example see *Daily Express*, 9th December 1918, p. 1; 16th December 1918, p. 1; *Star*, 17th January 1919, p. 3.

186 Sax Rohmer, *Dope: the Story of Chinatown and the Drug Traffic* (London, 1919, 2002).

187 Rohmer, *Dope*, p. 78.

188 Auerbach, *Race, Law and the 'Chinese Puzzle'*, p. 147.

189 See Auerbach, *Race, Law and the 'Chinese Puzzle'*, pp. 143–8 for his perceptive analysis of *Dope*.

190 *Sunday Express*, 31st December 1922, p. 9; *Empire News*, 7th January 1923, p. 1.

191 *Illustrated Sunday Herald*, 31st December 1922, p. 2; *Sunday Express*, 31st December 1922, p. 9.

192 On Chinese on the Western Front see Xu Guoqi, *Strangers on the Western Front: Chinese Workers in the Great War* (Cambridge, MA, 2011); Paul J. Bailey, '"An Army of Workers": Chinese Indentured Labour in First World War France', in Santanu Das (ed.), *Race, Empire and First World War Writing* (Cambridge and New York, 2011).

193 *Empire News*, 7th January 1923, p. 1.

194 *The Times*, 8th January 1923, p. 7, *Sunday Express*, 31st December 1922, p. 9. 'Independent' is presented in inverted commas by the *Times* but not by the *Sunday Express*.

195 *Empire News*, 7th January 1923, p. 1.

196 *Shorter Oxford English Dictionary* (Oxford, 1973), p. 502.

197 *Illustrated Sunday Herald*, 21st January 1923, p. 19.

198 *Reynolds's News*, 14th January 1923, p. 11; *Illustrated Sunday Herald*, 21st January 1923, p. 19. A number of deviant women were given the sobriquet 'Queen', for example Kate Meyrick was known as the 'Night Club Queen', and see 'West End Cocaine Arrests: Woman Said to be Known as "Dope-Fiend Queen"', *Star*, 4th March 1919, p. 5. The leader of the 'Forty Elephants' or 'Forty Thieves', a gang of female shoplifters in Elephant and Castle, South London, was also known as 'Queen'. Brian McDonald, *Gangs of London: 100 Years of Mob Warfare* (London, 2010), pp. 221–2.

199 *Reynolds's News*, 14th January 1923, p. 11.

200 *Reynolds's News*, 14th January 1923, p. 11.

201 *The Times*, 14th June 1919, p. 8. The letter is from Ralph Williams, a former British colonial administrator, who had worked in Bechuanaland and been governor to the Windward Islands.

202 *John Bull*, 8th December 1923, p. 10.

203 *Reynolds's News*, 2nd December 1923, p. 6; *People*, 2nd December 1923, p. 11.

204 *Empire News*, 2nd December 1923, p. 5.

205 *The Times*, 29th November 1923, p. 9. She was lucky not to have been given a stiffer sentence, because the recent Dangerous Drugs (Amendment) Act 1923 extended the maximum penalty to ten years penal servitude. The new law was thought greatly to reduce the extent of drug dealing.

206 *Reynolds's News*, 2nd December 1923, p. 6.

207 *Reynolds's News*, 2nd December 1923, p. 6.

208 *John Bull*, 8th December 1923, p. 10.

209 *Empire News,* 2nd December 1923, p. 5. In December 1918 the *Daily Express* had commented on how it was now becoming difficult to tell the background of a woman from her appearance: 'Ten years ago there was a definite hard-and-fast line between the woman of this class ['dope fiend'] and the ordinary Bohemian woman artist, actor or writer. Today it is not so easy to distinguish the dividing line.'

210 Compare the press's respect for the skill of women who cross-dressed as men in this period, explicitly termed a masquerade. Alison Oram, *Her Husband was a Woman! Women's Gender-Crossing in Modern Britain's Popular Culture* (London, 2007)

3

The tribulations of Edith Thompson: sexual incitement as a capital crime

I n late January 1923 several newspapers reported the disturbing story of
a young entomologist, Gilbert Wickham, who had hanged himself from
a beam in his lodgings in Barnes, South London. He had been totally
naked save for a strapped-on 'false bust', a white hood over his head, and a
rope tying his hands behind his back. In the previous months, to quote the
Empire News, he had 'found himself gripped by the most compelling crime
story of the century' – that of Edith Thompson and Frederick Bywaters,
accused of the murder of Mrs Thompson's husband – and 'by the time the
long trial had come to an end, Mrs Thompson had displaced the insects
as the centre of his existence.' According to this newspaper: 'he hanged
himself in circumstances as nearly as he could make them like those of Mrs
Thompson'.[1] Like most stories of cross-dressing in this period, Wickham's
actions were not understood first and foremost in terms of gender inversion or sexual pathology.[2] As someone who had apparently 'read and reread
every published detail' of the case, his plight was seen as illustrative of the
danger of imaginative over-identification – a 'danger' that had in fact been
regularly alluded to throughout the Thompson/Bywaters trial.

Gilbert Wickham might have been obsessed by the trial, but so too,
according to the *Daily Express*, was everyone else: 'No trial in the records of
the Central Criminal Court has gripped the public mind and imagination
in such a manner', the paper dramatically announced, a sentiment echoed
throughout the popular press.[3] The case is of interest to historians not
simply because it was a famous *cause celebre*, but also because it touches on
a spectrum of issues, raised in this book, of crucial importance in the years
after the Great War including adjustment to a post-war economy, blurring
of class boundaries, ambivalences towards the spread of mass culture, including the expansion of the popular press, and above all, deep anxiety
about gender roles and the modern woman. The trial was also central to
the introduction of a bill to prohibit court photography.

The bare bones of the Thompson/Bywaters case are as follows. Prior to his murder in October 1922, thirty-two year old shipping clerk Percy Thompson, and Edith, his twenty-eight year old wife, a book-keeper, manageress, and buyer for a wholesale milliners in the City, were living in a London suburb – Ilford in Essex – and had been married for nearly seven years. For the last fifteen months or so Edith had been having a passionate affair with sailor and shipping steward Freddy Bywaters, eight and a half years her junior. On 3rd October 1922 the Thompsons were returning late from the theatre and nearing home when Bywaters ran up, had angry words with Percy, and stabbed him with a knife several times. Percy died from the wounds. There was no evidence that Edith anticipated the attack; on the contrary, she appeared distressed and bewildered. However, on the discovery of sixty-two letters from Edith in Bywaters' seaman's box, and another five in his room, Edith and Freddy were jointly charged with murder.

As well as being jointly charged with murder, Edith and Freddy were jointly tried. The case was first heard at Stratford Police Court in East London, in the same month of the killing, then transferred to the Old Bailey two months later. In court, the well-known barrister acting for Edith Thompson, Sir Henry Curtis-Bennett, objected to the letters' admissibility on grounds that they had no connection with the actual murder. However the judge, Justice Shearman, ruled them admissible, as evidence of motive and intention. These letters, the central evidence used in Edith's conviction, were her undoing. Because of the way in which they were presented by the prosecution, they appeared to implicate her in a conspiracy to poison her husband or kill him through the administering of glass particles. The post-mortem concluded that the body showed no traces of poison or glass, but her apparent murderous intent (such as her descriptions of trying to poison Percy) was held to constitute incitement and conspiracy to murder. The *Daily Sketch* organised a petition for the reprieve of Bywaters (not Thompson) that generated more than a million signatures. However, when the case went to the Appeal Court on 21st December, the sentence for both defendants was upheld. Thompson and Bywaters were hanged on 9th January 1923.

Wickham's obsession with Edith Thompson was not unique; the press covered the case extensively. All the daily newspapers gave lengthy court reports each day of the Thompson/Bywaters case (weekly in the case of the Sundays), and continued serving up commentary in the form of letters, opinion pieces from experts and from the great and the good, 'exclusive' interviews, editorials, and exposés from investigative reporters, right up to, and beyond, the couple's final hour. Photographs and line drawings of

Edith were on the front and sometimes the back too of all the popular papers (unsurprisingly, since visual representations of attractive women were now a key ingredient for the popular press, particularly the 'picture' papers, like the *Daily Mirror* and *Daily Sketch*). All these different forms of press reportage offered different versions of the same case at the same time. Endless footage was devoted to Edith's appearance, her background, her personality, her likes and dislikes, her motives, her modernity, and the pros and cons of capital punishment. Everyone seemed to have a view on Thompson/Bywaters, indeed a number of leading public figures – prominent journalists, novelists, society ladies, actresses, well-known feminists – were keen to divulge their opinions to the competing newspapers. As feminist Cicely Hamilton reflected: 'I never read murder cases, but one cannot help hearing the discussions that are taking place on this particular case.'[4] Through a kind of mass voyeurism, a huge audience was able to watch/read the narrative(s) of the trial unfold.

Initially the press was positive in its representations of Edith, indeed the intricate detailing of her clothing and general appearance read like a veritable media love affair. As the trial proceeded however, and particularly as some of her letters were dissected in court, the tide largely turned against her. At the trial's end, and while the defendants waited for the appeal, many of the newspapers printed critical articles. The public also thought Edith more responsible for the crime than Bywaters, if the press's claims are to be believed (the *Daily Sketch* for example, undertook an opinion poll straight after the trial, which apparently found much antagonism towards Edith). Press and public appeared to follow the Solicitor General (the main prosecutor in this trial) in seeing her as 'the mind that conceived the crime'.[5]

Despite the apparent growing hostility towards Edith in the days before her hanging, subsequent to her death there has been widespread recognition of a miscarriage of justice – that the claim of incitement or conspiracy to murder had never been established in court.[6] In fact in the write-up of the trial in the 'Notable British Trials Series', published the same year as the hangings, criminologist Filson Young asserted her innocence in his Introduction.[7] So, why, in addition to the court jury (which included one woman), did much of the press at the time, and the public too, think Edith guilty? Barrister Curtis-Bennett, writing later about the case, declared that 'Mrs Thompson was hanged for immorality.'[8] How could this be? And what was it about her that fascinated – that both attracted and repelled the press and its readers?

The Thompson/Bywaters story – told not simply within the court-room but also on the pages of the press – was constructed in such a way that Edith's culpability spilled out beyond the act of murder. Edith was

THE DAILY MIRROR, Thursday, December 7, 1922.

MAIMED MAN'S PROTEST AFTER DEATH SENTENCE. See Page 3

The Daily Mirror

NET SALE MUCH THE LARGEST OF ANY DAILY PICTURE NEWSPAPER

20 PAGES

No. 5,959.   Registered at the G.P.O. as a Newspaper.   THURSDAY, DECEMBER 7, 1922   One Penny.

TENSE DRAMA OF ILFORD MURDER TRIAL

Mr. William Graydon, father of Mrs. Thompson, said she would be twenty-nine on Christmas Day.

Mrs. Edith Thompson on trial on the charge of her husband's murder.

Frederick Bywaters, jointly charged with murder and conspiracy to murder.

Sir H. Curtis Bennett, K.C., Mrs. Thompson's counsel, on his way to court.

Dr. Maudsley, an Ilford physician, was a witness.

Miss D. Pittard said Mrs. Thompson called to her after her husband fell.

Mr. J. Laxton said he was with the Thompsons at theatre

Mr. P. E. Cleveley, who saw Mr. Thompson dying.

Mr. T. W. H. Inskip, K.C., Solicitor-General, who prosecuted.

View of some of the extraordinarily large crowd which sought admission to the court. Inset, Mr. Justice Shearman, who is trying the case.

Many women were seen in the large crowd that besieged the Old Bailey yesterday in an endeavour to hear the dramatic Ilford murder trial, in which Mrs. Edith Thompson and Frederick Bywaters are charged with the murder of Mrs. Thompson's husband and with conspiracy to kill him. The Solicitor-General, in opening the case, said, while Bywaters' was the hand that struck the blow, Mrs. Thompson was the dominant partner and conceived the crime. At times during the day Mrs. Thompson was in tears.

8 *Daily Mirror*, 7th December 1922, Thompson/Bywaters trial
© British Library Board (MLD4)

on trial not just for murder but arguably also for her modernity, her consumption of mass culture – her seeking of sensation – and above all for her sexual agency. Further, the theme of incitement ran throughout the trial – not simply in relation to Edith's incitement of Freddy, and what that might entail, but also mass culture's incitement of the public, particularly its female half, to consume the sensational. The Thompson/Bywaters case clearly demonstrates how trials were a central cultural site for the contesting of societal moral boundaries.[9]

Edith Thompson as a modern woman

Edith in many ways was thought to epitomise the modern woman-cum-flapper. She was notably fashionable; over sixty years after the trial, one of Edith's acquaintances could still remember the visual impact she made: 'she was very smart, she loved clothes, she knew how to dress'.[10] Edith's hairstyle too was at the cutting edge of fashion, for she sported a fringed bob the last six months of her life.[11] Although married, in many ways Edith pursued the lifestyle of an unmarried young woman, untrammelled by childcare (she was childless) or many domestic duties, and committed to the pursuit of pleasure: she smoked, danced, betted on the horses, and read an inordinate amount of books, mostly what would be termed low- or middle-brow, such as romances and thrillers (although she was not a reader of the new 'sex novels' which were causing such a stir, preferring pre-war romances).[12] She moved confidently through urban space, commuting daily from the suburbs (where she lived), to the City (where she worked as a successful businesswoman), and on to the West End, where she regularly attended plays, shows and dance-halls where she danced, the latter being a very public display of her physical prowess.[13] As already discussed, the modern woman-cum-flapper represented both modernity *and* immorality, engendering deep ambivalence. Such ambivalence was apparent in relation to press reportage of Edith Thompson.

Many of the descriptions of Edith in the earlier part of the trial were sympathetic, even positive. To the *Daily Express*: 'The woman in the dock was without question the personality of the court, attractively feminine in every way.'[14] When the trial transferred to the Old Bailey, the *Express* was still waxing lyrical: 'A thrill passed through the court as Mrs Thompson walked slowly down the steps of the dock.'[15] It was as if she were a starlet making a stage entrance. The positive press representations of Edith chiefly involved her stylishness and elegance, her prowess as a dancer, and her capability as a businesswoman. Each day that she appeared in court, the popular press relished every detail of her ever-changing attire. The media's new deployment of photography contributed to the period's heightened scrutiny of the female body. One day in the Police Court she was wearing 'a brown coat with mole fur collar and cuffs, a hat also of fur, and plain white gloves. Beneath her brown coat was a grey crepe de chine dress trimmed with black silk.'[16] (Gloves and hats were essential wear for respectable middle-class women in the 1920s; fur also was widely worn by the middle-classes.)[17] Other days in court, Edith's coat generally appeared to be the same, but the hats changed: 'a large velour hat', 'a small hat and veil', 'a velvet Tam-o-Shanter', 'a black velvety hat with black quills'.[18]

While the press was attentive to the details of Edith's dress, so too was she. Although positioned as a largely mute witness to her and Freddy's trial, apart from the agonising moments of cross-examination, her careful dressing spoke loudly of her respectability and her femininity. It does not sound as if her court clothes were the height of fashion; they were 'lady-like', set on conveying a particular impression to the onlooker. As historian Liz Conor observes, with the rise of modernity, and particularly by the 1920s, 'women were invited to articulate themselves as modern subjects by constituting themselves as spectacles'.[19] But of course women had long taken care over how they dressed, for they learned the (class-specific) codes as to the signification of different outfits and combinations.[20] In relation to Edith, she occasionally wore black in court (she was, after all, a recent widow) but more usually grey, brown, navy blue, cream or white. She does not appear to have worn bright colours, which presumably would have been seen by her and the court spectators as inappropriate.[21]

As a manifestation of her mobility – mobility was a key trope of the flapper – Edith's love of dancing was frequently commented upon. As we have seen, dance was emblematic of the modern woman/flapper. The comments were benign, even flattering. For example, the *Daily Express* noted that she 'was fond of dancing and other forms of harmless gaiety.'[22] The *World's Pictorial News* reported that she was 'an exquisite dancer ... Night after night she went to dances.'[23] Unlike the women discussed in Chapter 2, Edith did not attend nightclubs but respectable dance halls and dances taking place in hotels. Edith's close friend since childhood, Bessie Aitken, writing in *Lloyd's Sunday News* anonymously as 'a Lifelong Friend of Mrs Thompson', mentioned the many trophies Edith had won in competitions, noting that 'above all she was a superb waltzer.'[24] Waltzing, unlike the tango or the foxtrot, was respectable and traditional. Thus her dancing was presented as an innocent, respectable pleasure – 'harmless gaiety' – and a skill – she was 'an exquisite dancer'.

Edith was also presented as a committed and talented businesswoman who had done very well for herself and was much respected in the firm she worked for – Carlton and Prior, a wholesale milliners in Aldersgate Street in the City. She had started working there in late 1911, aged nearly eighteen, having worked previously as a junior clerk in a couple of whole-sale clothiers.[25] Such was her flair for the work that she had risen rapidly to the positions of manageress and chief buyer, in addition to that of book-keeper.[26] (Book-keeping had, until recently, been a male preserve, as was the City.)[27] The *Daily Express* quoted the manageress of a neighbouring firm: 'Mrs Thompson is one of the keenest businesswomen in the City ... Her engaging manner has undoubtedly contributed to her success in busi-ness.'[28] Edith travelled to Paris on a number of occasions as a buyer for her firm; it helped that she spoke good French, which she must have taken the initiative to study, for her elementary school would not have taught lan-guages.[29] She used her maiden name, Graydon, at work – another aspect of her unmarried, independent, flapper persona.

These representations of Edith as well-dressed, professional, and highly dance-proficient had their negative counterparts, which in relation to Edith took the form of accusations of extreme extravagance and indul-gence, and over-commitment to work at the neglect of marital duties.[30] There was no direct attack on her dancing, although at the same time as the trial the press was publishing articles castigating 'the dance craze'.[31] There was however a hint of disapproval, for in noting that her husband did not dance, the press implied that she danced with other men. For a married woman to dance without her husband was thought not quite 'proper'. Indeed, on marriage most women stopped dancing altogether, since women of the period saw dance halls as potential 'pick-up' places.[32]

The most vitriolic account of Edith came from her husband's brother, Richard Thompson, who clearly hated his sister-in-law. (He is described by Edith's biographer as of a 'vindictive disposition.')[33] In *Lloyd's Sunday News* Richard Thompson narrated how Edith was 'a flighty, forward flirt, pleasure-loving and extravagant ... untruthful ... loud and vulgar'.[34] (This was in blatant contradiction to a (ghosted) article by Edith's father, William Graydon, which had appeared two weeks earlier in the *Weekly Dispatch*, claiming that 'she was never a girl to flirt ... Her husband and Bywaters were the only two men who ever played a part in her life'.)[35] Poor dull, slow Percy (for even his own brother, in his depiction of the man who longed for nothing but a 'humdrum', 'quiet, steady home life', did not disguise the dull-ness) was no match, Richard argued, for his hard-drinking, hard gambling, extravagant wife, who surrounded herself with male admirers, covered herself in expensive scent, wore endless new hats, and dressed in clothes well beyond her means. Even the less antagonistic accounts stressed the couple's incompatibility.[36] Richard claimed that prior to the trial he had never seen Edith without overt make-up: 'the woman who stood in the dock, with white face and pale lips, was a new creature to me'. (Edith's paleness – and frailty – was widely commented upon by the press.)[37] Make-up was only just taking hold in Britain in the early inter-war years, but its immediate effect was to erode the boundaries between different types and classes of women. According to writers Robert Graves and Alan Hodge: 'The course was from brothel to stage, then on to Bohemia, to Society, to Society's maids, to the mill-girl, and lastly to the suburban woman'.[38] But according to Richard, Edith (a 'suburban woman' in that she lived in the suburbs) had long used make-up: 'I had always known her as a woman with bright pink cheeks and carmined lips.' If this implied that Edith was akin to a prostitute (although it could also be read as a sign of her modernity) the connotations of prostitution went further: 'I do know that at times she had more money than could be accounted for by her office salary ... Edith had a mind very far from pure.'[39]

In the same newspaper the following week, Edith's friend Bessie Aitken rallied to her defence, emphasising that she was not a woman of loose morals, that she barely drank alcohol, only betted in moderation, and that she 'wore a lot of hats as advert for her millinery business'.[40] Yet the same day as this article appeared, a rival Sunday paper, the *Empire News*, presented a counter-narrative, one that reinforced the Richard Thompson line – unsurprisingly, since the paper's so-called 'commissioner' had been talking to the Thompson family:

> Edith Thompson was a woman passionately fond of money, not for the purpose of hoarding it up, but for what it would bring ... it was a perpetual mystery to her relations, especially those on her husband's side, who did not like her, where she found the money to buy the endless number of new things she was always wearing ... she received money from other men ... Everybody who knew her said she dressed like a woman with £2,000 a year to spend, while her husband went about like a poor man.[41]

Edith did not earn anything like £2,000 a year, but through her access to a regular supply of hats, and her excellent 'dress sense', she might indeed have masqueraded as a high earner. Although not rich by any means, her wages were good, double the country's average.[42] She had done well all through the war – her income rising steadily as she rose in the firm. She earned more than her husband, her lover and her father (and had done so in relation to her father since 1913): £6 a week plus a £30 annual bonus, i.e. £342 a year.[43] Her husband earned the same but without the bonus; Freddy earned considerably less. She was a woman who had 'made good'; it helped of course that her field of work was booming, for as historian Catherine

Horwood points out: 'The trade in women's hats ... was robust between the wars.'[44] Edith's work had not been war-work, but the production of 'unnecessary' hats. When men returned, a million found their pre-war jobs held by someone else, sometimes a woman.[45] Working women were frequently taunted by men.[46] The economic crisis of 1921 exacerbated the situation, and in 1922 male unemployment had passed the two million mark.[47] Some of these demobbed men queued all night outside the Old Bailey during the week of the trial in order to sell their places the next morning – frequently to women. There was widespread resentment of women who had prospered in the war, yet had 'done nothing for their country', to quote a letter from 'Disgusted', published in the *Western Mail*.[48]

If the working woman was married, the resentment was greater still. In fact the 1921 economic crisis had led many local authorities to introduce a marriage bar, especially in relation to teaching and the civil service.[49] A married woman who was voluntarily childless, as in Edith's case, was also deemed unacceptable. To Richard Thompson, Edith had selfishly deprived her husband of children, because they would have interfered with her business career.[50] The prosecuting Solicitor General's unnecessary comment that '[p]erhaps because there were no children, perhaps for other reasons, she was carrying on her employment', could be read as criticism of both her status as a working wife and as a wife who remained childless.[51] The press asserted that she 'steadfastly declined to have any children'.[52] It was implicitly a comment on her selfishness and her unnaturalness. Since the 1870s there had been national concern with the falling British birth rate, an anxiety that had intensified after the carnage of the Great War. Proponents of eugenics noted with anguish that the fall was class-specific, being far greater amongst the middle and upper classes. It was middle-class women – women such as Edith – who were seen as the most blameworthy.[53]

Edith Thompson as modern sexual woman

The aspect of the modern woman that was most contentious was her sexuality, both in the sense of her appearance as sexual spectacle, and in the sense of her capacity for sexual agency. The Modern Girl Around the World Research Group suggests that 'explicit eroticism' and 'pursuit of romantic love' were two of the modern girl's key characteristics.[54] Edith was of course immediately read in sexual terms, not simply because of her attractiveness, but also because of her engagement in an adulterous relationship. Lawyer Gerald Sparrow, who attended the trial out of interest, remembered that 'the first thing I noticed in that packed court at the Old Bailey was her physical attraction and her lovely neck. She exuded sex.'[55] Edith claimed that despite much pleading, Percy had adamantly refused to give her a divorce. The double moral standard enshrined in the idea of a woman's adultery being more serious than a man's had been codified in the 1857 Divorce and Matrimonial Causes Act. This stipulated that a wife's adultery was sufficient cause for divorce, while the woman required proof of an additional matrimonial offence. The 1912 report of Royal Commission recommended the equalisation of men and women's access to divorce, a recommendation brought into effect in the Matrimonial Causes Act of 1923, the year of Edith Thompson's execution. But as historian Anne Sumner Holmes convincingly argues, this did not represent a lessening of the idea that a woman's adultery was a serious offence. Rather, it reflected a shift in thinking about a *man's* adultery, namely the growing belief that men's infidelity contributed to such national problems as prostitution, illegitimacy and the spread of venereal disease.[56]

As mentioned earlier in this chapter, Barrister Curtis-Bennett believed that 'Mrs Thompson was hanged for immorality'.[57] By 'immorality' he meant adultery, a 'crime' magnified further by the age difference between the two culprits. Bywaters was characterised as an innocent young 'boy' led astray by an older, predatory, sexual seductress. Edith's behaviour was deemed triply inappropriate and unacceptable: initiating, adulterous and cross-generational. The judge was openly disapproving of what he called their 'sordid affair', the *Daily Sketch* likewise: 'Human life is sacred … But sacred also are "household laws" and marital faith … the "right" to love anyone and anywhere is the spear-head of social anarchy.'[58] (Ironically, the *Daily Sketch* had been Edith's favoured newspaper.) In several papers Edith was referred to as the 'Messalina of Ilford'.[59] ('Messalina', the wife of the Roman Emperor Claudius, was notorious for sexual profligacy and put to death for plotting against her husband.)[60] Thus although on the verge of a new marriage law that on the face of it appeared to represent a significant shift in thinking, it seems that in the early 1920s there was still much hostility towards the adulterous wife.

If Edith as sexual subject was on trial for adultery, it was because of the evidence of such given by her passionate, extraordinary letters. Long extracts from these letters were read out in court and produced mixed reactions. Curtis-Bennett described them as containing 'the most beautiful language of love'.[61] In contrast, the judge referred to them as 'full of the outpourings of a silly, but at the same time wicked affection'.[62] Once deemed admissible, some of the letters were first read out in Stratford Police Court on 24th October, and were immediately printed in all the newspapers. James Douglas, Ulsterman, high moralist, and editor of the *Sunday Express*, headed his editorial 'Love Letters', and gushed in his usual excessive, bombastic manner: 'Like all the world, I have been amazed and astounded by the letters … No novelist could imagine or invent letters like these. The subtlest literary art could not put into words a tithe of the emotion with which they pulse and throb in every line.'[63] Douglas is best known today for his infamous remarks in 1928 on Radclyffe Hall's *The Well of Loneliness* that led to its prosecution for obscenity, namely: 'I would rather give a healthy boy or a healthy girl a phial of prussic acid than this novel. Poison kills the body, but moral poison kills the soul.'[64] In fact Douglas had been in the business of sniffing out 'obscenity' for many years, and he always used this body/soul dichotomy. For example in May 1922 in a review of James Joyce's *Ulysses* he opined: 'I regard the traffic in cocaine as infinitely less dangerous than this traffic in moral poison. Cocaine destroys the body, but books like "Ulysses" destroy the soul.'[65] As the Old Bailey trial opened in early December, he continued in his gushing praise of Edith. But before the trial was finished Douglas turned violently against her, supporting the guilty verdict and her death penalty. Later still he shifted yet again, declaring, three days before her death, that 'the hanging of Mrs Thompson will be a miscarriage of justice'.[66] The swings in Douglas's verdict paralleled the vicissitudes of the public response. Many other journalists were likewise impressed by Edith's letters.[67] Beverley Baxter, briefly editor of Douglas's sister newspaper, the *Daily Express*, noted later: 'She wrote as if she were the first woman and Bywaters were the first man. She raised the love of her suburban self and the wandering steward to the level of an epic.'[68] Yet this was a woman who had left school at only fifteen.

Edith's letters are wonderfully expressive, written with great feeling and verve. She viewed them as her way of 'talking' to Freddy; it was in fact often her only way of talking to him, given that he was away at sea for long periods of time. The letters contain passionate declarations, witty observations, details of plays and dances she has attended, bets she has placed on the horses, and the clothes she has been wearing and buying, for Freddy was very interested in what she wore, and had strong likes and dislikes.[69] There is also the odd incriminating remark about Percy, of which more below. Greatest space is given over to lengthy and perceptive literary criticism of the various books that she and Freddy are currently reading. Their elaborate discussion of the books – it is clear that Freddy also engages in such discussion, although only three of his letters to Edith were discovered – offered a shared language, referred to by historian Matt Houlbrook, in his brilliant article on Edith Thompson's letters, as 'an intimate trans-national dialogue'.[70] Books were a central part of Edith's life – and she inhabited them, identifying with specific fictional characters: 'aren't books a consolation and a solace? We ourselves die and live in the books we read while we are reading them'.[71] This was not simply about escapism; as Houlbrook perceptively remarks: 'Moving into a fictional life affords an opportunity to find subjective composure. The act of writing temporarily allows Edith to resolve deep psychic fears and secure a reassuring sense of self as spiritual, selfless and heroic'.[72] Part of her analysis of books involves considering the morality of their characters – not dissimilar, ironically, to the way in which her own and Freddy's characters were later dissected by the press.

What possibly greatly scandalised many readers were the references to sexual behaviour and desire, oblique though they were. One jurist, writing to the *Daily Telegraph* thirty years after the trial, reflected back on the letters: '"Nauseous" is hardly strong enough to describe their contents … Mrs Thompson's letters were her own condemnation'.[73] For women to be 'knowing' about sex (as in the case of Maud Allan) and, worse still, to take the sexual initiative, was unacceptable. Indeed there was still much sexual ignorance across all social classes, despite the fact that Marie Stopes's 1918 *Married Love*, a purveyor of basic sex education for married couples, had sold over 400,000 copies by 1923.[74] In one letter Edith reflects back on her and Freddy's urgent love-making in an empty railway carriage and her active participation: 'darlingest boy you said to me "Say No Peidi" [his nickname for her] say "No" on Thursday didn't you – but at that very moment you didn't wish me to say "No" did you? You felt you wanted all me in exchange for all you. I knew this – felt this – and wouldn't say "No" for that very reason'.[75] (She claimed to have said 'no' to Percy however, writing to Freddy on several occasions of her resistance to Percy's sexual advances.) Edith even gives a description of what sounds like an orgasm: 'It seems a great welling up of love – of feeling, of inertia, just as if I am wax in your hands – to do with you as you will … Its physical, purely, and I can't describe it … You say you knew it would be like this one day'.[76] Unlike some letters which were withheld, this one formed part of the evidence presented at the trial and was reproduced by the press; readers must have been surprised, possibly shocked, by the audacity of a woman writing in such terms (although her description of an orgasm is uncannily similar to that given in Stopes's *Married Love*).

To her brother-in-law, Richard Thompson, her letters 'finally confirmed her as "a moral pervert"'.[77] Even her friend Bessie Aitken, despite her affection for Edith, had to distance herself from Edith's sexuality. In what was very probably a ghost-written account, Bessie accepted the guilty verdict as correct, and wrote of it, formulaically, in terms of a body/soul dichotomy: 'there were two Edith Thompsons … the Edith Thompson of the Body and … the Edith Thompson of the Soul … between the two the battle was waged. The Soul fell and was trampled; the Body triumphed'.[78]

The soul was destroyed by bodily lust, or what was here termed 'gratification of her illicit love'. Such was its power that 'at the last, the old Edith that we knew and loved, was dead'.[79]

Edith Thompson as modern suburban woman

Edith's class and geographical location arguably also contributed to her general vilification. This may seem a strange assertion; after all, she was earning a good salary which enabled her to buy an expensive lawyer for her defence. However, in terms of the dominant beliefs of the period, her lower-middle classness opened her up to ridicule. She was the daughter of a clerk, married to a clerk, in a job on a par with that of a clerk's, living in the suburbs. The Thompson murder took place a short distance away from Edith's home in the suburb of Ilford; in the press reportage it was always referred to as the 'Ilford murder', an epithet that was arguably meant to convey more than a mere geographic location. To the late Victorians, Edwardians, and on into the 1920s and 1930s, the lower-middle classes and the suburbs were closely identified. The suburbs were seen as dreary and unsightly. Although the lower-middle classes might have signified 'respectability', to those who saw themselves 'above' this class location, namely the upper- and upper-middle classes, the lower-middle classes were marked by vulgarity and pretension, narrow-mindedness, philistine culture and mediocrity. They were also disturbingly proliferating in numbers.[80]

While the lower-middle-class suburban male (a man such as Percy) was depicted by the intelligentsia as pottering about in the garden or sitting around aimlessly in his slippers – an image at the heart of the new, more domestic Englishness of the inter-war years that is so convincingly discussed by Alison Light – his female equivalent was the worse offender.[81] She was cast as sluttish, pleasure-seeking, without morals, engaged in sensational reading, consumption and cheap thrills. For example in the 1920s novel *The Suburban Young Man* by well-known diarist and novelist E.M. Delafield, Norah, the eponymous hero's sister-in-law, is depicted as greedy, lazy, stupid, vulgar, fond of shopping and frivolous pursuits.[82] No one called Edith stupid, but 'vulgar' and 'extravagant' were terms applied by her brother-in-law, and all commentators remarked on her penchant for pleasure-seeking. As cultural theorist Christopher Breward notes, there was an inter-war (upper-middle-class) anxiety about young lower-middle-class women adopting new products and lifestyles, yet having 'no truck with the stratified access to pleasure and luxury'.[83] Indeed newspaper editor James Douglas found it hard to reconcile Edith's 'illicit passion' with her class position: 'it would not surprise us in the higher strata ... where luxury and self-indulgence have sapped the will ... But it is staggering to discover it in the underworld of the humdrum clerks and humdrum milliners.' It was the equivalent, as he put it so wonderfully, of 'Madame Bovary in a bunshop!'[84] Edith was not in fact a milliner – a more lowly post than her position of book-keeper, buyer and manageress – but the press was always referring to her as such.[85] If not a milliner, then she was referred to in the press as a 'suburban housewife'. Both were persistent misrepresentations (and attempts to fit her into specific cultural frameworks) that indicated an inability to accept her as a successful businesswoman, and an anxiety as to the social mobility of women.

Reflecting on why Edith and Freddy had not simply gone away together and let Percy live, Douglas suggested it was because 'they were too respectable! They wanted to keep their posts and their reputations. They preferred the risk of murder to the risk of scandal.'[86] (Douglas always made prolific use of explanation marks.) Writer Harrison Owen in *Reynolds's Newspaper* remarked: 'Reading these remarkable letters ... one might imagine her to be a woman ... ready to risk anything to be with her lover. Actually she would not even risk the displeasure of Ilford society.'[87] ('Ilford society' suggests mockery: a juxtaposition of suburban Ilford and high society.) Richard Thompson likewise argued that the reason that Edith had never left Percy was her love of 'ostensible respectability' and her fear of job loss, penury and ostracism.[88] Thus lower-middle-class respectability was turned against Edith: her desire to retain her professional life and standing in the community was presented as the reason why she chose murder as the preferred option.

Modern woman as consumer of cheap fiction

London suburbs grew hugely in the inter-war years, accelerated by expansion in transport. The inhabitants of 'commuterland', as they sat daily in trains and buses on their way to work, represented a sizeable number of the consumers of not simply the expanding daily popular press, but also cheap, easy-to-read novels, so-called 'railway fiction'.[89] According to Bessie Aitken: 'Day by day, sitting on the crowded third-class carriage that took her to work, she [Edith] read omnivorously'; in contrast, 'her husband never opened a book'.[90] Edith often read a book a day, generally romantic fiction.[91] If part of Edith's vilification involved ambivalence towards her suburban lower-middle classness, another contributor to this vilification, one inherently interlinked, was her love of romantic fiction.

By the inter-war years, in addition to the new body of commuters, it was young women from the lower-middle and working classes (often indeed part of the commuting body, as in Edith's case) who were seen as central to the rising demand for cheap literature. Women readers of fiction from the eighteenth century onwards had been accused of indulging in unhealthy sensationalism.[92] Reading 'light' literature during the war had been seen as understandable: a way to escape the anxieties of the times and an available form of leisure in the face of few alternatives.[93] But out of wartime, romantic fiction, the main staple of Edith's literary taste, was singled out by the middle-class intelligentsia as especially undesirable.[94] The literature was characterised as 'cheap' in more senses than one: inexpensive to buy, and worthless in its content. But it was deemed more than worthless: it appealed to 'base' emotion over reason, it encouraged dangerous fantasy.[95] Madame Bovary, to whom Edith had been compared by Douglas, was a lover of romantic fiction, embracing its delusions as a way of side-stepping the banality of everyday life.[96]

During the trial, Edith's love of reading was presented as a crucial element in both her defence *and* her prosecution. When Cecil Whiteley, Bywaters' counsel, asked Bywaters whether he believed that Edith had in fact given poison to her husband, Bywaters replied: 'No, it never entered my head at all. She had been reading books.'[97] The next day he elaborated: 'She read a book and had a way of imagining herself as a character in the book.'[98] (No mention was ever made of the fact that Freddy had also been reading books.) Throughout the trial Edith's defence lawyer stressed that she inhabited a world of fantasy, fostered by the reading of novels: 'She was a woman who lived an extraordinary life of make-believe.'[99] The defence counsel argued that the 'make-believe' remained at the level of pure fantasy. Criminologist Filson Young in his write-up of the trial agreed, contrasting the two lovers: 'Bywaters ... was totally devoid of imagination; actions were his only realities. Edith Thompson had an excess of imagination. To her, actions were unimportant.'[100] The prosecution however claimed that the fiction had 'given her ideas' which she had acted upon. Much was made of her letter discussion of Robert Hichens' *Bella Donna*, a novel whose plot in part involves the slow poisoning of a husband by his wife.[101] This was a well-known 1909 desert romance-cum-thriller, set in Egypt; it had been turned into a play starring Mrs Patrick Campbell in 1911 and again in 1916.[102] While the prosecution suggested that the book was read as an aid to her murderous intentions, the defence countered with the claim that it simply fed her vivid imagination.[103]

Books, in the context of the trial, were thought either to have contributed to the murder through suggestion, even inspiration, as those who thought her guilty argued, or simply to have fed a fantasy life that did not spill over into reality, but yet had given an unfortunate impression to the readers of her letters. What appeared to unite the two positions was a belief in the dangerous power of cheap fiction. Even Edith's old friend Bessie Aitken appeared to agree (although words might have been put into her mouth): she held that books, along with plays, had 'worked upon a mind neurotic and unbalanced'.[104] It was the familiar trope of the woman reader as highly impressionable, with the additional element of 'neurosis', a term that pre-dated psychoanalysis and referred to 'morbid psychic activity'. The term 'war neurosis' had developed during the war as an alternative to 'shell-shock', but by the 1920s, 'neurosis' without the qualifier of 'war' was being widely applied to women.[105]

Edith Thompson as poisoner and inciter

Books and their influence were central to Edith's trial because books featured so prominently in her letters, and were thought a crucial element in her thoughts about poisoning. As already stated, Edith's letters to Freddy were the key evidence used in her conviction, held not simply to reveal her murderous intent, but also to constitute incitement to murder. If the books that Edith read were held to have incited *her* to evil thoughts, she in turn was thought to have incited Freddy. The prosecutor argued that she had tried to persuade Freddy to kill Percy by continuous innuendo and suggestion, and through claiming that she was prepared to risk trying to kill him herself.[106] For not only do the letters involve discussion of poisoning incidents in books such as the above mentioned *Bella Donna*, but a number mention her attempts to poison Percy. As criminologist Anette Ballinger points out, a false impression as to the centrality of these passages in the correspondence was created through their being endlessly repeated, despite constituting only 1 per cent of the entire correspondence. In addition, only half the letters were entered as evidence, and they were presented out of sequence, further creating the potential to confuse the jury. What is more, the fact that the poison and glass references (in her letters she claims to have put ground light bulbs in his food) occur five months prior to the murder was not clarified in court.[107] And the prosecuting Solicitor General sowed further doubt in the minds of the jury by disingenuously stating that 'a post mortem examination showed that there were *practically* no traces of any poison'.[108] (There were in fact no traces at all.) Edith also sent with her letters a few newspaper cuttings about poisonings. Although the other cuttings she enclosed had nothing to do with poison (and there were over fifty cuttings in total, including one on Freda Kempton) these 'poison' cuttings were singled out by the prosecution and helped predispose the jury to reading something sinister into various innocuous phrases in her letters, such as 'If I do not mind the risk why should you?'[109] Poisoning was a quintessentially 'female' crime, and the wife who poisoned her husband's food committed a kind of domestic treason – a deadly reversal of her traditional role as carer and nurturer.[110]

Edith and Freddy also had great difficulty in explaining the letters' references to 'bitter tea', and Percy getting the 'wrong porridge'. Ironically, these incidents referred not to any attempt to poison Percy, but Edith's attempts to take an abortifacient.[111] This was never admitted in court, the defence fearing that it would stain her moral character still further (and indeed procurement of abortion was a crime) although instead, absence of explanation reinforced the image of Edith as poisoner.[112] Had she not entered the witness-box, as Curtis-Bennett strongly advised, she would not have been questioned as to the meaning of these and other various passages in the letters, and conviction would have been a great deal harder. In court, Edith explained the references to poisoning as a pretence, in order to keep Bywaters' love: 'I wanted him to think I would try to help him in order to keep him to me.'[113] And Bywaters admitted that he never for a moment thought she was actually engaged in poisoning: he read it as fantasy, make-believe, what he called 'melodrama'.[114]

If Bywaters, and indeed Curtis-Bennett, thought of Edith as spinning tales of melodrama, the popular papers were not adverse to spinning such tales themselves. The ways in which Edith, Freddy, and husband Percy were presented were in terms of classic melodramatic narrative, with victim (Percy), villain (*femme fatale* Edith) and hero (Freddy).[115] True, there was not huge sympathy for Percy; the *World's Pictorial News*'s characterisation of him as 'simply a plodding, uncommunicative clerk' was not atypical.[116] But Freddy in many ways represented a kind of hero. He was good-looking: to the *Daily Express*, for example, he was 'a handsome youth, with a clear skin, a keen, finely carved profile, a trenchant, high forehead, brilliant eyes … virile and vigorous in his gait'.[117] (Given the large number of demobbed men in Britain who were physically or psychically disabled, there was a general tendency to fetishise vigorous young men.)[118] Freddy was also seen as brave and patriotic, for it was noted that though underage (only fifteen) he had joined up as a sailor in February 1918. His father was gassed in the war and subsequently died, and Freddy, though still only a teenager, had become head of the household. (In contrast, Percy had been discharged from the army as unfit, never seeing active service.)[119] Freddy's bravery could be seen in his bearing: 'Bywaters … stood like a soldier on parade, head up, eyes steady, and never flinched.'[120] The press were effectively elevating his status to that of an officer or gentleman. Like all true heroes, Freddy loved his mother: 'Bywaters' affection for his mother is one of the most touching incidents in this dramatic case', opined the *Daily Mail*.[121] His virility was never in doubt: his 'well-cut lounge coat, double collar and neat tie bespoke carefulness rather than dandyism'.[122] Yes, he had been violent – the size of the knife he had used clearly shocked the jury – but there was a popular 'understanding' of violence in men who had been through the war and had had brutality 'unleashed' 'for the purpose of killing Germans'.[123] He evoked such affection in Revd Hugh Chapman that in his sermon to the Chapel Royal, the Savoy, he confessed that he wanted 'to go to that boy, put my arms round his neck, kiss him on the forehead'.[124]

An incited audience

The female audience attending the Thompson/Bywaters trial were heavily criticised from many quarters. They were deemed to be equally as sensation-seeking as Edith in her consumption of popular fiction. Cheap literature incited Edith, Edith incited Freddy, the couple's tale – as narrated in court and in the popular press – incited the general public, above all, women, who thrilled to the sexually and morally illicit. (Edith had also incited wretched Gilbert Wickham, who, according to the press, desired to *live out* Edith's fate, such was his over-identification). Women of all classes were apparently now present: 'matrons of Mayfair swaddled in costly furs, trim young typists or dressmakers, a blue-stocking or two, haggard and eager-eyed'.[125] The products of modernity, they were all part of the new public audience keen to consume the drama of the court.[126] Thus unlike the Victorian period, when female spectators in the high court were largely restricted to 'fashionable' ladies, women of all classes and ages were now attending.[127] Despite the judge's reprimand that '[t]his is a vulgar and common crime. You are not listening to a play from the stalls', the parallels to the theatre were endlessly drawn.[128] The *Daily Mirror* noted that '[t]he diffused electric lights round the oak-panelled room and the presence of hatless but well-dressed women, chatting and munching chocolates, were reminiscent of a theatre scene between the acts'.[129] To *Sunday Express* editor James Douglas: 'It was like sitting through a series of putrid plays, drenched with stale melodrama'.[130] The *Daily Chronicle* spied 'a woman in furs smiling ... as if she were going to see a music comedy at a West End theatre'.[131] Men were present in court in equal if not greater number, but it was women who were singled out for especial condemnation, such as the 'many women of fashion ... [who] followed with breathless interest ... driven by morbid curiosity ... by a lust for the sensational'.[132] The concept 'fashionably dressed women' had negative connotations at the time, implying ostentation and conspicuous consumption – an affront to a world

9 Freddy Bywaters, Edith Thompson and Percy Thompson

of male unemployment and war-inflicted disabilities. Their wearing of fur also indicated their middle- or upper-class location. 'One woman in a fur coat never took her lorgnette from her keen dark eyes. She looked the kind of person who would bully her maids and nag her husband.'[133] Such women were seen as akin to those who during the French Revolution 'knitted peacefully while the guillotine cut off ... heads'.[134] (Disapproval of female trial audiences was nothing new: the Victorian press was full of similar admonishments.)[135] These criticisms of the female audience implicitly raised the question of their potential suitability as jurors: if they were so obsessed with seeking sensation, how could they judge impartially?

Society beauty Lady Diana Cooper (formerly Manners) defended the public's keen interest in the Bywaters/Thompson case:

> People are not reproached for going to 'gloat' over the suffering of Lear; not taunted with morbid curiosity for studying the criminal psychology of Macbeth ... Those were poetic dramas, we may be told, and this was merely an ordinary vulgar crime. But ... the insight of a poet can detect the germ of beauty where the lawyer's eye sees nothing but the squalor of crime.[136]

But although Diana Cooper may have credited the ordinary man and woman with the 'insight of a poet', to the majority of commentators, women's consumption of court-as-theatre was indicative of a growing sensationalism, linked to the rise of mass culture. Mass culture and 'the masses' were associated with women; 'real' culture was the preserve of men. Literary critic Andreas Huyssen suggestively proposes that the fear of the crowd-as-mass was indistinguishable from a male fear of women – of raging, hysterical, uncontrollable, engulfing femininity.[137]

Condemning the 'goggling at monsters as an entertainment', the *Manchester Guardian* had 'a good deal more sympathy with the unemployed workmen who exploited the decadence of public taste by holding places in the line, which they sold for £5'.[138] (Quite a sum, given that the average weekly wage was about £3 10s.)[139] The newspaper was referring to the lengthy queues waiting outside the court every night of the trial. The implicit juxtaposition of unemployed workmen on the one hand and the 'trim young typists or dressmakers' on the other resonates with historian Sally Alexander's observation of the 'two visual images of the working-class [which] vie for attention in the popular memory of the inter-war years: the cloth cap and spare frame of the unemployed man … and the young working girl – lipsticked, silk-stockinged, and dressed, in the phrase of … J.B. Priestley "like an actress"'.[140] One could add that at the time of the trial, the former of these two gendered images was linked to the tragedy of the recent past (the war), while the latter spoke of the future, of modernity, and of the allure of popular culture.

Writing in the 1930s, author and journalist Rose Macaulay suggested that the reading public had long had an obsession with the three 'Ss': 'sensation, sentiment and the sordid': 'Most of us like to enjoy with our reading a shudder of excitement, a tear and a smile of sympathy, and a feeling of superiority to the sordid persons read about.'[141] The audience at Edith's trial, along with the readers of the newspaper reports, commentaries, letters, editorials and interviews, had no difficulty in finding all the ingredients to satisfy this so-called pleasurable 'obsession'. The popular press was blamed by the 'class' press, such as *The Times,* for this 'whipping up of public emotion'.[142] To many male intellectuals, the 'mass media', like 'cheap' literature, was catering to the lowest common denominator, namely women searching for quick thrills.[143] Indeed the popular newspapers' presentation of the Thompson/Bywaters narrative paralleled their instalments of serialised sensational novels. The extensive space given by the popular press to drawings and photographs of the trial's protagonists was held to contribute to this 'whipping up of public emotion', and seen as pandering to the female reader. Some of these pictures were 'intrusively' sketched or taken in the courtroom. Cultural historian Lynda Nead suggests that the press's visual reportage of the Thompson/Bywaters trial was central to the introduction of a bill to prohibit court photography, such was the cross-party concern with growing press tyranny, and its invasion into hallowed legal spaces. A Criminal Justice Bill introduced in 1923 finally became law in 1925, forbidding a photographer or artist from making an image inside the court or its precincts. (The courtroom sketch, undertaken from memory, is still today the only permitted visual courtroom representation in Britain.)[144]

Freddy as incited boy

Immediately following the trial's verdict, the *Daily Sketch* chose to publish an anonymous letter calling for Bywaters' reprieve: Freddy was

> just a boy ... swayed by the love of a woman many years older, a woman who knew how to ... mould his passion into a slave of her every impulse ... But when he might have cried out 'She, the woman tempted me!' ... he cried out instead: 'She, the woman, is innocent!' ... Will the *Daily Sketch* lead the way?[145]

The letter contained the three elements that were endlessly to occur in all subsequent *Daily Sketch* reporting, namely Bywaters' youth, his chivalry, and Edith Thompson's ultimate responsibility for the murder. Freddy as 'boy' did not of course quite fit with the melodramatic narrative, in which he was heroic, virile, and soldier-like. The 'boy' epithet did not fit either with what one knew of him from Edith's letters as a 'man of the world', dominant and aggressive. These contradictory representations seem to have gone unnoticed however.

As the letter requested, The *Daily Sketch* did indeed 'lead the way', launching a nationwide campaign on behalf of Bywaters. No public steps were taken at the time on behalf of Edith. Feminists did not rally to her defence, despite well-known feminist, novelist, and journalist Rebecca West pronouncing in the popular press that she did not believe Edith had tried to poison her husband (the claims 'were simply day-dreams').[146] And although Cicely Hamilton and the feminist journal *The Vote* were both against her execution, it was on grounds of opposition to capital punishment, rather than belief in her innocence.[147] From the start of the *Daily Sketch* campaign, the grounds for *Freddy's* reprieve rested on *Edith's* culpability. The paper undertook an opinion poll of a 'random' cross-section of people, 'in the City and suburbs, the region of the clubs, and the poorer households of the East'.[148] (The 'City and the suburbs' were probably used to denote Edith's dual identity as a woman of both Aldersgate and Ilford.)

Three out of four of these people favoured a petition. The reasons they gave were in terms of one, two or all three of the above mentioned representations of Bywaters (his youth, chivalry, and lack of responsibility for the killing). A waitress, for example, was reported to have said: 'she instigated him to the crime', while a shop assistant commented: 'he proved himself such a man in standing by his sweetheart at all costs'. To three soldiers: 'it was the woman who was to blame ... he was coerced. He proved himself a man afterwards.' Author W.L. George suggested that the older woman with her powerful personality 'may have reduced Bywaters to ... a state of mental slavery', akin to hypnotism.[149] And it was reported that Revd Chapman pleaded for Bywaters' reprieve in his sermon on the grounds that Freddy was 'a youth subject since boyhood to the influence of an hysterical ... unbalanced self-centered woman'.[150] Beverley Nichols, journalist and writer, later referred to Edith as 'the suburban syren [sic]'.[151] In classical mythology, sirens – half-woman, half-bird – lured sailors to death with their songs of enchantment.

The *Daily Sketch* claimed that requests for the petition, said to be available in all cinemas, theatres and principal shops, were overwhelming. By the end of the campaign the paper had procured more than a million signatures – the largest petition for a convicted prisoner that Britain had ever seen.[152] The desire to sign apparently came from all classes: 'quiet, unemotional City men, clerks in offices, burly carters, mothers from the suburbs, shopkeepers and typists', ladies who 'stepped from their limousines'.[153] Indeed women in particular were making the campaign into what the *Daily Sketch* termed a 'veritable crusade'.[154] The *World's Pictorial News* asserted: 'tens of thousands of women declare they would "hang her and not him"'.[155] The irony of this crusade was that Bywaters had explicitly directed his counsel not to argue his defence in court in terms of the mitigating circumstances of incitement. He had always claimed sole responsibility for the murder, yet now the campaign for his reprieve was predicated on precisely that which he had repudiated, namely that Percy's death had been stage-managed by his *femme fatale* mistress.

The cost of female modernity

One refrain running through all the reporting of and reflections on the case was the preoccupation with morbidity. Edith was characterised in this way – one of her greatest friends (Bessie Aitken) and one of her greatest foes (Richard Thompson) effectively in agreement that she was suffering some kind of 'morbidity'. (In contrast, Edith's father, William Graydon, in a ghost-written account in the *Weekly Dispatch*, was a lone voice of denial:

'There was never anything morbid in her tastes. She was too healthy and high-spirited for that.')[156] The spectators in court, especially the women, were labelled 'morbid', and the broadsheets accused the tabloids of encouraging the 'morbid appetite' of the general public. To Cicely Hamilton, one of the reasons to oppose capital punishment lay in 'the unhealthy morbid excitement which is created amongst a section of the public'.[157] An extreme example of this 'morbid excitement' – and indeed of *in*citement – was that of Gilbert Wickham. We cannot understand the specificity of Wickham's obsession with Edith, but in a sense he was trying to inhabit her story in a manner parallel to the way in which she was depicted as inhabiting the stories that she herself read. Wickham's desire to become Edith Thompson in her/his final moment echoes a controversial statement that Rebecca West had written about Edith the previous month: 'there is nothing in her that is not in us, and if we … gave ourselves up to morbid day-dreaming we might find ourselves where she is'.[158]

That morbidity was spoken of so frequently possibly had much to do with the problem of how to come to terms with the death of millions of young men in the recent war. Thus, a further part of the vilification of Edith Thompson related not simply to what she did or might have done, but what she stood for in the post-war world: a successful businesswoman, acting above her station, who had supposedly done well out of the war while young men fought and died, and who had both calculatingly seduced and brought about the downfall of a young man in his prime (the cream of what was left of British youth) while sadistically encouraging the killing of her unwanted husband. The murder of Percy Thompson in a London suburb might have meant little to a country still grieving the loss of so many. But the subsequent killing of a fit young man with his future ahead of him (Bywaters) had resonances of the killing of the millions of fit young men on the fields of Flanders. In the case of Thompson and Bywaters, the blame for the killing of *both* men was laid at the feet of the ideological scapegoat, the *femme fatale*. Literary critic Rebecca Stott suggests that the *femme fatale* is emblematic of chaos and rooted in anxieties over women, especially their sexual emancipation.[159] Edith Thompson might also have brought to mind the more recent construct of the vampire woman or 'vamp'. The 'vamp' figure was prominent throughout popular culture during this period, especially in pulp novels and the cinema. Whether seen as vamp or *femme fatale*, both represented an immoral, predatory, sexual woman who seduced innocent men and left ruined lives and homes in her wake.[160]

On the face of it, Edith Thompson was a young, good-looking, lower-middle-class, married woman with a successful career, who dressed fashionably and well, and lived respectably. But behind the 'façade' – behind the lace curtains of suburbia – there was the 'other' Edith (referred to by Bessie Aitken or her ghost writer as 'the Edith Thompson of the Body') who lived a double life, a female Jekyll and Hyde. Here was a woman who made her own choices and acted on her own desires, and whose pleasure-seeking entailed not just the refusal of children, the reading of sensational literature, and the purchase of fashionable clothes, but also cross-generational sex, adultery, even incitement to murder. Edith represented the danger of the post-war sexual modern woman. It has been noted that: 'Implicitly or explicitly, feature stories about homicide convey powerful messages about morality, respectability and normality.'[161] In relation to the Thompson/Bywaters case, the most powerful message conveyed was about the undesirability of women's sexual agency. As a 'woman of the world', Edith had seduced a far younger man – a mere 'boy'. She had inflamed his passions and in remaining with her husband, had unforgivably inflamed his sexual jealousy too. In the end, Edith was on trial – in the law courts, in the press, in the pulpit, in the discussions of the general public – not simply for incitement to murder, but also for *sexual* incitement – inappropriate incitement to, and expression of, dangerous, indeed deadly, sexual passion. And possibly too, the anxiety prompted by the trial as to how to 'know' and 'read' the ordinary 'modern woman' in the ordinary suburbs related to deep anxiety about the erosion of social boundaries in the aftermath of the war, and the rapidity of modernity. Arguably, Edith became a (transitory) hate object who carried and reflected these fears.

Notes

1 *Empire News*, 28th January 1923, p. 5.
2 See Oram, '*Her Husband was a Woman!*' for cross-dressing in this period. See McLaren, *Trials of Masculinity*, Chapter 9 on 'transvestites'.
3 *Daily Express*, 7th December 1922, p. 1, and see *News of the World*, 10th December 1922, p. 9; *World's Pictorial News*, 16th February 1923, p. 1.
4 Quoted in *Daily Sketch*, 13th December 1922, p. 19. Hamilton had had a huge impact in 1909 with the publication of her biting critique of marriage, *Marriage as a Trade*.
5 Quoted in *Daily Chronicle*, 7th December 1922, 1.
6 See Lewis Broad, *The Innocence of Edith Thompson: a Study in Old Bailey Justice* (London, 1952); René Weis, *Criminal Justice: the True Story of Edith Thompson* (London, 1990). I am indebted to Weis's excellent book for much of the information on Edith.
7 Young, *Trial of Frederick Bywaters and Edith Thompson*, Introduction. At the time of the trial there were voices of opposition to capital punishment, although they were not necessarily claiming Edith's innocence, for example, Cicely Hamilton, *Daily Sketch*, 13th December 1922, p. 2; letters in the *Manchester Guardian*, 9th January 1923, p. 4, and 10th January 1923, p. 5; *The Vote*, 19th January 1923, p. 20.
8 Roland Wild and Derek Curtis-Bennett, '*Curtis': the Life of Sir Henry Curtis-Bennett KC*

(London, 1937), p. 149.

9 See Robb and Erber (eds), *Disorder in the Court*; Matt Cook, 'Law', in Matt Houlbrook and H.G. Cocks (eds), *Palgrave Advances in the Modern History of Sexuality* (London, 2005).

10 Quoted in Weis, *Criminal Justice*, p. 134.

11 Weis *Criminal Justice*, p. 116. The bob first appeared during the war, but only reached the height of fashion in 1924. Doan, *Fashioning Sapphism*, p. 234. In having a bob cut two years before this high point, Edith was a fashion forerunner.

12 On betting see Edith Thompson to Freddy Bywaters, 15th May 1922, and Edith Thompson to Freddy Bywaters, 14th June 1922, in Young, *Trial of Frederick Bywaters and Edith Thompson*, pp. 189, 201. See Ross McKibbin, 'Working-class Gambling in Britain, 1880–1939', in *The Ideologies of Class: Social Relations in Britain, 1880–1950* (Oxford, 1991).

13 On women, modernity and mobility in urban space see Elizabeth Wilson, *The Sphinx in the City* (London, 1991); Walkowitz, *City of Dreadful Delight*; Rita Felski, *The Gender of Modernity* (Cambridge, MA, 1995); Ana Parejo Vadillo, 'Phenomena in Flux', in Ann L. Ardis and Leslie W. Lewis (eds), *Women's Experience of Modernity, 1875–1945* (Baltimore, MD and London, 2003); Matthews, *Dance Hall and Picture Palace*.

14 *Daily Express,* 24th November 1922, p. 5.

15 *Daily Express,* 9th December 1922, p. 4.

16 *Daily Mirror,* 7th October 1922, p. 2.

17 Catherine Horwood, *Keeping up Appearances: Fashion and Class between the Wars* (Gloucester, 2005), p. 137. On fur see Carol Dyhouse, *Glamour: Women, History, Feminism* (London and New York, 2010).

18 *The Times,* 12th October 1922, p. 12; *Daily Express,* 18th October 1922, p. 4; *World's Pictorial News,* 4th November 1922, p. 2; *Daily Express,* 7th December 1922, p. 1.

19 Liz Coner, *The Spectacular Modern Woman* (Bloomington and Indianapolis, IN, 2004), p. 2.

20 See for example Mrs Eric Pritchard, *The Cult of Chiffon* (London, 1902).

21 One of her favourite items of clothing was a green jumper, that she mentions in her letters to Freddy. Jumpers were new and associated with the modern woman/flapper. Beddoe, *Back to Home and Duty*, p. 23.

22 *Daily Express,* 6th October 1922, p. 1.

23 *World's Pictorial News,* 16th December 1922, p. 1.

24 *Lloyd's Sunday News,* 24th December 1922, p. 5. Weis identifies the 'lifelong friend', Weis, *Criminal Justice*, p. 264, but in the second edition, with a new preface, he raises doubts and suggests it may have been Lily Vellender instead. Weis, *Criminal Justice,* 2002, pp. xx–xxv.

25 Weis, *Criminal Justice*, p. 12. She had started work on leaving school aged fifteen.

26 In the words of her boss, Mr Carlton, 'she did the work of three clerks'. *Reynolds's Newspaper,* 24th December 1922, p. 2.

27 See Meta Zimmeck, 'Jobs for the Girls: the Expansion of Clerical Work for Women, 1850–1914', in Angela V. John (ed.), *Unequal Opportunities* (Oxford, 1986).

28 *Daily Express,* 6th October 1922, p. 1.

29 *World's Pictorial News,* 16th December 1922, pp. 1–2, refers to her French as 'fluent'; Weis, *Criminal Justice*, p. 16, describes her French as 'quite competent'.

30 There was also an unfounded claim that she was 'a woman fond of the Bohemian way of life'. *Empire News,* 7th January 1923, p. 1.

31 For example see *Daily Sketch*, 13th December 1922, p. 17.

32 Langhamer, *Women's Leisure in England*, pp. 117, 137, 167. Edith Thompson must have also been thought on the old side to be dancing, for most women who danced regularly were under twenty-four years old. McKibbin, *Classes and Cultures*, p. 394.

33 Weis, *Criminal Justice*, p. 211.

34 *Lloyd's Sunday News*, 31st December 1922, p. 7.

35 *Weekly Dispatch*, 17th December 1922, p. 7.

36 For example *Empire News*, 17th December 1922.

37 For example *Daily Express*, 7th December 1922, p. 1.

38 Graves and Hodge, *The Long Weekend*, p. 39; see Matt Houlbrook, 'The Man with the Powder Puff' in Interwar London', *The Historical Journal*, 50, 1 (2007); Bingham, *Gender, Modernity, and the Popular Press*, p. 173; Dyhouse, *Glamour*, pp. 15–19 .

39 *Lloyd's Sunday News*, 31st December 1922, p. 7.

40 *Lloyd's Sunday News*, 7th January 1923, pp. 5, 7.

41 'Edith Thompson's Life in West End', *Empire News*, 7th January 1923, p. 7. Despite the title, the text barely mentions the West End at all. It was another attempt to caste aspersions on Edith, implying a 'wild life up West'.

42 The average annual earnings across seven occupational classes for the period 1922–24 were £180 for men and £103 for women. In 1924 the average pay for 'lower professionals' was £320 for men and £214 for women. Guy Routh, *Occupation and Pay in Great Britain, 1906–79* (London, 1980), pp. 70, 120.

43 Weis, *Criminal Justice*, p. 16.

44 Horwood, *Keeping Up Appearances*, p. 135. The middle classes did much better after the Great War than the working classes, despite a widely held belief to the contrary. McKibbin, *Classes and Cultures*, p. 52; Alan Jackson, *The Middle Classes, 1900–1950* (Nairn, 1991).

45 Graves and Hodge, *The Long Weekend*, p. 27.

46 Alexander, 'Men's Fears and Women's Work', p. 401. On male literary resentment towards women see Sandra M. Gilbert, 'Soldier's Heart: Literary Men, Literary Women, and the Great War', *Signs*, 8, 3 (1983), pp. 422–50.

47 Weis, *Criminal Justice*, p. 48.

48 *Western Mail*, 17th February 1920, quoted in Beddoe, *Back to Home and Duty*, p. 84, and see p. 49 on the aggression towards women who held on to their wartime jobs.

49 Beddoe, *Back to Home and Duty*, p. 82, Alison Oram, *Women Teachers and Feminist Politics, 1900–1939* (Manchester, 1996), pp. 45–72.

50 *Lloyd's Sunday News*, 31st December 1922, p. 7.

51 Young, *Trial of Frederick Bywaters and Edith Thompson*, p. 9.

52 *Reynolds's Newspaper*, 17th December 1922, p. 9.

53 See Richard Allen Soloway, *Birth Control and the Population Question in England, 1877–1930* (Chapel Hill, NC, 1982).

54 Modern Girl Around the World Research Group, 'The Modern Girl Around the World', p. 245. Liz Conor likewise points to her '"sporting" sexual "frankness" with men'. Coner, *The Spectacular Modern Woman*, p. 210.

55 Gerald Sparrow, *Vintage Murder of the Twenties* (London, 1972), p. 23. Nichols too noted 'her very beautiful neck … the physical symbol which set the seal on my hatred of capital punishment'. Nichols, *The Sweet and the Twenties*, p. 67.

56 Anne Sumner Holmes, 'The Double Standard in the English Divorce Laws, 1857–1923', *Law and Social Enquiry: the Journal of the American Bar Association*, 20 (1995), pp. 601–20. See

Hall, *Sex, Gender and Social Change in Britain since 1880*, p. 105.

57 Wild and Curtis-Bennett, 'Curtis', p. 149. There was a famous precedent: the conviction of Florence Maybrick in 1889 for the murder of her husband chiefly on the grounds of her adultery. Unlike Edith, Florence's case was taken up widely, especially by women, and the petition for commutation of the death penalty to life imprisonment was successful. Mary S. Hartman, *Victorian Murderesses* (London, 1977, 1985), Chapter 6, George Robb, 'The English Dreyfus Case: Florence Maybrick and the Sexual Double Standard', in Robb and Erber (eds), *Disorder in the Court*.

58 *Daily Sketch*, 12th December 1922, p. 7.

59 Weis, *Criminal Justice*, p. 188. The year after Edith's execution, E.M. Delafield wrote a novel, based on the case, called *The Messalina of the Suburbs* under her real name: Esmee de la Pasture, *Messalina of the Suburbs* (London, 1924).

60 Betty Radice, *Who's Who in the Ancient World* (London, 1973), p. 164.

61 *The Times*, 11th December 1922, p. 12. Transcripts of Edith's letters are held in the National Archives, MEPO 3/1582, but also collated in Young, *Trial of Frederick Bywaters and Edith Thompson*. The original letters are missing.

62 *The Times*, 12th December 1922, p. 8.

63 *Sunday Express*, 29th October 1922, p. 8.

64 *Sunday Express*, 19th August 1928, p. 10.

65 *Sunday Express*, 26th May 1922, p. 5.

66 *Sunday Express*, 17th December 1922, p. 8; *Daily Express*, 6th January 1923, p. 4.

67 For example, see *World's Pictorial News*, 16th December 1922, p. 1. See Gordon and Nair, *Murder and Morality in Victorian Britain* for discussion of an extraordinary 1857 trial featuring seventy-seven letters from Madeleine to her lover, whom she was accused of poisoning. Unlike Edith, she was acquitted.

68 Beverley Baxter, *Strange Street* (London, 1935), p. 154.

69 See for example Edith Thompson to Freddy Bywaters, 18th May 1922, in Young, *Trial of Frederick Bywaters and Edith Thompson*, pp. 195, 196.

70 Matt Houlbrook, 'A Pin to See the Peepshow: Culture, Fiction and Selfhood in the Letters of Edith Thompson', *Past and Present*, 207, 1 (2010).

71 Edith Thompson to Freddy Bywaters, 17 March 1922, in Young, *Trial of Frederick Bywaters and Edith Thompson*, p. 246.

72 Houlbrook, 'A Pin to See the Peepshow'.

73 Quoted in Weis, *Criminal Justice*, pp. 247, 315.

74 Melman, *Women and the Popular Imagination*, p. 3; Sally Alexander, 'The Mysteries and Secrets of Women's Bodies', in Mica Nava and Alan O'Shea (eds), *Modern Times* (London, 1996), pp. 161–75. Roy Porter and Lesley Hall, *The Facts of Life: the Creation of Sexual Knowledge in Britain, 1650–1950* (New Haven, CT and London, 1997), p. 209. And see Lesley A. Hall (ed.), *Outspoken Women: an Anthology of Women's Writings on Sex, 1870–1969* (London, 2005), Chapter 3.

75 Edith Thompson to Freddy Bywaters, 1st April 1922, in Young, *Trial of Frederick Bywaters and Edith Thompson*, p. 181.

76 Edith Thompson to Freddy Bywaters, no date [2nd October 1922], in Young, *Trial of Frederick Bywaters and Edith Thompson*, p. 214.

77 *Lloyd's Sunday News*, 31st December 1922, p. 7.

78 *Lloyd's Sunday News*, 24th December 1922, p. 5. Other newspapers also see Edith as having 'two sides', for example, *Reynolds's Newspaper*, 17th December 1922, p. 2.

79 *Lloyd's Sunday News*, 17th December 1922, p. 17.

80 See John Carey, *The Intellectuals and the Masses: Pride and Prejudice amongst the Intelligentsia* (London, 1992); Rita Felski, *Doing Time* (New York, 2000), Chapter 1; A. James Hammerton, 'The Perils of Mrs Pooter: Satire, Modernity and Motherhood in the Lower Middle Classes in England, 1870–1920', *Women's History Review*, 8, 2 (1999); Judy Giles, *The Parlour and the Suburb* (Oxford and New York, 2004).

81 Light, *Forever England*.

82 E.M. Delafield, *The Suburban Young Man* (London, 1928); Carey, *The Intellectuals and the Masses*, p. 52. And see Julie English Early, 'Keeping Ourselves to Ourselves: Violence in the Edwardian Suburb', in Shani D'Cruze, *Everyday Violence in Britain, 1850–1950* (London, 2000), including her discussion of the representation of Dr Crippen's wife Cora as sluttish and vulgar.

83 Breward, *Fashioning London*, p. 100.

84 *Sunday Express*, 10th December 1922, p. 8. See Summerscale, *Mrs Robinson's Disgrace* for another case evoking Mme Bovary.

85 This was something that Edith's father, William Graydon, took issue with, in his (ghosted) article in the *Weekly Dispatch,* 17th December 1922, p. 7.

86 *Sunday Express*, 17th December 1922, p. 8.

87 *Reynolds's Newspaper*, 24th December 1922, p. 2.

88 *Lloyd's Sunday News*, 31st December 1922, p. 7, and see *Empire News*, 17th December 1922, p. 7.

89 Melman, *Women and the Popular Imagination in the Twenties*, pp. 96–7. And see H. Llewellyn Smith, *The New Survey of London Life and Labour* (London, 1930), p. 171, on transport and the suburbs.

90 *Lloyd's Sunday News*, 17th December 1922, p. 5.

91 *Lloyd's Sunday News*, 17th December 1922, p. 17.

92 Markman Ellis, *The Politics of Sensibility* (Cambridge, 1996); Jane Flint, *The Woman Reader, 1837–1914* (Oxford, 1993).

93 Joseph McAleer, *Popular Reading and Publishing in Britain, 1914–1950* (Oxford, 1992), pp. 72–3.

94 For the leading contemporary critique of cheap literature see Q.D. Leavis, *Fiction and the Reading Public* (London, 1932, 1979). Many women writers and feminists were appalled by the popularity of romantic fiction. Anthea Trodd, *Women's Writing in English: Britain, 1900–1945* (London and New York, 1998), p. 120. The popular press however, in their attempts to expand their female readership, regularly serialised romance novels.

95 See Houlbrook, 'A Pin to See the Peepshow'.

96 Andreas Huyssen, *After the Great Divide: Modernism, Mass Culture, Post Modernism* (London, 1986), pp. 44–5; Flint, *The Woman Reader*, p. 140.

97 *The Times*, 8th December 1922, p. 17.

98 *Daily Express*, 9th December 1922, p. 4.

99 *The Times*, 11th December 1922, p. 19.

100 Young, *Trial of Frederick Bywaters and Edith Thompson*, p. xv.

101 The *Empire News* cynically began the serialisation of this book on 7th January 1923, despite having so criticised Edith.

102 *London Stage*, 1910–1919, pp. 193, 644.

103 *The Times*, 8th December 1922, p. 17, and other newspapers for that day.

104 *Lloyd's Sunday News*, 24th December 1922, p. 5.

105 See Tracey Longhran, 'Shell-Shock in Britain, c.1860–c.1920' (unpublished Ph.D. thesis, London University, 2006). Various other commentators referred to Edith as 'neurotic', for example James Douglas, *Sunday Express*, 10th December 1922, p. 8; Rebecca West, *Reynolds's Newspaper*, 17th December 1922, p. 2.

106 See William Twining, *Rethinking Evidence* (Oxford, 1990), Chapter 8.

107 Anette Ballinger, *Dead Woman Walking: Executed Women in England and Wales, 1900–1955* (Aldershot, 2000), pp. 226–7.

108 Young, *Trial of Frederick Bywaters and Edith Thompson*, p. 17, my emphasis.

109 See Ballinger, *Dead Woman Walking*, p. 227.

110 Ann-Louise Shapiro, '"Stories More Terrifying than the Truth Itself": Narratives of Female Criminality in Fin de Siècle Paris', in Margaret L. Arnot and Cornelie Usborne (eds), *Gender and Crime in Modern Europe* (London, 2003), p. 207.

111 Filson Young, writing the year of the executions, was aware of what these references really referred to: 'measures to counteract the results of intercourse'. Young, *Trial of Frederick Bywaters and Edith Thompson*, p. xxv. On abortion in this period see Barbara Brookes, *Abortion in England, 1900–1967* (London, 1988).

112 See Lesley A. Hall, *Sex, Gender and Social Change in Britain Since 1880* (London, 2000), p. 11. In January 1920 Justice Darling had given an abortionist ten years penal servitude. *People*, 25th January 1920, p. 9.

113 *Daily Mail*, 9th December 1922, p. 5.

114 See *The Times*, 8th December 1922, p. 17.

115 See Young, *Trial of Frederick Bywaters and Edith Thompson*, p. xiv, for the way in which the criminal lawyers resorted to melodrama.

116 *World's Pictorial News*, 23rd December 1923, p. 10.

117 *Daily Express*, 7th December 1922, p. 1, And see *World's Pictorial News*, 16th December 1922, p. 2. Not everyone was so praising. Beverley Nichols later referred to him as 'an amiable ape', 'rigid with sex'. Nichols, *The Sweet and Twenties*, p. 67.

118 See Bourke, *Dismembering the Male*.

119 Weis, *Criminal Justice*, p. 27.

120 *Daily Mail*, 18th October 1922.

121 *Daily Mail*, 18th October 1922. Once the verdict was passed however, the *Daily Mail* took a hard line, condemning both the prisoners. Poet T.S. Eliot congratulated the paper, seeing it 'in striking contrast with the flaccid sentimentality of other papers I have seen'. *Daily Mail*, 8th January 1923.

122 *Daily Sketch*, 8th December 1922, p. 2.

123 Philip Gibbs, *Now It Can Be Told* (1920), quoted in Kingsley Kent, *Making Peace*, p. 99. Freddy has not actually fought in the war, although that may have not been clear to readers and spectators. Newspapers carried many accounts of violence committed by men upon women in the immediate years after the war, yet convictions were low and sentences lenient. See Judith A. Allen, *Sex and Secrets: Crimes Involving Australian Women since 1880* (Melbourne, 1990), Chapter 6, for the parallel Australian situation.

124 *Daily Sketch*, 18 December 1922, p. 2.

125 *Illustrated Sunday Herald*, 10th December 1922, p. 8.

126 Nead, 'Visual Cultures of the Courtroom', p. 122.

127 Hartman, *Victorian Murderesses*, p. 268. Working-class women attended local courts as spectators however. Shani D'Cruze, *Crimes of Outrage: Sex, Violence and Victorian Working Women* (London, 1998).

128 *Weekly Dispatch*, 10th December 1922, p. 1; *Sunday Express*, 10th December 1922, p. 1.

129 *Daily Mirror*, 12th December 1922, p. 2.

130 James Douglas, 'The Pale Woman', *Daily Express*, 7th December 1922, p. 1.

131 *Daily Chronicle*, 11th December 1922, p. 7.

132 *Lloyds' Sunday News*, 10th December 1922, p. 1.

133 *Daily Graphic*, 7th December 1922, p. 3.

134 *Daily Chronicle*, 11th December 1922, p. 7.

135 See for example press response to the 1857 murder trial of Madeleine Smith, and 1889 murder trial of Florence Maybrick, in Hartman, *Victorian Murderesses*, pp. 84, 251; Gordon and Nair, *Murder and Morality in Victorian Britain*.

136 *Weekly Dispatch*, 17th December 1922, p. 8.

137 Huyssen, *After the Great Divide*, pp. 47, 52. Fear of young women was apparent in the war too, as discussed in the introduction.

138 *Manchester Guardian*, 12th December 1922, p. 8.

139 Routh, *Occupation and Pay in Great Britain*, p. 120.

140 Sally Alexander, *Becoming a Woman and Other Essays in 19th and 20th Century Feminist History* (London, 1994), p. 203.

141 *Spectator*, 23rd August 1935, p. 289.

142 See *The Times*, 6th January 1923, p. 9; *Manchester Guardian*, 12th December 1922, p. 8.

143 Carey, *The Intellectuals and the Masses*, pp. 7–8.

144 Nead, 'Visual Cultures of the Courtroom'.

145 *Daily Sketch*, 13th December 1922, p. 2.

146 *Reynolds's Newspaper*, 17th December 1922, p. 2.

147 *Daily Sketch*, 13th December 1922, p. 2; *Lloyd's Sunday News*, 14th January 1923, p. 10; *Vote*, 19th January 1923, p. 20. And see article against capital punishment by 'the Elderly Gent', *Illustrated Sunday Herald*, 17th December 1922, p. 7.

148 *Daily Sketch*, 14th December 1922, p. 3.

149 *Daily Sketch*, 15th December 1922, p. 13.

150 *Daily Sketch*, 18th December 1922, p. 2.

151 Nichols, *The Sweet and Twenties*, p. 67.

152 Weis, *Criminal Justice*, pp. 255–6.

153 *Daily Sketch*, 15th December 1922, p. 2.

154 *Daily Sketch*, 16th December 1922, p. 2.

155 *World's Pictorial News*, 16th December 1922, p. 2.

156 *Weekly Dispatch*, 17th December 1922, p. 7. The paper published three instalments by her father, ghosted by Beverley Nichols, who had just begun work as a journalist. Weis, *Criminal Justice*, pp. 353–4; Nichols, *The Sweet and Twenties*, pp. 75–8.

157 *Lloyd's Sunday News*, 14th January 1923, p. 10. A woman had not been hanged in Britain since 1907; many women had been reprieved.

158 *Reynolds's Newspaper*, 17th December 1922, p. 2.

159 Rebecca Stott, *The Fabrication of the Late-Victorian Femme Fatale: the Kiss of Death* (Basingstoke, 1992), pp. 30, 37; and see Hanson and O'Rawe (eds), *The Femme Fatale*.

160 See Bram Dijkstra, *Evil Sister: the Threat of Female Sexuality in Twentieth-Century Culture* (New York, 1996). The vamp was epitomised by the silent screen Hollywood actresses Theda Bara and Pola Negri. See Eve Golden, *Vamp: the Rise and Fall of Theda Bara* (New York, 1996); Sheila Rowbotham, *Century of Women* (London, 1997), p. 110.

161 L. Perry Curtis, *Jack the Ripper and the London Press* (Yale, 2001), p. 9.

4

Mme Fahmy's vindication: Orientalism, miscegenation fears and female fantasy

The autobiography of Mrs Kate Meyrick, 1920s Soho nightclub owner, is peppered with references to club visits from famous names – entertainers, actresses, artists, writers. Royalty too make an appearance – the Crown Prince of Sweden, Prince Nicholas of Romania, and 'one princely signature in the visitors' book … associated with a grim tragedy … that of Fahmy Bey'.[1] The 'grim tragedy' to which she referred was his untimely death, for in the early hours of 10th July 1923, in the corridor of London's Savoy hotel, the French wife of Egyptian Ali Fahmy had shot her husband dead.

As told in a London courtroom and on the pages of the British press, this was an Orientalist tale, for the narrative relied in its telling on a wide repertoire of Orientalist tropes in which East and West were polarised, the Oriental man demonised, and the assumed lowly status of the Eastern woman taken as central to the Orient's vilification. But while being a tale of the Orient in all its mystery, horror, romance and dread, it was also a cautionary tale directed at British women, in which the inadvisability, even danger, of miscegenation was the key moral. However some of the women themselves 'read' the narrative rather differently. Their preferred reading and the pleasure they took from that reading, became a bone of contention.

Ali Kamel Fahmy Bey, a twenty-two year old press attache at the French Legation in Cairo, was one of Egypt's richest men, having inherited much of his father's wealth on his sixteenth birthday. He was the only son of a rich deceased engineer who had 'made his fortune through irrigation schemes and deals in cotton'.[2] Raw cotton was Egypt's key export crop at this time, and the Fahmy wealth had carried on expanding after the father's death in 1907, for the industry did very well out of the Great War. Ali Fahmy had been made a 'Bey', an honorary title similar to 'Lord', for his donations to charity; he was not a 'prince', although the British press often referred to him as such.[3] He had first glimpsed Marguerite Marie Laurent, a divorcée ten years his senior, in Egypt in December 1921, where she was accompanying a rich businessman. He was very taken with this striking, elegant Frenchwoman. He caught sight of her again in Paris on several more occasions, and finally managed an introduction in July 1922. They travelled round 'the wealthy watering holes of Europe, where they had spent lavishly', namely Deauville, Biarritz, and Paris.[4] He returned to Egypt, but enticed her out there on the fraudulent pretext that he was critically ill and could not live without her. They married in a civil ceremony in December of that year, and in an Islamic ceremony the following January.[5]

On 1st July 1923, having been married six months, the Fahmys arrived in London with his male secretary, his black valet, and her French maid. They had come for a month's holiday (indeed their life was one of constant holidaying) and occupied a suite of rooms on the fourth floor of the Savoy Hotel, the leading London hotel, fashionable and expensive.[6] On 9th July the Fahmys, along with the male secretary, Said Enani, went out in the evening to the operetta *The Merry Widow* (an ironic choice, given the subsequent events), returned to the Savoy for a late supper, and argued violently (yet again).[7] At 2.30 a.m., now upstairs on the fourth floor, during one of the city's most violent thunderstorms in living memory, Marguerite Fahmy aimed her pistol at her husband and shot three times, hitting his back, neck and head from behind.[8] He was taken to Charing Cross Hospital but was dead within an hour.

Two months later Marguerite appeared at the Central Criminal Court (better known as the Old Bailey) on trial for murder. She admitted to the killing but in defence claimed firstly that it was an accident, believing that she had disengaged the pistol earlier in the evening, and secondly, and contradictorily, that it was an act of self-defence, as he had threatened to kill her. The third plank to her plea, which only became established as the trial proceeded, was that she was 'driven to desperation' by the 'brutality and beastliness' of her Oriental husband – in effect that she had been provoked.[9] The six-day trial ended in a verdict of 'not guilty' not simply to murder, but to manslaughter as well, even though evidence that the shooting was either accidental or that she acted in self-defence, was, to say the least, unconvincing. And the suggestion that she had been provoked was explicitly discounted by the judge.[10] The *Daily Chronicle* explained the verdict as 'one of those cases, so rare in English law, of justifiable and excusable homicide'.[11] So what were the determinants of this extraordinary statement, and indeed the trial's extraordinary outcome?

While the trial centred on both the treatment of a specific Western woman by an Eastern man, and, as will become evident, on the general treatment of women in the Orient, newspaper commentary on the trial also focused on women in Britain: on the one hand their presence and behaviour at the Old Bailey (the female audience refused to leave the court despite being advised to on several occasions because of the nature of the case), on the other hand their infatuation with racially 'other' men. If the first question here concerns the determinants of the trial's outcome, the second set of questions relate to press commentary on women. Why was women's presence in court seen as a concern, and what was thought to draw them there? And in relation to young British women more generally, how was their fascination with 'Orientals' presented? It will be demonstrated that press commentary was pervaded by a combination of fear of miscegenation and outrage at its contemplation.

The Old Bailey trial

Five days after the death of Fahmy, the *Illustrated Sunday Herald* was describing the case as 'destined to rank among the most amazing dramas in the country', due to 'its romance, its association with the beautiful and the bestial'.[12] Such a view was in line with the general Western attitude to the East: fascination combined with revulsion. In the press reportage of the inquest and the Bow Street police court hearing, both held in July, the 'beautiful' was the main focus, with the couple's wealthy lifestyle a source of fascination.[13] The popular Sunday paper the *People* took pleasure in detailing the extravagance: 'The young pair are said to have spent over £100 a day [equivalent to a labourer's yearly pay] and the "Princess" lived up to her reputation of being one of the world's best-dressed women. Everyday she went shopping in a luxurious car and spent money like water, while her husband whiled away his time with costly luncheons, extravagant dinners and wonderful evening parties'.[14] Just before the Old Bailey trial opened two months later, the newspapers returned again to the splendorous life of the Fahmys, but it was wealth which was at once 'Orientalised': the *Daily Chronicle* for example wrote of the 'luxurious surroundings that lent all the glamour of an Eastern romance', while the *Daily Sketch*'s front page headlines read: 'From Oriental Luxury to Old Bailey Dock'.[15] The *Sunday Express* dramatically summed up the fate of the Fahmy 'romance': 'From Luxor to Cairo, from Cairo to London, living all the time with the magnificence of a prince and princess in a fairy tale, these two seemed attended by fortune until – Revolver shots in a hotel corridor in the midst of a crashing storm, and the fairy tale was ended.'[16]

The trial at the Old Bailey opened on Monday 10th September and concluded the following Saturday. It was noted that of the huge numbers queuing to enter the court the majority were women, many of whom were

SPECIAL ST. LEGER NUMBER TO-MORROW : ORDER NOW

DAILY SKETCH.

No. 4,517　Telephones {London—Holborn 6510. / Manchester—City 6501.　LONDON, TUESDAY, SEPTEMBER 11, 1923.　(Registered as a Newspaper.)　ONE PENNY.

KING OF EGYPT'S FRIEND: OLD BAILEY MURDER TRIAL

A studio portrait of Ali Kemal Bey Fahmy. He was 23.

Ali Kemal Bey Fahmy, the dead man, is here seen with the King of Egypt at the laying of the foundation-stone of a hospital built at Fahmy's expense.—(Exclusive).

This exclusive portrait of Ali Kemal Bey Fahmy was taken at his Cairo home.

Mr. Justice Rigby Swift, who is trying the case.

Two portraits of the wife. On the left she is in Egyptian dress. She is French and is 32 years of age.

Stories of life in an Eastern Palace, of motor-cars and yachts, were features of the Old Bailey trial when Marie Marguerite Fahmy was brought to trial for the alleged murder of her young Egyptian husband, Ali Kemal Bey Fahmy, the rich friend of the King of Egypt, who was found shot at the Savoy Hotel on July 10, the night of the great London thunderstorm. She pleaded "Non Coupable" or "Not Guilty." Sir Edward Marshall-Hall took the responsibility of not having the evidence translated for the accused.

10 *Daily Sketch*, 11th September 1923, Fahmy trial
© British Library Board (MLD19)

'fashionably dressed'. There were women in the body of the court as well, for of the twelve person jury, two were women (women having been admitted to jury service in 1919).[17] Their appearance in court was rare enough still to receive comment, as too was the presence of England's first two women barristers, Ivy Williams and Helena Normanton, who had been called to the Bar the previous year; they were attending the Fahmy trial out of general interest.[18] The press noted the cosmopolitan air of the court: in addition to 'many Egyptians' (which included Egyptians lawyers holding watching briefs for members of Fahmy's family), they spotted 'an Indian woman and an elegant man with the mark of Paris stamped on his clothes'.[19] On the last day of the trial it was noted that 'most of the crowd were foreigners, and many were French'.[20]

The prosecution was led by Percival Clarke (son of the famous Sir Edward Clarke, QC, who had unsuccessfully defended Oscar Wilde in 1895) while the defence was headed by the most well-known (and expensive) defence lawyer of the day, Sir Edward Marshall Hall.[21] Now aged nearly sixty-five, Marshall Hall was still handsome, a brilliant orator, with a theatrical and commanding presence, helped by his height (he was 6ft 3in). He saw his profession as akin to acting, and it was thus no surprise that he was a member of the actors' club, the Garrick. He was known as 'the Great Defender', having defended, and sometimes won, a number of seemingly hopeless murder trials in his long legal career.[22] His back-up, Sir Henry Curtis-Bennett, had recently been less successful, having failed to save Edith Thompson from the gallows at the beginning of the year.[23]

In presenting the background to the case the prosecution counsel Percival Clarke offered a sense of the couple's extravagant lifestyle: their time in the resorts of Europe, where they had spent wildly, then on to Fahmy's beautiful palace on the Nile, where they had travelled around in his numerous motor-cars (he possessed nine) and his magnificent yacht.[24] While united in their love of luxury, the couple had nevertheless been incompatible, suggested Clarke: 'Fahmy was supposed to have been a quiet, retiring man, while his wife was fond of a gayer life.'[25] Keener to party, Clarke suggested, but possibly also keener to pick a fight. He reported that at supper on the night of the killing they had quarrelled, and Marguerite had apparently said to her husband (in French, for that was the language they held in common): '"You shut up. I will smash the bottle over your head".'[26] Clarke emphasised that the post-mortem revealed Fahmy to have been shot from behind, and the bullets fired from some distance. These observations alone should have demolished the claim of self-defence or provocation, but Clarke's dry delivery did not, it appears, convey the findings' full weight.[27] He went on to relate the eye-witness account of the hotel's night porter John-Paul Beattie. On the night in question, Beattie had observed the couple in an 'excited' state, and, to quote the *Evening News*, had asked them

> not to create a disturbance in the corridor. Just as the porter was going away he heard a slight whistle behind him, and looking back, saw the husband stooping down whistling … at a little dog [it belonged to Marguerite] which had come out of the suite. The porter did not at that moment see Mme Fahmy and he continued his way along to another suite. A moment later he heard three shots fired in quick succession.[28]

Fahmy had last been seen alive by Beattie in the corridor, thirty feet away from his wife's bedroom door. The narrative was substantiated later on in the day, when the night porter gave his evidence in person. Marshall Hall, defence counsel, in his cross-examination of Beattie, asked little (he knew when *not* to ask questions) but discredited the night porter somewhat by suggesting that it would have been impossible to hear the whistling to a dog over the roar of the storm. Most newspapers made little of Beattie's account, although his observations were surely critical to the prosecution's case. Possibly by the time of writing up the case at the day's end the press was already being won round by the persuasiveness of the 'Great Defender'.

In his summary of the case, Clarke's objective was to present Mme Fahmy as a violent, quick-tempered woman, in contrast to her 'calm' husband, who at the time of his death had been doing nothing but calling to a pet dog.[29] But such a representation would not have convinced the members of the public who attended the Old Bailey trial or read the press, for in addition to Marshall Hall's counter presentation of Fahmy that followed later that day, all the newspapers stressed the wife's apparent passivity and vulnerability, for example the *Daily Chronicle* was typical in referring to her as 'a tragic, drooping figure, dressed in black and veiled … leaning for support against a wardress, whose arm encircled her waist'.[30]

One of Clarke's prosecution witnesses was Said Enani, 'a short dapper figure in a well-tailored blue suit'.[31] Enani had been Fahmy's secretary for the last five years, had travelled to England with the Fahmys, indeed went everywhere with them. The press barely reported the exchanges between Clarke and Enani, but focused instead on Marshall Hall's four-hour cross-examination, the outcome of which was wholly to the benefit of the defence.[32] Enani was asked by Marshall Hall about his employer's brutality; he admitted to recollecting that Fahmy had once dislocated the defendant's jaw, but denied general cruelty. Fahmy was simply 'a bit unkind'. He had never heard Fahmy earlier in the year swearing on the Koran to kill his wife, nor recently threatening to throw her into the Thames. Despite the denials, mention of these various incidents presented a picture of Fahmy as a violent man. His cruelty was further illustrated by a letter read out in court written to the defendant's sister about the defendant in which he refers to being 'engaged in training her'.[33]

Recounting Fahmy's cruelty and violence was not the only way in which Enani was deployed to the benefit of the defence; he was also asked about his own relationship with Fahmy. The secretary admitted that he had been very attached to his employer, seven years his junior – not in a master/servant relationship but as a great friend. Marshall Hall suggested however that their relationship had been something more: that in Egypt their association had been 'notorious', and that before Fahmy had come into his money, they had 'lived together'. Enani denied it. (Given that Fahmy came into his money at the age of sixteen, six years prior to his death, the implication was that Enani as an older man had lived with a mere boy.) Marguerite had informed Marshall Hall that much against her wishes, her husband visited Enani's room for an hour every night before coming to bed. In suggesting earlier co-habitation, mentioning Fahmy's nightly visits to his secretary, and referring to the men's relationship as 'notorious', Marshall Hall appeared to imply a sexual relationship between the two men.[34] But Marshall Hall was sailing close to the wind in his defamation of Enani: to attack the secretary's character in court in theory allowed the prosecution to do likewise in relation to the defendant.[35] Under the 1898 Criminal Evidence Act, section 1(f), casting imputations on the character of a prosecution witness permitted the presentation of evidence of the defendant's 'bad character'.[36] None of this was spoken of publicly, but the unconvincing denial of his employer's behaviour and the inference of impropriety and 'unnatural' behaviour acted to discredit the secretary and to question his reliability as a witness.[37] Enani's cross-examination had helped significantly to suggest Fahmy's violence and sexual perversion.

On the second day of the trial, there was a queue of several hundred people in the street an hour before the court opened, the majority of whom were again women.[38] The court was packed as gun expert, Robert Churchill, entered the witness box to discuss Mme Fahmy's pistol. He was adamant that the pistol, a Browning Belgian, could *not* go off accidentally. He noted that the gun was in perfect working order, and when loaded, the weight of the pull was heavy – eight and a quarter pounds – and the trigger had to be pulled for each shot. At this stage the gun evidence was not going in the defendant's favour. When Marshall Hall cross-examined Churchill, he made much of the fact that Marguerite claimed to know nothing about guns and to have never fired one until the night of the killing. (This seemed unlikely if Enani was correct in his claim that both Fahmys always carried pistols. And there was also the evidence that the gun had been shot from some distance, possibly 30 feet, yet hit its target each time, which was no mean feat.) Part of the defence was that she had fired a shot out of the window earlier in the evening, believing that this dislodging of a cartridge rendered the gun inoffensive. A cartridge was indeed found near the window. (She changed the timing: at Bow Street police station she had claimed to have fired out of the window immediately before the killing. Neither defence counsel, prosecution nor press commented on this change of story. Presumably changing the time acted to counter any suggestion that her shooting the gun out of the window just before killing Fahmy was to test its being in working order.) She announced that she had 'often' seen her husband unload his own pistol in this manner, and did not know that once a bullet was discharged, another replaced it. Her husband had threatened to kill her, Mme Fahmy insisted, and thus she wanted the gun in order to frighten him. The fact that she had fired at him three times with a trigger that had to be pulled with some force for each shot clearly undermined her claim of accidental shooting, yet the press made no mention of this contradiction. What was reported instead was Churchill conceding to Marshall Hall's suggestion that 'an inexperienced person might easily reload the weapon thinking that in fact he was emptying it'.[39]

On this second day of the trial, once the prosecution witnesses had been examined and cross-examined, Marshall Hall presented the case for the defence. He was seeking to prove that '"Mme Fahmy killed her husband in legitimate self-defence ... driven to despair by the cruelty and brutality of the man, and shot him when she believed he was about to kill her."'[40] To illustrate the danger under which she was living, he quoted an anonymous letter received by Mme Fahmy at the Savoy Hotel:

> Please permit a friend who has travelled widely among Orientals and who knows the craftiness of their acts to give you some advice. Don't return to Egypt ... Rather abandon fortune than risk your life. A journey means a possible accident, poison in the flower, a subtle weapon that is neither seen nor heard.[41]

The press quoted the letter with relish, and it was clear that for the newspapers, the Fahmy narrative was fast becoming not simply a desert romance, but also a mystery, thriller and horror story in one, peopled with dangerous, even deadly, Orientals.

Marshall Hall presented the husband not simply as one such dangerous Oriental, but also as a man who was fundamentally sexually perverse: 'a beast whom the vilest words known cannot adequately describe', 'abnormal and a brute'.[42] This perversity, already hinted at on day one, was expanded upon in the examination of the hotel's doctor who had attended Mme Fahmy while at the Savoy.[43] Dr Edward Gordon confirmed that the defendant was suffering from a 'painful condition' requiring surgery, which was 'consistent with her story of her husband's cruel conduct'.[44] She had told him that 'Fahmy had brutally handled her and pestered her.'[45] The doctor had advised an operation in London, to which her husband was adamantly opposed, and she had thus decided to return to Paris for the surgery, planning to leave with her maid on 10th July. In the end their journey was cancelled, for it was in the early hours of 10th July that she shot her husband dead.

In what way had Fahmy 'brutally handled' his wife? Marshall Hall informed the court, according to the *Daily Express*, that the Egyptian 'attacked his wife like a raving, lustful beast because she would not agree to an outrageous suggestion he made – a suggestion which would fill every decent-minded person with utter revulsion'.[46] Did he expand further? The trial transcripts unfortunately no longer exist, and given press censorship one cannot know for certain what was actually said in court.[47] And was the 'painful condition' she was suffering from explained? Amongst depositions lodged in the National Archives, evidence of three doctors clarifies her medical problem: inflamed external haemorrhoids, one of which was described as 'thrombosed', and a fissure of the anus. The doctors suggested that the condition was 'very painful and distressing', and that Marguerite believed it due to her 'husband's practices'.[48] Clearly the husband had practiced buggery, as later press references to 'unnatural sexual intercourse' implied.

Once effectively established as a sexual pervert (although this was hinted at rather than made explicit, as far as can be ascertained) – engaged in something sexually unspeakable with his wife, and possibly also in homosexual relations with his male secretary – Fahmy's 'sadism' was elaborated upon. The 'sadist', explicitly defined by Marshall Hall as 'the man who enjoyed the sufferings of women', was also Orientalised, as seen in Marshall Hall's reconstruction of the fatal night.[49] According to the defence counsel, Fahmy had made a vile suggestion, and when she had refused, he had rushed at her and attempted to strangle her. 'Then in sheer desperation, as he crouched for the last time – crouched like an animal, like an Oriental … she put the pistol to his face, and to her horror the thing went off.'[50] In his statement 'like an animal, like an Oriental' Marshall Hall was explicitly defining the Oriental male as inherently bestial, reinforced by his declaration that Fahmy was a 'treacherous Eastern beast'.[51] As for the claim that she killed in self-defence, no reference was made by Marshall Hall to the night porter's evidence of the previous day that Fahmy had been shot moments after being observed thirty feet along the corridor from the couple's suite, stooping down and whistling to a dog, and not, as she maintained, as he attacked her in her bedroom. There was also nothing said here about the difficulty of firing the gun 'accidentally'. But already the die was cast and the establishment of the Egyptian husband as sexually perverse and ruthlessly cruel – central tropes in the West's construction of the Oriental male – acted to render marginal any evidence contrary to the developing verdict: the guilt of Ali Fahmy, rather than that of the defendant. The character assassination was total and Fahmy – deemed a sexually perverse Eastern sadistic monster – was effectively presented as deserving of his death, his wretched wife having performed not a crime but a public service.

Mme Fahmy as 'woman of the world'?

On day three prosecutor Clarke announced that he intended to question Mme Fahmy about her relations with other men in order to prove her an immoral 'woman of the world'. Marshall Hall immediately called for a point of law. On the dismissal of the jury, he argued that all such questioning should be rendered inadmissible, since it would 'prejudice the jury unfavourably'.[52] Justice Swift agreed that cross-examination should focus solely on the defendant's relations with her husband, pointing out that Marshall Hall had been careful not to present Marguerite as a total saint, for he had mentioned in passing that 'the accused is perhaps a woman of not very strict morality'.[53] But he added that Marshall Hall, in his inimitable way, had given the impression to everyone that 'she was an innocent and most respectable lady'.[54] As the law stood, the defendant's bad character was only admissible if it were directly relevant to the specifics of the case, or if she or her defence counsel had attacked the character of a prosecution witness. Clarke might have held the latter to have taken place, given Marshall Hall's treatment of Enani. Clarke might also have thought the former a possibility, for he had 'evidence' given to him by an Egyptian lawyer, A. Ragai, acting for Ali Fahmy's sister and brother-in-law (the Saids), that Mme Fahmy had specific premeditated murderous intentions towards her husband, and was known to be a violent woman. The 'evidence' took the form of sworn statements from two friends of the Fahmys, Mahmoud Abdel Fath and Mme Fanny Luis, both of which referred to how she had confessed to hating her husband, and had a 'programme' that she was going to carry out in Europe that would result in her obtaining Ali's money. They interpreted this as her intention to kill Ali. She had also told Fath of how she had stabbed a former male lover seven times with a dagger; nothing was said as to whether he had survived! Potentially all this amounted to explosive ammunition against the defendant.

Indeed the prosecution team had a great deal of material on Marguerite – information which largely never entered the public domain and was not made known to the jury. In addition to the report given to them by Ragai, evidence had been gathered by their own detectives and police. The police and detective reports established that she had been born Marguerite Marie Alibert on 9th December 1890, in Paris, her father a cab-driver or coachman, her mother a char woman, and that a month after her sixteenth birthday she had borne an illegitimate daughter, Raymonde, at present at a boarding school in Hertfordshire. (The press did mention that she had a sixteen-year old daughter, which meant that anyone could have calculated that she had had her at a young age.) Marguerite Alibert was said to have been on the streets for the next eight to ten years (her daughter being looked after by Marguerite's mother) and was then taken up by a Mme Denant who ran a high-class brothel, and a 'Maison de Rendezvous', who taught her to be a 'lady'. At this establishment she entertained a number of wealthy clients.[55] Although Marguerite claimed in court to have married and later divorced a Charles Laurent, a rich captain in the French flying service five years her junior, the detective could find no evidence of either the marriage or the divorce, which she held occurred in 1919 and 1920 respectively.[56] The detective was also informed that it was well known that Marguerite was 'addicted to committing certain offences with other women'.[57] This was not elaborated upon.

It is unknown if Clarke challenged the judge and raised the issue of the defaming of Enani (defaming Fahmy, the dead and voiceless murder victim, was acceptable in the eyes of the law).[58] As for the incriminating 'evidence' he had received concerning Mme Fahmy, he might well have been distrustful of evidence collected by Egyptians and thus not have given it much weight. That certainly appears to be the case as far as the Director of Public Prosecutions, Sir Archibald Bodkin, was concerned. In the month before the Old Bailey trial, Bodkin had been approached by Fahmy's brother-in-law, Dr Said, who had come to London with his wife (Fahmy's sister) and his lawyer, Ragai, but Bodkin had rather rudely refused to meet them. He replied to their London solicitor, W. Ewart Craigen: 'I do not think that at present it will be necessary to trouble you or them'.[59] Ten days before the trial was to open Craigen tried again: 'My clients have expressed surprise that you have not thought it necessary to interview them … They are willing and anxious to see you'.[60] Craigen sent Ragai's report, but there is no evidence that Bodkin or Clarke ever consulted the Saids or their lawyer in person (although all three came every day to court, as witnessed by the press and its photographers).[61] As to why Bodkin refused to meet with them, one can speculate that he might have seen Egyptians as unreliable – he (and Clarke?) in effect buying into the dominant Orientalist representation of the Eastern male as wily, cunning and untrustworthy.

When Marguerite entered the witness box she had a male interpreter by her side, for she spoke no English. Marshall Hall was concerned that the interpreter assigned to her was not doing a very good job; as a fluent French speaker himself, he was not convinced by the exactness of the man's interpretation.[62] He had heard from barrister Helena Normanton that there was in court a young French lawyer, Maitre Odette Simon, who was willing to help. He applied for her to act as a substitute interpreter and she was duly sworn in. According to Marshall Hall's biographer, 'the romantic situation … of one gifted young Frenchwoman helping another in her hour of extreme peril in a strange country, made an irresistible appeal to him'.[63] Simon was a feminist, active in the Union Francaise pour le Suffrage des Femmes.[64] Her feminism may have contributed to her desire to help an abused woman, and she and Marguerite apparently became good friends.[65]

Marshall Hall's examination of Mme Fahmy concentrated on the ways in which she had been brutalised and her civil liberties denied. The defendant told of how her husband had once sworn on the Koran to kill her, and another time had threatened her with a horsewhip. The conditions under which Fahmy had made his wife live were presented by Marshall Hall as insupportable and as inherently Oriental – in contradistinction to the freedoms of the West. She told the court of some of the threats to her liberty: 'One day … Fahmy and Enani took me in a car to the outskirts of Paris … they stopped and told me they were looking for a house in which to imprison me.'[66] On his yacht she was indeed locked in and guarded: 'alone on board and surrounded by black men'.[67] The contradiction within this statement appears to have gone unrecognised; many in the courtroom might well have subscribed to Ali Fahmy's own view of his black servants. Marguerite told the court that when she complained about a black valet who regularly entered her room while she was dressing, her husband replied: 'He does not count. He is nobody'.[68] (This was the valet who had accompanied the Fahmys to the Savoy, but was never called as a witness, such was the acceptance of his total insignificance.) The defendant was not simply involuntarily confined, she was effectively reduced to the same status as her guards, for 'he demanded a slave-like obedience'.[69] Should she think of disobeying, there was the threat of Costa, a powerfully built black servant who Fahmy claimed was beholden to him for saving his life. Costa, Fahmy warned, would disfigure her should Fahmy so order, and should she escape, Costa would always seek her out. (He may have been well-built, but it transpired that Costa was only 5ft tall, as Clarke later pointed out.) Positioned between two male figures imbued with abnormal sexuality – the sadist Oriental and the 'primitive' black – the Frenchwoman was presented as facing a fate worse than death. And when she suggested to her husband that 'she preferred to die than go on living in the way she was doing, her husband replied: "You have a revolver."'[70]

If in this instance, when set against his servants, Fahmy was something other than 'black', in another instance the distinction disappeared. For example the previous day Marshall Hall claimed that Fahmy had attempted to 'cow her into the state of obedience that a black man wants of the woman who is to be her chattel'.[71] This slippage in one context between the Oriental as distinct from the 'primitive' black African, and in another equating the two, was typical of the indistinctness and fluidity of the terms used. For while Arabs were classified as primitive in one instance, in another they were degenerate. In relation to Egypt, literary critic Joseph Boone's discussion of its liminality adds an extra dimension to this issue of indeterminancy. Boone argues that Egypt has 'acted as a conduit between East and West, Europe and Africa', with the consequence that 'it never functioned merely or solely as the Occident's Other', but 'has come to represent in the Western imagination an intermediate zone'.[72]

Marguerite's helplessness in the face of Eastern tyranny was central in the trial to the demonisation of the Orient and it was underscored by the defence's and the press's frequent references to the fragility of her appearance. Over the East/West divide were superimposed the similarly polarised stock characterisations of melodrama – the overpowering male villain and the weak female victim.[73] (Melodrama informed both the Billing and Thompson/Bywaters trials too, as seen in Chapters 1 and 3.) Ali Fahmy was presented by the press as 'a great, hulking, muscular fellow', violent, with 'abnormal tendencies'.[74] Marguerite was depicted as small, frail, frightened and cowered, given to almost constant weeping and occasional swooning, with the press repeatedly referring to her as 'pale and drooping', her 'two frightened eyes, barely visible beneath the deep brim of the small cloche hat'.[75] She wept so 'copiously', according to *Reynolds's News*, that 'several women in the public gallery were crying too'.[76] The butterfly analogy which we saw used so widely in the reportage of young women and drugs was made here too, the *Empire News* commenting that when she spoke 'it was like the fluttering of the gossamer wings of a butterfly on the wheel'.[77] Marshall Hall mentioned more than once that she had formerly been 'a charming attractive woman' changed by fear into 'a poor quaking creature'.

She was also described by the press however as beautiful and elegant if demure, and here the referents of melodrama combined with her French 'stylishness' (Paris had been seen as the heart of haute couture since at least the mid-nineteenth century).[78] Day by day the popular press carefully detailed her clothes and general appearance, as it had with Edith Thompson. It was no accident that the popular press paid close attention to her outfits; by the 1920s, eager to attract and keep the female reader, fashion had become one of its staples.[79] Marguerite was always in Western dress; indeed she had apparently made the wearing of such a condition of her marriage. In court her clothes were fashionable, but simple, black and funereal. Some of the newspapers however managed to reproduce a photograph of her in what they termed a yashmak.[80] (Depositions at the National Archives reveal this to have been taken at the Islamic marriage ceremony.) The inclusion of this photograph alongside trial reportage acted to reinforce her claim of wretched subordination. The fact that she spoke no English, and thus supposedly did not understand what was happening during the trial, save when given occasional briefings by the interpreter, added to the image of her as helpless and tragic. Her Frenchness, which could well have worked against her (for France had long been seen as a key rival of Britain as well as the site of sexual deviancy), added to both her glamour and her vulnerability.[81]

Clarke began his cross-examination of the defendant with an ill-judged question about whether her father was a Parisian cab-driver. Judge Swift testily responded: "Does it matter whether he was a cab-driver or a millionaire? I do not want a long inquiry into the lady's ancestry.'"[82] To Clarke's next question: was she 'a woman of the world', her reply cleverly deflected the implication of immorality: 'I have had experience of life.'[83] And when he inquired 'were you not very ambitious to become his wife?' she answered, according to the *Daily Chronicle* as she was 'wiping her tear-stained cheeks': "Ambitious, no ... I loved him so very much and wished to be with him".[84] The prosecution was not going well, not only because of Clarke's inept questioning and Mme Fahmy's disarming replies, but also because Marshall Hall was creating a distracting side-show. As Clarke was cross-examining, the defence counsel had walked over to Churchill, the gun expert, and whispered to him about partridge shooting. Churchill remembered:

> At first, I imagined that he was resting his mind by talking about sport in the middle of a difficult case. Later I recollected that I had never heard a word of the prosecution's case while we were together. I have little doubt now that his conversation ... was a diversion to distract the attention of the jury ... Instead they were watching us'[85]

(Apparently Marshall Hall was fond of creating diversions at moments where he feared the case might go against him. He would start using his throat spray for example, which made odd hissing and gargling noises.)[86] When the court adjourned for the day, Marguerite promptly swooned (again) and had to be carried down to the cells.

Closing addresses

On the fourth day of the trial, Marguerite's younger sister, Yvonne Alibert, recounted the bruises she had seen and the threats of strangulation that she had heard, Mme Fahmy's French maid, Amy Pain, corroborated the claims of the husband's violence, telling of how she had had to use cream and powder to hide bruises on her mistress's back and neck, and Marguerite's chauffeur, Eugene Barbay, informed the court that his mistress had always been crying.[87] That afternoon, Marshall Hall began his lengthy closing address. He drew on a well-known repertoire of Orientalist tropes when he remarked: 'The curse of this case is the atmosphere which we cannot understand. The Eastern feeling of possession of the woman, the Turk in his harem, the man who is entitled to have four wives if he liked for chattels', 'which to we Western people with our ideas of women is almost unintelligible.'[88] The public might well have expected Fahmy to have had a harem, for the press was regularly filled with stories about harems, mostly cautionary tales, set in Egypt or Turkey.[89] Marshall Hall had asked Enani if Fahmy had been entitled to four wives and was answered in the affirmative. That Fahmy had had only the one wife was not seen as relevant, for he had had the possibility of taking others. Although Marguerite had tried to insert a clause into her marriage contract giving her the right to divorce, she had been persuaded by Fahmy's relatives to sign without it. She thus had no right to divorce her husband, yet he could divorce her by repudiation.[90] (England's Divorce Act of that year may at this point have come to mind, for at last divorce had been equalised between the sexes.)[91] 'It is common knowledge that the Orient's treatment of women does not fit in with the ideas of the Western woman', Marshall Hall confidently asserted.[92] As feminist scholar Leila Ahmed points out, Islam's particular treatment of women has long been central to the West's condemnation of the Orient. British colonialists, and Lord Cromer especially (British Consul-General in Egypt from 1883 to 1907) had appeared to champion the emancipation of Egyptian women from the harem despite condemning female suffragists back in Britain.[93] (Cromer was the president of the National League for Opposing Women's Suffrage.) The claim that Eastern men oppressed Eastern women 'justified' the undermining of the culture of the colonised. Historian Tim

Mitchell suggests that British colonialists' concern with harems was not about the condition of women's lives but the fact that the harems' inaccessibility frustrated the colonialist project of policing the population.[94] The status of women (by which was meant the degree of approximation of relations between the sexes to the British model) was taken as a key index of a country's 'civilisation' and hence capacity for self-rule. In reality (and unbeknown to the vast majority of the British population) Egyptian women were not the pathetic and passively oppressed creatures of Orientalist mythology; their activism in the 1919 nationalist struggles boosted an already existing Egyptian feminism, which thrived in the 1920s.[95]

In Marshall Hall's closing address, unsurprisingly nothing was said of the gun expert's evidence that Marguerite's pistol could *not* have gone off accidentally, and he never mentioned the night porter's evidence of the incident of Fahmy and the dog in the corridor, which directly contradicted her story. Instead, he dramatically reconstructed the version of events which he and his client claimed as the truth. He imitated the crouching Fahmy by himself crouching down in the court, then he switched to imitating Fahmy's wife. Taking up the gun, he pointed it at the jury, rapped three times on wood to represent the three shots, then 'amid a tense and hushed court the pistol rattled to the floor as it had fallen from the hands of Mme Fahmy'.[96] To the *Daily Sketch*: 'it was almost like a scene from Grand Guignol' (a theatre in Paris specialising in naturalistic horror shows which was at its peak of popularity in the early 1920s).[97] According to Marshall Hall's biographer: 'No words can describe the effect of this daring demonstration.'[98]

Marshall Hall's theatrical displays were not over yet. The East/West binary was rolled out once again in his finale through reference to Robert Hichens' *Bella Donna*, which he termed 'that wonderful work of fiction'.[99] The book had featured in the Thompson/Bywaters trial, discussed by Edith in a letter to Freddy, its plot in part involving the slow poisoning of a husband by his wife. No mention had been made in that trial however of the novel's anti-hero, the cruel Egyptian-Greek sheik Mahmoud Baroudi. There were obvious parallels between Fahmy and Baroudi, for the latter had 'like a good many of his smart, semi-cultured, self-possessed and physically attractive young contemporaries ... gloried in his triumph among the Occidental women'.[100] The *Empire News* had serialised the book at the beginning of the year of the trial, and the actress Pola Negri was about to appear in a Hollywood film version.[101] Marshall Hall addressed the jury:

You will remember the influence of Mahmoud over the Englishwoman, who, under his inspiration, poisons her English husband. You will remember the final scene where this woman goes out of the garden into the dark night of the desert. Members of the jury, I want you to open the gates where the Western woman can go – not into the dark night of the desert, but back to her friends ... let this Western woman go back into the light of God's great Western sun.[102]

As he spoke the sun streamed into the courtroom.[103] Why the sun should be claimed as 'Western' Marshall Hall did not clarify (other than implying that the East was benighted in its violence, godlessness and ignorance), and his 'reading' of the book was somewhat misleading. The English woman, the terrible, unscrupulous, money-obsessed Ruby Chepstow, does not attempt to poison her husband under the inspiration of the unpleasant Mahmoud Baroudi: although strongly attracted to the seductive Baroudi, the poisoning is all her own doing. As for the representation of the desert as darkness and despair, the book on the contrary presents the desert as a site of freedom, light and spirituality, although it is true that at the end of the narrative Mrs Chepstow is forced out into the night. Marshall Hall however chose quite deliberately to misrepresent, for it served as a dramatic reinforcement of the East/West divide.

In the end, what was largely responsible for condemning Ali Fahmy and vindicating his wife was not the claim of accidental shooting or her act of self-defence, but his vilification as an Oriental. 'I dare say Egyptian civilisation is one of the oldest and most wonderful civilisations in the world' suggested Marshall Hall sarcastically, 'but if you strip off the external civilisation ... you get the real Oriental underneath'.[104] He implied that the 'real Oriental' was despotic, sinister, bestial and sexually perverted. Yet perhaps Marshall Hall's most quotable statement as far as the press were concerned related to the danger of miscegenation: 'Her great mistake – possibly the greatest mistake a woman could make – was as a woman of the West in marrying an Oriental'.[105] It was a logical conclusion to the demonisation of the Orient which had been propagated throughout the trial.

Clarke's final address could not have been more different to that of Marshall Hall, indeed Clarke explicitly distanced himself from 'the theatrical atmosphere which has prevailed in this court for the last four or five days'. His speech for the Crown was low key, delivered in a measured, quiet tone. He reminded the jury that in *Bella Donna*: 'The woman who went out into the desert ... was the woman who had planned, and very nearly succeeded, in murdering her husband. It may be that the simile is somewhat alike.'[106] He attempted to include a disparaging remark about the defendant's morals, drawing the jury's attention to the age of her daughter: 'evidence that from sixteen upwards the woman had had experience of men and the world'.[107] And he tried to counter Marshall Hall's account of the killing:

Fahmy was shot while bending down playing with a dog. Was there any doubt that what really happened was that madame – angry, cross, quarrelling – went back, lost her temper and her head, seized the pistol which she knew was in working order, and fired?[108]

The judge's summing up, although deemed 'a masterpiece of lucidity' by the *Daily Chronicle,* was clearly weighted in favour of the defendant.[109] He did advise the jury that the dead man being 'depraved' and despicable was not a sufficient excuse for homicide and must not cloud their judgment.[110] But he never pointed out the defence's logical flaws, indeed he asserted that Mme Fahmy's story had been consistent throughout and well corroborated. He found 'certain aspects of the case ... shocking, sickening, disgusting', and made an especial point of noting his disapproval of Eastern attitudes towards women: 'We in this country put our women on a pedestal' he boasted disingenuously, 'but in Egypt it is different'.[111] He pointed out that a verdict of manslaughter could only be given where there had been extreme and immediate provocation in the form of 'some physical act, such as a blow', which he thought did not apply in this case. He clarified that 'a verdict of not guilty was only permissible if the jury thought homicide justifiable', that is, if they believed that Mme Fahmy had shot her husband in self-defence or by accident. In effect he directed the jury to precisely this verdict.[112]

After just over one hour, the jury followed the judge's directing and returned with a verdict of 'not guilty' to murder and to manslaughter. The court audience cheered wildly, as too did crowds outside waiting in the street. The press might have claimed her acquittal 'a universally popular verdict', and certainly the French public were said to be delighted, but the Egyptians were far from happy. A written protest was sent by barristers from Cairo, objecting to 'the inaccurate assertions and rash generalisations'. It was published in the *Daily Chronicle* and *Manchester Guardian:* 'Contrary to wild stories circulated in connection with the trial of Mme Fahmy, the Oriental has the greatest respect for women.' But they were quick to dissociate themselves from Fahmy himself: 'All here know that Ali Fahmy was of modest extraction and practically uneducated except for the veneer acquired in the demi-monde. Chance gave him a fortune, which he misused'.[113] Also from Cairo came a furious letter from the radical Women's Wafd Party Central Committee, accusing Marguerite's lawyers and the British press of 'a deliberate campaign of hostility, a new form of defamation of Oriental peoples in order to justify British colonial policy'.[114]

Explaining the verdict: the role of the actors

To return to the first question: what were the determinants of the trial's outcome? Clearly the trial's main actors – Marguerite, Marshall Hall and Clarke – each played a crucial role in the final verdict above and beyond the 'facts' of the case. To call them 'actors' is appropriate, for as pointed out in the cases of Maud Allan and Edith Thompson, the courtroom trial was a theatrical spectacle and space par excellence. Not only did the language and style of theatre permeate the courtroom, but the architecture too was reminiscent of a theatre with a stage and audience, and actors performing on elevated platforms. And the theatricality of the narrative could be fully played out in an English court, given the adversarial nature of English law where confrontation and rhetorical swordplay are permitted, and a brilliant defence lawyer has the opportunity to sway the jury. The system is known as 'adversarial' because it is, in effect, a battle between the defence and the prosecution: 'not to establish the truth of what happened but to establish a case that convinces the jury'.[115] The existence of a court jury of one's peers – twelve laymen and women – was/is seen as the hallmark of the English justice system. The English legal system places a greater burden of proof on the Crown prosecution than does the 'inquisitorial' legal system operating on the Continent (where a group of judges together investigate serious cases such as murder); the consequence is a lower conviction rate.[116] Mme Fahmy may well have been relieved to have been tried in England rather than France (although the French defence of *crime passionnel* might have worked in her favour). She indeed expressed her gratitude for 'British justice', which she described as 'too wonderful for words'.[117]

In an excellent article comparing the trial of Marguerite with that of Ruth Ellis (who in the 1950s was the last woman to be hanged in Britain, found guilty of shooting her lover dead), criminologist Anette Ballinger argues that the verdict in the Fahmy trial was due to the Frenchwoman's strategic use of 'appropriate' femininity: she gave the impression of being a helpless, dazed and grieving victim.[118] She certainly presented herself, and was presented by her defence counsel and the press, as weak, fearful, prone to fainting, endless crying and clearly no match for her 'abnormal' and brutish husband.[119] When Mme Fahmy was handed her gun in court by Marshall Hall she appeared unable to pull the trigger back at all (although she had of course done so several times on the night of the killing). Such a self-presentation was clearly an important factor in the final verdict, but so too were the prosecution counsel's incompetence and the defence counsel's impressive ability to 'work' the jury.

Clarke proved an inept prosecutor. There were numerous points of evidence working against Marguerite which he could have drawn to the jury's attention. In his final address, while he noted that Fahmy was killed while bending down playing with a dog, it appears from press reports that he omitted to mention that the three shots had hit the Egyptian from behind, from a distance of thirty feet. He could have reminded the jury that the gun had to be pulled back with force and that a Browning pistol required skill, and thus at that range the accuracy of the shots clearly demonstrated her familiarity with the gun. In other words, he could have established her dishonesty in claiming never to have fired a pistol before, as well as forcefully challenging her claim of self-defence. He could also have pointed to the shift in her statement on the timing of the first shot near the window, raising the question of why she had changed her story. And he could have challenged her self-presentation as weak and helpless. It goes without saying that Clarke's omissions were of great benefit to the defence.

Marshall Hall was obviously the 'leading man' in this particular show, playing his part to the full. His theatrical orations, his staged diversions, his care to omit questions at moments where evidence would have worked against his client, and above all his whipping up of emotions, all contributed to his winning the case. Perhaps most important of all was Marshall Hall's deployment of ideas about the Orient: his emphasis on Fahmy's racial 'otherness', and his representation of the East, and in particularly Egypt, as a site of bestial cruelty, especially as directed towards women.

Explaining the verdict: the role of Orientalism

To cultural critic Edward Said, 'Orientalism' refers both to the discipline by which the Orient was (and is) approached as a topic of learning and discovery (the original meaning of the term), and as a site of domination, where the West's imperialist attitudes and practices negatively impact on the East. He also uses the term to refer to the collection of dreams, images, racial stereotypes and vocabularies available to the Westerner to talk about the East.[120] That Marshall Hall was able to say what he did (such statements as 'If you strip off the external civilisation … you get the real Oriental underneath') and be *permitted* to say as much, was a clear example of Orientalism in action – its embeddedness in 'common sense' and everyday culture. He drew on a repertoire of negative Orientalist tropes which had been in circulation for many years.[121] In relation to Egypt however there were two additional, more contemporary referents, one wholly negative, relating to Egyptian politics, the other more contradictory, relating to the recent discovery of the tomb of Tutankhamen.

Britain had occupied Egypt in 1882 and on the outbreak of war in 1914 had made Egypt a British protectorate. In 1919 there was a nationalist revolution in which nearly a thousand Egyptians died and seventy-five British were injured. It was feared that any concessions made to Egypt would encourage nationalism elsewhere, for Britain was simultaneously confronting nationalist movements in Ireland and India.[122] Eventually, with the Allenby declaration of 1922 (Lord Allenby was the High Commissioner), Britain conceded nominal independence to Egypt, granting a degree of internal self-government. But it retained supervision of Egypt's foreign policy, maintained a British military presence and kept its control over the Suez Canal.[123]

Tutankhamen's tomb had been discovered by two Englishmen, Howard Carter and Lord Carnarvon, in November 1922. The first unplundered tomb, it revealed something of the extent of ancient Egypt's extraordinary wealth and splendour. 'Treasures so rich and wonderful that the first to behold them uttered cries of amazement', dramatically reported the *People*.[124] But this 'new cave of Aladdin' was soon believed to carry a fatal curse. The burial chamber was unsealed on 16th February 1923 and in just over six weeks Lord Carnarvon was dead from a poisoned mosquito bite. Explanations were rife, especially those of the occult. The best-selling romance writer Marie Corelli had given a warning two weeks previously that 'the most dire punishment follows any rash intruder into a sealed tomb'.[125] To Sir Arthur Conan Doyle, Carnarvon's death was the work of 'an evil elemental' acting as guard.[126] Certain scientists were more attracted to the idea that the fatal bite was from a many-centuries-old mosquito, reawakened by the fresh air. But the death of anyone even faintly connected with the discovery was taken as further evidence of Tutankhamen's 'vengeance'. At the moment of Lord Carnarvon's death in Cairo, his dog in England apparently howled and dropped dead.[127] Other supposedly mysterious deaths followed.[128] Even Ali Fahmy was later cited as yet another victim of the curse, for he and his wife had visited the tomb soon after its opening in February, and they had had Lord Carnarvon and Howard Carter to lunch on their yacht.[129] The Fahmys had been spotted near the tomb by travel writer and journalist H.V. Morton, who while noting that 'Fahmy impressed me as a very polished upper-class Egyptian, not very dark, clean shaven', sneeringly added: 'He was too well-dressed to look exactly right. Like most Oriental men, he reeked of scent.'[130] In other words, he could never have passed as an Englishman. Although no direct connection was made at the time between ancient Egypt and the Egypt of the Fahmys, Marshall Hall's sarcastic statement about the 'real Oriental underneath' can be read as a reference to the sinister, supernatural qualities attributed to Ancient Egypt – primitive horror beneath the veneer of civilisation. There was at this time a thriving genre of popular fiction centred upon the demonic powers of mummified corpses, who punished if disturbed, for example Bram Stoker's Ancient Egyptian-themed thriller, *The Jewel of the Seven Stars,* which had been posthumously re-issued in 1912.[131] Along with the view of contemporary Egyptians as politically troublesome, the idea of Egypt's ancestral evilness was a further contribution to the vilification of Ali Fahmy and the nation of Egypt as a whole.

Explaining the verdict: the role of sexual perversity

Not only was Fahmy represented as a troublesome, sinister Egyptian, but he had been revealed to be a sexual pervert. In Britain, attitudes towards 'sexual perversity' had been formed in part by the Oscar Wilde trials of 1895 (the spectre of the decadent homosexual).[132] But where sexual perversity meant sodomy, there was a much longer tradition. Fahmy fitted more the British picture of the sodomite, as opposed to the new category of homosexual: the sodomite, a concept linked to character, was a figure of excess, a close cousin to the rake. Fahmy was a racially 'other' Lord Castlehaven – the defendant in the notorious early modern sodomy trial, who had been accused of buggering his wife and his page.[133] Yet sodomy as a practice had also long been racialised. German sexologist Magnus Hirschfeld located the expression 'the Oriental vice' back in the Middle Ages.[134] Books on Islamic countries from the time of the Crusades onwards disseminated the image of widespread sodomy.[135] In explorer Richard Burton's 'Sotadic Zone', which corresponded to those countries defined as the Orient (today called the Middle East), 'le vice contre nature is popular and endemic'.[136] Egypt in particular was associated with homosexuality: 'that classical region of all abomination' to quote Burton again.[137] Sodomy in the Arab world was thought to be provoked by polygamy: that a man's over-indulgence stimulated a craving for diversity. The West was obsessed with the genital size of the Arab male. One Jacobus X (pseudonym of Jacob Sutor, a French army surgeon) wrote in 1893 that the Arab 'an active pederast, is provided with a genital organ which, for size and length, rivals that of the negro ... With such a weapon does the Arab seek for anal copulation. He is not particular in his choice, and age or sex make no difference.'[138] The Fahmy case confirmed and reinforced this representation of the highly sexed, sodomitic, and non-discriminatory Oriental male.

The astute self-fashioning of Marguerite, the incompetence of the prosecution, the brilliance of the defence, who was able and willing to draw on deeply negative representations of Egyptian men and of 'sexual perversity', and the directing of the judge, acted in combination to over-determine the outcome: Ali Fahmy's 'justifiable' killing, assuring Mme Fahmy's acquittal. It is probable, given Clarke's reticence to undertake an adequate prosecution, that all the legal parties involved subscribed to the 'common-sense' assumptions concerning the Orient and sexual perversity as presented by Marshall Hall.

Women at the trial

The second set of questions here relate to women and their representation in the press: why was there such concern about their presence in the court and why were they so drawn to the trial? Every day of the trial newspapers reported the predominance of women in the waiting queues and in the audience. For example, on day three of the trial there had been a queue outside the court from as early as 2 a.m., and when the court opened, the public stalls were crowded again with 'fashionable' women 'wearing earrings and ropes of pearls'.[139] But it was not just 'women who wore expensive clothes' who were present on the first day, according to a shocked *Daily Express*: 'After the luncheon interval the first three rows of the public gallery were filled by young girls who were unmistakably shop assistants.' And 'most astonishingly of all', to quote the *Daily Express* again, there were 'girls who did not appear to be more than eighteen years of age'.[140] There was often covert press disapproval, especially when women were seen to behave disgracefully: 'Several women sought to secure front positions by climbing over the backs of seats'.[141] Throughout the trial, women were witnessed listening to the 'revolting' evidence with 'breathless and unconcealed curiosity', refusing to leave the court despite warnings given by counsel. The fact that 'unpleasant things' would be heard did not seem to concern them.[142]

The 'unpleasant things' may not have concerned the female audience, but certain commentators were concerned about there being a female audience at the Fahmy trial in the first place (as they had at the Thompson/Bywaters trial). That any woman was behaving disgracefully in a court of law, a predominantly male sphere, which had only recently granted the right to women to serve as lawyers and jurors, was bad enough. But the class and age composition of the female audience had changed since the war, and now young women and lower-middle-class women (the shop-girls) were present as well (as was noted in Edith Thompson's trial). While it was not deemed desirable for any woman to hear sexual material, the youth or class of these newer recruits to the courtroom rendered them supposedly more susceptible to corruption. What seemed to disturb even more was the *attitude* the women brought to what they heard, namely seemingly treating the trial as they treated many other public spectacles – as popular entertainment. Ironically, the small, quiet, fragile and beautiful Mme Fahmy was implicitly counterpoised to the badly behaved women on the other side of the dock who scrambled over seats in their bid to secure a better view. A self-defined 'psychologist' writing in the *Daily Express* levelled attack against the upper- or upper-middle-class female spectator (the 'fashionably dressed' woman) who 'brings the atmosphere of a theatre into a court of justice'. The 'psychologist' had a theory for why such a woman was keen to attend the trial: 'She seeks an afternoon's entertainment and … sits through the most revolting evidence outwardly placid, inwardly indulging in an orgy of unhealthy sensation'. These women were 'female ghouls', who sought 'an outlet for their own repressed vileness'.[143] The 'psychologist' may have written out of class antagonism, and/or misogynistic resentment at women's greater access to the public sphere. The claim of 'repressed vileness' probably owed something to Freudian ideas of repression, which were slowly entering popular discourse at this time.[144] Discounting 'repressed vileness' as a plausible explanation, what alternative understanding do we have for why women were apparently so entranced by this 're- volting evidence'?

Women's fascination with the trial: Oriental romance

Part of the trial's attraction for women may have related to fantasises of revenge on tyrannical husbands. And the prospect of a hanging – the usual outcome of a guilty verdict for murder – may have drawn a few. But perhaps the main appeal lay with the idea of Oriental romance. As already pointed out, one of the meanings of Orientalism as defined by Edward Said is the collection of dreams, images, racial stereotypes and vocabularies which inform the Westerner's representation of an imaginary Orient. Said's work on Orientalism is hugely productive and important, but he operates with an assumed male subject, as well as inferring homogeneity, and for this he has been rightly critiqued.[145] Once we think about a female subject and the heterogeneity of Orientalism it is clear that one crucial aspect of the representation of the East is as quintessentially *romantic*, and it is this which is likely to have drawn the crowds, especially the women, to the Old Bailey.

What is meant by the 'romance' of the Orient? Part of this romance involved a fascination with ancient Egypt, greatly enhanced by the discovery of Tutankhamen's tomb. But those interested in ancient Egypt were often entirely uninterested in the Egypt of the present: ancient Egypt was pre-Islamic and reputedly non-Arab. It is unlikely that the appeal of

Egyptology alone drew the crowds to the trial, although the glamour, mystery and sinister danger surrounding the new archaeological finds were likely to have been part of the attraction.[146] The more contemporary Orient was also seen as glamorous: the middle classes had purchased various Oriental artefacts and materials in Britain, such as Turkish rugs and muslin, since the eighteenth century, and these were now available in department stores such as Liberty's and Selfridges.[147] In the years leading up to the Great War however there were new stimuli: the Ballets Russes' greatly acclaimed performance of *Sheherazade* in London in 1911, and couturier Paul Poiret's 'Oriental' clothing.[148] (Chapter 1 noted the contributions of dancer Maud Allan to this pre-war interest in Oriental dress and art, and the spy Mati Hara to the association of the Orient with dangerous sexual allure.) White middle-class British women might have worn Oriental-type outfits themselves for an evening out, but if they had flocked to the Old Bailey to see Egyptians dressed in traditional wear, they would have been disappointed. Newspapers commented frequently on the presence of 'Orientals' in court, where, to quote the *People*, 'East and West sat cheek by jowl', but they were all in European garb.[149] From 1910 onwards, unveiling amongst the Egyptian middle classes was on the increase.[150] As mentioned earlier in this chapter, some of the newspapers carried photographs of Marguerite wearing a veil/'yashmak', captioned 'Egyptian dress', which undoubtedly added to the trial's allure (for the veil, then and still today, is one of the key symbols of the 'otherness' of the East).[151] Yet when Marguerite wore a veil in court, it was of the short, European kind.

The 'fashionably dressed' women of the Fahmy trial were also likely to have been attending the many plays about the 'mysterious Orient' which were regularly showing in the West End. The new fashion in Orientalism in its many guises was an integral part of cultural modernity. During the same month as the trial, for example, *Hassan*, a play-cum-ballet with music by Delius, was highly praised for catching 'the colour and fantasy of the East, as well as its cruelty'.[152] Whether or not the trial audience had seen the above mentioned performance of *Sheherazade*, its narrative might have been familiar, for Sheherazade was the fictitious narrator of the widely known *Arabian* or *Thousand and One Nights*. Married to a king who has had all his previous wives executed after just one night, Sheherazade tells him a bedtime story, but stays her own execution by leaving it unfinished. The following night the story is completed but another begun, and so on for a thousand and one nights. Many people would have known something of either Edward Lane's translation of the *Nights* or at least some of the various abbreviated versions of such.[153] References to the *Nights* appear in many nineteenth- and twentieth-century novels, there were a huge number of selections and abridgements adapted for children, stories from the *Nights* regularly appeared in pantomime (tales such as 'Ali Baba and the Forty Thieves', 'Aladdin and his Wonderful Lamp', and 'Sinbad the Sailor'), and many newspaper articles on the Middle East referred to the tales as a matter of course.[154] By the early twentieth century, knowledge of the *Nights* was assumed to be so common that virtually any traveller's or journalist's account of the Middle East referenced the *Nights* as shorthand for that which he/she was witnessing, or, more likely, imagining. Though of ancient origin, the *Nights* was assumed to mirror a still existing present (part of the timelessness ascribed to the East). For example, in reporting on the Fahmy trial the *People* commented: 'Some of the revelations ... were suggestive of the fanciful romance of the Arabian Nights', while the *Empire News* claimed that Fahmy's palace was 'an Aladdin's palace glittering with priceless jewels'.[155] And Mme Fahmy, in the five part instalment of her 'own story' in the *Illustrated Sunday Herald*, referred on three separate occasions to her life with her Egyptian husband being 'such as one reads of in the *Thousand and One Nights*'.[156]

It was not simply press reports of the trial which drew inter-textually upon literary referents; as we have seen, Marshall Hall, as an evocation of the East, mobilised the fictional work of Robert Hichens. Hichens' 'romance' is primarily with the landscape, with the desert as the central love object, the site of symbolic freedom and spiritual quest, and such a romance was often at the heart of much travel writing, including work by women.[157] In romances of the desert, whether fictional or supposedly factual, this representation of the desert as the site of freedom of movement often overlapped with a fantasy figure of the Oriental male. On the one hand, the Oriental male was the object of homoerotic romance, recently fuelled by reports of T.E. Lawrence ('Lawrence of Arabia') and his Arab associates.[158] They were depicted as traditional, primitive, but courageous fighters and above all, sexually uninhibited.[159] They were the repositories of the escapist sexual fantasies of European homosexual men, such as the socialist Edward Carpenter and the novelist E.M. Forster, who journeyed to the East in search of the liberatory 'other', freed from Western sexual taboos.[160] On the other hand, and more pertinent for this discussion, there was the Oriental male of heterosexual romance, which in the early twentieth century took the form of the new sub-genre developed for the female reader, the 'desert romance'.[161]

Hichens' *The Garden of Allah*, published in 1904, is cited as the first novel in this new sub-genre; the book ran into five editions within its first few months, forty-three editions by 1929, and was filmed three times, firstly in 1917.[162] Hichens introduces the theme of the Englishwoman striking out into the desert, or the forbidden casbah (the male Arab quarter), but it is only with the desert romances written by women that a heroic Oriental male becomes the main object of desire. As historian Billie Melman points out, the desert romance novel was part of an enormous body of erotic literature (condemned as 'pornocracy' by *Sunday Express* editor James Douglas) written largely by women for women that blossomed in this period.[163] The demand for such literature related not simply to the increased spending power and leisure of many young women across class, but also to women's frustrations with, and the wartime throwing aside of, restrictions on their actions and their sexuality. The appeal of desert romances also related to a degree of disillusionment with British masculinity. Faced with a shortage of young men after the carnage of the war, and with many of the men who had survived suffering mentally if not physically, the soldier hero of much wartime romantic fiction was superseded by an alternative masculinity, that of the Arab sheik – highly potent as opposed to emasculated.[164] And Britain as a location was replaced by the exotic East, an imaginary timeless, stateless zone. But rather than some vague portrayal of the Orient, the novelists, in their keenness to convey scenic authenticity, commit to realism in their precise detailing of the environment, even while their human portrayals are wholly imaginary.

The desert romance Oriental hero, the Sheik (a term that entered popular parlance at the same time as the flapper), is typically handsome, rich, educated, meticulously clean, priapic, domineering and brutal (just the right balance of the civilised and the barbaric). Further, he is a law unto himself. The heroine falls for all these qualities, surrendering herself finally to her seduction, even her rape, thereby permitting sexual response, indeed sexual pleasure (and the *right* to such pleasure), without the burden of responsibility. There is an analogy between the exploration of unknown places and the heroine's discovery of her suppressed sexuality. The fact that the heroine frequently moves with speed across the desert on horseback conveys an additional metaphor of freedom and sexual liberation.[165] The heroine's sexual inquisitiveness and her new awareness of her sexuality (in the first instance thrust upon her by the hero's penetrating gaze) also mark her entry into full womanhood.[166] In the process (and this is formulaic to romantic fiction generally) the hero is 'civilised': transformed from brute to caring lover. While he gains the capacity for tenderness, she gains the capacity for passion.[167] But what of course is specific to most of the desert romances, and potentially so threatening to white men, is that the object of the heroine's desires and fantasies is deemed racially 'other'.

The women spectators at the Fahmy trial are likely to have been familiar with at least some of this literature. The best known of such women novelists were Kathlyn Rhodes, Joan Conquest and E.M. Hull. Rhodes' books included *Will of Allah* (1908), *Desert Dreamers* (1909), The *Lure of the Desert* (1911) (serialised in *Girls' Own Stories* in 1921), and *Under Desert Stars* (1921). In summer 1922 her 'specially written' *Desert Lovers* was serialised daily in the *Daily Sketch*. However it was E.M. Hull's 1919 *The Sheik*, contemptuously and snobbishly termed 'a typists' day-dream' by literary critic Queenie Leavis, which was *the* best-seller of the day, and had gone through 103 editions by the time of the Fahmy trial.[168] When H.V. Morton went to Biskra, Algeria in January 1924 to report for the *Daily Express* on what he termed 'the Garden of Allah', such was the emblematic status of *The Sheik* that he conveyed his intentions thus: 'I want sheiks. I want the real Edith M. Hull stuff.'[169]

E.M. Hull, the pseudonym of Edith Maud Winstanley, who apparently lived a quiet life married to a Derbyshire gentleman pig farmer, wrote a number of other desert romances including *The Shadow of the East* (1921), *The Desert Healer* (1923), *Sons of the Sheik* (1925) (which like *The Sheik* was made into a film) and *The Lion Tamer* (1928). None was anything like as successful as her debut, indeed they were all emblazoned with the by-line:

11 Rudolph Valentino as the Sheik

'by the author of *The Sheik*'. The 1921 Hollywood film of *The Sheik* starring Italian Rudolph Valentino opened in London in January 1923.[170] In the next few months it was a key topic of conversation. In June the satirical magazine *Punch* carried a cartoon portraying a balding, middle-aged, bespectacled city gent sitting at the dinner table about to be served something by his mild-looking wife. He is leaning forward in a paroxysm of fury, thumping his fist on the table: 'Great heavens, Amelia! Not a date pudding again! What do you take me for? A sheik?'[171] The joke of course lies in the idea that anyone could possibly mistake such a man for a handsome sheik. By July the film had been shown at over a thousand cinemas around the country.[172] But rather than portraying Hull's Sheik as highly masculine, Valentino's Ahmed Ben Hassan is remarkably effeminate in his dress and heavy eye make-up (referred to by literary critic Karen Chow as a 'foppish sheik').[173] It is Ahmed/Valentino, rather than the heroine, Diana/actress Agnes Ayres, who is the filmic object of the gaze – predominantly a *female* gaze, for this is a film addressing a female spectator and is part of the growing leisure market for women. Valentino does however follow the book's plot-line in forcefully asserting his will over the wilting Diana, thereby managing to combine virility with effeminacy.[174] The film resulted in an outburst of 'sheik mania' with women fainting in cinema aisles, and buying 'Arab'

"GREAT HEAVENS, AMELIA! NOT A DATE PUDDING AGAIN? WHAT DO YOU TAKE ME FOR? A SHEIK?

12 *Punch*, 27th June 1923

fashions and motifs.[175] 'Shriek for the Sheik', the placards read in the USA (but the rhyming did not work in Britain, where 'sheik' was pronounced 'shake'). The song 'The Sheik of Araby' was written in response to the film and became a jazz hit in both the USA and Britain.[176] The film made Valentino a Hollywood 'heart-throb'. When he married (for the second time) in March 1923, it was front-page news for the popular British dailies.[177] When in 1926 he died suddenly of peritonitis aged thirty-one, hundreds of thousands lined the streets of New York to watch his coffin pass by.[178] Beverley Nichols equated women's interest in Valentino with their interest in the Thompson trial: 'Valentino strode through reel after reel, hurling women about as though they were sacks of potatoes, snarling at them, smacking them on the bottom. The women of the twenties lapped it all up ... perhaps they were experiencing the same masochistic excitement which they had found in the case of Edith Thompson.'[179]

Although desert romances increasingly depicted the hero as not wholly or even partly of Arab descent – the most famous example, then and now, being the above mentioned Sheik Ahmed, who is revealed late in the book to be the son of a Spanish woman and an English aristocrat – some of the heroes of the novels are 'pure blood' Arabs. Joan Conquest's best-selling 1920 *Desert Love* for example, set in Egypt, has as her hero Hahmed, Camel King (the novel has much to say about camels) who wins the heart and hand of seventeen-year-old Englishwoman Jill Carden, a classic desert romance heroine: young, beautiful, with red-gold hair and blue eyes, independent and wealthy, but sexually inexperienced (in *The Sheik* the heroine is represented similarly, with overtones of the boyish flapper). Jill's idea of love is 'utter submission to the man she should love'. Hahmed is a powerful and civilised Arab, over 6ft tall, with 'thick virile hair' and dressed 'in spotless white robes sweeping to his feet', who has spent many years in England, but still insists on women's absolute submission. He kills easily, anyone or anything that displeases him, and when aged fourteen had strangled the young female lover of his eleven-year-old betrothed, and supported the latter's stoning to death. The narrative shocks Jill, but it does not lessen her adoration, and the book ends with her giving birth to his child in the desert.[180] Melman suggests that Conquest's novels are parodies of the genre. Be that as it may, she is the only desert romance writer acknowledged positively by literary magazines, the *Times Literary Supplement* for example, in its review of *Desert Love*'s sequel, *The Hawk of Egypt* (about the son of Jill and Hahmed) praising her 'exceptional power of pouring into her pages the picturesque glamour of Egypt and the desert'.[181] We cannot know for certain the class background of her readers, but the location of this review suggests that many would have been middle- and upper-middle-class – possibly including the 'fashionably dressed' women of the Fahmy trial.

What one cannot fail to note are some of the obvious parallels between the classic desert romance narrative and that of the Fahmys. Like the typical desert romance heroine, Marguerite was a beautiful European woman who was independent and rich (although not born into wealth, she was already wealthy on meeting Fahmy, from money gained from her various rich lovers). Like the fictitious heroine, once she was under the spell of the Oriental male, she was violated and locked up, unable to escape. Ali Fahmy likewise met many of the criteria of the desert romance hero. Photographs showed him as handsome, he was very rich, educated (he spoke French and English as well as Arabic and Turkish), brutal and sexually rapacious (although not in the manner appropriate to a fictitious hero). *The Sheik's* heroine, Diana, realises that Ahmed is 'a brute, but she loved him, loved him for his very brutality', and like Fahmy, he is referred to as an 'Oriental beast'.[182] Fahmy inspired complete loyalty from servants, and had written of being engaged in 'training' the Western woman into submission, another trope of the desert romance novel, in which analogy is made to the breaking-in of a horse.[183] A letter from him to her read out in court displayed great devotion, she described his pursuit of her as 'ardent a wooing as any woman ever experienced', and she herself during the trial said that she had not hated him, 'only what he wanted me to do', and that on the contrary, she had loved him.[184] In all these ways then, the story of the Fahmys could be read as a desert romance. There were of course important differences. They had lived together in great grandeur, in palaces and on yachts, rather than simply and in the desert, which was a hallmark of the classic desert romance. She had not managed to civilise her husband out of his brutality. She was older than him by ten years (something else that the prosecution counsel could have made much of, had he chosen to) and she most definitely was not sexually inexperienced. Most significant of all, once she was confined and violated ('violation' was her version of the events; we cannot know to what degree their sex was consensual, although the evidence does appear to support her version), she did not submit, but rebelled and killed. The Fahmy narrative was thus open to different readings. It could be read as a cautionary tale of the dangers of inter-racial marriage; it could be read as signifying the awfulness of the Orient: the violence, despotism, sexual perversity, one-sided divorce, the seclusion of women; or it could be read as a desert romance, which although manifesting all the above ingredients, was also a story of mystery, exoticism, and women's sexual pleasure and desire. In all three readings, gender and race were bound together, and in each the figure of the white woman was central: as victim of miscegenation, as an implicit referent against which the Eastern woman was compared, and as the heroine in a romantic drama.

Anti-miscegenation

After the Fahmy trial there were many commentators keen to support Marshall Hall's line on the inadvisability of miscegenation. James Douglas, editor of the *Sunday Express*, claimed as 'the lesson of this dreadful trial' that 'East is East and West is West and that never the twain shall meet in marriage.'[185] (He was of course drawing on Rudyard Kipling.) *Illustrated Sunday Herald* wrote likewise: 'it comes back to the "one fatal error", the attempted mingling in matrimonial bonds of East and West'.[186] This simplistic polarisation was drawn on widely. Mme Fahmy herself, in an interview for the *People*, 'pointed out the folly of marriage between East and West', and her five-part account of her 'own story' for the *Illustrated Sunday Herald* opens with the statement: 'Underlying all is the ever-recurring theme of the fundamental difference between East and West.'[187] The *Daily Mirror* editorial, taking the 'moral of the [Fahmy] case' as 'the undesirability of the marriages which unite Oriental husbands to European wives', was explicit in its allocation of blame:

> Too many of our women novelists, apparently under the spell of the East, have encouraged the belief that there is something specially romantic in such unions. They are not romantic, they are ridiculous and unseemly; and the sensational revelations of the trial … will not be without their use if they bring that fact home to the sentimental, unsophisticated girl.[188]

Thus commentary on the trial became a vehicle for attacking not only miscegenation, but also women's production and consumption of certain kinds of popular culture. The press media were blatantly contradictory: they condemned desert romance novels and their misleading, enticing fantasies, but they simultaneously serialised these very novels.[189]

It would be wrong however to assume that the majority of female desert romance novelists were in favour of miscegenation. As already pointed out, in many desert romances the hero is not wholly or even partly of Arab descent, including in Hull's *The Sheik*, and inter-racial relationships are often presented as undesirable, with 'natives' frequently described as dirty and animal-like. What strikes Hull's heroine as so odd about the Sheik, until his 'true' heritage is revealed, is that he is so clean and spotless, compared to the filthy, slovenly Arabs surrounding him. If Joan Conquest and a few other desert romance novelists present a 'real' Arab hero, the majority attempt to have their cake and eat it, depicting a passionate, wild and virile 'Eastern' man who is in truth partly or wholly of good British 'stock'.

Some desert romance novelists went out of their way to condemn 'marriages which unite Oriental husbands to European wives'. The well-known traveller writer and desert romance novelist Lady Dorothy Mills, although photographed in the *Daily Express* in 1922 in 'Southern Tunisian costume', and described in her obituary as having 'her heart always in the Sahara', nevertheless responded negatively to an announcement in 1927 that an English girl guide had married an Arab sheik and had gone to live with him in the desert.[190] Despite claiming that 'flapper hearts all over England have fluttered at the news', the *Daily Express* quoted Mills's baleful prediction: 'The odds are against such a marriage being happy'. She explained:

> The life of a white woman married to an Arab is not enviable. She will have to be veiled all the time … if she displeases her husband … he will probably knife her. When he tires of her he just says two words in front of an Arab lawyer, and she is divorced … then as she grows older and her looks leave her he is sure to take other wives. She leads an extremely confined life.[191]

In her desert romance *The Tent of Blue*, published in 1922, with a second popular edition two years later, the hero is not an 'Oriental', but an Englishman who, like the English heroine, adores the desert and its sense of freedom. He might have the heart of an Arab, but he has the mind and body of an honest, clean-limbed Anglo-Saxon.

Although the press frequently condemned inter-racial relationships (including those witnessed in British ports, as seen in Chapter 2), its reportage of certain liaisons between English women and upper-class Egyptian men was, on occasion, relatively neutral. The Sunday paper the *People* in 1921 for example cited two such cases. One was the announcement of the forthcoming marriage of thirty-three year old bachelor Prince Mohammed Mahmoud, brother of the ex-Khedive of Egypt and nephew of the present Egyptian ruler (King Fuad), to Mrs Evelyn Ellis, in a London registry office. Readers were assured that he 'has lived principally in England, where he was educated' and that he was 'very tall' and 'thoroughly European in appearance'.[192] In other words, no diminutive, ill-educated Arab in bizarre, effeminate clothes, but a prince who was virtually an English gentleman. The second citing was of another Egyptian prince, Ibrahim Said Fazil, as co-respondent in an English divorce suit. He was described as 'at present a cadet in the Army' and 'an old Brightonian' (an alumni of Brighton College, a public school.)[193] *Reynolds's Newspaper* had a photograph of him in a bowler hat.[194]

But if the thoroughly Westernised royal Egyptian man was potentially acceptable as the husband of a Western woman (although note that
the two women mentioned were both divorcées/about to be divorcées and
thus seen as 'soiled') his acceptability vanished once he over-stepped certain limits. Race might have been temporarily marginalised or trumped
by class, but such marginalisation was always conditional. In the case
of Ali Fahmy, it was not the fact of his violence alone, for British courts
regularly discounted the seriousness of men's brutality against wives and
partners.[195] Ali Fahmy's actions may have been indefensible, but the odds
stacked against him went much deeper than anything relating to his actual
behaviour. His violence was seen as exceptional and unacceptable because
it transgressed certain taboos: it was perpetrated by an Oriental man on an
Occidental woman, and it was combined with sexual perversity. Percival
Clarke's half-hearted attempts to prosecute were surely due precisely to his
subscribing to such a view.

From the early nineteenth century until the end of the Second World
War, Britain and France dominated the Orient. The three geographical do-
mains were 'represented' in the trial: Britain by the legal counsel, France by
the defendant, and the Orient by the dead Egyptian husband. In practice,
differences between Britain and France were submerged, and the defendant was taken as emblematic of 'Western Womanhood', standing against
the brutality of the East. Marguerite's undesirable past – once an unwed,
underage mother, once a prostitute – was concealed, replaced by that of
the pathetic and terrorised victim of the Oriental male. She was aided and
abetted by cultural fears – of the 'otherness' of the East, of sexual perversity, of miscegenation. In contrast, the Western women who appeared on
the other side of the dock, in the audience, were vilified for their seeking
of sensation, their desire for pleasure, their interest in Oriental romance,
their Schadenfreude. The trial and the commentary surrounding it became
a vehicle for the critique not simply of the East and its treatment of women,
but also of the modern Western women's search for sexual and sensational
pleasures, fictional or otherwise. Cultural modernity, in the form of new
fiction and new cinema for women, was as much a concern as the imaginary racially 'other' priapic Arab sheik; indeed the latter figured significantly in the former. With the appearance of the said sheik in the flesh, or
rather on the mortuary slab, distinctions between fact and fiction blurred,
as the modern woman in effect extended her dangerous pleasure to the
realm of the courtroom.

Notes

1 Meyrick, *Secrets of the 43*, p. 81.

2 *Daily Mail*, 10th September 1923, p. 7.

3 In Egypt he would have been known as Ali Bey, for the title was used only with first names, not family names. The British press did not appear to know this.

4 *The Times*, 11th September 1923, p. 7.

5 Apparently his full inheritance from his deceased mother was conditional on his marrying a Muslim, and Marguerite reluctantly consented to renouncing her Catholicism for Islam, taking the name of Munira, his mother's name. *Daily Mirror*, 11th September, 1923, p. 2.

6 See Arnold Bennett *Imperial Palace, Vol. 1 and 2* (London, 1930), for a fictional celebration of the Savoy hotel. The Savoy had been built in 1889 by Richard D'Oyly Carte, the impresario behind Gilbert and Sullivan.

7 The play was being performed at Daly's Theatre, Cranbourne Street.

8 "'For over two hours the sky was illuminated by brilliant, continuous flashes … Equally dramatic were the heavy clashes of thunder'". *Daily Telegraph*, 10th July 1923, quoted in Edward Marjoribanks, *The Life of Sir Edward Marshall Hall* (London, 1929), p. 433. And see *Illustrated Sunday Herald*, 16th September 1923, p. 5: 'It seemed … as though the elements themselves conspired to give the last act of the actual drama a setting of primitive intensity.'

9 Sir Edward Marshall Hall, quoted in *Daily Mirror*, 12th September 1923, p. 2.

10 *The Times*, 17th September 1923, p. 6.

11 *Daily Chronicle*, 17th September 1923, p. 1.

12 *Illustrated Sunday Herald*, 15th July 1923, p. 5.

13 The inquest was held at Westminster Coroner's Court on 12th July under Samuel Ingleby Oddie, the coroner who had presided over Billie Carleton's inquest. The Bow Street police court hearing was held on 10th, 18th and 21st July.

14 *People*, 15th July 1923, p. 7.

15 *Daily Chronicle*, 11th September 1923, p. 1; *Daily Sketch*, 12th September 1923, p. 2; and see *Daily Express*, 11th September 1923, p. 1.

16 *Sunday Express*, 9th September 1923, p. 3.

17 The inclusion was one provision of the Sex Discrimination (Removal) Act, 1919. See Anne Logan, *Feminism and Criminal Justice: a Historical Perspective* (London, 2008), p. 87.

18 See Helena Normanton, *Everyday Law for Women* (London, 1932), and Hall, *Outspoken Women*, pp. 171, 191 for two extracts from Normanton's book.

19 *Daily Express*, 11th September 1923, p. 1. And see *Daily Chronicle*, 15th September 1923, p. 5.

20 *Sunday Express*, 16th September 1923, p. 1.

21 See Montgomery Hyde, *The Trials of Oscar Wilde*. Clarke refused a fee for his defence of Wilde in his second and third trials. Marshall Hall was paid 652 guineas for the Fahmy case, one of the highest fees he had ever earned at the Bar. Marjoribanks, *Life of Sir Edward Marshall Hall*, p. 435.

22 Marjoribanks, *Life of Sir Edward Marshall Hall*.

23 See Edward Grice, *Great Cases of Sir Henry Curtis-Bennett* (London, 1937), pp. 56–8 for discussion of the Fahmy case.

24 His palace's interior was apparently a copy of Fontainebleau. *Illustrated Sunday Herald*,

30th September 1923, p. 5.

25 *Evening News*, 10th September 1923, p. 1.

26 *The Times*, 11th September 1923, p. 7.

27 Today (as a result of feminist campaigning) the defence of provocation has been to some extent redefined to allow for the situation of 'battered women' who kill their abusers even when not under immediate threat. From the evidence there is a case to be made that Mme Fahmy fell into such a category. Thanks to Judy Greenway for pointing this out.

28 *Evening News*, 10th September 1923, p. 5. *The Times* did not mention the dog incident.

29 *Evening News*, 10th September 1923, pp. 1, 5.

30 *Daily Chronicle*, 11th September 1923, p. 1; and see *Evening News*, 10th September 1923, p. 1.

31 *Daily Express*, 11th September 1923, p. 1.

32 'Sir Edward Marshall Hall for four hours directed the full battery of his forensic skill on the dead man's secretary.' *Daily Express*, 11th September 1923, p. 1.

33 Fahmy to Yvonne Alibert, 18th January 1923, PRO CRIM 1/247, National Archives.

34 Marshall Hall added further to Enani's discrediting by producing a large coloured cartoon from an Egyptian weekly entitled 'the Light, the Shadow, and the Shadow of the Shadow'. It depicted line drawings of three men in profile: Fahmy, Enani, and his own 'shadow'/secretary, with the letter press describing Enani as 'the Evil Genius of Fahmy.' *Daily Chronicle*, 11th September 1923, p. 1; *Daily Express*, 11th September 1923, p. 1; *Daily Mail*, 11th September 1923, p. 4.

35 See Marjoribanks, *Life of Sir Edward Marshall Hall*, p. 438.

36 Thanks to Caroline Derry and Nigel Richardson for their legal advice.

37 Marshall Hall had access to information about Enani that revealed the man's own violent disposition. A former detective in Egypt informed Mme Fahmy's Egyptian lawyer that in 1918 Enani had 'brutally' beaten both Dolly, an English music hall artist whom he had married, and Fanny, his Italian mistress. Further, he had acted as his employer's pimp'. DPP1/74, letter to Freke Palmer, solicitor, send Maitre Assouad: statement from Selim Nakhla, 17th August 1923.

38 *Evening News*, 11th September 1923, p. 1.

39 *The Times*, 12th September 1923, p. 7.

40 *Daily Chronicle*, 12th September, p. 1.

41 *The Times*, 12th September 1923, p. 7. There appears to have been no attempt to trace the author of this anonymous letter, or to question how the author might have known of Mme Fahmy's arrival at the hotel.

42 *Daily Express*, 12th September 1923, p. 1; *The Times*, 12 September 1923, p. 7.

43 Although the term 'sexual perversity' was not reported as being used during the trial, the term was not anachronistic, having been deployed, as we have seen, in the 1918 Maud Allan libel trial.

44 *Evening News*, 11th September 1923, p. 1.

45 *The Times*, 12th September 1923, p. 7. And see *Daily Mirror*, 12th September 1923, p. 2, 'Poison Hidden in Flowers'.

46 *Daily Express*, 12th September 1923, p. 8.

47 For example, *Daily Sketch*, 12th September 1923, p. 2: 'much that he [Marshall Hall] indicated could not be printed.' There was censorship in court as well, according to the *People*, 16th September 1923, p. 7: 'the actual details of his [Fahmy's] conduct was too sordid and disgusting to be minutely described even in court'.

48 Deposition of Dr Gordon, 10th July 1923, DPP1/74; deposition of Dr Henri Leu, 17th August 1923, DPP1/74; depositions of Dr Gordon and Dr Morton, PRO CRIM 1/247, National Archives.

49 *The Times*, 12th September 1923, p. 7; also in *Daily Mirror*, 12th September 1923, pp. 2, 15 and *Daily Mail*, 12th September 1923, p. 6. Most newspapers did not mention the words 'sadism' or 'sadist' however.

50 *The Times*, 12th September 1923, p. 7. Similar wording in all the papers.

51 *Daily Express*, 12th September 1923, p. 8.

52 *The Times*, 13th September 1923, p. 7.

53 *The Times*, 13th September 1923, p. 7.

54 *Evening News*, 12th September 1923, p. 1.

55 DPP1/74, National Archives.

56 The account is confusing: a report to the Metropolitan Police Superintendent of 23rd September 1923, sent by A. Grosse, DD Inspector, relates that through the French police they had learnt that Marguerite had married Laurent in Venice in 1919. She claims to have divorced him in 1920, disagreeing with his insistence on going to Japan to live. But a report sent on 1st September 1923 states that there is no record of any marriage or divorce, and that Laurent was killed in the Great War! DPP1/74, National Archives.

57 DPP1/74, National Archives.

58 According to the press, the judge noted that 'although he thought there was going to be an attack on the character of Said Enani ... there was really none.' *Evening News*, 12th September 1923, p. 1. It seems he was deaf to what appears, to today's reader at least, as a clear attack.

59 DPP to Craigen, 23rd August 1923, DPP1/74.

60 Craigen to DPP, 31st August 1923, DPP1/74.

61 See for example *Evening News*, 10th September 1923, p. 1; *Daily Sketch*, 11th September 1923, p. 1 and 15th September 1923, p. 1.

62 Marjoribanks, *Life of Sir Edward Marshall Hall*, p. 442, *Evening News*, 13th September 1923, p. 1; *The Times*, 14th September 1923, p. 7.

63 Marjoribanks, *Life of Sir Edward Marshall Hall*, pp. 442–3.

64 See Sara L. Kimble, 'No right to Judge: Feminism and the Judiciary in 3rd Republic France', *French Historical Studies*, 31, 4 (2008), pp. 609–41.

65 Andrew Rose, *Scandal at the Savoy* (London, 1991), p. 165.

66 *Daily Chronicle*, 13th September 1923, p. 1.

67 *The Times*, 13th September 1923, p. 7.

68 *Daily Mirror*, 14th September 1923, p. 2; *Daily Chronicle*, 13th September 1923, p. 1; *Daily Sketch*, 13th September 1923, p. 1. What would of course have horrified the British public was the thought of a *white* woman's nakedness open to the gaze of a black man, or indeed an Oriental.

69 *Daily Mirror*, 12th September 1923, p. 2. On Islam's black slaves, see Ronald Segal, *Islam's Black Slaves: A History of Africa's Other Black Diaspora* (London, 2002); Diane Robinson-Dunn, *The Harem, Slavery and British Imperial Culture* (Manchester, 2006).

70 *Daily Sketch*, 13th September 1923, p. 2.

71 *Daily Chronicle*, 12th September 1923, p. 1.

72 Joseph Boone, 'Vacation Cruises; of the Homoerotics of Orientalism', *PMLA*, 110 (1993), p. 93.

73 See Walkowitz, *City of Dreadful* passim for a discussion of the use of melodrama.

74 *Daily Mirror*, 15th September 1923, p. 2.

75 *Daily Express*, 12th September 1923, p. 8.

76 *Reynolds's News*, 16th September 1923, p. 7

77 *Empire News*, 16th September 1923, p. 5.

78 See Elizabeth Wilson, *Adorned in Dreams: Fashion and Modernity* (London, 1985, 2005). On the relation of French fashion to France's colonies, see Michelle Tolini Finamore, 'Fashioning the Colonial at the Paris Expositions, 1925 and 1931', *Fashion Theory*, 7, 3/4 (2003), pp. 345–60.

79 See Bingham, *Gender, Modernity, and the Popular Press*, Chapter 5; Horwood, *Keeping up Appearances*.

80 See *Daily Mail*, 10th September 1923, p. 7; *Daily Mail*, 12th September 1923, back page; *Daily Chronicle*, 12th September 1923, p. 1; *Sunday Chronicle*, 16th September 1923, p. 6.

81 As Raphael Samuel has noted, France was 'represented as a moral pit, a place of sexual adventure and infidelity'. Raphael Samuel, 'Introduction: The Figures of a National Myth', in R. Samuel (ed.), *Patriotism: the Making and Unmaking of British National Identity, Vol. III, National Fictions* (London, 1989), p. xxv. See R. and I. Tombs, *That Sweet Enemy: the French and British: from the Sun King to the Present* (London, 2006); Oram, *Her Husband was a Woman!*, pp. 90–1; Stefan Slater, 'Pimps, Police and Filles de Joie: Foreign Prostitution in Interwar London', *The London Journal*, 1 (2007): 'everything French had become metonymic for sex' (p. 60), and some non-French prostitutes would adopt French sobriquets: it was widely held that French prostitutes were willing to cater for 'more exotic sexual tastes' (p. 63).

82 *Daily Chronicle*, 13th September 1923, p. 9.

83 *Daily Chronicle*, 13th September 1923, p. 9.

84 *Daily Chronicle*, 13th September 1923, p. 9.

85 Macdonald Hastings, *The Other Mr Churchill*, 1963, quoted in Rose, *Scandal at the Savoy*, p. 145.

86 See Nina Warner Hooke and Gil Thomas, *Marshall Hall: a Biography* (London, 1966), p. 224.

87 *Daily Mirror*, 14th September, 1923, p. 2.

88 *The Times*, 14th September 1923, p. 7; *Daily Chronicle*, 14th September 1923, p. 1.

89 See *Weekly Dispatch*, 16th July 1922, p. 6; *World's Pictorial News*, 25th November 1922, p. 12; *People*, 25th November 1922, p. 3, 3rd June 1923, p. 4, 10th June 1923, p. 7; *Illustrated Sunday Herald*, 12th August 1923, p. 8.

90 *The Times*, 14th September 1923, p. 7.

91 Sumner Holmes, 'The Double Standard in the English Divorce Laws'. Egyptian feminist groups were trying to restrict polygamy and male access to divorce, but without success. Leila Ahmed, *Women and Gender in Islam* (New Haven, CT, 1992), p. 175.

92 *Daily Chronicle*, 14th September 1923, p. 10.

93 Leila Ahmed, 'Western Ethnocentrism and perceptions of the Harem', *Feminist Studies*, 8 (1982).

94 Tim Mitchell, *Colonising Egypt* (Cambridge, 1988), pp. 111–13.

95 Ahmed, *Women and Gender in Islam*, Chapter 9; Beth Baron, *The Women's Awakening in Egypt* (New Haven, CT, 1994); Margaret Badran, *Feminists, Islam, and Nation* (Princeton, NJ, 1995), Parts 1 and 2.

96 *Evening News*, 14th September 1923, p. 1; *Daily Sketch*, 15th September 1923, p. 5.

97 *Daily Sketch*, 15th September 1923, p. 5. *People*, 16th September 1923, p. 7 also saw a likeness

to 'Grand Guignol horrors'.

98 Marjoribanks, *Life of Sir Edward Marshall Hall*, p. 444.

99 *Bella Donna* was written in 1909, with a popular version appearing in 1911; it was reprinted many times. It was Hichens' best known work, although his *The Garden of Allah* (1904) was also a huge success.

100 Robert Hichens, *Bella Donna* (London, 1909, 1911), p. 188.

101 *Empire News*, 23rd September 1923, p. 8.

102 *Daily Mirror*, 15th September 1923, p. 15; similar versions of this speech in *Evening News*, *Daily Sketch*, *Daily Express* and *Daily Chronicle*.

103 The *Daily Sketch* took up the sun analogy: 'All day long the sun streamed in and out of the glazed roofing of the court, symbolising the alternate spasms of despair and hope shaking the woman in the dock.' *Daily Sketch*, 15th September 1923, p. 5.

104 *Daily Chronicle*, 14th September 1923, p. 10; and see the *People*, 16th September 1923, p. 7.

105 *The Times*, 14th September 1923, p. 7; there are similar versions of this statement in many other newspapers.

106 *Daily Mirror*, 15th September 1923, p. 15.

107 *Evening News*, 15th September 1923, p. 1; *Daily Express*, 15th September 1923, p. 5.

108 *Daily Mirror*, 15th September 1923, p. 15.

109 *Daily Chronicle*, 17th September 1923, p. 2.

110 *The Times*, 15th September 1923, p. 5.

111 *The Times*, 17th September 1923, p. 6; *Evening News*, 15th September 1923, p. 1. In March 1923 Huda Sha'rawi had founded the Egyptian Feminist Union in an attempt to tackle women's various grievances, including their lack of suffrage. Ahmed, *Women and Gender in Islam*, p. 176.

112 *Daily Chronicle*, 17th September 1923, p. 2.

113 *Daily Chronicle*, 18th September 1923, p. 1, *Manchester Guardian*, 18th September 1923, p. 14. The *Daily Chronicle* editorial conceded that there were 'some grounds to the Egyptian protest ... The Mohammedan laws of marriage and of the treatment of women are different from our own, but they are based upon strict ethical principles'. It referred however to 'the retarded civilisation of most parts of the Orient'. *Daily Chronicle*, 18th September 1923, p. 6.

114 Quoted in Yunan Labib Rizk, 'Warped Justice', *Al-Ahran Weekly*, 479 (27th April–3rd May 2000).

115 Shani D'Cruze, Sandra Walklate and Samantha Pegg, *Murder: Social and Historical Approaches to Understanding Murder and Murderers* (Collompton, 2006), p. 4.

116 Robb and Erber (eds), *Disorder in the Court*, p. 4. On French trials see Ruth Harris, *Murders and Madness: Medicine, Law, and Society in the Fin de Siecle* (Oxford, 1989); Shapiro, 'Stories More Terrifying than the Truth Itself'.

117 *Illustrated Sunday Herald*, 16th September 1923, p. 3.

118 Anette Ballinger, 'The Guilt of the Innocent and the Innocence of the Guilty: the Cases of Marie Fahmy and Ruth Ellis', in Alice Myers and Sarah Wright (eds), *No Angels: Women who Commit Violence* (London, 1996).

119 The occasional newspaper however realised that she had been a force to be reckoned with, before being 'subdued' by her husband. For example, *Illustrated Sunday Herald*, 16th September 1923, p. 5: 'She is, indeed, the exact antithesis to the clinging, fairylike embodiment of sweet simplicity'.

120 Edward Said, *Orientalism* (London, 1978, 1991).

121 See Rana Kabbani, *Europe's Myth of Orient* (London, 1986); John M. McKenzie, *Orientalism: History, Theory and the Arts* (Manchester, 1995).

122 See Hobsbawn, *Age of Extremes*.

123 See R.L. Tignor, *Modernism and British Colonial Rule in Egypt, 1882–1914* (Princeton, NJ, 1966); John Darwin, *Britain, Egypt and the Middle East* (London, 1981). Another Fahmy – Abdel Rahman Bay Fahmy – along with twenty-eight others, was accused of plotting to kill Lord Allenby in July 1920. Marshall Hall was invited to defend him out in Cairo. *Manchester Guardian*, 29th July 1920.

124 *People*, 18th Febuary 1923, p. 1.

125 *People*, 8th April 1923, p. 4.

126 Nicholas Reeves, *The Complete Tutankhamun* (London, 1990), p. 63. Rider Haggard however felt such speculation about magic was 'dangerous nonsense'.

127 Reeves, *The Complete Tutankhamun*, p. 63.

128 For example see *Empire News*, 1st July 1923, p. 1.

129 Letter from Ali Fahmy to his wife's sister 16 March 1923: PRO: CRIM 1/247. On the theory that Fahmy died from the curse of Tutankhamen, see Mark Beynon, *London's Curse: Murder, Black Magic and Tutankhamun in the 1920s West End* (Stroud, 2011), Chapter 3.

130 *Sunday Express*, 16th September 1923, p. 5.

131 Susan D. Cowie and Tom Johnson, *The Mummy in Fact, Fiction and Film* (London, 2002), p. 157.

132 See Montgomery Hyde (ed.), *The Trials of Oscar Wilde*; Alan Sinfield, *The Wilde Century* (London, 1994); Matt Cook, *London and the Culture of Homosexuality, 1885–1914* (Cambridge, 2003).

133 Cynthia Herrup, *A House in Gross Disorder: Sex, Law and the 2nd Earl of Castlehaven* (Oxford, 1999).

134 Magnus Hirschfeld, *Racism* (London, 1938) quoted in Lucy Bland and Laura Doan (eds), *Sexology Uncensored: the Documents of Sexual Science* (Oxford, 1998), p. 228.

135 Rudi C. Bleys, *The Geography of Perversion* (London, 1996), p. 163.

136 Burton in his terminal essay to *The Arabian Nights Entertainments*, quoted in Boone, 'Vacation Cruises', p. 93.

137 Quoted in Boone, 'Vacation Cruises', p. 93. And see Mark Harrison, 'The British Army and the Problems of Venereal Diseases in France and Egypt during the First World War', *Medical History*, 39 (1995), p. 149.

138 Quoted in Boone, 'Vacation Cruises', p. 94. As Boone points out, if the figure of the effeminate Asiatic is one side of the Orientalist fantasy of men, the other is of the ultra virile, hugely endowed sheik. The representation of the highly sexed, sodomistic Oriental male also featured in nineteenth-century pornography, for example *The Lustful Turk* of 1828. See S. Marcus, *The Other Victorians* (London, 1964), pp. 197–203.

139 *Daily Chronicle*, 13th September 1923, p. 1; *Evening News*, 12th September 1923, p. 1.

140 *Daily Express*, 11th September 1923 , p. 1.

141 *Evening News*, 15th September 1923, p. 5.

142 *Daily Express*, 13th September 1923, p. 1. At the beginning of his summing up, the judge, referring to the public gallery, noted: 'These things are horrible; they are disgusting. How anyone could listen to these things who is not bound to listen to them passes comprehension.' *Daily Mirror*, 15th September 1923, p. 2.

143 *Daily Express*, 13th September 1923, p. 4. The article led to two letters of support, *Daily Express*, 15th September 1923.

144 See Dean Rapp, 'The Reception of Freud by the British Press: General Interest and Literary Magazines, 1920–1925', *Journal of the History of Behavioural Sciences*, 24 (1988), pp. 191–201; Mathew Thomson, *Psychological Subjects: Identity, Culture, and Health in Twentieth-Century Britain* (Oxford, 2006), pp. 20–3.

145 See James Clifford, review of *Orientalism* in *History and Theory*, 12, 2 (1980), pp. 204–23; Robert Young, *White Mythologies: Writing History and the Rest* (London, 1990), p. 129; Lisa Lowe, *Colonial Terrains: French and British Orientalisms* (Ithaca, NY, 1991); Dennis Porter, 'Orientalism and its Problems', and Aijaz Ahmed, 'Orientalism and After', in Patrick Williams and Laura Chrisman (eds), *Colonial Discourse and Post-Colonial Theory* (Hemel Hempstead, 1993), pp. 17–22; Kenan Malik, *The Meaning of Race* (London, 1996), p. 227: Ania Loomba, *Colonialism/Postcolonialism* (London and New York, 1998), pp. 48–9. For discussion of how Western women are differently placed in relation to Orientalism, see Billie Melman, *Women's Orients: English Women and the Middle East, 1718–1918* (Ann Arbor, MI, 1992); Lewis, *Gendering Orientalism*.

146 The Egyptian find was however influencing dress fashion, see *Daily Mirror*, 6th January 1923, back page.

147 John Brewer and Roy Porter (eds), *Consumption and the World of Goods* (London, 1993), pp. 133–4; Mackenzie, *Orientalism*, p. 116; Nava, 'The Cosmopolitanism of Commerce and the Allure of Difference'; Mica Nava, *Visceral Cosmopolitanism* (Oxford and New York, 2007), Chapter 2.

148 Wollen, 'Fashion/Orientalism/the Body', pp. 5–33.

149 *People*, 16th September 1923, p. 7.

150 Ahmed, *Women and Gender in Islam*, p. 172. And see 'From Harem Trousers to Paris Frocks', *Illustrated Sunday Herald*, 9th March 1924, p. 6 on how Turkish women were modernising their dress.

151 Joanna de Groot, '"Sex" and "Race": the Construction of Language and Image in the Nineteenth Century', in Susan Mendus and Jane Rendall (eds), *Sexuality and Subordination* (London, 1989); Judy Mabro, *Veiled Half-Truths* (London, 1991); Nadia Wassef, 'On Selective Consumerism: Egyptian Women and Ethnographic Representations', *Feminist Review*, 69 (2001); Joan Scott, *The Politics of the Veil* (Princeton, NJ, 2007).

152 'Hassan': 'a Poetic Arabian Nights Drama', *People*, 23rd September 1923, p. 5. And note 'Tents of Allah': 'a Serious Rival to "The Shiek" [*sic*]', *People*, 20th May 1923, p. 5. *Omar Khayyam* was performed in August 1923, and *The Oriental Impressions* in September 1923. *London Stage* (1920–29), pp. 401, 409.

153 Edward Lane undertook an English translation in 1838–41, with large sections omitted. See Robert Irwin, *The Arabian Nights: A Companion* (London and New York, 1994, 2004); Malcolm C. Lyons with Ursula Lyons, *The Arabian Nights: Tales of 1,001 Nights* (London, 2008). Few British people would have had access to the privately printed sixteen-volume translation of the *Nights* by explorer Richard Burton, which appeared in the 1880s, and whose readership was mainly confined to Orientalist scholars and pornographers. Richard Burton, *Plain and Literal Translation of the Arabian Nights Entertainments* (1919 [1884–86]). See Dane Kennedy, '"Captain Burton's Oriental Muck Heap": The Book of the Thousand Nights and the Uses of Orientalism', *Journal of British Studies*, 39 (July 2000), pp. 317–39.

154 Mabro, *Veiled Half-Truths*, p. 28. For an example of a children's book referencing the *Nights*, see Frances Hodgson Burnett, *A Little Princess* (London, 1905, 1961), p. 156; on pantomime see Witchard, *Thomas Burke's Dark Chinoiserie*, pp. 84–5; for an example

of newspaper articles see H.V. Morton's articles in the *Daily Express*, 23rd January–1st February 1924.

155 *People*, 16th September 1923, p. 7. *Empire News*, 15th July 1923, p. 5. The satirical magazine *Punch* had numerous pictorial and literary references to the *Nights*. See for example *Punch*, 21st January 1921, p. 60; 18th February 1920, p. 121; 12th April 1922; 8th October 1924, pp. 398–9.

156 *Illustrated Sunday Herald*, 30th September 1923, p. 5, and see 7th October 1923, p. 6 and 14th October 1923, p. 6.

157 On travel writings by women see Hsu-Ming Teo, 'Clean Spaces, Dirty Bodies: the Middle Eastern Desert in British Women's Travel Writing, 1890–1914', in Patricia Grimshaw and Diane Kirkby (eds), *Dealing with Difference* (London, 1997). See 'Sahara Secret', *People*, 24th July 1921, p. 10, about a new book by Mrs Rosita Forbes. She complains about how the desert dries your skin and hair, but 'one does not mind … She [the desert] destroys while she enthralls.' While landscape might be glamorised, its very alienness could be seen as sinister. See *Daily Mail*, 14th September 1923, p. 4, where in its commentary on the Fahmy trial, it noted: 'here, in 1923 in the midst of London' the threat of the East might seem unreal, 'but let them think of Egypt, of the long journey up the Nile, into the desert'.

158 His *Seven Pillars of Wisdom* did not appear until 1926, but accounts of his exploits long preceded this autobiography, for example with Lowell Thomas's illustrated lectures at Covent Garden in 1919, and the showing of Thomas's film *With Allenby in Palestine and Lawrence in Arabia*.

159 See Graham Dawson, *Soldier Heroes* (London, 1994), Chapters 6–8.

160 See Jane L. Pinchin, *Alexandria Still: Forster, Durrell, and Cavafy* (Princeton, NJ, 1977); Parminder Kaur Bakshi, 'Homosexuality and Orientalism: Edward Carpenter`s Journey to the East', in Tony Brown (ed.), *Edward Carpenter and Late Victorian Radicalism* (London, 1990); Boone, 'Vacation Cruises'; Robert Aldrich, *Colonialism and Homosexuality* (London and New York, 2003), Chapters 5 and 10.

161 Melman, *Women and the Popular Imagination*, Chapter 6.

162 Mary Cadogan, *And Then Their Hearts Stood Still* (London, 1994), pp. 117–22. The play of the book was appearing at Drury Lane in January 1924. *Daily Express*, 23rd January 1924, p. 5.

163 James Douglas, *Daily Express*, 29th November 1927, quoted in Melman, *Women and the Popular Imagination*, p. 44. The 1920s was the heyday for the desert romantic novel.

164 On men's experiences of the Great War, see references in Chapter 2, note 104. On British men's sexual 'inadequacies' see Lesley A. Hall, *Hidden Anxieties: Male Sexuality, 1900–1950* (Oxford, 1991).

165 Melman, *Women and the Popular Imagination*, pp. 95, 99.

166 See Evelyn Bach, 'Sheik Fantasies: Orientalism and Feminine Desire in the Desert Romance', *Hecate*, 23, 1 (1997), pp. 9–40.

167 On romantic fiction generally see Tanya Modelski, *Loving with A Vengeance* (New York, 1984); Rosalind Coward, 'An Overwhelming Desire' in Coward, *Female Desire*; Jean Radford (ed.), *The Progress of Romance* (London, 1986); Catherine Belsey, 'True Love', in *Women: a Cultural Review*, 3, 2 (1992); Jay Dixon, *The Romantic Fiction of Mills & Boon 1909–1990s* (London, 1999); Lynne Pearce and Jackie Stacey (eds), *Romance Revisited* (London, 1995).

168 Leavis, *Fiction and the Reading Public*, p. 116. E. M. Hull, *The Sheik* (London, 1919, 1996).

D.H. Lawrence disapprovingly saw *The Sheik* as pornography for women. D.H. Lawrence, *Pornography and Obscenity* (London 1929), pp. 12–13. On *The Sheik* see Patricia Raub, 'Issues of Passion and Power, in E.M. Hull, 'The Sheik', *Women's Studies*, 21 (1992), pp. 119–28; Karen Chow, 'Popular Sexual Knowledges and Women's Agency in 1920s England: Marie Stopes's Married Love and E.M. Hull's The Sheik', *Feminist Review*, 63 (1999), pp. 64–87. According to Melman, its sales surpassed 'those of all the contemporary best-sellers lumped together'. Melman, *Women and the Popular Imagination*, p. 90. The term 'best-seller' came into common parlance in the 1920s. *The Sheik* was serialised in *Betty's Paper* in winter 1922.

169 *Daily Express*, 23rd January 1924, p. 5.

170 Valentino had been a paid dancing partner before he began acting – the male equivalent of Freda Kempton. See Emily W. Leider, *Dark Lover: the Life and Death of Rudolph Valentino* (London, 2004), Chapter 3.

171 *Punch*, 27th June 1923, p. 604. And see *Punch*, 13th February 1924, p. 167 and 20th August 1924, pp. 214–15 for more jokes about sheiks.

172 Rose, *Scandal at the Savoy*, p. 130. According to Melman, the film was seen by 125 million viewers, the majority of whom were women. Melman, *Women and the Popular Imagination*, p. 90. Paramount estimated that five million people in Britain saw the film.

173 Chow, 'Popular Sexual Knowledges', p. 78.

174 On Valentino's appeal see Miriam Hansen, 'Pleasure, Ambivalence, Identification: Valentino and Female Spectatorship', in Christine Gledhill (ed.), *Stardom: Industry of Desire* (1991); Gaylyn Studlar, 'Valentino, "Optic Intoxication", and Dance Madness', in Steven Cohan and Ina Rae Hark (eds), *Screening the Male* (London, 1993).

175 Chow, 'Popular Sexual Knowledges', p. 79.

176 The words of the song were reproduced in *Reynolds's News*, 8th July 1923, p. 8.

177 See *Daily Express*, 16th March 1923, p. 1; *Daily Mirror*, 16th March 1923, p. 1.

178 Leider, *Dark Lover*, p. 394.

179 Nichols, *The Sweet and the Twenties*, p. 143.

180 Joan Conquest, *Desert Love* (London, 1920), pp. 15, 21, 107–8.

181 *Times Literary Supplement*, 20th April 1922; 'The Hawk of Egypt by Joan Conquest', p. 262. See Ahdaf Soueif, *The Map of Love* (London, 1999) for a rare example of what could be seen as a high-brow desert romance. It was shortlisted for the Booker Prize. See interesting review by Clarissa Burt, *Feminist Review*, 69 (2001), p. 153.

182 Hull, *The Sheik*, p. 112.

183 See Hull, *The Sheik*, p. 96 where the Sheik says he will break her in like a horse.

184 *Illustrated Sunday Herald*, 30th September 1923, p. 5; *Daily Mirror*, 14th September 1923, p. 2.

185 *Sunday Express*, 16th September 1923, p. 6.

186 *Illustrated Sunday Herald*, 16th September 1923, p. 5.

187 *People*, 23rd September 1923, p. 9; *Illustrated Sunday Herald*, 23rd September 1923, p. 2. The weekly *John Bull* posed the question: 'Is it ever without danger for a Western girl to associate with a man of the East?' The answer was 'no'. *John Bull*, 22nd September 1923, p. 11. See *Sunday Express*, 16th September 1923, p. 5.

188 *Daily Mirror*, 17th September 1923, p. 7.

189 For example Rhodes' *Desert Lovers* was serialised daily in the *Daily Sketch* in summer 1922, Conquest's *Zarah the Cruel* was serialised in the *Daily Sketch* in winter 1922 and Hichens' *Bella Donna* was serialised in *Empire News* in early 1923.

190 *Daily Express*, 7th December 1922, p. 7. Perhaps unsurprisingly, her 'Tunisian costume' appears to be that worn by men. Obituary in *The Times*, 16th December 1959, p. 13.

191 *Daily Express*, 10th June 1927, p. 9. In addition to *The Tent of Blue*, Mills' writings included a travel book *The Road to Timbaktu*, 1924.

192 *People*, 25th September 1920, p. 8.

193 *People*, 2nd October 1921, p. 1.

194 *Reynolds's Newspaper*, 26th February 1922, p. 10.

195 See Shani D'Cruze (ed.), *Everyday Violence in Britain, 1850–1950* (London, 2000). For case of the acquittal of Edwin Semmens for the murder of his wife see *The Times*, 24th July 1920, p. 7.

5

'Hunnish scenes' and a 'Virgin birth': the contested marriage and motherhood of a curious modern woman

In March 1923 the *Illustrated Sunday Herald* informed readers that news of the divorce case *Russell* v. *Russell* had 'spread around the world. It has been more than a divorce case. It has been an intimate drama with the curtain rising and falling on climax after climax.'[1] The sexual innuendo here may have been inescapable, for the case had at its heart a debate over sex: how to speak it, and how to perform it. The case involved not only sex, but also aristocrats behaving badly, court-room drama, sensation, revelation – everything in fact that sold newspapers. Divorce reports were a preoccupation of the popular papers at this time, but the press was especially obsessed with this case – it featured on the front page, along with photographs, in several of the dailies, and covered many inside pages too. At the end of the first trial a Sunday paper called it 'the most remarkable cause celebre of recent times'; at the end of the second (the first being inconclusive) the same paper claimed it as 'probably *the* most talked of divorce case of a generation.'[2] So what was so extraordinary about the Russell case and why was it such an object of fascination?

The key players were distinctively odd, as too was their marital relationship. They apparently battled furiously over sex, she condemning their intercourse as 'Hunnish' (that is to say 'barbaric'). Then there was the bewildering fact that she had conceived with an intact hymen. Yet another facet to this strange tale was John Russell's regular and incongruous cross-dressing as a woman. If this did not already add up to a rich brew of upperclass oddity, there was at the heart of the narrative the figure of Christabel Russell: represented as an exceptional and exceptionally modern woman, she was also depicted as possessing a profound ignorance of, and intense dislike for, anything to do with sex. In this asexual portrayal she appears to go against the grain of historians' assumptions about the modern girl/woman as decidedly sexual in behaviour and inclination, for as discussed in previous chapters, part of the modern woman's representation involved

THE DAILY MIRROR, Friday, March 2, 1923.

KEEN RIVALRY IN "DAILY MIRROR" BEAUTY CONTEST

The Daily Mirror

NET SALE MUCH THE LARGEST OF ANY DAILY PICTURE NEWSPAPER

No. 6,030.   Registered at the G.P.O. as a Newspaper.   FRIDAY, MARCH 2, 1923   One Penny.

MR. RUSSELL'S STORY OF HIS MARRIED LIFE

Another charming study of Mrs. Russell and her baby.—(*Daily Mirror* photograph.)

A portrait of Mrs. Christabel Russell, daughter of the late Colonel John Hart.

Mr. Russell, who gave evidence at the continued hearing before Mr. Justice Hill.   The Hon. John Hugo Russell. A photograph taken at an early age.   The baby boy, born on October 15, 1921, whose paternity is disputed.   Sir Edward Marshall-Hall, K.C., finished his opening statement yesterday.

The Hon. John Hugo Russell went into the witness-box in the Divorce Court yesterday and gave an account of his engagement and his married life. He stated that in June, 1921, he and his wife were convinced their relations had not been such as to result in the birth of a child. He added that it was not until after he saw the announcement of the birth of the child that he started divorce proceedings, and that he consulted his wife's doctor as a kind of forlorn hope, because "I wanted it to be mine."

13 *Daily Mirror*, 2nd March 1923, Russell case,
© British Library Board (MLD4)

her sexual agency. But Christabel Russell – an ultra-modern woman in every other respect – disavowed all knowledge of, and interest in, sex and the erotic.

As with the Maud Allan libel trial, the opportunity to compare the trials as presented in the newspapers with the supposedly verbatim trial transcripts (the transcript of the second trial being lodged at the Parliamentary Archives) enables us to see what was designated publicly unprintable, the self-censoring press replacing the explicit courtroom discussions of sex and reproduction with euphemism and innuendo.[3] Christabel was castigated in the courtroom for her sexual ignorance, but in its account of divorce trials, the press was anxious to avoid the presentation of any actual sexual knowledge. Yet the 'suggestiveness' of its reporting of the Russell case was deemed a step too far, infuriating George V and instigating a crucial change in the law – another reason for the case's historical importance.

For a number of reasons therefore this trial is worthy of detailed analysis. Firstly, it raises questions about how the 'modern woman' was caricaturised at the time. Christabel Russell, in presenting herself as simultaneously non-sexual, maternal *and* modern (and being seen as such by her contemporaries), complicates our accepted narrative of the 1920s modern woman. Secondly, the trial's reportage illustrates the self-imposed parameters of contemporary press discussion of sex and the body (newspapers being concerned to claim suitability for a family readership).[4] Finally, the deemed *un*suitability of the reportage of this particular trial led to a significant legal shift in press censorship.

Pregnancy as instigator of divorce

The narrative of the case, as presented in the press of July 1922, began with Christabel Russell's visit to a clairvoyant in June of the previous year. Christabel, a striking, stylish, woman in her mid-twenties, married to the son of the second Lord Ampthill (her junior by a year), frequently consulted clairvoyants, but this time she received startling news, for the 'psychological expert', as Mrs Naismith preferred to call herself, informed her that she was five months pregnant. Mrs Naismith could tell from the 'vibrations of the hormones'.[5] Once a doctor had confirmed the diagnosis, Christabel told her husband of the pregnancy, but he denied paternity and petitioned for divorce on grounds of adultery.[6] The Hon. John Russell asserted that the few times that they had slept in the same bed in their (then) two-and-a-half years of marriage, his method of 'incomplete relations' (of which, more later) could not possibly have led to pregnancy. What added to the sensational nature of the case was the revelation that although she was pregnant, Christabel's hymen was unbroken.

The two divorce trials and two appeals that followed were known as the 'Russell baby case', for at stake was the legitimacy of Christabel's baby Geoffrey, who had been born in October 1921. The first trial in July 1922 was nine days long, the second in March 1923 was eleven, but both covered periods of two-and-a-half weeks as the court did not sit every day. Both trials were extensively covered by all the papers, bar one or two exceptions, such as the right-wing *Morning Post* which prided itself on not stooping to report sensational divorces.[7] The first trial ended inconclusively: the jury dismissed the two named co-respondents, but could not agree about the third, so-called 'unknown man'.[8] The second trial was won for John Russell however by the eminent barrister Sir Edward Marshall Hall (who was to successfully defend Mme Fahmy later that year). Again the named co-respondent was dismissed but this time the jury declared there must indeed have been adultery with some man unknown. In July 1923 the Court of Appeal upheld the verdict, but on the second appeal, in May 1924 in the House of Lords, drawing on an 1869 Act, it was ruled inadmissible for a husband or wife to give evidence which would have the effect of bastardising a child born in wedlock. The decree nisi was rescinded and the baby was formally legitimised in 1926, and thereby in line for the title of Lord Ampthill.

The co-respondents consisted of two men in the first trial, Gilbert Bradley and Lionel Cross, a man called Edgar Mayer in the second, and an unknown man in both. The cases against the named men were dealt with and dismissed fairly quickly and conclusively. Christabel had stayed over one night at Bradley's flat, having returned with him from a dance at two in the morning to find that she had lost her front-door key. At the time John readily believed that Bradley slept on two chairs in his sitting-room, while Christabel occupied Bradley's bed. As barrister for the co-respondents Sir Ellis Hume-Williams (who had acted for Maud Allan in 1918), asked rhetorically of the jury: 'If the husband did not mind, why on earth should we?'[9] Christabel had been in Paris with Cross, and had returned on an overnight sleeper. They had been forced, through lack of space, to share a berth, but neither had undressed. As for Mayer, four servants who worked at his block of flats claimed that Christabel had visited him frequently and had had a bath with him, but on being exposed as either liars, drunks or thieves, their evidence was discredited.[10]

The Russell divorce trials were atypical, for at their heart was not so much an exploration of the evidence in relation to the co-respondents (mere sidekicks in the narrative), as a focus on the two protagonists: their veracity, their behaviour and their lifestyle. In that sense the trials had more in common with rape trials, where the verdict depends on whether to believe his account or hers, with the woman's sexual history regularly deemed admissible. For the Russell case, as barrister Marshall Hall expressed it: 'The whole crux of the case will hang on which of these two people the jury believe.'[11] Much time was taken up in both of the Russell divorce trials with claims and counterclaims as to what constituted acceptable male and female attributes and behaviour. In addition, particularly in the second trial, there were lengthy discussions of sex and reproduction, although most of this was not reproduced in the press.

Both trials took place at the Probate, Divorce and Admiralty Division of the High Court (known as the site of 'wills, wrecks and wives'). The press reported that the court was 'crowded to suffocation', especially with the familiar 'fashionable' women, who 'literally fought at the doors for a footing inside.'[12] Again there was comment about the wide social mix: 'Young women, old women, women with paint and powder besmirching their complexions, flappers, men about town, people of the modern world, famous actresses', 'men-out-of-work by the look of them'.[13] The *News of the World* gave a sense of the rather grim location: 'no less attractive setting could be found for an enthralling drama. Around the double oak-panelled walls are hundreds of musty law books behind wire netting ... Prominent on the wall ... is a golden anchor ... A much begrimed map of Jutland and the North German coasts ... hangs ... behind the jury'.[14] Reference to the case as 'an enthralling drama' was linked to the usual complaint about the public treating trials as theatre: 'Day by day since the hearing began', observed the *News of the World*, 'fashionable women and blasé young men have clamoured for admission to the court as though it were some popular place of entertainment.'[15]

Christabel Russell in the public eye

As was the case with both Edith Thompson and Marguerite Fahmy, the popular press was full of photographs and drawings of Christabel and detailed descriptions of her appearance. Christabel was described as attractive, tall (she was 5ft 11in), slim, supple, walking gracefully 'with a sinuous swing', chic, 'Sphinx-like' with 'personal magnetism', self-possessed, 'a woman of unbelievable poise,' 'always at her ease', who 'replied to questions with her left hand poised assuredly on her hip'.[16] She was 'exceedingly unconventional', vivacious, very modern in dress, speech, behaviour and hair style (her hair had been bobbed since autumn 1920).[17] The *Illustrated Sunday Herald* described her 'of great athletic activity ... above all physically strong. She is not mannish. She is boyish, which is quite a different thing'.[18] She danced, hunted, played tennis, could drive a car and a motorcycle, had a pilot's licence to fly an aeroplane. In the 1920s the athletic woman was being celebrated in the press as a symbol of modernity, although there were always counter voices warning of the threat to motherhood of active sport.[19] Christabel managed to combine the two. Some papers thought her beautiful; many singled out her voice: 'flutelike and pure', 'so languid, so slow – almost a drawl'.[20] She dressed simply but fashionably, in dresses of her own design. A so-called 'intimate friend' writing in *Reynolds's News* elaborated: 'The clothes she wore during the case were chosen with great care and with an eye to their psychological effect on the jury. In fact her dresses were inspected by her leading counsel.'[21]

In court, her flirtatiousness and indiscretion were under the spotlight from the start. As she herself wrote in a letter to a woman friend, read out in court: 'I have been so frightfully indiscreet all my life that he [John] has enough evidence to divorce me about once a week'. 'Do think of the rows of Cos [co-respondents] lined up for the trial.'[22] In court she spoke openly about her rackety 'Bohemian' lifestyle of unchaperoned adolescent years. She was born in 1895; her Colonel father, a career soldier, had died when she was 14, and she had then moved from England with her sister and widowed mother to Paris's Left Bank, where she and her sister had attended life drawing lessons (not an acceptable undertaking for respectable middle-class girls). She had later returned to England to undertake war work, and in October 1918 she had married, largely, she said, to stop men pestering her with proposals. Her parents-in-law however, particularly Lady Ampthill, JP and Lady of the Bedchamber to Queen Mary, had been horrified that their son had married 'beneath' him, and they had refused to attend the wedding.[23] Lady Ampthill had had her sights on his marriage to royalty.[24] Christabel had insisted on a separate bedroom from her husband, and generally had had very little to do with him, going out every evening with some other man, frequently to nightclubs and nearly always to dance. Dancing was a great passion of hers. Her husband was not invited along, being a very poor dancer.[25] She teased him too, and letters were read out in court as illustration. For example, she wrote to him from Switzerland, where in January 1920 she had gone on a long holiday with her mother, but without her husband, to recover from pleurisy: 'your wife has a vast following of adoring young men ... several of the type after my very own heart. Dark, sleek Argentines and Greeks who dance like dreams of perfection.' (These would have been paid dance partners, the male equivalent of Freda Kempton.) She writes of one in particular: 'I am so in love with my Dago young man! ... He looks very ill and his hair is beautifully marcel-waved ... Can't I just *see* my husband of mine shuddering at the thought ... Your *very* naughty wife.'[26] In another letter she asked: 'You don't mind wife having the most awful amount of young men, do you? ... You take them so seriously and are not able to realise like mother that they make about as lasting an impression on me as ice-cream in hell.'[27] It should be noted however that many of these letters from Switzerland were very affectionate (and she wrote to him several times a week during her more than three-month stay).

Friends and relatives who appeared as witnesses testified to her absolute truthfulness (she referred to herself as 'distressingly truthful') but also to her frequent use of superlatives.[28] The *Illustrated Sunday Herald* commented that she used a form of slang 'common among the younger generation. The words "tremendous", "terrific" ... "priceless" ... "absolutely dreadful."'[29] 'Topping' was another of her favourites. In his summing up towards the end of the first trial, Christabel's counsel Patrick Hastings explained that she was 'essentially a modern product'.[30] Ellis Hume-Williams elaborated: she was 'a curious product of the age in which we lived. The Bohemianism of pre-war days had developed into the heroism of the war, and Mrs Russell was a highly-developed type of the class of woman produced by modern education and the war combined.' She was also 'absolutely fearless'.[31] In the second trial Hume-Williams again stressed that Christabel was a 'product of the war', adding that she was 'one of those women who led a life that neither the jury nor himself could have contemplated ten or fifteen years ago.'[32] Presumably none of the jurors was young, or at least not seen as such by Hume-Williams, for he placed them with him as remembering a pre-war world where women's lives were entirely different. Christabel was thus presented by her counsel as a typical post-war flapper, if rather posher and more bohemian than most.

The shadow of war

The frequent references to the war illustrate how, several years after the Armistice, the war still shadowed and informed explanations of behaviour, especially those of women. Indeed the motif of the war was everywhere, cited as the central explanation for a new kind of femininity. According to the *People* women who worked during the war had been permanently damaged – in health and in morals, the latter 'alloyed by the laxity of discipline and decorousness in those busy, hectic days'. Now many of them still craved pleasure: they danced, drank and smoked.[33] Reflecting negatively on the trials' female audience, 'Lady Mab' of the *Sunday Express* observed that 'most of the women were that thin, neurotic type which ... remind us that

there was once a war. They are nearly all young ... with that feverish thin-
ness which speaks of too many cocktails and not enough healthy food, of
sleep taken chiefly during the hours of sunlight ... these sinuous creatures
are what the war produced.'[34] (I have been unable to establish Lady Mab's
identity, but a play by Arnold Bennett called *Body and Soul* had recently
been performed featuring a Lady Mab – young, beautiful, eccentric, and a
subject of the gossip columns.)[35] Hume-Williams took a more sympathetic
view of the post-war woman:

> Women had done men's work during the war; they dressed like men and
> were working in conditions in which sex was subordinated and forgotten.
> That had a profound effect on their manners, though not on their morals
> ... No woman who had lived that kind of life ... could entirely shed it
> when she came out of it, and therefore to such women must be applied a
> different standard.[36]

The *Daily Express* editorial however took issue with this excuse of the war:
'it is unfair even to the war to saddle it with the responsibility of the Russell
case.'[37]

Against her frivolous leisure pursuits of nightclubs and dancing,
Christabel's war work was presented as serious and valuable. She had over-
seen 2,000 female munitions workers at Woolwich Arsenal, and in 1916
had become buyer for Whitworth Engineering Company.[38] As her barrister
expressed it, she 'had done all sorts of venturesome things during the war.'[39]
However, her practical side had not extended to her decision to marry: to
the judge of the second trial, Justice Hill, hers was 'a wartime marriage
[they had married in October 1918] in which little thought was given to
how the home was to be carried on after the war.'[40] The huge rise in the
divorce rate in 1919 was frequently laid at the door of the 'hasty wartime
marriage.'[41]

In addition to her war work, Christabel was praised for her sound
business sense. With borrowed capital of £500, she and her mother had
started a fashionable London dress shop in 1920, in the heart of Mayfair,
for which she designed original, expensive, and sought-after clothes. It
was proving extremely successful, and workers at the shop vouched for
how hard she worked. One of her aunts sweetly described her niece as 'a
super-woman, extremely clever, extremely lively, and extremely good.'[42]
But Marshall Hall, counsel for John Russell, was determined to demonstrate her extravagance. When her husband was about to leave the Navy in
April 1920, he was given the choice of taking £158 and a pension, or a lump
sum of £1,200. He asked his wife's advice. She replied:

Darling Old Thing – can you be sane? … I may as well set your mind at rest … I prefer a 'Rolls' to a Ford, a 15-ton yacht to a punt … Of course take the £1,200. We will pay our debts with £200, blow about £400 on a Hammond coupe [a sports car], put £25 or £30 in the bank, invest the rest and get about 8d a year interest.

Marshall Hall, after reading out this letter, commented: 'They got the £1,200 and spent the lot.'[43] Whatever her virtuous war work, her modernity was at the extreme end of flightiness and immoderation, John's counsel implied.

John Russell: cross-dressing, unassertive and unemployed

If Christabel's behaviour was under scrutiny, so too was that of her husband. The Hon John Russell had been a midshipman and then in 1917 an officer in the submarines, but it is unclear whether he ever actually saw active service. He was described as tall and handsome, he gave his evidence 'in soldiery fashion', and was 'the very embodiment of what we all like to think of as a typical young Englishman. Fair of feature and clean of limb'.[44] He might at first glance have looked the 'typical young Englishman', but Christabel's counsel attempted to undermine his credibility by demonstrating his lack of manliness, as exemplified in his cross-dressing. A photograph was produced in court of John Russell, 6ft 6in (known to his friends as 'Stilts') dressed as a woman. Other such photos made it into the popular press, including on the front page of the *Daily Mirror*. John apparently kept 'an entire trousseau' at home of stays, stockings and so forth, and when he had lived with his parents, he had regularly dressed up in his mother's clothes.[45] His mother noted the difficulty: he took size twelve in shoes. He didn't dress up simply to attend fancy dress parties – all the rage amongst the upper classes at this time – which might have been seen as excusable.[46] He admitted that he cross-dressed 'lots of times' simply for fun, including at the flat of a Mrs 'S' (her identity was not revealed) where for a joke, as he put it, he passed himself off as one of her female relatives when visitors came round.[47] As mentioned in the chapter on Edith Thompson, in the early 1920s for men to cross-dress was not yet seen as an obvious sign of gender inversion, sexual pathology or homosexuality, at least not for upper- or middle-class men as opposed to lower-class men and boys hanging around street corners.[48] But regular cross-dressing, whatever the class of the man, was thought to indicate effeminacy. Magnus Hirschfeld, leading German sexologist, had coined the term 'transvestism' in his 1910 book *Die Transvestiten*. Here he had asserted that the behaviour was a sexual variation unrelated to homosexuality.[49] In 1920s England however, Hirschfeld's book was not yet translated and the term 'transvestism' appears not to have

14 John Russell dressed as a woman

been generally known. Nevertheless John Russell's masquerade as a woman acted to compromise his masculinity. When asked sarcastically whether he thought 'that sort of thing would increase your wife's regard for her husband's manliness?' (the implied answer was 'of course not') John replied that he believed it had made no difference.[50] Christabel however told the court that his dressing as a woman 'became rather more than legitimate fun. In the end it revolted me.'[51] His effeminate cross-dressing stood in stark contrast to her fashionable boyishness.[52]

John's masculinity was also compromised by his apparent lack of assertiveness. He was presented by many witnesses and counsel alike as by far the weaker of the two in the marriage.[53] Hastings, Christabel's barrister, pronounced Christabel 'just the sort of girl who wanted to marry a man. Instead she married the petitioner – day after day, querulous, complaining – asking for what ought to have been taken, beseeching what he ought to command ... If only he had taken her and said "You have married a man, not a mouse; this will have to stop!" she might have respected him'. This was substantiated when Hastings asked of Christabel: 'Did he ever say he was going to give you a shaking or a beating?' to which she disturbingly replied: 'No, I think I should have admired him more if he had.'[54] The fact that he had been unemployed since March 1921 did not help his case. His claim that he had spent many days in London 'tramping the streets in search of a job' did not convince the *Empire News* which wryly noted: 'Mr Russell did not look like a man who would have tramped the streets ... He is, indeed, a born aristocrat.'[55] But his parents, although titled, were not rich, and John received a relatively small yearly allowance of £100. (This is according to Christabel's biographer, but the verbatim report of the appeal before the House of Lords in 1924 states that he received a £300 allowance. There is either an error, or possibly his allowance was increased three-fold between 1918 and 1924.)[56] Marshall Hall tried to engender sympathy for his plight: 'He used to sit at home like Cinderella and mend the taps and paint the doors and all that kind of thing.' Hastings sardonically replied: 'it sounds like an interesting home life'.[57] Christabel meanwhile worked hard all day at her shop. 'The pity of it' reflected Hastings 'is that this man did not get on with life – on with work – on with the real things, and get rid of his stays and his acting'.[58] The gender reversal in terms of waged work and authority was presented by Christabel's counsel as a means to John's discrediting, but the ploy risked an unintended consequence: the representation of Christabel as a woman who had emasculated her husband.

Hunnish scenes

John's masculinity was also implicitly undermined by the constant references to his and his wife's sexual relations, which were referred to variously in the press as incomplete relations, attempted relations, partial intercourse, or 'Hunnish scenes' (Christabel's term). For it was not entirely clear from press accounts (or indeed from the transcripts) whether John sometimes attempted full intercourse and was rebuffed (as the term 'attempted relations' implies) or whether the partial intercourse was always a conscious form of birth control. Christabel did remark that she was 'disgusted with my husband's general attitude in not insisting on his full rights', but it was she who had got John to agree, just before their marriage, that they would delay the having of children.[59] And when cross-examined by Marshall Hall as to the nature of her marital sexual relations, the barrister suggested: 'He was restraining himself from complete penetration?' to which she replied: 'I restrained him … It was more my effort than his, I daresay.'[60] Sir Henry Duke, judge in the first trial, must have agreed with this view, commenting that there was 'no obstacle to consummation save the respondent's impregnable self-will'.[61] But of course neither her self-will nor indeed her hymen turned out to be impregnable.

In the summer of 1919 John had given his wife a copy of Marie Stopes's *Married Love* – 'a book that was exciting a good deal of comment at the moment', according to the *Daily Mirror* – but she had said that she did not like the idea of using 'preventives' and he had agreed.[62] On the mention of preventives, one of the two women jurors asked if she could be discharged.[63] As was noted in earlier chapters, Stopes's 1918 *Married Love* was a huge best-seller and by 1923 had sold more than 400,000 copies.[64] Lamenting the extent of sexual ignorance, *Married Love* hoped to break the silence with its presentation of clear and basic sex education to married couples. It openly used the words 'penis', 'vagina' and 'clitoris', advocated mutual sexual pleasure, and pointed to the periodicity of women's sexual desire.[65] No other marriage manual had been so accessible and explicit. As will become evident, it seems unlikely that the Russells had actually read much of the book.

When asked about the expression 'Hunnish scenes', John replied that everybody was using 'Hun' at that time (another relic of the war), and his wife used to describe anything she didn't like as 'Hunnish'. Although mentioned the first day of the first trial, no clear definition of the phrase was ever given, the newspapers' varied terms reflecting the confusion. When John was asked by a counsel whether the term 'Hunnish scenes' had 'any particular meaning between you?', he replied 'No'; the barrister was presumably trying to discover if it was the couple's shared sexual code or agreed euphemism.[66] Christabel said the Hunnish scenes were like nightmares, but when John's counsel for the first trial, Sir John Simon, asked if by Hunnish scenes she meant that she was overpowered or assaulted, she haughtily replied: 'No, that would be quite ridiculous.'[67] She said that she used the term to refer to John's attempts at relations 'which were usually preceded by threats to shoot himself and once to shoot my cat who slept on the bed'. She informed the court that he used to lie on his bed with a shotgun balanced on his feet, his toe on the trigger, 'to blow his brains out if she did not consummate the marriage.'[68]

Marie Stopes had also had an unsatisfactory marital sex life; it had prompted her to write *Married Love*. In the preface she notes: 'In my first marriage I paid such a terrible price for sex-ignorance that I feel that knowledge gained at such a cost should be placed at the service of humanity.'[69] The 'terrible price' had been her unconsummated marriage, although this is not spelt out in the book. In 1911 Marie had married a fellow botanist, Reginald Ruggles Gates. She claimed that it was only on reading medical texts on sex in the restricted access area of the British Museum's Reading Room that she had realised the lack of consummation.[70] In their annulment suit in 1916, Marie informed the court that her husband's 'parts' had never become rigid, and to the question 'he never succeeded in penetrating into *your* private parts?' she replied 'No.'[71] One is struck by the parallels to the Russell case: the invasive questions, the sexual ignorance, the unsatisfactory sex.[72]

The reason why John Russell insisted that he could not be the father of Christabel's child rested firstly on his assumption that his practiced form of partial intercourse could not lead to pregnancy. 'We all took the view', declared John, 'that these relations were not in fact a consummation of the marriage in the strict sense of the word.' Indeed before the discovery of the pregnancy, the couple had discussed the possibility of annulment, as had also his parents and her mother. The 'incompleteness' of the sexual intercourse was medically established in court by the revelation that Christabel's hymen during pregnancy had been unbroken. Prior to the first divorce trial, John Russell had never been informed of this; judge Sir Henry Duke commented on this 'fateful silence': 'I cannot conceive of anything more unfortunate for these young people than that the respondent had not the advantage of having told to her husband … the all-important fact of her bodily state.'[73] With this fact before the court, John's assertion that he could not be the father was weakened. His other claim was that on the date when they had shared a bed in December 1920, at his parents' house, no form of sex had taken place. He insisted that there had been no intimacy, not even a kiss, since August 1920. Christabel on the contrary was adamant that they had had the usual and hated incomplete relations. ('Complete' relations were implicitly taken as the term for 'proper' marital sexual intercourse, that of 'full'/'complete' penetration.) In this dispute over what occurred in December, it was his word against hers.

At both trials, witnesses included an impressive line-up of medical experts for the respondent, brought in to establish the veracity of her claims.[74] Various questions were asked of them: could the form of 'incomplete relations' practiced by the couple lead to pregnancy? Could a woman conceive with an unbroken hymen? Could a woman not know she was pregnant for as long as five months? Could a pregnancy last ten months (for the baby had been conceived in December, according to Christabel, and was born the following October)? The answer was 'yes' on each count. Gynaecologist Dr Stanley Dodd, who had examined Christabel when she was seven months pregnant, 'had in his experience met with several cases in which conception had occurred without penetration'.[75] Fellow gynaecologist Dr Thomas Eden agreed.[76] ('Without penetration' was ambiguous; did they mean without *full* penetration? for Christabel claimed that there was 'slight' penetration, which always caused her pain.[77] This question of the degree of penetration was to become significant in the second trial.)

Reading the body

That a woman with an intact hymen could conceive was likely to have been seen as remarkable by most; that a woman could be pregnant for five months without knowing it, possibly less so, at least by women. Christabel had noticed that she was getting fatter, but that, she said, was all. She had suffered neither morning sickness nor increased appetite.[78] Her mother was asked how it was that *she* didn't suspect her daughter's pregnancy; could she not read her daughter's body? 'You must remember the fashion at the time – there was not a waist in sight' was her wonderful reply.[79] During the second trial she added that she had been unaware of her own first pregnancy for several months. And obstetric surgeon Dr Herbert Spencer told the court about a 'very experienced' married nurse of his who had asked him to remove an ovarian tumour, but on examination was found to be pregnant with twins and about to go into labour![80] But when Dr Eden started to mention cases he knew of, Justice Hill intervened: 'if we are to go into individual cases we shall be here through the Long Vacation'.[81]

Christabel's assertion that she had first learnt about her pregnancy from a clairvoyant was treated by John's counsel as risible. (Spiritualism, including clairvoyance, had enjoyed a revival during the Great War, with people desperate to contact their killed sons, husbands and lovers, and it continued to be popular into the 1920s.)[82] Sir John Simon enquired incredulously of Mrs Hart: 'Did your daughter believe in occult disclosures?' Her reply was non-committal: 'I think they all believe them at some time, and at other times they don't.'[83] The barristers effectively belittled Mrs Naismith, including her attempt to claim scientific credibility with her talk of being a 'psychological expert' and reading the hormones. 'Is that Latin or Greek?' John Simon asked sarcastically, playing to the Classics-educated upper-middle-class men present in court. 'Hormones' in fact came from the Greek for 'excite' or 'arouse', but Mrs Naismith did not seem to know. She defensively responded: 'It is a very good word' and the technique was 'a new phase of therapeutics'.[84] She denied that she surmised pregnancy from visual indicators; it was all due to her being able to sense the hormonal 'vibrations'. She was asked mockingly by Sir John Simon whether her psychological science 'had advanced to the extent that you can tell ... who is the father of the child?' 'I might if I was able to concentrate', she bravely replied.[85] When the same question arose in the second trial, she was more assertive: 'it could be done by the electronic principle'.[86] The 1920s were the 'golden years' for the study of internal secretions, named 'hormones' in 1905 by British physiologist, Ernest Starling.[87] Mrs Naismith's attempt to modernise her pre-modern occult practices with the language of this new scientific development was a bold refashioning.[88] But it convinced neither the barristers nor the press, and in one press description she was implicitly condemned as a sham by her appearance alone: 'A woman with bright gold hair, who bore a bunch of artificial red rosettes in her hat'.[89]

Whatever the reason for the clairvoyant knowing that Christabel was pregnant, John's counsel were determined to throw doubt on Christabel's claim that she herself had no such knowledge. They questioned her apparent lack of concern with the cession of her menstrual periods. (Periods did not make it into the press.) Christabel claimed that she had ceased having periods on at least one previous occasion. When Marshall Hall cross-examined Christabel's mother on this issue, he began with a warning for the men in court: 'Now I must ask you about this unpleasant subject which is always unpleasant to men – the question of periods.' He continued: 'Your daughter has told us that on ... certainly one occasion she had missed for a whole twelve months?' Mrs Hart replied: 'For many months, I cannot say twelve months.' 'Did she consult a doctor?' 'No.' Marshall Hall feigned surprise and implied she was neglectful: 'Do you mean to say, as a mother, a watchful affectionate mother, it did not give you any anxiety that your daughter's monthly periods should be suppressed for, say, nine months?' 'No, I did not worry about it at all', was her off-hand reply.[90] As for the question of whether a pregnancy could last ten months, obstetric surgeon Dr Trevor Davies testified that he had found Christabel's baby exceptionally well developed, well beyond full term, and weighing ten and a half pounds.[91]

For the second trial, John Russell's counsel, now knowing of the unbroken hymen, called their own medical experts. They questioned John's paternity through trying to establish that his sexual relations with his wife had involved little or no penetration, that he had ejaculated 'at the orifice of her person' as opposed to inside her vagina, and that therefore it was highly unlikely that his sperm could have impregnated her. Further, they engaged in a long discussion with the doctors – both those for the respondent and those for the plaintiff – about the nature of Christabel's hymen, suggesting that it was feasible for a lover likewise not to have broken it, either because its elasticity meant that full or nearly full penetration was compatible with lack of rupturing, or because she had persuaded the lover to penetrate only partially as a form of birth prevention. Marshall Hall tried to establish that it was highly unlikely that John Russell's very limited penetration, which he claimed involved ejaculation 'at the orifice of her person', would have led to conception. But Dr Dodd insisted: 'If coitus took place in the position … in which I understood it to take place [their lying on their sides] the penis would be between the lips of the vulva, and it is quite possible that the semen might be almost injected through the hymen'.[92] Hastings took up the debate, asking of Dr Eden: 'if in fact the emission took place at the orifice of the person, is it possible to say whether in fact it is ejaculated right on to the hymen or not?' He got the desired reply: 'It could be driven through the hymen'.[93] Even the evidence of the medical men brought in by John's counsel did not fully support Marshall Hall's claim of unlikely conception. In response to the question about whether emission taking place at the 'orifice of her person' could lead to pregnancy, obstetric surgeon Sir Maurice Abbot-Anderson replied: 'if the penis was engaged in the smallest degree with the vulva … that is quite possible'.[94] Such a view was echoed by Marie Stopes, who in her book *Marriage in My Time* claimed that if she 'had been able to give evidence for the wife [Christabel] I could have demonstrated such vital physiological laws' that the jury would have concluded that John was indeed the father. Spermatozoa were not hampered by the flimsy silk of modern women's underwear, which to them was 'as large as a railway tunnel'.[95]

Marshall Hall tried unsuccessfully to establish Christabel's hymen as being 'elastic' and thus able to accommodate nearly full penetration by a lover without its rupture. Dodd, who had examined Christabel when she was seven months pregnant, denied there was much elasticity, and was certain that: 'the particular hymen we are discussing ... will not permit anything the size of a penis'.[96] (The word 'penis' was used a lot in the cross-examination of the doctors, but never reproduced in the press.) The barristers were reluctant to openly contradict the doctors, but Marshall Hall quoted numerous medical books at them to try and challenge their claims, and was occasionally somewhat tongue-in-cheek in his asides. For example, he unctuously remarked to Dr Eden: 'You medical men have seen thousands of hymen ... Of course we unfortunate people have never seen one.'[97] Relinquishing his elastic hymen claim, Marshall Hall changed tack: 'Here is a woman who ... has a lover ... She does not want children by that man ... She promised that sort of partial intercourse on the distinct understanding that there is no penetration sufficient to put her in the family way.' Dodd would have none of it: 'I think ... that when a woman becomes a man's mistress ... I do not think they stop at half measures.'[98] In his summing up, at the end of the second trial, Justice Hill presented both sides of the argument, although appeared more convinced by Dodd's.[99]

Sexual ignorance

Neither of the Russells apparently knew that their form of limited penetration followed by withdrawal (not a term they appeared to use), let alone withdrawal that didn't even break the hymen, could result in pregnancy. Did other people know of its unreliability? Kate Fisher's invaluable oral history demonstrates that many people at this time favoured withdrawal and thought it a generally foolproof method, and if pregnancy *did* result, it was due to user-error.[100] Marie Stopes also thought the method prevented conception, although she presented it as harmful to the woman, leaving her 'mid-air', and without the advantage of 'the partial absorption of the man's secretions'.[101] (Stopes was very keen on secretions.) Hastings however surprisingly asserted: 'Any man in England knew that in what in fact did take place there was always the risk of a child.'[102] This surely implied that John Russell must have known, or at least should have known. And in saying any *man*, women were not necessarily assumed to have such knowledge. Indeed, too much sexual knowledge in a woman, especially an unmarried woman, compromised her respectability.[103]

Christabel certainly did not have such knowledge, or at least she disavowed such knowledge. Despite her 'Bohemian', 'unconventional' upbringing, Christabel proclaimed that she 'knew absolutely nothing about [matters of sex]. They did not interest me and I never discussed them with anybody.'[104] Even after her marriage, her apparent lack of knowledge – and of interest – continued, as revealed in the following extract from her cross-examination by Marshall Hall:

> MH: Did you notice what is the main difference between a man and a woman on that night when he was in bed with you? [their wedding night]
>
> CR: How should I?
>
> MH: Do you mean to tell us that you did not know whether your husband was differently made?
>
> CR: That is a most ridiculous question. I have been an art student in Paris, and I have studied anatomy from the age of 12 …
>
> MH: So you had seen a nude man?
>
> CR: Constantly …
>
> MH: Have you never had the smallest curiosity to know what that portion of the man's body was intended by nature for?
>
> CR: I had not the smallest curiosity.
>
> MH: Do you know that in moments of passion that portion of the man's body gets large?
>
> CR: I did not know that.
>
> MH: Do you know that now?
>
> CR: You have told me.
>
> MH: Never mind about my telling you …
>
> CR: No, I did not know until you have just told me …
>
> MH: During this partial intercourse, when you say that your husband had emissions, do you say that that you did not realise that his person became rigid?
>
> CR: No, I did not.
>
> MH: Has he ever had this partial intercourse with you that you suggested?
>
> CR: He has told you so.
>
> MH: And yet you noticed no difference?
>
> CR: No difference in what?
>
> MH: Between the person in quiescence and the person in excitement. I use the word 'person'; you know what I mean?
>
> CR: This is – Oh! …
>
> …
>
> MH: Did you know the object for which he wanted to put his person inside yours?
>
> CR: It seemed to be objectless; it seemed to have no object. I could see no satisfaction from it.[105]

None of this exchange was reproduced in the press. While mention was made in the press of her lack of sexual knowledge, there was little clarification as to what this entailed.

Marshall Hall claimed to be puzzled by her ignorance: 'When you worked with two thousand girls at Woolwich, did you not hear about sexual matters?' She tellingly replied: 'I think they were always very careful in my presence. They looked upon me as being from another world because I was not of the same class as theirs, and they used to treat me with enormous deference and respect.'[106] Dr Eden confirmed this class difference: 'The women of the industrial classes talked with more freedom about such matters [sex], and they generally know more than educated women did.'[107] ('Educated' was surely a misnomer in this case.) Such a claim as to working-class women's sexual knowledge is not borne out in contemporary personal testament or autobiography, at least as far as respectable working-class girls and women were concerned. The oral history testimony of eighty-nine middle- and working-class British men and women born slightly later than the Russells (between 1902 and 1931) largely substantiates this claim of pre-marital sexual ignorance, especially in the case of women.[108]

Sexlessness and motherhood

If lacking sexual knowledge, Christabel presented herself as also lacking sexual desire: 'all sexual subjects disgust me.'[109] Her 'intimate friend' writing in a Sunday paper noted that 'she is fond of male society, but has no interest in men from the point of view of sex', while the judge in the first trial suggested that she had a 'resentful distaste for anything in the nature of sexual intercourse'. And when asked by Marshall Hall: 'You have no sex love?' she replied: 'I do not think I can have or it has not been brought forth yet.'[110] Marshal Hall deemed her 'abnormal' and castigated her with the epithet 'super-sexless'. To Marshall Hall, her sexlessness rendered her emotionally barren but highly manipulative: 'she glories in having a train of men dancing attendance to her'.[111] But to others, her non-sexual self-presentation may have been read positively as indicating respectability and sexual innocence. No one openly mentioned the word 'frigid' in relation to the trial; the term was not yet widely in use. Although Walter Gallichan, popular writer on 'sex psychology', had asserted back in 1898 that 'frigidity' was a frequent cause of 'conjugal calamity', in the subsequent years up until the war the idea of 'temperamental coldness' was applied more to the 'unhealthy' celibacy of the chaste spinster than to the married woman.[112] But when in 1927 Gallichan pointed to 'the paramount problem of the sexually anaesthetic woman ... unable to experience that perfect sense of oneness with her husband', there was greater reception to his ideas. (Had he been thinking of Christabel?)[113]

Pregnancy had initially been Christabel's downfall, but to many, her embrace of motherhood was central to her redemption. She herself acknowledged motherhood's transformative power. In one of her letters to her husband, read out in court, and written soon after the birth of her son, she reflected: 'It is extraordinary how it changes ones outlook having a baby. I feel quite different ... Will you for his sake ... start afresh?'[114] He refused to even see the child. In court she said that she would do anything for her son, work for him, even die for him.[115] *Lloyd's Sunday News* depicted Christabel, during her four-hour interrogation by Marshall Hall, as displaying 'primitive mother-love', which 'burst ... through the armour of her iron self-control, and at those times her fine teeth would be startlingly bared, and you saw ... the female of the species, snarling defiance over her offspring'.[116] Beverley Baxter of the *Daily Express* was so moved by Christabel-as-mother that he announced he could not bear to go back to the court: 'It is too cruel ... it is not as if only Mrs Russell were in the box – it is motherhood.'[117] For both newspapers, the threat of the modern woman was thereby implicitly reduced to and contained by a common and essentialist denominator: primitive instinctual motherhood. She was basically the same as all women, her modernity simply a façade.

In both trials the baby was carried in and shown to the jurors; in a time before DNA testing, it was one way, although inadequate, of trying to establish paternity. The judges in both trials were sceptical of this search for similarities; Justice Hill's summing up warned that such comparisons 'would be very unsafe and conjectural. Science is only groping to find out the laws which govern the transmission of likeness from one generation to another.'[118] Hastings however got John to show his ears to the jury (he did so reluctantly) suggesting they were exactly like those of the baby. His ears were 'somewhat square, and stand out a little from his head'.[119] Lady Ampthill denied *any* likeness to her son, but the popular press thought otherwise. They filled their pages with photographs of Geoffrey, some noted his similarity to John, and they called him 'a dear little fellow' – the Russell case's 'real victim'.[120]

The case lost

Christabel lost the second trial, much to surprise of the press, the *Daily Express* for example commenting that it was 'out of tune with the sentiment and conviction of most'.[121] As she left the court after the verdict, 'there were loud cheers and several women cried "Plucky woman. Hard lines." One woman threw a bunch of flowers into the car'.[122] (There were cheers too for John and his parents however.) Marshall Hall's biographer, writing in the late 1920s, also notes the verdict as surprising 'in face of the great public prejudice which had been excited in favour of the "mother fighting for her child"'.[123] This was clearly the key factor in her public support. Her self-presentation as a doting mother, concerned above all for the future of her son, countered the image of her as frivolous and spoilt. She was a modern woman but tamed by motherhood. As already mentioned, other factors worked in her favour, including her husband's questionable masculinity. Although the press presented him as essentially honest, in many ways he was likened to the typical modern post-war young man regularly ridiculed in the papers: effeminate, asexual and impotent, both literally and metaphorically.[124] However, the attempt to question his masculinity could have backfired against Christabel, for if he were truly impotent, how could he have fathered a child? Working in Christabel's favour was her war work as a supervisor of munitions workers, her business sense, possibly her class versus that of her husband (he upper-class, she middle-class 'trade', snubbed by his titled family), and her disarming frank admission of ignorance about sex and conception. Christabel as maternal figure co-existed with her more modern persona: stylish, lover of modern dance, sport and fashion, habitué of nightclubs, able to make a living for herself without the help of any man (John was out of work for nearly half of their married life), and flaunting a total disregard for convention. She was a very modern woman but one that defied the dominant image, for she lacked both sexual knowledge and desire, and she happily embraced maternity once it unexpectedly came her way. She was an *asexual* modern woman, in contrast to the vilified highly sexual and sexualised Edith Thompson, who had been hanged only two months before Christabel's second trial. Her apparent asexuality, along with her maternity, were no doubt the key reasons for her public support.

So why did she lose the second trial? The key to her defeat was Sir Edward Marshall Hall. Christabel kept the same barrister, Patrick Hastings, for both trials, and Ellis Hume-Williams similarly stayed on to represent the co-respondents, but John Russell's previous counsel, Sir John Simon, was unavailable in March 1923 so could not resume his advocacy. When seeking an alternative, John Russell and his family were apparently advised by the Attorney General: 'Well, there's one man at the Bar who might pull it off and win a brilliant victory for you or he might make a terrible mess of it. That's Marshall Hall.'[125] As was mentioned in Chapter 4, Marshall Hall was possibly the most famous (and expensive) British barrister of the day. Known largely for defending in murder trials, he regarded the Russell trial as 'his greatest victory in a civil case'.[126]

Marshall Hall was ruthless in his cross-examination of Christabel – all the papers said as much. 'Again and again his questions forced her into a corner just as a boxer trying for a knock-out will manoeuvre his opponent against the ropes.'[127] Christabel held her own admirably; The *News of the World* noted that 'she NEVER MISSED A CHANCE OF REPARTEE' (capital letters in the original), as the short example reproduced earlier demonstrated.[128] She was subjected to continual bullying and accusations of lying and play-acting. She stood for all four hours in the dock (she refused to sit) subjected to Marshall Hall's constant barrage, but 'never did she show signs of exhaustion'.[129] *Lloyd's Sunday News* called the cross-examination 'the greatest court duel in memory', continuing: 'When it is remembered that counsel conducted her through all the privacies of her married life, cast doubt upon her girlish beliefs, brought out the broad facts of sex – all before an audience mostly of strangers, and in terms that were not minced ... – it will be realised that there were many things that might have shaken the composure of an ordinary woman.'[130] But the fact that she was *not* an ordinary woman, or rather, did not masquerade as one, was largely responsible for her defeat, according to 'Lady Mab' of the *Sunday Express*. Writing a column entitled 'How we lost Mrs Russell's case', 'Lady Mab' claimed that 'Mrs Russell largely lost her case because she chose to fight with a rapier rather than a powder puff.'

> If she had acted I am certain she would have won her case. Supposing she had shed a few tears every time Marshall Hall went it a bit rough? Supposing she had swooned from exhaustion? ... Supposing her lips had quivered whenever the baby was mentioned ... All women know the effect of tears and blushes and quivering lips on men ... Yet Mrs Russell fought fearlessly and honestly and asked no quarter for her sex.[131]

Hastings tried to appeal to the jury's concern for the fate of baby Geoffrey, ending his summing up with the plea: 'Don't go to your homes with the thought that in twenty years time, when this child has grown up into the living image of this man, he will be branded with the infamy that cannot be redressed that his mother was a woman of no reputation, and he was a nobody's child.'[132] But Marshall Hall, famous for his melodramatic orations, outdid Hastings, both with the length of his summing up – four and a half hours to Hastings's forty minutes – and with his theatrical finale to what Hume-Williams thought was the best speech he had ever heard him make.[133] He implored the jury 'to free this young man from a tie which he hoped would be a bond of pleasure but is nothing but a rusty chain that burns into his soul. He is entitled to a divorce from this woman who has never been a wife.' The co-respondents did not feature; as Hume-Williams had pointed out, the case against Mr Mayer was 'not sufficient to hang a dog on'.[134] For the case was no longer about adultery – at that time the only rationale for divorce – but entitlement for a man in a sexless marriage. This was not grounds for divorce. A plea of non-consummation would have been grounds for annulment, but was not of course admissible in this case, given the respondent's pregnancy. Yet Marshall Hall got away with misleading the jury (as we saw in the Mme Fahmy trial as well) and was never reprimanded by the judge. The jury may indeed have felt that a young man in a loveless, sexless marriage *was* entitled to freedom from the 'rusty chain' of what writer A.P. Herbert was later to refer to as 'Holy Deadlock'.[135]

The case condemned

Not all the press was in favour of Christabel. At the end of both trials, the *Daily Express*, which had lauded Christabel-as-mother and waxed lyrical about her lily-like neck, turned on both Russells, referring to their lives as 'empty, selfish, sordid', their manners and morals 'freakish'. The paper smugly played the populist card: 'the saving grace [is] that the antics of a few have little influence on the decent, hard-worked folk', the 'humdrum, happier lives of those who travel side by side in tube and omnibus', namely the decent lower-middle-class and respectable working-class readers of the *Daily Express*.[136] Christabel had many letters from those opposed to her, but even more from those in her favour, including one from a long-term prisoner who promised that once he was out 'his heart and hand were hers and he would see "the boy was brought up right"'.[137] But she was snubbed too. Her friend Eileen Hunter narrates the case of a tennis-party in Sussex where one mother refused to bring her girls because they 'should not, would not, meet that woman', and when Christabel arrived at the Berkeley Hotel one evening to dine and dance, a number of people stood on chairs in order to stare at her.[138]

George V was also concerned about the morals portrayed in the Russell case. He got his private secretary to write on his behalf to the Lord Chancellor in July 1922 complaining about the disappearance of the 'unwritten code of decency' that used to keep 'repulsive' matters 'out of the range of public eye or ear'. He proposed that such cases be heard *in camera*. While the publicity arising in divorce courts had once been seen as a deterrent to divorce – the sanction of public humiliation – now with mass education (the 1870 Education Act) and the development of a mass market in newspapers, there was concern with the potential tarnishing of marriage as an institution, and the corruption of impressionable youth and the working classes. Part of this 'corruption' entailed the jeopardising of social hierarchies, for given the expense, divorce was largely a middle- and upper-class affair, allowing social inferiors the opportunity to pour over the private sexual misconduct of their supposed superiors. As historian Gail Savage perceptively observes, the reading public's consumption of the daily and Sunday papers transformed the divorce narrative from what was meant to be a *moral* lesson into an erotic, entertaining story, while the press barons reaped the profits.[139] Further, the *frisson* of the narrative had been heightened by the daily 'picture' papers' relatively new and extensive use of photography.[140]

As the first Russell trial was coming to its inconclusive end, the *Sunday Express* presented the views of three 'outstanding men of their professions' on this issue of publication of divorce details. All three men (an MP, the surgeon to the King, and a clergyman) were against publication of details, but interestingly, only the Reverend was against legislation, believing that trials *in camera* were 'breeding grounds for abuses'. He wanted the press to exert restraint: 'the poison pervades the whole of the daily Press, and ... the most influential papers are now the worst offenders'.[141] The following day the *Daily Express* editorial picked up on this theme of poison:

> some minds, and not only of the young, may be poisoned by certain tes-
> timony if given in full, and every newspaper in such trials as the Russell
> case must bear its own responsibility and use its discretion ... on the one
> hand not to pander to the prurient, on the other not to permit evil to
> nestle in the dark shadows.[142]

The *Daily Express* was as capable of pandering to the prurient as any popular newspaper, but it hypocritically liked to take the moral high ground versus the rest of the press. In fact its partner paper the *Sunday Express* was at the forefront in suggestive reporting of the Russell case. One example of such can be found in its account of Christabel's cross-examination:

> Questions were asked [by Sir Edward] which would have embarrassed a
> woman alone with her physician ... She said she did not understand ... he
> repeated the question ... she answered again that she did not know what
> he meant. 'Then I am very sorry to have to explain,' he said quietly. He did
> so. No newspaper could possibly repeat his words.[143]

The transcripts however do allow us to repeat his words. When Christabel indicated that she was unclear of the difference between being examined 'visually' or 'digitally' by a doctor, Marshall Hall responded: 'Well, I will tell you; I am sorry I must tell you. Digitally is by putting his fingers into your private parts to examine in that way; visually is by looking to see your private parts.' She sensibly replied: 'One could not do one without the other,

I should imagine.'[144] The exchange was in fact possibly rather less obscene than anything the reader had been encouraged to imagine.

In 1923 a select committee was set up on this issue of divorce reporting, its eleven witnesses including Sir Henry Duke (judge in the first of the Russell trials), Ellis Hume-Williams (the counsel for the Russell co-respondents, who was also a Tory MP), and the Bishop of London.[145] The latter marshalled behind him the London Public Morality Council of which he was chair, and which included such groups as the Mothers' Union and the National Council of Women. Those in favour of restriction could not point to actual *instances* of obscenity, given the care the press took to use euphemisms and to censor their reports, but it was the prominence given to the divorce trials, and as Adrian Bingham notes, the 'suggestiveness' of the reports, which was objected to – examples such as that of the *Sunday Express* report.[146] Despite opposition from Hume-Williams and thirty-odd other MPs, in 1926 the Judicial Proceedings (Regulation of Reports) Act prohibited the publication of detailed press reporting of divorce cases.[147]

Film and fame

In July 1923 the Court of Appeal upheld the Russell verdict, but on the second appeal, in May 1924 in the House of Lords, it was ruled that evidence questioning the legitimacy of a child born in wedlock was inadmissible, and the decree nisi was reversed. They cited the Evidence Amendment Act of 1869 whereby a husband and wife were not permitted 'to bastardise any issue of their marriage'. Soon after this 1924 appeal Christabel took fictional revenge on her husband. She wrote the screenplay for a film called *Afraid of Love*, released in 1925, which she claimed was based on her own experience of married life. She also played the star part – Rosamund, married to the philandering Anthony Bond, a wealthy stockbroker. Determined to be self-supporting, Rosamund opens a dress-shop, with the help of money borrowed from her friend Philip Brymer. (Incidentally, the co-respondent in the second trial, Edgar Mayer, had lent her money for her own dress-shop, or rather he had invested in her business as a shareholder). When Anthony brings his mistress to the shop, Rosamund, affronted, moves to the countryside with their small son, where she becomes a writer. Five years later, Anthony, tired of his debauched life, visits Rosamund with a view to taking away their son. He returns alone to London, full of remorse, and conveniently shoots himself. Rosamund marries Philip and they devote themselves to raising her son.

Unfortunately no copy of the film now appears to exist, but two contemporary reviews indicate its reception. That of *Bioscope* was

15 Christabel Russell in *The Beauty Book*, 1926

uncompromisingly bad, labelling the film an 'indifferent production of a dull and disjointed story of the penny novelette type ... Of the Hon Mrs John Russell one can say only that she walks through the part of Rosamund with more apparent concern for the many elaborate gowns than for the emotional demands of the character. To be candid, her performance is that of an untrained and unpromising amateur.'[148] (So much for Marshall Hall's attempt to discredit her through labelling her an excellent actress, capable of effortless lying.) The *Kinematograph Weekly* was kinder. It tactfully made no mention of Christabel's acting ability (although praised the other actors) but suggested that 'the celebrity of the central player should make this a box-office proposition ... The curiosity value of this picture is obvious and exceptional', not least because of the 'strong feminine appeal in the mannequin parades'.[149] *Bioscope* also thought 'the dresses worn by Mrs Russell will doubtless interest women', though added snidely: 'it seems unnecessary to advertise their source in the main title'.[150] Presumably Christabel used the film to publicise her dress shop. And in cathartically disposing of the husband through an act for which she was not responsible – his suicide – she may have felt vindicated. Remember that John Russell, on her refusal of sex, had threatened to shoot himself on a number of occasions; here his fictional equivalent carries through the threat.

The *Kinematograph Weekly* referred to 'the celebrity of the central player'. The following year, the same year as the Regulation of Reports Act, Christabel appears to have been reaccepted into 'society', for a photograph of her featured in fashionable photographer Hugh Cecil's *Beauty Book*, alongside other society celebrities such as Lady Diana Cooper. To have been 'through the divorce courts' debarred women from attending Court (capital C) or Ascot's Royal Enclosure, yet Christabel had managed to turn her notoriety into fame and glamour. It appears that she had also maintained her honour – a gendered and class specific issue at stake for both Russells. For Christabel, honour referred to her sexual respectability and her baby's legitimacy (and of course his entitlement to a peerage); for John it referred to the family name of Ampthill: his own honour was bound up in this heritage, and no bastard child without the Ampthill blood should ever have a claim.[151]

A forum for speaking sex?

Writing about the Victorian divorce court, historian Kali Israel notes: it 'stands ... as one of the great social spaces for the enactment of access to the secrets of sex and marriage'.[152] Her observation is just as applicable to the divorce court of the early 1920s. So, what secrets of sex and marriage did the Russell case reveal? The trials gave a glimpse of a dysfunctional marriage and the rather wild, exotic and frenzied life of an exceptional woman, whose self-presentation was decidedly contradictory. The two versions of her 'self' – modern flapper and devoted mother – had an edgy, jarring quality. That she was both seen as the epitome of a modern woman, and saw herself in such terms, necessitates our rethinking of this key 1920s female representation as necessarily sexualised and childless.

The trials also exposed the two protagonists' apparent extreme sexual ignorance. The latter would have elicited recognition in many of the public: memoirs, autobiographies and letters from the upper and middle classes of the time reveal a level of ignorance on par with that of the Russells.[153] As for the working classes in the 1920s, from all accounts they were unlikely to be any more knowledgeable, especially the women who, like Christabel, lacked a language in which to talk about either sex or their bodies.[154] With this level of widespread sexual ignorance, the trials' questions concerning sex and reproduction, although questions for the petitioner, respondent and witnesses, must also have interested and perplexed the courtroom audience and newspaper readers alike. Those who managed to fight their way into the divorce court (possibly several hundred) would have had much more of a 'sex education' (such as a detailed biology lesson about the life expectancy and journey of sperm) than those who only had access to the press.[155] As indicated earlier in this chapter, newspapers heavily censored their reports. The word 'hymen' was only mentioned by the *News of the World*, and no newspaper mentioned periods, sperm, semen, penises, vaginas or breasts.[156] The numerous euphemisms were more titillating and 'suggestive' than educational. Yet the literally millions of people who read the details in their newspapers day by day (an even larger readership than Stopes's *Married Love*) were likely to have discussed and debated such issues amongst themselves. This erotic, amoral, entertaining divorce narrative (the likes of which were to be banned with the 1926 Act) was thus not simply a challenge to the sanctity of marriage and to the superiority of the upper classes; its wide press reportage also inadvertently generated a public space for talking about one of the things that the British are still meant to find the most embarrassing and difficult, namely sex. The print media might have been self-censoring and euphemistic, but their reports of the Russell case would undoubtedly have generated discussion of how to speak sex, how to do it, how not to do it, and with what consequences.

Notes

1 *Illustrated Sunday Herald*, 18th March 1923, p. 2.
2 *Reynolds's News*, 23rd July 1922, p. 1; 4th March 1923, p. 5.
3 I have been unable to read original transcripts of the first trial, which do not appear to exist, but transcripts of the second trial are bound with the transcripts of the House of Lords appeal. Parliamentary Archives, HL/PO/JU/4/3/754 (henceforth transcript of second trial). Many thanks to Mari Takayanagi, who alerted me to this invaluable resource.
4 Bingham, *Family Newspapers?*
5 Lord Ampthill, a second cousin of Bertram Russell, had been Governor of Madras in

1900, and briefly Viceroy of India in 1904. He had co-founded the xenophobic National Party in 1917, intent on interning enemy aliens. His father, the 1st Baron Ampthill, was Odo Russell, son of the Duke of Bedford.

6 Routine pregnancy testing did not exist in the 1920s and doctors generally refused to confirm early pregnancy by pelvic examination. Thanks to Jesse Olszynko-Gryn for this information.

7 Eileen Hunter, *Christabel: the Russell Case and After* (London, 1973), p. 161.

8 Edith Thompson wrote to Freddy Bywaters on 4th August 1922, enclosing a cutting about the Russell case from the *Daily Express*: 'I've wished and wished all the time it has been on that she could be proved innocent'. Young, *Trial of Frederick Bywaters and Edith Thompson*, p. 238.

9 Ellis Hume-Williams, *The World, the House and the Bar* (London, 1930), p. 152.

10 Apparently Mayer sported 'dazzling white buckskin shoes banded with brown broguing, "co-respondent shoes" they used to be called'. Hunter, *Christabel*, p. 11.

11 *News of the World*, 4th March 1923, p. 5.

12 *Daily Express*, 1st March 1923 p. 1; *News of the World*, 18th March 1923, p. 4.

13 *Reynolds's News*, 23rd July 1922, p. 1; 4th March 1923, p. 5.

14 *News of the World*, 16th July 1922. p. 4.

15 *News of the* World, 16th July 1922. p. 4.

16 *Illustrated Sunday Herald*, 18th March 1923, p. 4; *Weekly Dispatch*, 18th March 1923, p. 3; *Empire News*, 18th March 1923, p. 2; *Sunday Express*, 11th March 1923, p. 3; *News of the World*, 11th March 1923, p. 5; *News of the World*, 16th July 1922, p. 4.

17 *People*, 4th March 1923, p. 1; *The Times*, 9th March 1923, p. 5.

18 *Illustrated Sunday Herald*, 18th March 1923, p. 4.

19 *Daily Express*, 2nd March 1922, p. 6; *Daily* Mail, 1st June 1922, p. 8. See Bingham, *Gender, Modernity, and the Popular Press*, pp. 69–72; Barbara Burman, 'Racing Bodies: Dress and Pioneer Women Aviators and Racing Drivers', *Women's History Review*, 9, 2 (2000), pp. 299–326; Huggins, 'And Now for Something for the Ladies'; Soland, *Becoming Modern*, Chapters 2 and 3.

20 *Lloyds's Sunday News*, 16th July 1922, p. 5; *Illustrated Sunday Herald*, 18th March 1923, p. 4.

21 *Reynolds's News*, 18th March 1923, p. 10. On fashion see Coner, *The Spectacular Modern Woman*.

22 *The Times*, 14th July 1922, p. 4.

23 Thanks to Anne Logan for the information that Lady Ampthill was a JP.

24 Hunter, *Christabel*, p. 36.

25 Christabel's mother, Mrs Hart, suggested to John that he learned to dance: 'It might mend matters'. *News of the World*, 23rd July 1922, p. 2.

26 *The Times*, 12th July 1922, p. 5.

27 *The Times*, 1st March 1923, p. 5.

28 *The Times*, 15th July 1922, p. 4; *Daily Express*, 10th March 1923, p. 5.

29 *Illustrated Sunday Herald*, 18th March 1923, p. 4.

30 *Daily Mirror*, 24th July 1922, p. 2.

31 *People*, 23rd July 1922, p. 7.

32 *The Times*, 15th March 1923, p. 5.

33 *People*, 14th January 1923, p. 5.

34 *Sunday Express*, 18th March 1923, p. 7.

35 Arnold Bennett, *Body and Soul: a Play in Four Acts* (London, 1922).

36 *The Times*, 21st July 1922, p. 5. To this John Simon, John Russell's counsel in the first trial, quipped: 'the war ... has apparently provided counsel for the respondent and co-respondents ... with an every-ready explanation of every possible irregularity'. *The Times*, 22nd July 1922, p. 5.

37 *Daily Express*, 24th July 1922, p. 6.

38 Her salary there was £400 a year – much more than her husband's, who earned £275 when he worked at Vickers. *Reynolds's Newspaper*, 25th March 1923, p. 1.

39 *Daily Mirror*, 24th July 1922, p. 2.

40 *Empire News*, 18th March 1923, p. 2.

41 See *Manchester Guardian*, 25th January 1917: 'the extraordinary jumble that has taken place in the ranks of society through hasty war marriages ... young men and young women have married very much "above" and "below" their former station in life ... and bewildered parents have given up all attempts to control their children's matrimonial careers'.

42 *People*, 23rd July 1922, p. 14.

43 *Empire News*, 4th March 1923, p. 5. Most papers, including *The Times*, did not report this.

44 *Daily Mirror*, 15th March 1923, p. 2; *People*, 4th March 1923, p. 1; *Reynolds's News*, 4th March 1923, p. 5.

45 Christabel denied giving the press the photographs. When Marshall Hall asserted: 'I suggest that only you and your mother had that photograph?' She replied: 'Well, really, I should have thought that the photographer who took it might also have it.' Parliamentary Archives, HL/PO/JU/4/3/754, p. 323.

46 See Taylor, *Bright Young People*, for examples of the upper classes cross-dressing for fancy-dress parties.

47 *Daily Mirror*, 3rd March 1923, p. 1.

48 Matt Houlbrook, *Queer London: Perils and Pleasures in the Sexual Metropolis, 1918–1957* (Chicago and London, 2005), pp. 224–7.

49 This was in contrast to the argument posed in Krafft-Ebing's earlier *Psychopathia Sexualis*. Havelock Ellis introduced the term 'eonism' (after the cross-dressing eighteenth-century chevalier d'Eon) but the term never caught on. Havelock Ellis, 'Eonism', in *Studies in the Psychology of Sex: 7* (Philadelphia, PN, 1928).

50 *Daily Sketch*, 3rd March 1923, p. 2.

51 *The Times*, 8th March 1923, p. 5.

52 For fashionable female boyishness see Doan, *Fashioning Sapphism*.

53 For example, Mrs Hart, Christabel's mother, told the court that she had suggested to Lady Ampthill 'that the secret of the whole trouble was that her son was not man enough, and if he would assert himself all their little quarrels would be at an end'. *Daily Express*, 21st July 1922, p. 5.

54 *The Times*, 14th July 1922, p. 4.

55 *Empire News*, 4th March 1923, p. 5. *People*, 4th March 1923, p. 1. *Reynolds's News* was impressed by him however: 'he told without a falter of pride or shame of his long and fruitless search for work'. *Reynolds's News*, 4th March 1923, p. 5.

56 Hunter, *Christabel*, p. 53; House of Lords appeal. HL/PO/JU/4/3/754, p. 17.

57 *Daily Express*, 14th March 1923, p. 5.

58 *Daily Express*, 15th March 1923, p. 5.

59 *Empire News*, 11th March 1923, p. 6.

60 Parliamentary Archives, HL/PO/JU/4/3/754, p. 271.

61 *Empire News*, 16th July 1922, p. 2.

62 *Daily Mirror*, 1st March 1923, p. 19.

63 *The Times*, 8th July 1922, p. 4. She was permitted to leave.

64 Melman, *Women and the Popular Imaginatio*n, p. 3.

65 The need for sex education was starting to be voiced in the press, for example see Dr Elizabeth Sloan Chesser, *Sunday Express*, 16th October 1921, p. 8.

66 *News of the World*, 9th July 1922, p. 5.

67 *Daily Mail*, 15th July 1922, p. 4.

68 *The Times*, 15th July 1922, p. 4.

69 Stopes, *Married Love*, preface, p. xvii.

70 A counter statement by Gates, left posthumously to the British Library, argues that intercourse had indeed occurred, but that they had used contraceptives on her insistence. As Lesley Hall perceptively notes: 'Annulment may have seemed like the only way that she could free herself while retaining both her respectability and the chance of a second and better union.' Lesley Hall, '"The Subject is Obscene: No Lady would Dream of Alluding to it": Marie Stopes and her Courtroom Dramas', *Women's History Review*, 22, 2 (2013)

71 Quoted in Ruth Hall, *Marie Stopes: a Biography* (London, 1978), p. 80.

72 In both cases, both couples were virgins on marriage, although John Russell's virginity was never mentioned in the press. Parliamentary Archives, HL/PO/JU/4/3/754, p. 6. There was another link between Marie Stopes and the Russells. As the second Russell trial was beginning in March 1923, Marie's libel suit against the Roman Catholic Dr Halliday Sutherland was coming to an end. Patrick Hastings acted for both Marie and Christabel. Both trials also shared a witness: obstetric surgeon Sir Maurice Abbot-Anderson, called by Sutherland and by John Russell. Muriel Box, *The Trial of Marie Stopes* (London, 1967).

73 *Times*, 24th July 1922, p. 6.

74 Medicine increasingly entered the courtroom from the late nineteenth century in the form of specialist testimony. See Harris, *Murders and Madness*.

75 *The Times*, 19th July 1922, p. 5.

76 *The Times*, 20th July 1922, p. 5.

77 Transcript of second trial, pp. 296–7.

78 In the second trial, Marshall Hall asked her if she 'noticed a certain amount of colour coming around the nipples of your breast?' She denied it. This exchange was not reported in the press. Transcripts of second trial, p. 300.

79 *The Times*, 20th July 1922, p. 5.

80 Transcript of second trial, p. 437; *Daily Mirror* 10th March 1923, p. 2.

81 *The Times*, 10th March 1923, p. 4.

82 On the popularity of clairvoyants in the West at this time see Willem de Blecourt and Cornelie Usborne, 'Women's Medicine, Women's Culture: Abortion and Fortune-Telling in Early Twentieth Century Germany and the Netherlands', *Medical History*, 43, 3 (1999), pp. 376–92. On their popularity in Britain during the war, see Emma Tennant, *Strangers: a Family Romance* (London, 1998), p. 46. There were numerous prosecutions of fortune-tellers during the war: see the popular press and *The Times* 1916–18.

83 *Empire News*, 23rd July 1922, p. 2.

84 *The Times*, 20th July 1922, p. 5; *Daily Sketch*, 20th July 1922, p. 2. She said she was neither

a clairvoyant nor a fortune-teller, but had 'passed examinations conducted by a medical man'. *The Times*, 20th July 1922, p. 5.

85 *Daily Sketch*, 20th July 1922, p. 2; *News of World*, 23rd July 1922, p. 4.

86 *The Times*, 9th March 1923, p. 5.

87 Chandak Sengoopta, *The Most Secret Quintessence of Life: Sex, Glands, and Hormones, 1850–1950* (Chicago, 2006). Also see Diana Long Hall, 'Biology, Sex Hormones and Sexism in the 1920s', *Philosophical Forum* 5, 1–2 (1973/4), pp. 81–96.

88 See Michael Saler, '"Clap if You Believe in Sherlock Holmes": Mass Culture and the Re-Enchantment of Modernity, c.1890–1940', *The Historical Journal*, 46, 3 (2003), pp. 599–622 for a wonderful discussion of Holmes's reconciliation of modernity and enchantment, in contrast to Conan Doyle's resort to spiritualism. See Cornelie Usborne, *Cultures of Abortion in Weimar Germany* (New York and Oxford, 2007) for a fascinating account of the way that women of Weimar Germany combined traditional and modern scientific discourses in the representation and understanding of their bodies.

89 *Empire News*, 11th March 1923, p. 6.

90 Transcript of second trial, pp. 493–4.

91 Under cross-examination however, he admitted that this did not decisively prove that the baby had been carried more than the normal period. *The Times*, 20th July 1922, p. 5; 10th March 1923, p. 4. And see evidence of Dr Eden, transcript of second trial, p. 431.

92 Transcript of second trial, p. 396.

93 Transcript of second trial, p. 432.

94 Transcript of second trial, p. 587. Abbot-Anderson had been medical inspector for nullity cases for fifteen years and was presumably used to making these fine distinctions. Transcript of second trial, p. 41.

95 Marie Stopes, *Marriage in My Time* (London, 1935), pp. 153, 155. Thanks to Angus McLaren for drawing my attention to this reference.

96 Transcript of second trial p. 392, and see p. 428 for Dr Eden on this question.

97 Transcript of second trial, p. 427.

98 Transcript of second trial, pp. 388–90.

99 Transcript of second trial, pp. 392, 388–90, 606.

100 Kate Fisher, *Birth-Control, Sex and Marriage in Britain, 1918–1960* (Oxford, 2006), p. 182; Angus McLaren, *A History of Contraception* (Oxford, 1990), p. 235.

101 Stopes, *Married Love*, p. 52. And see Marie Stopes, *Contraception: Theory, History and Practice* (London, 1923).

102 *News of the World*, 16th July 1922, p. 4.

103 Fisher, *Birth-Control, Sex and Marriage in Britain*, p. 27; Judy Giles, '"Playing Hard to Get": Working-Class Women, Sexuality and Respectability in Britain, 1918–40', *Women's History Review*, 1, 2 (1992).

104 *The Times*, 8th March 1923, p. 5.

105 Transcript of second trial, pp. 268–70.

106 Transcript of second trial, p. 276.

107 *Daily Mirror*, 10th March 1923, p. 2.

108 Simon Szreter and Kate Fisher, *Sex before the Sexual Revolution* (Oxford, 2010); and see Simon Szreter, *Fertility, Class and Gender, 1860–1940* (Cambridge, 1996), p. 425; Sally Alexander suggests that *protection* from sexual knowledge was 'the equivalent among the poor of chaperonage: Alexander, 'The Mysteries and Secrets of Women's Bodies', p. 166.

109 *Empire News*, 11th March 1923, p. 6. See Lesley A. Hall, 'Sexuality', in Ina Zweiniger-

Bargielowska, *Women in Twentieth-Century Britain* (London, 2001), p. 53 on a woman telling writer Leonora Eyles in the early 1920s that 'I shouldn't mind married life so much if it wasn't for bedtime.'

110 Transcript of second trial, p. 262.

111 *The Times*, 16th March 1923, p. 5.

112 Geoffrey Mortimer (pseudonym for Walter Gallichan), *Chapters on Human Love* (1898), quoted in Walter Gallichan, *Sexual Apathy and Coldness in Women* (London, 1927), p. 20. For example of feminist debates on celibacy, see *The Freewoman* (1912), quoted in Bland, *Banishing the Beast*, pp. 281–3.

113 Gallichan, *Sexual Apathy and Coldness in Women*, p. 18. In one of Christabel's letters read out in court she writes to John: 'there is nothing more distasteful to me than the idea … that anyone should feel merged into one with me'. Marshall Hall asked her: 'Does that mean that anything like complete sexual intercourse between you was horrible?' 'Perfectly horrible' was her reply. Transcript of second trial, p. 287.

114 *The Times*, 2nd March 1923, p. 4.

115 *The Times*, 8th March 1923, p. 5.

116 *Lloyd's Sunday Newspaper*, 11th March 1923, p. 11.

117 *Sunday Express*, 11th March 1923, p. 3.

118 *The Times*, 16th March 1923, p. 5.

119 *People*, 4th March 1923, p. 1. One is reminded of those nineteenth-century anthropological mug-shots of prostitutes' ears that were said to indicate degeneracy. Gilman, 'Black Bodies, White Bodies'.

120 *Empire News*, 16th July 1922, p. 2 had as a strap-line: 'Child's amazing resemblance to the Hon John Hugo Russell'. The paper was quoting Hastings, but choosing it as a strap-line could be read as support for the view.

121 *Daily Express*, 17th March 1923, p. 3.

122 *Daily Sketch*, 17th March 1923, p. 2.

123 Marjoribanks, *Life of Sir Edward Marshall Hall*, p. 428.

124 Melman, *Women and the Popular Imagination*, p. 24.

125 Quoted in Hunter, *Christabel*, p. 106.

126 Marjoribanks, *Life of Sir Edward Marshall Hall*, p. 426.

127 *Sunday Express*, 11th March 1923, p. 3.

128 *News of the World*, 11th March 1923, p. 5.

129 *Empire News*, 11th March 1923, p. 6.

130 *Lloyd's Sunday News*, 11th March 1923, p. 11.

131 *Sunday Express*, 18th March 1923, p. 7.

132 *Daily Sketch*, 15th March 1923, p. 2

133 Hume-Williams, *The World, the House and the Bar*, p. 157. Christabel formed an intense dislike for Marshall Hall, especially 'repelled by his flamboyant theatrical demeanour in court'. Hunter, *Christabel*, p. 111.

134 *Daily Express*, 15th March 1923. Hastings, in his short summing up, implied jokingly that the co-respondents had been picked almost randomly: 'Someone … in this front bench where I sit lives in Curzon Street and he is most grateful he has not been dragged into this case as co-respondent (laughter) [he is referring to himself]. I don't suppose that there is a single male acquaintance of Mrs Russell who does not thank God he has not been made a party to this suit.' *The Times*, 15th March 1923, p. 5.

135 A.P. Herbert, *Holy Deadlock* (London, 1934).

136 *Daily Express*, 24th July 1922, p. 6, 17th March 1923, p. 6
137 Hunter, *Christabel*, p. 109.
138 Hunter, *Christabel*, pp. 110, 161.
139 Gail Savage, 'Erotic Stories and Public Decency: Newspaper Reporting of Divorce Proceedings in England', *The Historical Journal*, 41, 2 (1998), p. 527.
140 Bingham, *Family Newspapers?*, pp. 136–7.
141 Revd Norwood, *Sunday Express*, 23rd July 1922, p. 8.
142 *Daily Express*, 24th July 1922, p. 6.
143 *Sunday Express*, 11th March 1923, p. 3.
144 Transcripts of second trial, p. 303.
145 Duke was also President of the Probate, Divorce and Admiralty Division.
146 Bingham, *Family Newspapers?*, p. 135.
147 Savage, 'Erotic Stories and Public Decency'; Hume-Williams, *The World, the House and the Bar*, pp. 154–5.
148 *Bioscope*, 19th March 1925, p. 48.
149 *Kinematograph Weekly*, 19th March 1925, p. 80.
150 *Bioscope*, 19th March 1925, p. 48.
151 He even said: 'I might not have brought proceedings if it would have been possible for me to resign my succession in favour of my brother.' *The Times*, 14th March 1923, p. 5.
152 Kali Israel, 'French Vices and British Liberties; Gender, Class and Narrative Competition in a Late Victorian Sex Scandal', *Social History*, 22, 1 (January 1997), pp. 1–26.
153 See Naomi Mitchison, *All Change Here; Girlhood and Marriage* (London, 1975); Frances Partridge, *Memories* (London, 1981), Hall, *Hidden Anxieties*; Hera Cook, *The Long Sexual Revolution English Women, Sex and Contraception, 1900–1975* (Oxford, 2004), pp. 167–77.
154 See Diana Gittins, *Fair Sex: Family Size and Structure, 1900–39* (London, 1982); Elizabeth Roberts, *A Woman's Place: An Oral History of Working-Class Women, 1890–1940* (London, 1984); Alexander, 'The Mysteries and Secrets of Women's Bodies'..
155 It is difficult to arrive at even an approximate number for the courtroom audience. *The Daily Express*, 1st March 1923, p. 1 mentioned that 'The retrial of the Russell case began yesterday in a court crowded to suffocation. So great was the array of counsel, witnesses and relatives of the parties that room could be found for only thirty-six members of the public.' But the *People*, 4th March 1923, p. 1 noted that 'The audience which has listened each day to the Russell case has consisted of nearly 500 members of the general public.' This suggests that the trial was moved to a larger court.
156 *News of the World*, 23rd July 1922, p. 4 referred to Dr Mackenzie finding 'traces of virginity, the hymen not being ruptured'.

Afterlives

Throughout this book I have been looking not just at the female protagonists of a series of trials, but also how they were looked at, 'explained' and categorised by the press and other commentators at the time. I have attempted to delineate the cultural salience of these categorisations. But what happened later to these women, after their trials were over? And was there also an afterlife to the memory of each trial? These women were not merely the various 'types' that the press made them out to be, they were of course real people, whose collisions with the law had an impact on the rest of their lives. For some of these women, their afterlives were long, Maud Allan, Margot Asquith, Marguerite Fahmy and Christabel Russell all living into their eighties. Maud Allan never regained her previous fame, making a living through teaching dance rather than performing it. By the late 1920s Maud had been joined in her grand apartment near Regent's Park by Verna Aldrich – her secretary-cum-companion-cum-lover. Margot Asquith stopped paying for the apartment in the early 1930s, but Allan stayed on with Aldrich until 1938 – her longest relationship with either sex. When Allan returned to the USA in 1941, Margot generously paid off her large debts. Allan died fifteen years later aged eighty-three.[1] Margot Asquith became Countess of Oxford and Asquith on the ennoblement of her husband in 1925. Henry Asquith died three years later, but Margot lived until she was eighty-one, writing prolifically over the years, including numerous memoirs. None mentions the 'cult of the clitoris' trial.

Billie Carleton and Freda Kempton lived on in drug mythology. For example, in Kate Meyrick's 1933 memoir, appearing eleven years after Freda's death, it was assumed that their names would be familiar to readers as 'figures of tragedy', while Brilliant Chang was presented as 'undoubtedly the master-mind behind the drug traffic in England'.[2] Ada Ping You, who had been sent to Holloway prison in December 1918, having received five months imprisonment with hard labour for the possession and preparation of opium, did not feature in this public list of famous drug villains and their victims. She entered prison suffering from tuberculosis, and after her release lived for only a year-and-a-half, dying in November 1920 aged twenty-nine.[3] In 1922 there was a repeat raid on the home of her husband, Lsu Ping You, and opium utensils were again found. While he had been fined only £10 on the previous occasion in late 1918, this time he was recommended for deportation by a less compassionate magistrate, namely J.A.R. Cairns.[4] I unfortunately have no information as to what happened to May Roberts and Julia Kitt.

The fate of Edith Thompson prompted Fryn Tennyson Jesse to write up her story thinly veiled in the moving 1934 novel *A Pin to See a Peepshow*.[5] When Tennyson Jesse edited the Alma Rattenbury/George Stoner case for the 'Notable British Trial Series' the following year, she observed how 'the uneasy memory of Edith Thompson' was a factor safeguarding Mrs Rattenbury (who like Edith, was accused of murdering her husband in collaboration with her younger lover, but unlike Edith was acquitted).[6] I mentioned that subsequent to Edith's death there has been widespread recognition of a miscarriage of justice. By the early 1950s, the wrongful execution of Edith Thompson had become a key plank to the movement for the abolition of capital punishment.[7] In 1971 her body was exhumed from Holloway prison; she is now buried, with an engraved headstone, in Brookwood Cemetery, Surrey.[8] With Jill Dawson's *Fred and Edie*, shortlisted in 2000 for the Whitbread and the Orange Prize, and the 2001 film *Another Life*, many of the present generation are now likely to have heard of Edith.[9]

What happened to Marguerite Fahmy after she was acquitted? In April 1924 the story of a 'bogus baby' emerged: that she had planned to pretend to be pregnant by her late husband, then to make it appear that she had given birth to a male child, who would conveniently die, but not before she had claimed Fahmy's vast fortune in the name of the son. Under Muslim law, a posthumous son could inherit a quarter to a half of his father's estate. Marguerite denied that this idea had ever been hers, but had been suggested to her in a series of letters sent by a Syrian moneylender and carpet merchant, Yusuf Cassab Bey, who had said he would lay on a doctor to verify the birth (and subsequent death) of the child. He also, she claimed, proposed getting a share of the fortune. She took the matter to the Parisian police (she had moved back to Paris after the trial) and Cassab Bey was put on trial, but released for lack of evidence. It became apparent to journalists that the idea had indeed been (at least partly) Marguerite's, but recognising its likely failure, she had set up Cassab Bey as the fall-guy. The affair 'caused an enormous sensation throughout Paris, and indeed, throughout France'.[10]

In February 1926 *World's Pictorial News* informed its readers that in the previous two-and-a-half years Mme Fahmy had had many proposals of marriage, and had been approached by music-hall magnates both in Britain and on the Continent, but had rejected all offers, including the suggestion from a film company that she appear in a reconstructed scene of the night she shot her husband. She was currently training as an opera singer, as well as being in dispute with her sisters-in-law over the possession of 'an elaborate dressing case' (covered in diamonds, with fittings of tortoise shell, and bottles with stoppers of pure gold) which she claimed had been given to her by her late husband and thus was rightfully hers.[11] Whether she ever obtained the dressing-case is unclear, but she remained wealthy, living in a fashionable Parisian suburb until January 1971, where she died aged eighty, never having remarried.[12]

Memory of Christabel Russell's notorious case lived on for a time – at least until the Second World War – for in Nancy Mitford's 1945 *Pursuit of Love*, Linda announces that she 'knew the laws of divorce from having read the whole of the Russell case off newspapers with which the fires in the spare bedrooms were laid.'[13] Mitford must have assumed that even if her readers did not know the 'laws of divorce', they would at least have heard of the Russell case. Christabel and John had finally divorced in 1937; she never remarried and had no more children. She continued with her highly successful dress shop, was costume designer for several British films, but later moved to a dilapidated castle in Galway, Ireland, where she became an active member of the local hunt. John remarried twice. On his father's death in 1935, John succeeded to the title of Lord Ampthill. By his third wife John had another son, also called John, and on the death of John senior in 1973, John junior contested the title of Lord Ampthill. Christabel's son Geoffrey declined a DNA test, and three years later, a House of Lords committee confirmed him as lawful heir to the title, ruling that what had been decided in court fifty years earlier could not now be rescinded. His mother never lived to hear the judgment, for she had died aged eighty a few weeks earlier. Christabel, ever the maverick, had spent her last years travelling the 'hippy trail' on precarious buses through Southern Asia.[14] Geoffrey, after playing an active role in the Lords as a cross-bencher, including as deputy speaker, died in April 2011.[15]

Comparisons: the trials

That the trials considered in this book all took place in the short period 1918–24 means that comparisons between them were inevitably made at the time. For example, on Marguerite Fahmy's acquittal the *People* asserted:

'The case differed at every turn from the Thompson murder [Edith's trial had been nine months earlier], and Mme Fahmy was justly entitled to her freedom.'[16] What did the newspaper mean by 'differed at every turn'? How are we to explain the contrasting verdicts of Edith and Marguerite? Despite certain parallels in press representation of the two women – both depicted as simultaneously elegant yet frail – one obvious difference between them lay with the representation of their sexuality. Edith was constructed in court and by the press as highly and deviantly sexual; Marguerite as sexually passive and sexually abused. Linked to this were contrasting melodramatic tropes: in Edith's trial Percy was the victim and she the villain, in Marguerite's the victim was the defendant herself and the villain her dead husband. The conduct and outcome of the trials were also crucially affected by the admissibility or otherwise of certain evidence. The admissibility of incriminating letters was Edith's undoing; the inadmissibility of background information about Marguerite contributed to her acquittal. The most obvious contrast though was the role of ethnicity: the way in which racially prejudicial Orientalist discourse was used to defame Ali Fahmy and construct a polarised East/West divide. As Anette Ballinger rightly points out, if Marguerite's husband had been a member of the British aristocracy instead of an Egyptian, she would have been the one constructed as 'the uncontrollable and passionate foreigner'.[17] And if Edith had been a Frenchwoman, Filson Young suggests, 'she would have been taken out of her humble working life and been at once the slave and the ruler of some connoisseur in extravagant caprice'.[18]

The trials may have been compared and contrasted at the time, but there were a number of thematic similarities that ran through most if not all of them. Press reports of all the trials paid close attention to the women's appearance, and in relation to the four more significant cases (Maud Allan, Edith Thompson, Marguerite Fahmy and Christabel Russell) many papers filled their columns with numerous photographs. In addition to this focus on the visual, there were two linked themes that ran through nearly all the trials, namely dance and sensation-seeking. Maud Allan not only made her living as a dancer, but was an important catalyst in the rise of the 'dance craze'. Freda Kempton also made her living from dance. While Freda spent all her work-time dancing, Edith Thompson and Christabel Russell spent most of their leisure-time doing likewise, for both were excellent dancers and adored to dance. Dance was emblematic of the modern woman-cum-flapper, and along with jazz was a crucial signifier of the 1920s. The 1920s press constructed a special term for the dancing flapper of the nightclub: she was labelled the butterfly woman/girl. The term sounds benign but as we have seen, it reduced the butterfly woman's agency, pinning her down to a superficial and transitory life of flitting aimlessly from nightclub to nightclub, sipping the deadly nectars of drink and dope.

Although dance was not explicitly attacked in press reports of the trials, women's sensation-seeking was, particularly as exhibited by the female audience. The trials of Edith, Marguerite and Christabel all involved press complaints about the cross-class, cross-generational female audiences – that they were 'neurotic' 'female ghouls' who came to the court as they would to a theatre, seeking entertainment, cheap thrills and an outlet for their 'repressed vileness'. Their inappropriate sensation-seeking was seen as part of the modern woman's frivolous lifestyle: her seeking of pleasure in quick fixes of instant delight, be it drugs, drink, nightclubs (the pursuit of the butterfly girls), the thrill of relations with racial 'others', the foolish escapist consumption of popular 'cheap' literature (as in Edith's case and the readers of 'desert romances') or of Hollywood cinema (the likes of the *Sheik*). Criticism of women's 'consumption' of all the above was in effect an attack on cultural modernity, the intensity and sheer viciousness of some of the commentary indicating deep disquiet about the modern woman, the spread of mass culture and the instability of class definers. Young women in their dress and behaviour confounded class distinctions, for many, across class, now donned make-up and dressed like the actresses they saw in bright lights at the 'pictures'. As for class-inappropriate behaviour, James Douglas had found it difficult to reconcile Edith's lower-middle-class back-ground with her 'illicit passion', awarding her the bizarre epithet 'Madame Bovary in a bunshop'.

Comparisons: the newspapers

The presence or absence of photographs was one importance difference between the newspapers in their reports of the trials, and it was of course the 'picture' press who featured the most photographs, the 'class' papers the least. Photographs were thought to appeal to the female reader in par-ticular; 'When men think pictorially', claimed journalist Holbrook Jackson, 'they unsex themselves.'[19] The 'class' newspapers, aimed at the upper- and middle-class man, were, as yet, unconcerned with providing photographs. As for editorials, the *Daily* and *Sunday Express* tended to provide a number of editorial comments on each trial, as opposed to simply one, and they were generally written by the opinionated and moralistic James Douglas. The other main difference between the newspapers lay not so much with the contents of the reports as with the nature of the headlines. The 'class' papers had factual headlines such as 'Trial of Mme Fahmy', while divorce cases came under the title 'Law reports'. The popular 'Sundays' and dailies varied in the degree of sensationalism in their headlines; in the Russell case, for example, the *News of the World*'s 'His Bohemian Wife', and 'Married Ignorance' were possibly more enticing than the *People*'s 'The Amazing Case of the Russell Baby', and 'Russell Baby Drama'. The *Daily Express* included quotes from Christabel's letters in some of its headings – 'My Dago Man', 'Vast Numbers of Adoring Men' – while the *Daily Mirror* had equally intriguing strap-lines such as 'Husband Told he had Walked in Sleep', 'Bohemian Life of Peer's Daughter-in-law'. But did the press report the cases differently? Generally not greatly, although in my examination of several Sunday newspapers' accounts of the two 'drug fiends', May Roberts and Julia Kitt, I demonstrated internal inconsistencies in the papers, which I suggested was an indication of the inconclusiveness of press responses to the modern woman.

If the newspapers were inconsistent in their presentation of the modern woman, were they similarly inconsistent on the issue of censorship? In the 'cult of the clitoris' case, Judge Darling directed the press to self-censor sexual material 'in the interests of public decency'. Most newspapers were indeed attentive to such a request, the popular press trying to juggle its presentation as a 'clean', 'family' read on the one hand with the commercial pull of sensational copy on the other, the 'resolution' frequently being that of euphemism (which was objected to by some as too 'suggestive').[20] In relation to the Maud Allan case, we have seen that *The Times* was the one newspaper (apart from the subscription-only *Vigilante*) to reproduce the term 'lesbian'; it also mentioned 'homosexualists' and 'sodomy'. The *Manchester Guardian* used the terms 'homosexual' and 'sadism', but not 'sodomy'. Presumably these two 'class' newspapers did not think of themselves as 'family' papers, and assumed that their (upper- and middle-class male) readers had no need of 'protection' from explicit sexual terms. The only two popular papers to reproduce any of these concepts were the *News of the World*, who like *The Times* referred to 'homosexualists' (this was, after all, a paper renowned for sensationalism), and the *Daily Sketch*, who like the *Manchester Guardian*, referred to 'sadism' (the term might have been thought fairly unobjectionable). Most of the papers most of the time in their reporting of this trial wrote of 'sexual perversions', 'a certain vice', or 'moral pervert' – terms that were vague in their non-specificity but highly suggestive. Maud Allan, in her defence of the play *Salome*, commented on this issue of suggestiveness: she argued that the paragraph headed 'the Cult of the Clitoris' was more harmful than the play in its greater suggestiveness, and 'the curiosity of man is such that they will go and find out'. The play in contrast was 'so veiled as not to be obvious'.[21]

Insufficient veiling and too much suggestiveness were precisely the accusations made by George V and others against the press reportage of the Russell case. I gave an example of just such press suggestiveness – of how the *Sunday Express*, in referring to an exchange between Marshall Hall and Christabel, asserted that 'no newspaper could possibly repeat his words', thereby conjuring up a host of unspeakably dreadful possibilities. As I pointed out, the clinical sexual terms used in the two Russell trials were never reproduced in either popular or 'class' press – terms like periods, sperm, semen, penis, vagina or breasts. As for why these terms (all appearing in Marie Stopes's *Married Love*) were seen as less printable by papers such as *The Times* than words such as 'lesbian' and 'homosexual', possibly related to contemporary reservations on naming the body. Possibly too it indicated the inability to 'speak' heterosexuality: as historian David Halperin provocatively suggests: 'heterosexuality not homosexuality … is truly the "love that dare not speak its name".'[22]

The Russell divorce case was one of the last to be publicly reported. But if George V and others keen to ban sex from newspapers thought that the 1926 Act would transform the press, they were to be disappointed. Details of divorce trials may have gone, but in the inter-war years the number of visual depictions of the sexualised female body increased dramatically, with photographs of cinema stars, modern sportswomen, titled ladies, debutantes, and fashion models. If the female reader was to be wooed, so too was the male, and not simply with sport. 'Bathing belles' also became a regular in some of the popular papers.[23] Yet the inter-war was a contradictory period as far as depictions of sex were concerned. There was much censorship in theatre, film and literature. And from 1924 for the next five years, Britain had the most notorious 'guardian of public morality' for its Home Secretary that it has ever had: Sir William Joynson-Hicks ('Jix').[24]

Morality tales and the defining of Britishness/Englishness

There were two key didactic aspects to the ways in which the press wrote about the trials, and they both spoke to contemporary fears – about sexual morality on the one hand, national identity on the other. All the trials were represented by the press as morality tales. Reports of the Maud Allan trial warned that dangerously mixing sexual perversion, decadence and modernity inevitably spelt treachery. Chapter 2 revealed the morality tales spun around drugs and race: that women were far more susceptible to drugs than men, drug-taking would lead to ill-health and imprisonment if not death, and relations with 'Chinamen', to which they were 'lured', would likewise compromise looks, health and happiness, demonstrating the inadvisability of miscegenation. The fate of Edith Thompson warned women of the terrible consequences of acting on their sexual desires. The trial of Marguerite Fahmy did likewise in relation to women attracted to Oriental men. Despite Christabel's eventual victory, the Russell case cautioned women against reckless pursuit of pleasure at the expense of nurturing their marital home and submitting to the sexual and other needs of their husbands. The overall moral message of these various trials was that young women needed to curb their selfish sensation-seeking and their transgressive sexual desires. And they all were too frivolously insubstantial to be worthy of the vote.

The trials were also sites for the contestation of Britishness/ Englishness. In the Maud Allan trial, while her counsel accused Billing of being 'un-English' in his lack of chivalry, Billing and his radical right colleagues reconfigured 'true' Englishness in terms of family-orientated heterosexuality, with those falling outside this definition cast as the 'enemy within'. The image of the sadistic Orient was also a crucial factor in this defining of Britishness/Englishness. Before embarking on the research for this book, I had not anticipated the centrality of Orientalist discourse to the majority of these trials. Part of the way in which Maud Allan was demonised was in terms of the 'treachery' of her dancing the dance of a young sadistic, sexually perverted Oriental woman. During the three drug trials of Ada Ping You, May Roberts and Julia Kitt, the magistrates' pronouncements and the press reports evoked the inappropriateness of their marriages to Chinese men – men of the 'far Orient' – and in representing Chinese men in Britain as 'un-British', they contributed to shoring up an imagined national British identity. Marguerite Fahmy's defence was crucially predicated on the vilification of her Oriental dead husband, the case leading to wider debate on the inadvisability of relations of white women and Eastern men. After Edith Thompson's hanging, there were murmurings as to the fallibility of judgment, and the irreversibility of capital punishment, but the Fahmy trial reconfirmed the superiority of the British (implicitly in contrast to the French) judicial system – Marguerite describing 'British justice' as 'too wonderful for words'. Such a verdict must have sounded hollow and ironic to those who believed Edith innocent.

During uncertain, tumultuous times in the immediate aftermath of the Great War, the modern woman-cum-flapper was constantly under the spotlight, as seen in the trials discussed here. The press attempted to circumscribe her representation, to slot her into a typology. Thus I have suggested that the nightclub-attending, drug-taking young woman was 'contained' by the category 'butterfly woman/girl' – the sting (to carry on with the insect analogy) removed by her reduction to a harmless, fluttering, insubstantial being lacking all agency. Young women who formed relations with Chinese men ('lured' young women, another sub-category of the flapper, but one more consistently working-class), also had their agency challenged in their depiction as sad, pathetic and physically transformed, the bearers of 'handicapped' offspring. Where a modern woman displayed agency that was seen as threatening, as in the case of Edith Thompson, represented as highly and inappropriately sexual, the general verdict was that she should be punished accordingly. Christabel Russell, on the other hand, although seen as ultra-modern, impetuous and independent, presented an asexual persona, and thereby was thought less problematic by the press; combined with her 'primitive' maternity, her modernity was perceived as 'tamed'. It was not the female figure of Marguerite Fahmy who caused consternation during her trial, but the woman in the audience – the 'female ghoul', 'indulging in an orgy of unhealthy sensation' – and the foolish woman who read desert romances and yearned for relations with a sadistic Oriental sheik. In examining these trials and the ways in which the women concerned, and women more generally, were minutely and obsessively observed and categorised, we have been able to chart how the figure of the flapper was a personification of the upheavals of the time. She 'carried' a series of fears and anxieties about modernity, and instabilities of gender, class, race and national identity. The figure of the flapper came later to stand for the 'roaring' 1920s, but in the period immediately after the Great War she represented not only newness, hedonism and 'anything goes', but also disruption, change and a frightening, uncertain future.

Notes

1 Cherniavsky, *Salome Dancer*, pp. 264–5, 280.

2 Meyrick, *Secrets of the 43*, p. 55. Also in *Sunday Sentinel*, 3rd February 1929, p. 12. Her memoir, published posthumously, for she died the year of its publication, largely reproduced the ten episodes of her 1929 reminiscences written for the *Sunday Sentinel*. There were many articles in the press concerning the idea of a powerful Chinese syndicate reaching out from Limehouse across the world. See for example *Daily Express*, 1st October 1920, p. 1, which invokes a 'Chinese Moriaty' in control.

3 Kuhn, *Dope Girls*, p. 116; Auerbach, *Race, Law and the 'Chinese Puzzle' in Imperial Britain*, p. 183.

4 *The Times*, 30th July 1921, p. 7. Deportation of Chinese men for opium offences had begun in 1916, when a number of men were deported under the Aliens Restriction Act 1916 and Article XII of Aliens Restriction (Consolidation) Order 1916. PRO: HO45/24683. The Act was made permanent in 1919 with the Aliens Restriction (Amendment) Act.

5 F. Tennyson Jesse, *A Pin to See a Peepshow* (London, 1934, 1984).

6 F. Tennyson Jesse (ed.), *Trial of Alma Victoria Rattenbury and George Percy Stoner* (London and Edinburgh, 1935), p. 13.

7 In 1952 Broad's *The Innocence of Edith Thompson* was serialised in the *Sunday Dispatch*

and contributed to the contemporary debate on the abolition of capital punishment. A Royal Commission on Capital Punishment sat 1949–53 and the death penalty was finally abolished in 1965.

8 Weis, *Criminal Justice* (2001), new preface.

9 Jill Dawson, *Fred and Edie* (London, 2000); *Another Life*, written and directed by Philip Goodhew (2001).

10 *World's Pictorial News*, 19th April 1924, p. 2; *World's Pictorial News*, 26th April 1923, p. 2; Rose, *Scandal at the Savoy*, pp. 186–90.

11 *World's Pictorial News*, 7th February 1926, p. 2. Thanks to John Carter Wood for drawing my attention to this article.

12 Rose, *Scandal at the Savoy*, p. 191.

13 Nancy Mitford, *The Pursuit of Love* (London, 1945, 2010), p. 64. Thanks to Laura Schwartz for reminding me of this reference.

14 Hunter, *Christabel*, pp. 180–2.

15 See obituary in *Daily Telegraph*, 26th April 2011.

16 *People*, 23rd September 1923, p. 9.

17 Ballinger, 'The Guilt of the Innocent and the Innocence of the Guilty', p. 11.

18 Young, *Trial of Frederick Bywaters and Edith Thompson* (1923), p. xvii.

19 Quoted in Bingham, *Gender, Modernity and the Popular Press*, p. 36.

20 Bingham, *Family Newspapers?*

21 *Verbatim Report*, p. 113.

22 David Halperin, *Saint Foucault: Towards a Gay Hagiography* (New York, 1995), p. 48.

23 See Bingham, *Gender, Modernity ,and the Popular Press*, Chapter 5.

24 Jeffrey Weeks, *Sex, Politics and Society* (London, 1981), p. 218; Ronald Blythe, *The Age of Illusion: England in the Twenties and Thirties* (London, 1963), Chapter 2.

Bibliography

Archives

National Archives, Kew

Crime: CRIM 1/247
Director of Public Prosecutions: DPP1/74
Home Office: HO 45/10724/251861
Home Office: HO 45/25404
Home Office: HO45/24683.

Parliamentary Archives

House of Lords: HL/PO/JU/4/3/754

Newspapers and journals

British Film Institute Library

Bioscope
Kinematograph Weekly

British Newspaper Library, Colindale

Daily Chronicle
Daily Express
Daily Graphic
Daily Herald
Daily Mail
Daily Mirror
Daily News
Daily Sketch
Daily Telegraph
Empire News
Evening News
Illustrated Police News
Illustrated Sunday Herald

Imperialist/Vigilante
John Bull
Lloyd's Sunday News
London Stage
Manchester Guardian
Morning Post
News of the World
New Statesman
New York Times
Pall Mall Gazette
People
Punch
Referee
Reynolds's Newspaper/News
Spectator
Star
Sunday Chronicle
Sunday Express
Sunday Graphic
Sunday Pictorial
Sunday Sentinel
Tatler
The Sunday Times
The Times
The Times Literary Supplement
Weekly/Sunday Dispatch
Western Mail
Westminster Gazette
World
World's Pictorial News

The Women's Library

Britannia
The Vote

Books, articles and theses

Ahmed, Aijaz, 'Orientalism and After', in Patrick Williams and Laura Chrisman (eds), *Colonial Discourse and Post-Colonial Theory* (Hertfordshire, 1993)

Ahmed, Leila, 'Western Ethnocentrism and Perceptions of the Harem', *Feminist Studies*, 8 (1982)

Ahmed, Leila, *Women and Gender in Islam* (New Haven, CT, 1992)

Abra, Allison Jean, 'On with the Dance: Nation, Culture and Popular Dancing in Britain, 1918–1945' (unpublished Ph.D. thesis, University of Michigan, 2009)

Aldrich, Robert, *Colonialism and Homosexuality* (London and New York, 2003)

Alexander, Sally, *Becoming a Woman and Other Essays in 19th and 20th Century Feminist History* (London, 1994)

Alexander, Sally, 'The Mysteries and Secrets of Women's Bodies', in Mica Nava and Alan O'Shea (eds), *Modern Times* (London, 1996)

Alexander, Sally, 'Men's Fears and Women's Work: Responses to Unemployment in London between the Wars', *Gender & History*, 12, 2 (July 2000)

Alexander, Sally, 'A New Civilization? London Surveyed 1928–1940s', *History Workshop Journal*, 64 (2007)

Allan, Maud, *My Life and Dancing* (London, 1908)

Allen, Judith A., *Sex and Secrets: Crimes Involving Australian Women since 1880* (Melbourne, 1990)

Allen, Trevor, *Underworld: the Biography of Charles Brooks Criminal* (London, 1932)

Anderson, Benedict, *Imagined Communities: Reflections on the Origins and Spread of Nationalism* (London, 1983)

Andrew, Christopher, *The Defence of the Realm: The Authorized History of MI5* (London, 2009)

Archer-Straw, Petrine, *Negrophilia: Avant-Garde Paris and Black Culture in the 1920s* (London, 2000)

Asquith, Cynthia, *Diaries 1915–1918* (London, 1968)

Auerbach, Sascha, *Race, Law and the 'Chinese Puzzle' in Imperial Britain* (New York, 2009)

Author of 'Nemesis Hunt', *Maudie* (London, 1909)

Bach, Evelyn, 'Sheik Fantasies: Orientalism and Feminine Desire in the Desert Romance', *Hecate*, 23, 1 (1997)

Badran, Margaret, *Feminists, Islam, and Nation* (Princeton, NJ, 1995)

Bailey, Paul J., '"An Army of Workers": Chinese Indentured Labour in First World War France', in Santanu Das (ed.), *Race, Empire and First World War Writing* (Cambridge and New York, 2011)

Baldwin, M. Page, 'Subject to Empire: Married Women and the British Nationality and Status of Aliens Act', *Journal of British Studies*, 40 (October 2001)

Ballinger, Anette, 'The Guilt of the Innocent and the Innocence of the Guilty: the Cases of Marie Fahmy and Ruth Ellis', in Alice Myers and Sarah Wright (eds), *No Angels: Women who Commit Violence* (London, 1996)

Ballinger, Anette, *Dead Woman Walking: Executed Women in England and Wales, 1900–1955* (Aldershot, 2000)

Baron, Beth, *The Women's Awakening in Egypt* (Yale, 1994)

Barton, Edith and Marguerite Cody, *Eve in Khaki: the Story of the Women's Army at Home and Abroad* (London, 1918)

Baxter, Beverley, *Strange Street* (London, 1935)

Beddoe, Deirdre, *Back to Home and Duty: Women Between the Wars, 1918–1939* (London, 1989)

Bell, Anne Olivier (ed.), *The Diary of Virginia Woolf, Vol. I, 1915–19* (London, 1977)

Bell, Anne Olivier (ed.), *The Diary of Virginia Woolf, Vol. II, 1920–1924* (London, 1978)

Belloc Lowndes, Mrs, *Good Old Anna* (London, 1915)

Belloc Lowndes, Mrs, *A Passing World* (London, 1948)

Belsey, Catherine, 'True Love', *Women: a Cultural Review* 3, 2 (1992)

Bennett, Arnold, *Body and Soul: a Play in Four Acts* (London, 1922)

Bennett, Arnold, *Imperial Palace, Vol. 1 and 2* (London, 1930)

Bennett, Daphne, *Margot: A Life of the Countess of Oxford and Asquith* (London, 1984)

Berenson, Edward, *Trial of Madame Caillaux* (Berkeley, CA and Oxford, 1992)

Berridge, Virginia, 'Drugs and Social Policy: the Establishment of Drug Control in Britain, 1900–30', *British Journal of Addiction*, 79 (1980)

Berridge, Virginia, 'The Origins of the English Drug "Scene", 1890–1930', *Medical History*, 32 (1988)

Berridge, Virginia, *Opium and the People* (London, 1981, 1999)

Berridge, Virginia and Griffith Edwards, *Opium and the People* (London, 1981)

Beynon, Mark, *London's Curse: Murder Black Magic and Tutankhamun in the 1920s West End* (Stroud, 2011)

Bingham, Adrian, *Gender, Modernity, and the Popular Press in Inter-War Britain* (Oxford, 2004)

Bingham, Adrian, *Family Newspapers? Sex, Private Life and the British Popular Press, 1918–1978* (Oxford, 2009)

Blake, Andrew, 'Foreign Devils and Moral Panics: Britain, Asia and the Opium Trade', in Bill Schwarz (ed.), *The Expansion of England* (London, 1996)

Bland, Lucy, 'In the Name of Protection: the Policing of Women in the First World War`, in J. Brophy and C. Smart (eds), *Women in Law* (London, 1985)

Bland, Lucy, *Banishing the Beast: English Feminism and Sexual Morality, 1885–1914* (London, 1995)

Bland, Lucy, 'Trial by Sexology? Maud Allan, *Salome* and the "Cult of the Clitoris" Case', in Lucy Bland and Laura Doan (eds), *Sexology in Culture: Labelling Bodies and Desires* (Oxford, 1998)

Bland, Lucy, 'White Women and Men of Colour: Miscegenation Fears in Britain after the Great War', in *Gender & History*, 17, 1 (2005)

Bland, Lucy, 'British Eugenics and "Race Crossing": a Study of an Interwar Investigation', in Special Issue on 'Eugenics Old and New', *New Formations*, 60 (2007)

Bland, Lucy and Laura Doan (eds), *Sexology Uncensored: the Documents of Sexual Science* (Oxford, 1998)

Bland, Lucy and Frank Mort, 'Look out for the "Goodtime" Girl: Dangerous Sexualities as Threat to National Health', in *Formations of Nation and People* (London, 1984)

Bleys, Rudi C., *The Geography of Perversion* (London, 1996)

Bloom, Clive, *Cult Fiction* (London, 1996)

Blythe, Ronald, *The Age of Illusion: England in the Twenties and Thirties* (London, 1963)

Bonham Carter, Mark and Mark Pottle (eds), *Lantern Slides: the Diaries and Letters of Violet Bonham Carter, 1904–1914* (London, 1996)

Boone, Joseph, 'Vacation Cruises; of the Homoerotics of Orientalism', *PMLA*, 110 (1993)

Bourke, Joanna, *Dismembering the Male: Men's Bodies, Britain and the Great War* (London, 1996)

Box, Muriel, *The Trial of Marie Stopes* (London, 1967)

Braybon, Gail, *Women Workers in the First World War* (London, 1981)

Breward, Christopher, *Fashioning London: Clothing and the Modern Metropolis* (Oxford, 2004)

Brewer, John and Roy Porter (eds), *Consumption and the World of Goods* (London, 1993)

Brittain, Vera, *Testament of Youth* (London, 1933, 1978)

Broad, Lewis, *The Innocence of Edith Thompson: a Study in Old Bailey Justice* (London, 1952)

Brookes, Barbara, *Abortion in England, 1900–1967* (London, 1988)

Burke, Thomas, *Nights in Town* (London, 1915, 1925)

Burke, Thomas, *Limehouse Nights* (London, 1916, 1926)

Burman, Barbara, 'Racing Bodies: Dress and Pioneer Women Aviators and Racing Drivers', *Women's History Review*, 9, 2 (2000)

Burrows, Jon, '"A Vague Chinese Quarter Elsewhere": Limehouse in the Cinema, 1914–1936', *Journal of British Cinema and Television*, 6, 2 (August 2009)

Burt, Clarissa, review of 'Map of Love', *Feminist Review*, 69 (2001)

Burton, Richard, *Plain and Literal Translation of the Arabian Nights Entertainments* (1919 [1884–86])

Cadogan, Mary, *And Then Their Hearts Stood Still* (London, 1994)

Cairns, J.A.R., *The Loom of the Law: the Experiences and Reflections of the Metropolitan Magistrate* (London, 1922)

Carey, John, *The Intellectuals and the Masses: Pride and Prejudice amongst the Intelligentsia* (London, 1992)

Carter, Everett, 'Cultural History Written with Lightening: the Significance of the Birth of a Nation', *American Quarterly*, 12, 3 (Autumn 1960)

Carter Wood, John, *The Most Remarkable Woman in England: Poison, Celebrity and the Trials of Beatrice Pace* (Manchester, 2012)

Charmley, John, *Duff Cooper: the Authorised Biography* (London, 1986)

Cherniavsky, Felix, *The Salome Dancer: The Life and Times of Maud Allan* (Toronto, 1991)

Childers, Erskine, *The Riddle of the Sands: a Record of Secret Service* (London, 1903, 1978)

Chow, Karen, 'Popular Sexual Knowledges and Women's Agency in 1920s England: Marie Stopes's Married Love and E.M. Hull's The Sheik', *Feminist Review*, 63 (1999)

Clifford, Colin, *The Asquiths* (London, 2002)

Clifford, James, review of Orientalism in *History and Theory* 12, 2 (1980)

Cline, Sally, *Radclyffe Hall: a Woman called John* (London, 1997)

Cohler, Deborah, 'Sapphism and Sedition: Producing Female Homosexuality in Great War Britain', *Journal of the History of Sexuality*, 16, 1 (2007)

Coner, Liz, *The Spectacular Modern Woman* (Bloomington and Indianapolis, IN, 2004)

Conquest, Joan, *Desert Love* (London, 1920)

Cook, Hera, *The Long Sexual Revolution: English Women, Sex and Contraception, 1900–1975* (Oxford, 2004)

Cook, Matt, *London and the Culture of Homosexuality, 1885–1914* (Cambridge, 2003)

Cook, Matt, 'Law', in Matt Houlbrook and H.G. Cocks (eds), *Palgrave Advances in the Modern History of Sexuality* (London, 2005)

Cooper, Artemis (ed.), *A Durable Fire: the Letters of Duff and Diana Cooper, 1913–1950* (London, 1983)

Cooper, Diana, *The Rainbow Comes and Goes* (London, 1958, 1961)

Coward, Rosalind, 'An Overwhelming Desire', in Rosalind Coward, *Female Desire* (London, 1984)

Cowie, Susan D. and Tom Johnson, *The Mummy in Fact, Fiction and Film* (London, 2002)

Curran, James and James Seaton, *Power without Responsibility: the Press and Broadcasting in Britain* (fifth edition, London, 1998)

Curtis, L. Perry, *Jack the Ripper and the London Press* (New Haven, CT, 2001)

Darwin, John, *Britain, Egypt and the Middle East* (London, 1981)

Das, Santanu, '"Kiss Me, Hardy": Intimacy, Gender, and Gesture in World War I Trench Literature', *Modernism/Modernity*, 9, 1 (2002)

Das, Santanu, *Touch and Intimacy in First World War Literature* (Cambridge, 2008)

Das, Santanu (ed.), *Race, Empire and First World War Writing* (Cambridge and New York, 2011)

Daunton, Martin and Bernhard Rieger (eds), *Meanings of Modernity: Britain from the Late-Victorian Period to World War II* (Oxford and New York, 2001).

Dawson, Graham, *Soldier Heroes* (London, 1994)

Dawson, Jill, *Fred and Edie* (London, 2000)

D'Cruze, Shani, *Crimes of Outrage: Sex, Violence and Victorian Working Women* (London, 1998)

D'Cruze, Shani (ed.), *Everyday Violence in Britain, 1850–1950* (London, 2000)

D'Cruze, Shani, Sandra Walklate and Samantha Pegg, *Murder: Social and Historical Approaches to Understanding Murder and Murderers* (Cullompton, 2006)

de Blecourt, Willem and Cornelie Usborne, 'Women's Medicine, Women's Culture: Abortion and Fortune-Telling in Early Twentieth Century Germany and the Netherlands', *Medical History*, 43, 3 (1999)

de Groot, Joanna, '"Sex" and "Race": the Construction of Language and Image in the Nineteenth Century', in Susan Mendus and Jane Rendall (eds), *Sexuality and Subordination* (London, 1989)

de la Pasture, Esmee, *Messalina of the Suburbs* (London, 1924)

Delafield, E.M., *The Suburban Young Man* (London, 1928)

Dijkstra, Bram, *Idols of Perversity* (Oxford, 1986)

Dijkstra, Bram, *Evil Sister: the Threat of Female Sexuality in Twentieth-Century*

Culture (New York, 1996)

Dixon, Jay, *The Romantic Fiction of Mills & Boon 1909–1990s* (London, 1999)

Doan, Laura, *Fashioning Sapphism: the Origins of Modern English Lesbian Culture* (New York, 2001)

Dudgeon, Jeffrey, *Roger Casement: the Black Diaries* (Belfast, 2002).

Duncan, Isadora, *My Life* (London, 1928)

Dyhouse, Carol, *Glamour: Women, History, Feminism* (London and New York, 2010)

Ellis, Havelock, *Sexual Inversion* (Watford, 1897)

Ellis, Havelock, *Studies in the Psychology of Sex: 7* (Philadelphia, PN, 1928)

Ellis, Markman, *The Politics of Sensibility* (Cambridge, 1996)

English Early, Julie, 'Keeping Ourselves to Ourselves: Violence in the Edwardian Suburb', in Shani D'Cruze, *Everyday Violence in Britain, 1850–1950* (London, 2000)

English Early, Julie, 'A New Man for a New Century: Dr Crippen and the Principles of Masculinity', in George Robb and Nancy Erber (eds), *Disorder In The Court: Trials And Sexual Conflict At The Turn Of The Century* (London, 1999)

Ellmann, Richard, *Oscar Wilde* (London, 1988)

Evans, Neil, 'The South Wales Race Riots of 1919', *Llafur*, 3 (1980)

Felski, Rita, *The Gender of Modernity* (Cambridge, MA, 1995)

Felski, Rita, *Doing Time* (New York, 2000)

Ferris, Paul, *Sex and the British* (London, 1993)

Fisher, Kate, *Birth-Control, Sex and Marriage in Britain, 1918–1960* (Oxford, 2006)

Fleming, R.M., 'Anthropological Studies of Children', *Eugenics Review* (January 1927)

Flint, Jane, *The Woman Reader, 1837–1914* (Oxford, 1993)

French, David, 'Spy Fever in Britain, 1900–1915', *Historical Journal*, 21, 2 (1978)

Frost, Ginger, *Promises Broken: Courtship, Class and Gender in Victorian England* (Charlottesville, VA and London, 1997)

Fryer, Peter, *Staying Power: the History of Black People in Britain* (London, 1984)

Gagnier, Regenia, *Idylls of the Marketplace: Oscar Wilde and the Victorian Public* (Aldershot, 1987)

Gallichan, Walter, *Sexual Apathy and Coldness in Women* (London, 1927)

Garnett, David, *The Golden Echo: 2: The Flower of the Forest* (London, 1955)

'A Gentleman with a Duster' [Harold Begbie], *The Glass of Fashion: Some Social Reflections* (London, 1921, 1922)

Gibson, Margaret, 'Clitoral Corruption: Body Metaphors and American Doctors' Construction of Female Homosexuality, 1870–1900', in Vernon Rosario (ed.), *Science and Homosexualities* (London, 1997)

Gilbert, Sandra M., 'Soldier's Heart: Literary Men, Literary Women, and the Great War', *Signs*, 8, 3 (1983)

Giles, Judy, '"Playing Hard to Get": Working-Class Women, Sexuality and Respectability in Britain, 1918–40', *Women's History Review*, 1, 2 (1992)

Giles, Judy, *The Parlour and the Suburb* (Oxford and New York, 2004)

Gilman, Sander, 'Black Bodies, White Bodies: towards an iconography of female sexuality in late nineteenth-century act, medicine and literature', in James Donald and Ali Rattansi (eds), *'Race', Culture and Difference* (London, 1992)

Gilman, Sander, 'Salome, Syphilis, Sarah Bernhardt and the Modern Jewess', in Linda Nochlin and Tamar Garb (eds), *The Jew in the Text* (New York, 1996)

Gittins, Diana, *Fair Sex: Family Size and Structure, 1900–39* (London, 1982)

Glicco, Jack, *Madness after Midnight* (London, 1952)

Glucksmann, Miriam, *Women Assemble: Women Workers and the New Industries in Inter-war Britain* (London, 1990).

Golden, Eve, *Vamp: the Rise and Fall of Theda Bara* (New York, 1996)

Gordon, Eleanor and Gwyneth Nair, *Murder and Morality in Victorian Britain: the Story of Madeleine Smith* (Manchester, 2009)

Graves, Robert and Alan Hodge, *The Long Weekend; a Social History of Great Britain, 1918–1939* (New York, 1940, 1963)

Grayzel, Susan R., *Women and the First World War* (London, 2002)

Grayzel, Susan, 'Liberating Women? Examining Gender, Morality and Sexuality in First World War Britain and France', in Gail Braybon (ed.), *Evidence, History and the Great War* (New York and Oxford, 2003)

Grice, Edward, *Great Cases of Sir Henry Curtis-Bennett* (London, 1937)

Gullace, Nicoletta F., *'The Blood of our Sons': Men, Women, and the Renegotiation of British Citizenship during the Great War* (New York, 2002)

Guoqi, Xu, *Strangers on the Western Front: Chinese Workers in the Great War* (Cambridge, MA, 2011)

Halberstam, Judith, 'Technologies of Monstrosity: Bram Stoker's *Dracula*', in Sally Ledger and Scott McCracken (eds), *Cultural Politics at Fin de Siecle* (Cambridge, 1995)

Hall, Lesley A., 'Sexuality', in Ina Zweiniger-Bargielowska, *Women in Twentieth-Century Britain* (London, 2001)

Hall, Lesley A., *Hidden Anxieties: Male Sexuality, 1900–1950* (Oxford, 1991)

Hall, Lesley A., *Sex, Gender and Social Change in Britain since 1880* (London, 2000)

Hall, Lesley A., '"The Subject is Obscene: No Lady would Dream of Alluding to it": Marie Stopes and her Courtroom Dramas', *Women's History Review*, 22, 2 (2013)

Hall, Lesley A. (ed.), *Outspoken Women: An Anthology of Women's Writings on Sex, 1870–1969* (London, 2005)

Hall, Ruth, *Marie Stopes: a Biography* (London, 1978)

Halperin, David, *Saint Foucault: Towards a Gay Hagiography* (New York, 1995)

Hammerton, A. James, 'The Perils of Mrs Pooter: Satire, Modernity and Motherhood in the Lower Middle Classes in England, 1870–1920', *Women's History Review*, 8, 2 (1999)

Hansen, Miriam, 'Pleasure, Ambivalence, Identification: Valentino and Female Spectatorship', in Christine Gledhill (ed), *Stardom: Industry of Desire* (1991)

Hanson, Helen and Catherine O'Rawe (eds), *The Femme Fatale: Images, Histories, Contexts* (London, 2010)

Hardinge of Penshurst, Lord Charles, *My Indian Years* (London, 1948)

Harris, Ruth, *Murders and Madness: Medicine, Law, and Society in the Fin de Siecle* (Oxford, 1989)

Harrison, Mark, 'The British Army and the Problems of Venereal Diseases in France and Egypt during the First World War', *Medical History*, 39 (1995)

Hartman, Mary S., *Victorian Murderesses* (London, 1985)

Hekma, Gert, 'A Female Soul in a Male Body', in Gilbert Herdt (ed.), *Third Sex, Third Gender* (New York, 1994)

Herbert, A.P., *Holy Deadlock* (London, 1934)

Herrup, Cynthia, *A House in Gross Disorder: Sex, Law and the 2nd Earl of Castlehaven* (Oxford, 1999)

Hichens, Robert, *Bella Donna* (London, 1909, 1911)

Hoare, Philip, *Wilde's Last Stand: Decadence, Conspiracy and the First World War* (London, 1997)

Hobsbawn, Eric, *Age of Extremes: the Short Twentieth Century, 1914–1991* (London, 1995)

Hodgson Burnett, Frances, *A Little Princess* (London, 1905, 1961)

Holden, Katherine, *The Shadow of Marriage: Singleness in England, 1914–60* (Manchester, 2007)

Holland, Merlin, *Irish Peacock & Scarlet Marquess: the Real Trial of Oscar Wilde* (London, 2003)

Hooke, Nina Warner and Gil Thomas, *Marshall Hall: a Biography* (London, 1966)

Horne, Peter, 'Sodomy to Salome', in Mica Nava and Alan O`Shea (eds), *Modern Times* (London, 1996)

Horner, Frances, *Time Remembered* (London, 1933)

Horwood, Catherine, *Keeping Up Appearances: Fashion and Class between the Wars* (Stroud, 2005)

Houlbrook, Matt, *Queer London: Perils and Pleasures in the Sexual Metropolis, 1918–1957* (Chicago and London, 2005)

Houlbrook, Matt, 'The Man with the Powder Puff in Interwar London', *The Historical Journal*, 50, 1 (2007)

Houlbrook, Matt, 'A Pin to See the Peepshow: Culture, Fiction and Selfhood in the Letters of Edith Thompson', *Past and Present*, 207, 1 (2010)

Huggins, Mike, '"And Now for Something for the Ladies": Representations of Women's Sport in Cinema Newsreels, 1918–1939', *Women's History Review*, 16, 5 (2007)

Hull, E.M., *The Sheik* (Londno, 1919, 1996)

Hume-Williams, Ellis, *The World, the House and the Bar* (London, 1930)

Humphreys, Travers, *Criminal Days* (London, 1946)

Humphries, Steve and Pamela Gordon, *Forbidden Fruit: Our Secret Past, 1900–1960* (London, 1994)

Hunter, Eileen, *Christabel: the Russell Case and After* (London, 1973)

Huyssen, Andreas, *After the Great Divide: Modernism, Mass Culture, Post Modernism* (London, 1986)

Hynes, Samuel, *A War Imagined: the First World War and English Culture* (London, 1990)

Irwin, Robert, *The Arabian Nights: A Companion* (London and New York, 1994, 2004)

Israel, Kali, 'French Vices and British Liberties; Gender, Class and Narrative Competition in a Late Victorian Sex Scandal', *Social History*, 22, 1 (January 1997)

Jackson, Alan, *The Middle Classes, 1900–1950* (Nairn, 1991)

Jackson, Louise A., 'The Unusual Case of "Mrs Sherlock": Memoir, Identity and the "Real" Woman Private Detective in Twentieth-century Britain', *Gender & History*, 15, 1 (April 2003)

Jeffery, Tom and Keith McClelland, 'A World Fit to Live in: the *Daily Mail* and the Middle Classes, 1918–1939', in James Curran, Anthony Smith and Pauline Wingate (eds), *Impact and Influences: Essays in Media Power in the Twentieth Century* (London, 1987)

Jenkinson, Jacqueline, 'The 1919 Riots', in Panikos Panayi (ed.), *Racial Violence in Britain in the Nineteenth and Twentieth Centuries* (Leicester, 1996)

Jenkinson, Jacqueline, *Black 1919: Riots, Racism and Resistance in Imperial Britain* (Liverpool, 2009)

Kabbani, Rana, *Europe's Myths of Orient* (London, 1986)

Kaur Bakshi, Parminder, 'Homosexuality and Orientalism: Edward Carpenter's Journey to the East', in Tony Brown (ed.), *Edward Carpenter and Late Victorian Radicalism* (London, 1990)

Kennedy, Dane, '"Captain Burton's Oriental Muck Heap": *The Book of the Thousand Nights* and the Uses of Orientalism', *Journal of British Studies*, 39 (July 2000)

Kerner, Annette, *Further Adventures of a Woman Detective* (London, 1955)

Kettle, Martin, *Salome's Last Veil: The Libel Case of the Century* (London, 1977)

Kimble, Sara L., 'No Right to Judge: Feminism and the Judiciary in 3rd Republic France', *French Historical Studies*, 31, 4 (2008)

Kingsley Kent, Susan, *Making Peace: the Reconstruction of Gender in Interwar Britain* (Princeton, NJ, 1993)

Kingsley Kent, Susan, *Aftershocks: Politics and Trauma in Britain, 1918–1931* (London and New York, 2009)

Kohn, Marek, *Dope Girls: the Birth of the British Drug Underground* (London, 1992),

Koritz, Amy, 'Salome: Exotic Woman and the Transcendent Dance', in Antony Harrison and Beverley Taylor (eds), *Gender and Discourse in Victorian Literature and Art* (DeKalb, IL, 1992)

Koritz, Amy, 'Dancing the Orient for England: Maud Allan's "The Vision of Salome"', *Theatre Journal*, 46 (1994)

Koritz, Amy, *Gendering Bodies/Performing Art: Dance and Literature in Early Twentieth Century British Culture* (Ann Arbor, MI, 1995)

Koss, Stephen, *The Rise and Fall of the Political Press in Britain, vol.2: Twentieth Century* (London, 1984).

Kwee Choo, Hg, *The Chinese in London* (Oxford, 1968)

Lahiri, Shompa, *Indians in Britain: Anglo-Indian Encounters, Race and Identity, 1880–1930* (London, 2000)

Lambert, Angela, *Unquiet Souls: The India Summer of the British Aristocracy, 1880–1918* (London, 1984)

Langhamer, Claire, *Women's Leisure in England, 1920–1960* (Manchester, 2000)

Laqueur, Thomas, 'Amor Veneris', in Michel Feher (ed.), *Fragments for a History of the Human Body*, Part 3 (New York, 1989)

Lawrence, D.H., *Pornography and Obscenity* (London, 1929)

Leavis, Q.D., *Fiction and the Reading Public* (London 1932, 1979)

Leider, Emily W., *Dark Lover: the Life and Death of Rudolph Valentino* (London, 2004)

Lesage, Julia, '*Broken Blossoms*: Artful Racism, Artful Rape', *Jump Cut: A Review of Contemporary Media*, 26 (1981)

Levine, Philippa, '"Walking the Streets in a Way no Decent Woman Should": Women Police in World War One', *Journal of Modern History*, 66 (1994)

Levine, Philippa, 'Battle Colors: Race, Sex and Colonial Soldiery in World War I', *Journal of Social History*, 9, 4 (1998)

Lewis, Reina, *Gendering Orientalism* (London, 1996)

Light, Alison, *Forever England: Femininity, Literature and Conservatism between the Wars* (London, 1991)

Llewellyn Smith, H., *The New Survey of London Life and Labour* (London, 1930)

Lock, Joan, *The British Policewoman: Her Story* (London, 1979)

Logan, Anne, *Feminism and Criminal Justice: a Historical Perspective* (London, 2008)

Long Hall, Diana, 'Biology, Sex Hormones and Sexism in the 1920s', *Philosophical Forum* 5, 1–2 (1973/4)

Longhran, Tracey, 'Shell-Shock in Britain, c1860–c1920' (unpublished Ph.D. thesis, London University, 2006)

Loomba, Ania, *Colonialism/Postcolonialism* (London and New York, 1998)

Lovell, Julia, *The Opium War: Drugs, Dreams and the Making of China* (London, 2011)

Lowe, Lisa, *Colonial Terrains: French and British Orientalisms* (Ithaca, NY, 1991)

Lowndes, Susan (ed.), *Diaries and Letters of Marie Belloc Lowndes, 1911–1947* (London, 1971)

Lyall, H.G., *Press Circulations Analysed* (London, 1928).

Lyons, Malcolm C. with Ursula Lyons, *The Arabian Nights: Tales of 1,001 Nights* (London, 2008)

Mabro, Judy, *Veiled Half-Truths* (London, 1991)

McAleer, Joseph, *Popular Reading and Publishing in Britain, 1914–1950* (Oxford, 1992)

McDearmon, Lacy, 'Maud Allan: the Public Record', *Dance Chronicle*, 2, 2 (1978)

McDonald, Brian, *Gangs of London: 100 Years of Mob Warfare* (London, 2010)

MacKenzie, Jeanne, *The Children of the Souls: a Tragedy of the First World War* (London, 1986)

McKenzie, John M., *Orientalism: History, Theory and the Arts* (Manchester, 1995)

McKibbin, Ross, *The Ideologies of Class: Social Relations in Britain, 1880–1950* (Oxford, 1991)

McKibbin, Ross, *Classes and Cultures: England, 1918–1951* (Oxford, 1998)

McLaren, Angus, *A History of Contraception* (Oxford, 1990)

McLaren, Angus, *The Trials of Masculinity: Policing Sexual Boundaries, 1870–1930* (Chicago, 1997)

McLaren, Angus, *Twentieth Century Sexuality: a History* (Oxford,1999)

McPherson, Susan and Angela McPherson, *Mosley's Old Suffragette: a Biography of Narah Dacre Fox* (London, 2010)

Malik, Kenan, *The Meaning of Race* (London, 1996)

Mannin, Ethel,*Young in the Twenties: a Chapter in Autobiography* (London, 1971)

Marchetti, Gina, *Romance and the 'Yellow Peril': Race, Sex and Discursive Strategies in Hollywood Fiction* (Berkeley, CA, 1993)

Marcus, S., *The Other Victorians* (London, 1964)

Marjoribanks, Edward, *The Life of Sir Edward Marshall Hall* (London, 1929)

Martin, Gregory, 'The Influence of Racial Attitudes towards India during the First World War', *Journal of Imperial and Commonwealth History*, 14 (1986)

Matthews, Jill Julius, 'Dancing Modernity', in Barbara Caine and Rosemary Pringle (eds), *Transitions: New Australian Feminisms* (Allen & Unwin, 1995), pp. 74–87

Matthews, Jill Julius, *Dance Hall and Picture Palace: Sydney's Romance with Modernity* (Sydney, 2005)

May, Roy and Robin Cohen, 'The Interaction between Race and Colonialism: a Case Study of the Liverpool Race Riots of 1919', *Race and Class XVI* 2 (1974)

Medd, Josie, '"The Cult of the Clitoris": Anatomy of a National Scandal', *MODERNISM/Modernity*, 9, 1 (2002)

Melman, Billie, *Women and the Popular Imagination in the Twenties: Flappers and Nymphs* (New York, 1988)

Melman, Billie, *Women's Orients: English Women and the Middle East, 1718–1918* (Ann Arbor, MI, 1992)

Meyrick, Mrs, *Secrets of the 43: Reminiscences* (London, 1933)

Millman, Margaret, 'In the Shadow of War: Continuities and Discontinuities in the Construction of the Masculine Identities of British Soldiers, 1914–1924' (unpublished Ph.D. thesis, Greenwich University, London, 2003)

Mills, Dorothy, *The Tent of Blue* (London, 1922)

Mills, Dorothy, *The Road to Timbaktu* (London, 1924)

Mitchell, Tim, *Colonising Egypt* (Cambridge, 1988)

Mitchison, Naomi, *All Change Here; Girlhood and Marriage* (London, 1975)

Mitford, Nancy, *The Pursuit of Love* (London, 1945, 2010)

Modelski, Tanya, *Loving with a Vengeance* (New York, 1984)

Modern Girl Around the World Research Group, 'The Modern Girl Around the World: A Research Agenda and Preliminary Findings', *Gender & History*, 17, 2 (August 2005)

Modern Girl Around the World Research Group, *The Modern Girl Around the World: Consumption, Modernity and Globalization* (London, 2008).

Moles, Samantha, '"Going down the Pally": a Comparative Study of a Working Class "Girls' Night Out" at the Hammersmith Palais from the 1940s to 1980s' (MA dissertation, London Metropolitan University, 2007)

Montgomery Hyde, H. (ed.), *The Trials of Oscar Wilde* (London, 1948).

Moss, Stella, '"Wartime Hysterics"? Alcohol, Women and the Politics of Wartime Social Purity in England', in Jessica Meyer (ed.), *British Popular Culture and the First World War* (Boston, MA, 2008)

Nava, Mica, 'The Cosmopolitanism of Commerce and the Allure of Difference: Selfridges, the Russian Ballet and the Tango, 1911–1914', *International Journal of Cultural Studies*, 1, 2 (1998)

Nava, Mica, *Visceral Cosmopolitanism* (Oxford and New York, 2007)

Nava, Mica and Alan O'Shea (eds), *Modern Times: Reflections on a Century of English Modernity* (London and New York, 1996)

Nead, Lynda, 'The Magdalen in Modern Times: the Mythology of the Fallen Woman in Pre-Raphaelite Painting', in Rosemary Betterton (ed.), *Looking On: Images of Femininity in the Visual Arts and Media* (London, 1987)

Nead, Lynda, 'Visual Cultures of the Courtroom: Reflections of History, Law and the Image', *Visual Culture in Britain*, 3, 2 (2002)

Nichols, Beverley, *The Sweet and the Twenties* (London, 1958)

Nicholson, Virginia, *Singled Out* (London, 2007).

Nicolson, Juliet, *The Great Silence, 1918–1920: Living in the Shadow of the Great War* (London, 2009)

Normanton, Helena, *Everyday Law for Women* (London, 1932)

Nott, James, *Music for the People: Popular Music and Dance in Interwar Britain* (Oxford, 2002)

Oosterhuis, Harry, 'Richard von Krafft-Ebing's "Step-Children Of Nature": Psychiatry and the Making of Homosexual Identity', in Vernon A. Rosario (ed.), *Science and Homosexualities* (London, 1997)

Oosterhuis, Harry, *Step-Children of Nature: Krafft-Ebing, Psychiatry and the Making of Sexual Identity* (Chicago, 2000)

Oram, Alison, *Women Teachers and Feminist Politics, 1900–1939* (Manchester, 1996)

Oram, Alison, *Her Husband was a Woman! Women's Gender-Crossing in Modern Britain's Popular Culture* (London, 2007)

Panayi, Panikos, *The Enemy in our Midst* (New York and London, 1991)

Panayi, Panikos, 'Anti-German Riots in Britain during First World War', in Panikos Panayi (ed.), *Racial Violence in Britain in Nineteenth and Twentieth Centuries* (Leicester, 1996)

Parejo Vadillo, Ana, 'Phenomena in Flux', in Ann L. Ardis and Leslie W. Lewis (eds), *Women's Experience of Modernity, 1875–1945* (Baltimore, MD and London, 2003)

Parssinen, Terry M., *Secret Passions, Secret Remedies: Narcotic Drugs in British Society, 1820–1930* (Manchester, 1983)

Partridge, Frances, *Memories* (London, 1981)

Pearce, Lynne and Jackie Stacey (eds), *Romance Revisited* (London, 1995)

Pinchin, Jane L., *Alexandria Still: Forster, Durrell, and Cavafy* (Princeton, NJ, 1977)

Political and Economic Planning, *Report on the British Press* (London, 1938)

Porter, Dennis, 'Orientalism and its Problems', in Patrick Williams and Laura

Chrisman (eds), *Colonial Discourse and Post-Colonial Theory* (Hemel Hempstead, 1993)

Porter, Roy and Lesley Hall, *The Facts of Life: the Creation of Sexual Knowledge in Britain, 1650–1950* (New Haven, CT and London, 1997)

Pritchard, Mrs Eric, *The Cult of Chiffon* (London, 1902)

Pugh, Martin,'*We Danced all Night': a Social History of Britain Between the Wars* (London, 2008)

Radford, Jean (ed.), *The Progress of Romance* (London, 1986)

Radice, Betty, *Who's Who in the Ancient World* (London, 1973)

Rapp, Dean, 'The Reception of Freud by the British Press: General Interest and Literary Magazines, 1920–1925', *Journal of the History of Behavioural Sciences*, 24 (1988)

Raub, Patricia, 'Issues of Passion and Power in E.M. Hull's The Sheik', *Women's Studies*, 21 (1992)

Reeves, Nicholas, *The Complete Tutankhamun* (London, 1990)

Rich, Paul, *Race and Empire in British Politics* (Cambridge, 1986, second edition 1990).

Rizk, Yunan Labib, 'Warped Justice', *Al-Ahran Weekly*, 479 (27th April–3rd May 2000)

Robb, George, 'The English Dreyfus Case: Florence Maybrick and the Sexual Double Standard', in George Robb and Nancy Erber (eds), *Disorder in the Court: Trials and Sexual Conflict at the Turn of the Century* (London, 1999)

Robb, George, *British Culture and the First World War* (London 2002)

Robb, George and Nancy Erber (eds), *Disorder in the Court: Trials and Sexual Conflict at the Turn of the Century* (London, 1999)

Roberts, Elizabeth, *A Woman's Place: an Oral History of Working-Class Women, 1890–1940* (London, 1984)

Roberts, Mary Louise, *Civilization without Sexes: Reconstructing Gender in Postwar France, 1917–1927* (Chicago and London, 1994)

Robins, Jane, *The Magnificent Spilsbury and the Case of the Brides in the Bath* (London, 2010)

Robinson-Dunn, Diane, *The Harem, Slavery and British Imperial Culture* (Manchester, 2006)

Rohmer, Sax, *The Mystery of Dr Fu Manchu* (London, 1913, 1985)

Rohmer, Sax, *Dope: the Story of Chinatown and the Drug Traffic* (London, 1919, 2002)

Rose, Andrew, *Scandal at the Savoy* (London, 1991),

Rose, Sonya O., 'Sex, Citizenship and the Nation in World War II Britain', *American Historical Review*, 103, 4 (October 1998)

Rose, Sonja O., *Which People's War? National Identity and Citizenship in Wartime Britain, 1939–1945* (Oxford, 2003)

Ross, Cathy,*Twenties London: a City in the Jazz Age* (London, 2003)

Routh, Guy, *Occupation and Pay in Great Britain, 1906–79* (London, 1980)

Rowbotham, Sheila, *A Century of Women* (London, 1997)

Rowe, Michael, 'Sex, "Race" and Riot in Liverpool, 1919', *Immigrants and Minorities*, 19, 2 (2000)

Royal Commission on Marriage and Divorce, *Report, 1951–1955* (London, 1956, 1968)

Said, Edward, *Orientalism* (London, 1978, 1991)

Saler, Michael, '"Clap if you Believe in Sherlock Holmes": Mass Culture and the Re-Enchantment of Modernity, c.1890–1940', *The Historical Journal*, 46, 3 (2003)

Samuel, Raphael (ed.), *Patriotism: the Making and Unmaking of British National Identity, Vol. III, National Fictions* (London, 1989)

Sassoon, Siegfried, *Diaries, 1915–1918* (London, 1983)

Savage, Gail, 'Erotic Stories and Public Decency: Newspaper Reporting of Divorce Proceedings in England', *The Historical Journal*, 41, 2 (1998)

Scott, Joan, *The Politics of the Veil* (Princeton, NJ, 2007)

Searle, G.R., *Corruption in British Politics, 1895–1930* (Oxford, 1987)

Searle, G.R., *The Liberal Party. Triumph and Disintegration, 1886–1929* (London, 1992)

Seed, John, 'Limehouse Blues: Looking for Chinatown in the London Docks, 1900–1940', *History Workshop Journal*, 62 (2006)

Segal, Ronald, *Islam's Black Slaves: A History of Africa's Other Black Diaspora* (2002)

Sengoopta, Chandak, *The Most Secret Quintessence of Life: Sex, Glands, and Hormones, 1850–1950* (Chicago, 2006)

Shapiro, Ann-Louise, '"Stories More Terrifying than the Truth Itself": Narratives of Female Criminality in Fin De Siècle Paris', in Margaret L. Arnot and Cornelie Usborne (eds), *Gender and Crime in Modern Europe* (London, 2003)

Showalter, Elaine, *Sexual Anarchy: Gender and Culture at the Fin de Siècle* (London, 1991)

Silver, Kenneth, *Esprit de Corps: The Art of the Parisian Avant-Garde and the First World War* (London, 1989)

Simpson, Charlotte, 'Dope Girls, the Yellow Peril and Mormonism: Young Women and Moral Panics in the Early 1920s English Press'(MA dissertation, London Metropolitan University, 2008)

Sinfield, Alan, *The Wilde Century* (London, 1994)

Slater, Stefan, 'Pimps, Police and Filles de Joie: Foreign Prostitution in Interwar London', *The London Journal*, 1 (2007)

Smith, Harold L., *The British Women's Suffrage Campaign, 1866–1928* (London, 1998, second edition 2007)

Smith, Richard, *Jamaican Volunteers in the First World War* (Manchester, 2004)

Soland, Birgitte, *Becoming Modern: Young Women and the Reconstruction of Womanhood in the 1920s* (Princeton, NJ, 2000)

Soloway, Richard Allen, *Birth Control and the Population Question in England, 1877–1930* (Chapel Hill, NC, 1982)

Soueif, Ahdaf, *The Map of Love* (London, 1999)

Sparrow, Gerald, *Vintage Murder of the Twenties* (London, 1972),

Stoker, Bram, *Dracula* (London, 1897)

Stopes, Marie, *Married Love: a New Contribution to the Solution of Sex Difficulties* (London, 1918)

Stopes, Marie, *Contraception: Theory, History and Practice* (London, 1923)

Stopes, Marie, *Marriage in My Time* (London, 1935)

Stott, Rebecca, *The Fabrication of the Late-Victorian Femme Fatale: the Kiss of Death* (Basingstoke, 1992)

Studlar, Gaylyn, 'Valentino, "Optic Intoxication," and Dance Madness', in Steven Cohan and Ina Rae Hark (eds), *Screening the Male* (London, 1993)

Summerscale, Kate, *The Suspicions of Mr Whicher, or the Murder at Road Hill House* (London, 2008)

Summerscale, Kate, *Mrs Robinson's Disgrace: the Private Diary of a Victorian Lady* (London, 2012)

Summerfield, Penny, 'Women and War in the Twentieth Century', in June Purvis (ed.), *Women's History: Britain, 1850–1945* (London, 1995)

Sumner Holmes, Anne, 'The Double Standard in the English Divorce Laws, 1857–1923', *Law and Social Enquiry: the Journal of the American Bar Association*, 20 (1995)

Szreter, Simon, *Fertility, Class and Gender, 1860–1940* (Cambridge, 1996)

Szreter, Simon and Kate Fisher, *Sex Before the Sexual Revolution* (Oxford, 2010)

Tabili, Laura, *'We Ask for British Justice': Workers and Racial Difference in Late Imperial Britain* (Ithaca, NY, 1994)

Tabili, Laura, 'Outsiders in the Land of their Birth: Exomamy, Citizenship, and Identity in War and Peace', *Journal of British Studies*, 44, 4 (October 2005)

Tabili, Laura, *Global Migrants, Local Culture: Natives and Newcomers in Provisional England, 1841–1939* (New York, 2011)

Tate, Trudi, *Modernism, History and the First World War* (Manchester and New York, 1998)

Taylor, D.J., *Bright Young People: the Rise and Fall of a Generation: 1918–1940* (London, 2007)

Tennyson Jesse, F., *A Pin to See a Peepshow* (London, 1934, 1984)

Tennyson Jesse, F. (ed.), *Trial of Alma Victoria Rattenbury and George Percy Stoner* (London and Edinburgh, 1935)

Teo, Hsu-Ming, 'Clean Spaces, Dirty Bodies: the Middle Eastern Desert in British Women's Travel Writing, 1890–1914', in Patricia Grimshaw and Diane Kirkby (eds), *Dealing with Difference* (London, 1997)

Teo, Hsu-Ming, 'Women's Travel, Dance and British Metropolitan Anxieties, 1890–1939', *Gender & History*, 12, 2 (July 2000)

Thane, Pat, 'The British Imperial State and the Construction of National Identities', in Billie Melman (ed.), *Borderlines: Gender and Identities in War and Peace, 1870–1930* (London, 1998)

Thom, Deborah, *Nice Girls and Rude Girls: Women Workers in World War One* (London, 1998)

Thomson, Basil, *The Scene Changes* (New York, 1937)

Thomson, Mathew, *Psychological Subjects: Identity, Culture, and Health in Twentieth-*

Century Britain (Oxford, 2006)

Tickner, Lisa, *Modern Life and Modern Subjects* (New Haven, CT and London, 2000)

Tignor, R.L., *Modernism and British Colonial Rule in Egypt, 1882–1914* (Princeton, NJ, 1966)

Tinkler, Penny, *Smoke Signals: Women, Smoking and Visual Culture* (Oxford and New York, 2006)

Tinkler, Penny and Cheryl Krasnick Walsh, 'Feminine Modernity in Interwar Britain and North America', *Journal of Women's History*, 20, 3 (2008)

Todman, Dan, *The Great War* (London, 2005)

Tolini Finamore, Michelle, 'Fashioning the Colonial at the Paris Expositions, 1925 and 1931', *Fashion Theory*, 7, 3/4 (2003)

Tombs, R. and I., *That Sweet Enemy: the French and British: from the Sun King to the Present* (London, 2006)

Travis, Jennifer, 'Clits in Court: *Salome*, Sodomy and the Lesbian Sadist', in Carla Jay (ed.), *Lesbian Erotics* (New York, 1995)

Trodd, Anthea, *Women's Writing in English: Britain, 1900–1945* (London and New York, 1998)

Twining, William, *Rethinking Evidence* (Oxford, 1990)

Usborne, Cornelie, 'The New Woman and Generation Conflict: Perceptions of Young Women's Sexual Mores in the Weimar Republic', in Mark Roseman (ed.), *Generations in Conflict. Youth Revolt and Generation Formation in Germany, 1770–1968* (Cambridge, 1995)

Usborne, Cornelie, *Cultures of Abortion in Weimar Germany* (New York and Oxford, 2007)

Valverde, Mariana, *The Age of Light, Soap and Water* (Toronto, 1991)

Verbatim Report of the Trial of Noel Pemberton Billing, M.P., on a Charge of Common Libel (London, 1918)

Visram, Rosina, *Asians in Britain: 400 Years of History* (London, 2002)

von Krafft-Ebing, Richard, *Psychopathia Sexualis* (Philadelphia, PN, 1892)

Wachman, Gay, *Lesbian Empire: Radical Crosswriting in the Twenties* (New Brunswick, NJ, 2001)

Wadsworth, A.P. 'Newspaper Circulations, 1800–1954', *Transactions of the Manchester Statistical Society*, 9 (March 1955)

Walkowitz, Judith, *City of Dreadful Delight: Narratives of Sexual Danger in Late-Victorian London* (London, 1982)

Walkowitz, Judith, 'The "Vision of Salome": Cosmopolitanism and Erotic Dancing in Central London, 1908–1918', *American Historical Research*, 108, 2 (April 2003)

Walkowitz, Judith, *Nights Out: Life in Cosmopolitan London* (New Haven, CT and London, 2012)

Wassef, Nadia, 'On Selective Consumerism: Egyptian Women and Ethnographic Representations', *Feminist Review*, 69 (2001)

Waters, Chris, '"Dark Strangers" in Our Midst: Discourses of Race and Nation in Britain, 1947–1963', *Journal of British Studies*, 36 (April 1997)

Weininger, Otto, *Sex & Character* (London, 1910)

Weis, René, *Criminal Justice: The True Story of Edith Thompson* (London, 1990)

Weeks, Jeffrey, *Sex, Politics and Society* (London, 1981)

Wheelwright, Julie, *The Fatal Lover: Mata Hari and the Myth of Women in Espionage* (London, 1992)

White, Arnold, *The Hidden Hand* (London, 1917)

White, Rosie, "'You'll Be the Death of Me": Mata Hari and the Myth of the *Femme Fatale*', in Helen Hanson and Catherine O'Rawe (eds), *The Femme Fatale: Images, Histories, Contexts* (London, 2010)

Wild, Roland and Derek Curtis-Bennett, *'Curtis': the Life of Sir Henry Curtis-Bennett KC* (London, 1937)

Williams, Raymond, *The Long Revolution* (London, 1961)

Wilson, Elizabeth, *Adorned in Dreams: Fashion and Modernity* (London, 1985, 2005)

Wilson, Elizabeth, *The Sphinx in the City* (London, 1991)

Winter, J.M., *The Experience of World War I* (Oxford, 1988)

Winter, Jay and Antoine Prost, *The Great War in History* (Cambridge, 2005)

Witchard, Anne Veronica, *Thomas Burke's Dark Chinoiserie: Limehouse Nights and the Queer Spell of Chinatown* (Farnham, 2009)

Wollen, Peter, 'Fashion/Orientalism/The Body`, *New Formations*, 1 (Spring 1987)

Woollocott, Angela, "'Khaki Fever" and its Control: Gender, Class, Age and Sexual Morality on the British Home Front in the First World War', *Journal of Contemporary History* 29 (1994)

Wyles, Lillian, *A Woman at Scotland Yard* (London, 1952)

Young, Filson, *Trial of Frederick Bywaters and Edith Thompson* (Edinburgh and London, 1923)

Young, Robert, *White Mythologies: Writing History and the Rest* (London, 1990)

Zeigler, Susan, "'How far am I Responsible?" Women and Morphinomania in Late-Nineteenth Century Britain', *Victorian Studies*, 48, 1 (2005)

Zimmeck, Meta, 'Jobs for the Girls: the Expansion of Clerical Work for Women, 1850–1914', in Angela V. John (ed.), *Unequal Opportunities* (Oxford, 1986)

Index

Abbot-Anderson, Sir Maurice 191, 206n.72, 207n.94

abortifacient 118

adultery 90, 111, 125, 128n.57, 178–9, 198

Afraid of Love film 200

Ahmed, Leila 146, 169n.91, n.93, n.95, 170n.111, 172n.150

Aitken, Bessie 107–9, 113, 115, 117, 123, 125

alcohol 5, 55, 56, 60, 63–4, 109
  licensing hours 61, 64

Alexander, Sally 11, 94n.66, 121, 127n.46, 128n.74, 131n.140, 207n.108, 209n.154

Alibert, Raymonde 142

Alibert, Yvonne 146, 167n.33

Allatini, Rose 53n.168

aliens 38–40, 42–4, 67, 71–2, 79, 85, 98n.160, 204n.5

Allan, Maud 15–44, 52n.150, 53n.183, 63, 113, 150, 156, 167n.43, 178–9, 210, 213, 215–17

Allen, Judith A 130n.123

Ampthill, Lady Margaret 181, 195, 204n.23, 205n.53

Ampthill. Lord Oliver 178–9, 203n.5, 212

anti-semitism 17, 39, 40
  see also Jews and Jewishness

Arabian or *Thousand and One Nights* 156–7

aristocrats and aristocracy 23, 47, 83, 92n.43, 161, 176, 186, 213

Asquith, Cynthia 40, 43, 49n.85, 50n.122, 51n.126

Asquith, Herbert Henry 16, 19, 21–3, 29, 32–3, 40–1, 45n.6, 50n.97, 210

Asquith, Margot 16, 17, 19, 22–4, 27–9, 32–3, 40–1, 43–4, 47n.49, 48n.50, 49n.85, 210

Attorney General 196

Auerbach, Sascha 83, 92n.39, 95n.86, 96n.104, n.108, 99n.168, n.183, 100n.188, n.189, 218n.3

'bachelor girls' 3
  see also flapper

Ballets Russes 21, 156

Ballinger, Anette 117, 130n.107, n.109, 150, 170n.118, 213, 219n.17

Baroudi, Mahmoud 147–8

Baxter, Beverley 112, 128n.68, 195

Beaverbrook, Lord (Max Aitken) 8–9

Beddoe, Deirdre 7, 11n.13, 13n.31, 126n.21, 127n.48, n.49

Bell, Anne Olivier 11n.1, 47n.49

Belloc Lowndes, Marie 16, 45n.9, 47n.47, 48n.50, n.56, n.58, 52n.154

Bennett, Arnold 38, 51n.141, 166n.6

Body and Soul 183, 205n.35

Bernhardt, Sarah 45n.7

Berridge, Virginia 91n.12, n.14, 95n.88, n.98

Billing, Noel Pemberton 15–19, 23–44, 46n.16, n.18, 50n.122, 51n.130, n.141, 53n.165, 144, 217

Bingham, Adrian 3, 7, 11n.12, 12n.14, n.15, n.20, 13n.33, 14n.47, 49n.82, 94n.78, 98n.154, 127n.38, 169n.79, 200, 203n.4, 204n.19, 209n.140, n.146, 219n.19, n.21

Bioscope 200, 202, 209n.148, 150

Bishop of London 200

'Black Book' 15–16, 32–5, 38–40, 50n.118, 52n.163